KT-169-669

European
in a Chan...

102 040 100 1

REFERENCE

European Union Foreign Policy in a Changing World

3rd edition

KAREN E. SMITH

polity

First edition published in 2003 by Polity Press
This edition published in 2014 by Polity Press

Polity Press
65 Bridge Street
Cambridge CB2 1UR, UK

Polity Press
350 Main Street
Malden, MA 02148, USA

ISBN-13: 978-0-7456-6469-9 (hardback)
ISBN-13: 978-0-7456-6470-5 (paperback)

A catalogue record for this book is available from the British Library.

Typeset in 9.5 on 13 pt Swift Light
by Toppan Best-set Premedia Limited
Printed and bound in Great Britain by Clays Ltd, St Ives PLC

The publisher has used its best endeavours to ensure that the URLs for external websites referred to in this book are correct and active at the time of going to press. However, the publisher has no responsibility for the websites and can make no guarantee that a site will remain live or that the content is or will remain appropriate.

Every effort has been made to trace all copyright holders, but if any have been inadvertently overlooked the publisher will be pleased to include any necessary credits in any subsequent reprint or edition.

For further information on Polity, visit our website: www.politybooks.com

Contents

Tables

Boxes

Abbreviations

ACP	African, Caribbean and Pacific countries
AFSJ	Area of Freedom, Security and Justice
AMIS	African Union Mission in Darfur, Sudan
APEC	Asia-Pacific Economic Cooperation
ASEAN	Association of South-East Asian Nations
ASEM	Asia–Europe Meeting
AU	African Union
BEAC	Barents Euro-Arctic Council
BiH	Bosnia and Herzegovina
BSEC	Black Sea Economic Cooperation
CARICOM	Caribbean Community
CARIFORUM	Caribbean Forum of ACP States
CBSS	Council of Baltic Sea States
CCP	Common Commercial Policy
CEECs	Central and East European Countries
CEFTA	Central European Free Trade Agreement
CEI	Central European Initiative
CFSP	Common Foreign and Security Policy
CIS	Commonwealth of Independent States
CIVCOM	Committee for Civilian Aspects of Crisis Management
CJTF	Combined Joint Task Force
CMEA	Council for Mutual Economic Assistance
CMPD	Crisis Management Planning Directorate
Coreper	Committee of Permanent Representatives
CPCC	Civilian Planning Conduct Capability
CSCE	Conference on Security and Cooperation in Europe
CSDP	Common Security and Defence Policy
DCI	Development Cooperation Instrument
DDR	Disarmament, Demobilization and Reintegration
DG	Directorate-General
DG DEVCO	Directorate-General for Development Cooperation
DG RELEX	Directorate-General for External Relations
DRC	Democratic Republic of Congo

EBA	'Everything but Arms'
EC	European Community
ECHR	European Convention on Human Rights
ECJ	European Court of Justice
ECOWAS	Economic Community of West African States
ECSC	European Coal and Steel Community
ECU	European Currency Unit
EDC	European Defence Community
EDF	European Development Fund
EEA	European Economic Area
EEAS	European External Action Service
EEC	European Economic Community
EFTA	European Free Trade Association
EGF	European Gendarmerie Force
EIB	European Investment Bank
EIDHR	European Initiative for Democracy and Human Rights (through 2007); then European Instrument for Democracy and Human Rights
EMP	Euro-Mediterranean Partnership
ENI	European Neighbourhood Instrument
ENP	European Neighbourhood Policy
ENPI	European Neighbourhood and Partnership Instrument
EOM	Electoral Observation Mission
EP	European Parliament
EPA	Economic Partnership Agreement
EPC	European Political Cooperation
ESDP	European Security and Defence Policy
EU	European Union
EUBAM	European Union Border Assistance Mission
EUCAP	European Union Capacity Building Mission
EUFOR	European Union Force
EUJUST	European Union Rule of Law Mission
EUMM	European Union Monitoring Mission
EUMS	European Union Military Staff
EUPM	European Union Police Mission in Bosnia and Herzegovina
EUPOL	European Union Police Mission
EUTM	European Union Training Mission
Eurojust	EU Unit of Law Enforcement Officials
Europol	European Police Office
EUSR	European Union Special Representative
FAC	Foreign Affairs Council
FPI	Foreign-policy Instruments service
FRY	Federal Republic of Yugoslavia
FTA	Free Trade Agreement

FTAA	Free Trade Area of the Americas
FYROM	Former Yugoslav Republic of Macedonia
G8	Group of Eight
GAERC	General Affairs and External Relations Council
GATT	General Agreement on Tariffs and Trade
GCC	Gulf Cooperation Council
GDP	Gross Domestic Product
GNP	Gross National Product
GSP	Generalized System of Preferences
HRC	Human Rights Council
ICC	International Criminal Court
ICJ	International Court of Justice
ICTY	International Criminal Tribunal for the former Yugoslavia
IGAD	Intergovernmental Authority on Development
IGC	Intergovernmental Conference
ILO	International Labour Organization
IMF	International Monetary Fund
INTCEN	EU Intelligence and Analysis Centre
IPA	Instrument for Pre-Accession
IfS	Instrument for Stability
ISAF	International Security Assistance Force (Afghanistan)
JHA	Justice and Home Affairs
MEDA	Aid to Mediterranean countries
MEP	Member of European Parliament
MERCOSUR	Common Market of the South
NAFTA	North American Free Trade Agreement
NATO	North Atlantic Treaty Organization
NGO	Non-governmental Organization
OAS	Organization of American States
OAU	Organization of African Unity
ODIHR	Office of Democratic Institutions and Human Rights
OECD	Organization of Economic Cooperation and Development
OHCHR	United Nations Office of the High Commissioner for Human Rights
OJ	Official Journal (of the European Communities)
OOPEC	Office of the Official Publications of the European Communities
OSCE	Organization of Security and Cooperation in Europe
PHARE	Poland/Hungary Assistance for Reconstruction of Economies
PLO	Palestinian Liberation Organization
PMG	Political Military Group
PSC	Political and Security Committee
QMV	Qualified Majority Voting
RRM	Rapid Reaction Mechanism

SAA	Stabilization and Association Agreement
SAARC	South Asian Association for Regional Cooperation
SADC	Southern African Development Community
SALW	Small Arms and Light Weapons
SAP	Stabilization and Association Process
SCO	Shanghai Cooperation Organization
SEA	Single European Act
SFOR	Stabilization Force
SSR	Security Sector Reform
TACIS	Technical Assistance to the Commonwealth of Independent States
TEU	Treaty on European Union
UfM	Union for the Mediterranean
UK	United Kingdom
UN	United Nations
UNPROFOR	United Nations Protection Force
US	United States
USA	United States of America
USAID	United States Agency for International Development
WEU	Western European Union
WTO	World Trade Organization

Acknowledgements

The first edition of this book was published in 2003; revising it ten years on for the third edition has once again illustrated that change is the one constant in international affairs. In preparing this book, I have benefited greatly from conversations with colleagues at the LSE and beyond about the EU's international role, and from engaging with students trying to understand how the European Union works. Many thanks to two anonymous reviewers, whose suggestions for improving the draft manuscript were very helpful. Finally, thanks to Damiano de Felice for his very able assistance with the Appendix.

CHAPTER ONE

Introduction: Conceptualizing EU Foreign Policy

As recently as the end of the twentieth century, a variety of commentators and academics was heralding the European Union (EU) as a new and different power in international relations, whose values, economic model and approach to diplomacy and war were more appropriate in today's globalized world – and particularly more appropriate than the model offered by the United States, held in low esteem around the world after its wars in Afghanistan (from 2001) and Iraq (from 2003 to 2011). The EU was a 'quiet superpower', a 'normative power', a 'civilizing power'.[1] Although it took the EU most of the first decade of the twenty-first century to agree and then ratify a far-reaching institutional reform package – originally meant to be a 'constitutional treaty' but then revised into the Lisbon Treaty – there was considerable hope that once implemented, the new treaty would enable the EU to assume a leading position in international relations.

Some of that hope has dissipated. Since 2009, the EU has been struggling with the eurozone crisis – failing repeatedly to find a solution to it – which has drained attention away from global affairs, damaged the EU's image around the world, and affected the willingness and ability of the EU and its member states to devote resources to foreign policy. The implementation of the Lisbon Treaty, which entered into force on 1 December 2009, in the field of foreign, security and defence policy has been marked by turbulence, with turf wars and indiscreet mutterings about the weaknesses of the new High Representative for EU foreign policy. In sum, the focus of policy-makers has been inward-looking – long a complaint of EU-watchers. Meanwhile, the world has indeed been changing. A new administration in the USA signalled a 'pivot' away from Europe and towards Asia. Power in international relations has diffused to many more actors, including the so-called 'rising powers', such as Brazil, China and India. International relations is thus more multipolar, while still marked by interdependence and the demand for multilateral solutions to global problems: a situation Giovanni Grevi calls 'interpolarity'.[2] In 2011, popular uprisings broke out in north Africa and the Middle East (and beyond), bringing both violent upheaval and renewed questioning of the extent to which concerns for stability rather than democracy should guide policy-making.

The internal (EU) and external (the world) contexts have indeed changed since the second edition of *European Union Foreign Policy in a Changing World*. This third edition retains the original focus on analysing why and how the EU pursues five foreign-policy objectives, while adding an exploration of how the new realities are affecting the policy-making process. The five foreign-policy objectives are:

• the encouragement of regional cooperation and integration;
• the promotion of human rights;
• the promotion of democracy and good governance;
• the prevention of violent conflicts; and
• the fight against international crime.

The book examines the various internal and external pressures that led to agreement to pursue these particular foreign-policy objectives, which policy instruments the Union has used to try to achieve them, and how it has used those instruments. It considers how the Lisbon Treaty, which created new institutions such as the European External Action Service (EEAS) and revised decision-making procedures, has altered the way in which policies to pursue the five objectives are made. It explores how the transforming external environment and the euro crisis have affected the resources devoted to those policies, and the judgements made about their relative importance.

'Foreign policy' is defined widely here, to mean the activity of developing and managing relationships between the state (or in our case, the EU) and other international actors, which promotes the domestic values and interests of the state or actor in question.[3] Foreign policy can entail the use of economic instruments but its aims are explicitly political or security-related, in contrast with foreign economic policy, whose objectives *and* means are economic.[4] The scope of investigation is thus broadened beyond the EU's specific framework for foreign-policy cooperation, the Common Foreign and Security Policy (CFSP), to other aspects of EU 'external relations' that were conducted in what used to be called the 'pillars' of the European Community (EC) and Justice and Home Affairs (JHA), but are now part of a supranational EU framework. The EU is a 'foreign-policy system', composed of these various frameworks. Its member states have foreign policies too, of course, but the emphasis here lies with the EU, not national, level.

Foreign policy is *not* just the product of CFSP. The European Union has the competence to conduct external economic relations, and thus wields important foreign-policy instruments, while foreign policy increasingly addresses JHA issues (the fight against international crime, for example). There are different rules regarding, and institutions involved in, the decision-making process regarding the policy instruments used. For many economic instruments (such as aid or trade agreements), decision-making is supranational, meaning that member states vote by qualified majority voting (though reaching a consensus tends to be the norm), and central EU institutions such as the European Commission and European Parliament play key roles. The use of diplomatic and military instruments is decided on in the intergovernmental framework of CFSP, in which the member states retain more control over decision-making primarily because they can veto decisions. The system is complex, and coordination can be quite challenging. Chapters 2 and 3 discuss the EU's foreign-policy-making system in more detail.

1.1 The EU's foreign-policy objectives

The fact that the European Union has articulated common foreign-policy objectives is a step towards more effective 'international actorness'. For Gunnar Sjöstedt, a structural requirement for 'international actor capability' is the existence of commonly accepted goals, along with a system for mobilizing resources necessary to meet the goals. Goals are more precise than interests; in fact, they operationalize interests, and are principles that would be valid for a relatively long time.[5]

Naturally, once objectives have been identified, attempts have to be made to fulfil them. As Arnold Wolfers noted, what differentiates foreign-policy goals from mere aspirations is that sacrifices (in time, money, lives, and so on) must be made to realize goals.[6] Choices must be made, priorities decided (for international actors are normally pursuing numerous internal and external goals), and means deployed. Of course, this does not mean that objectives will indeed be fulfilled: even if the means are appropriate and the objectives reasonable, external circumstances (such as the amenability of other actors) may simply not be conducive to their realization.

But how well the EU can achieve its foreign-policy objectives does partly depend on the extent of its international actor capability. The member states have to agree to wield policy instruments that are expected to be effective, to devote the resources considered necessary to achieve the objective. Thus any exploration of the EU's foreign-policy objectives must consider how the EU tries to fulfil them. As discussed in later chapters, the EU has devoted resources towards meeting the objectives considered in this book, but these may not be sufficient or wielded in a consistent or coherent manner.

It took some time for the Union to articulate concrete foreign-policy objectives, in keeping with the gradual evolution of a more overtly political side to European integration. Sjöstedt argued in 1977 that the European Community (as it was known then)[7] had articulated vague and general interests (such as the maintenance of peace, or the desire to speak with one voice in international affairs), but that it had not yet specified goals. The 1958 Rome Treaty, which established the European Community, does not contain foreign-policy objectives, reflecting its origins as a project of economic integration. The Community can engage in external economic relations (namely trade), but the objectives of those relations are not laid down in the Treaty. It was only with the creation in 1970 of a separate framework for foreign-policy cooperation, European Political Cooperation (EPC), that the member states began to consider what they wanted to achieve collectively on the international stage.

The 'founding' documents of EPC – the 1970 Luxembourg Report, the 1973 Copenhagen Report, and the 1981 London Report – do not actually state what the EPC is for, what the member states intend to do together in foreign policy. They are instead concerned with setting out the basic modalities of cooperation, coordination and (possible) collective action. But in the 1970s and 1980s, there were attempts to map out the common interests and objectives of the member states, in a highly general way. In December 1973, the foreign ministers of the (then) nine EC member states published a Document on the European Identity. They declared that the Nine intended 'to contribute to ensuring that international relations have a more just basis; that the independence and equality of States are better preserved; that prosperity is more equitably shared; and that the security of each country is more effectively guaranteed'.[8] The Nine would try to define common foreign-policy positions to pursue these objectives.

The next grand attempt to set out international objectives came in the late 1980s. The provisions on EPC in the 1987 Single European Act (SEA) merely state that the member states 'shall ensure that common principles and objectives are gradually developed and defined' (Article 30.2). But the SEA preamble contains a hint of their common interests:

> Aware of the responsibility incumbent upon Europe to aim at speaking ever increasingly with one voice and to act with consistency and solidarity in order more effectively to protect its common interests and independence, in particular to display the principles of democracy and compliance with the law and with human rights to which they are attached, so that together that may make their own contribution to the preservation of international peace and security . . .

In December 1988, in the midst of international concern that the completion of the single European market (launched by the SEA) would result in a 'fortress Europe', the Rhodes European Council issued a Statement on the International Role of the European Community.[9] The heads of state or government pledged their commitment to greater liberalization of international trade, and to closer cooperation with third countries across the globe. The EC and its member states will:

- play an active role in the preservation of international peace and security, and in the solution of regional conflicts;
- demonstrate solidarity to the spreading movement for democracy and support for the Universal Declaration on Human Rights;
- strengthen the effectiveness of the United Nations and contribute to its peacekeeping role;
- improve social and economic conditions in less-developed countries; and

- work to overcome the division of Europe and to promote the Western values and principles that the member states have in common.

Another major attempt to specify foreign-policy objectives was made during the Maastricht Treaty negotiations in 1991. The member states were setting up a 'new and improved' mechanism for foreign-policy cooperation, the CFSP, and felt the need to indicate what it would do. They considered declaring specific objectives, but found it impossible to agree on a definite list.[10] So the objectives listed in the treaty are vague and general, and clearly reflect the earlier statements (see Box 1.1).

After the signing of the Maastricht Treaty, more progress was made in setting out objectives. In June 1992, the foreign ministers submitted a report to the European Council on potential areas for CFSP 'Joint Action'.[11] These include the five objectives discussed in this book:

- strengthening democratic principles and institutions, and respect for human and minority rights;
- promoting regional political stability and contributing to the creation of political and/or economic frameworks that encourage regional cooperation or moves towards regional or sub-regional integration;
- contributing to the prevention and settlement of conflicts;
- contributing to a more effective international coordination in dealing with emergency situations;

Box 1.1 Foreign-policy objectives in the 1993 Maastricht Treaty on European Union

Objectives of the *Common Foreign and Security Policy*:

- to safeguard the common values, fundamental interests, and independence of the Union;
- to strengthen the security of the Union in all ways;
- to preserve peace and strengthen international security;
- to promote international cooperation; and
- to develop and consolidate democracy and the rule of law, and respect for human rights and fundamental freedoms (Article J.1)

The Treaty does not lay out objectives for the external relations of the European Community pillar, but it does set out objectives for development cooperation. The Community will foster:

- the sustainable economic and social development of the developing countries, and more particularly the most disadvantaged among them;
- the smooth and gradual integration of the developing countries into the world economy;
- the campaign against poverty in the developing countries; and
- the development and consolidation of democracy and the rule of law, and respect for human rights and fundamental freedoms (Article 130u).

- strengthening international cooperation in issues of international interest such as the fight against arms proliferation, terrorism, and traffic in illicit drugs; and
- promoting and supporting good government.

In 2002–4, another round of specifying policy objectives occurred. In December 2003, the European Council agreed on a European Security Strategy (ESS).[12] The ESS can be viewed as a response to both the spectacular intra-European disagreements over the US–Iraq crisis in early 2003, and to US pressure for the EU to engage more with its agenda of pre-emptive action to counter security threats. The EU member states demonstrated solidarity in agreeing to the ESS, but also signalled differences with the US approach. The European Security Strategy declares that the EU has three core strategic objectives:

- addressing security threats: terrorism; proliferation of weapons of mass destruction; regional conflicts; state failure; and organized crime;
- enhancing security in the EU's neighbourhood, by, for example, building relations with the Mediterranean and East European states; and
- creating an international order based on 'effective multilateralism', which entails upholding international law and strengthening the United Nations.

The EU made it clear that none of the threats could be addressed with purely military means, and that 'preventive engagement' (not pre-emptive coercion) is the best way to try to ensure that situations do not escalate or deteriorate.

In 2002, the EU began what turned into a very long process of agreeing a new treaty (see Chapter 2). The 2009 Lisbon Treaty contains important reforms of the EU's machinery for making foreign policy (discussed in the next chapter), and sets out a by-now familiar list of foreign-policy objectives (see Box 1.2).

What is striking about most of the EU's objectives is that they appear to be what Arnold Wolfers called 'milieu goals' rather than 'possession goals'. Possession goals further national interests. Milieu goals aim to shape the environment in which the state – or the EU, in our case – operates. Milieu goals may only be means of achieving possession goals, but they may also be goals that transcend the national interest and are shared widely.[13] Judging solely from the objectives it has articulated, the EU seems to be more inclined to try to shape its surrounding environment than to protect particular interests. Whether this is actually the case in practice – and how conducive the environment is to being shaped by the EU – will be investigated further in this book.

The five objectives examined here have been chosen because they are *primarily* political and security-related (as opposed to promotion of sustainable

Box 1.2 Objectives for the EU's external action in the Lisbon Treaty

The EU shall define and pursue common policies and actions in order to:

- safeguard its values, fundamental interests, security, independence and integrity;
- consolidate and support democracy, the rule of law, human rights and the principles of international law;
- preserve peace, prevent conflicts and strengthen international security (in accordance with the UN Charter and CSCE principles, including those relating to external borders);
- foster the sustainable economic, social and environmental development of developing countries, with the primary aim of eradicating poverty;
- encourage the integration of all countries into the world economy, including through the progressive abolition of restrictions on international trade;
- help develop international measures to preserve and improve the quality of the environment and the sustainable management of global natural resources in order to ensure sustainable development;
- assist populations, countries and region-confronting natural or man-made disasters; and
- promote an international system based on stronger multilateral cooperation and good global governance (Article 21 (2), Treaty on the European Union).

development or abolishing trade restrictions), have been repeatedly affirmed at the highest levels of the EU (see above), and are precise enough to guide policy-making (as opposed to, arguably, pursuing effective multilateralism, or safeguarding fundamental interests). In some cases, the EU's adoption of the objectives pre-dates the attempts outlined above to list general foreign-policy aims. Furthermore, pursuing these five objectives requires considerable internal coordination, so an exploration of how the EU does this gives us a good overall view of how (and how well) the EU's foreign-policy system as a whole works.

The five chosen objectives are not the EU's only objectives, nor are they categorically the EU's top five priority objectives. As will be seen repeatedly throughout this book, pursuit of each of the five objectives chosen here often clashes with other policy objectives. This is to be expected in any system of government; what is of interest is how and whether the EU recognizes and resolves such clashes. What will become quite obvious later in the book is that the Union does not generally set priorities among its objectives, even though they can easily conflict with each other. For example, the fight against international crime may be incompatible with the promotion of human rights and democracy, if it entails tolerating authoritarian leaders who suppress international criminal networks. Furthermore, will the EU pursue all of these objectives *everywhere*? It clearly lacks the resources to do so, so what does it choose to do in practice? This will indicate which objectives are actually most important.

1.2 Theory and EU foreign policy-making: Obstacles to a common EU foreign policy

The process of choosing foreign-policy objectives and then devising policies to achieve them is, as might be expected in such a complex system, not a straightforward matter. Above all, the member states must all be in agreement. The Union does not come close to having exclusive jurisdiction over foreign policy, and the member states can still act autonomously in international affairs. They may agree to act collectively – but that agreement is not mandatory and is not always forthcoming. Even when decisions can be taken by qualified majority voting, the member states will seek to protect their vital interests and block decisions that contravene them. Tacit or explicit agreement of all the member states is needed for the Union to act internationally, or what is called 'vertical coherence'.[14] There can also be clashes among the EU institutions, most obviously the European Commission (with its supranational inclinations) and the Council of Ministers (protective of member state prerogatives), even though 'horizontal coherence' between the EU's frameworks has long been a requirement under the treaties.[15] Perhaps surprisingly, this complex system *does* produce common foreign policies though several quite serious obstacles lie in the way. This section considers those obstacles; the next discusses the potentially countervailing pressures that can lead the member states to agree common foreign policies.

For many observers, the fundamental – perhaps even insurmountable – obstacle to EU foreign-policy-making is that the member states still insist on pursuing their foreign-policy interests separately, or at least ensuring that any Union policy causes least damage to them. Any 'foreign policy' formulated at the EU level is inconsequential and weak, because it represents the lowest common denominator, or what the most reluctant member state could accept.

It is argued that the member states do not share extensive common interests, and this 'logic of diversity'[16] tends to block agreement on creating more supranational foreign-policy-making machinery, as well as the making of common foreign policies within the current framework. The EU's member states retain control of foreign-policy-making, and will not surrender that control in the name of a more effective common foreign policy.[17] They have not created collective capabilities to match the internal and external expectations of coherent, effective, collective international behaviour (a 'capabilities-expectations gap', in Christopher Hill's terms, is apparent).[18]

The tools and objectives of EU foreign-policy-making are necessarily limited to those which do not offend member state sensitivities or contradict their interests. As a result, the Union is weakest in the military field. For many observers, this means the Union cannot exercise much influence – if it cannot back up its diplomacy with the use of force, then it will never become a '*complete*, not merely a civilian power'.[19] Robert Cooper, for example, argues that the EU cannot protect its post-modern paradise much less spread its post-modern message if it is not prepared to play by the rules of the jungle outside it.[20] For Robert Kagan, a Europe without strong military capabilities (and a willingness to use them) will always have to rely on the USA to ensure international order and protect common interests.[21] The international system is not a post-modern, Kantian nirvana, but one with distinct Hobbesian characteristics; in such a system, power – and particularly coercive, military power – is the key currency, and the EU doesn't have it.

These arguments are consistent with either realist or intergovernmentalist theories. Realists emphasize the limits to cooperation, and argue that international institutions cannot overcome these limits. States have to survive in an anarchic international system, so they must perforce be concerned with whether or not other states (potential enemies) will gain more than they do from any cooperative venture. The accumulation, maintenance and use of power – especially military – are critically important, not only to ensure survival but to protect and promote other national interests.

Intergovernmentalists, in contrast, argue that international institutions can help overcome the limits to cooperation. But they see those institutions as a means of pursuing state interests, through bargaining, and large states will not accept outcomes that contravene those interests. Bargaining involves making side payments to small states and threatening sanctions to overcome resistance to an agreement. Only when cooperation brings benefits will states cooperate, and they will not make fundamental compromises just for the sake of agreement.[22]

Institutions, though, can also pose obstacles to common foreign-policy-making. Ulrich Krotz considers the complexity of the EU's foreign-policy-making system to be a serious impediment to its political actorness – 'a multitude of actors, units and institutions share fragments of political authority and may be involved in the formulation of positions or in decision-making processes'.[23] What foreign-policy analysts long ago described as bureaucratic politics and turf wars can complicate, slow down and even inhibit the formulation and implementation of common foreign policies.

Other theorists concentrate on identity, and the lack of a European identity, as the primary obstacle to a European foreign policy. Several observers deny that European interests can develop in the absence of a European state. They argue that foreign policy is the expression of the identity and interests of a particular community, and until the Union becomes such a community, it will never be able to formulate and implement effective, legitimate foreign policy. David Allen maintains that foreign policy is intrinsically linked to the 'idea of a state with a set of interests identified by a government'.[24] Jean-Marie Guehenno goes beyond the problematique of a common government and links the lack of European interests to the absence of a European polity:

> If there is to be a European foreign policy, it is not enough to overcome the national interests of the Member States. Common European interests are as much political

constructs as the national interests they are expected to supersede: national interests were produced by national polities therefore a European foreign policy requires a European polity, which will produce European interests.[25]

This is echoed in the assertion by Christopher Hill and William Wallace that '[e]ffective foreign policy rests upon a shared sense of national identity, of a nation-state's "place in the world", its friends and enemies, its interests and aspirations. . . . The European Community rests upon a relatively weak sense of shared history and identity . . .'[26] The emergence of a sense of common identity is difficult in economic hard times (as the EU has experienced since 2008–9), particularly because the EU is blamed – sometimes rightly, sometimes wrongly – for the economic malaise.

Finally, it must be noted that even if the member states and the institutions agree and implement coherent foreign policies, the EU may not exercise influence – it may not fulfil its policy objectives. As Daniel Thomas has argued, 'coherence may be necessary for the EU to exert its influence abroad, but it clearly is not sufficient in a multi-centric world order where many others do not share the EU's collective policy preferences and are ready to deploy vast resources in pursuit of their goals'.[27] The changing world may make it more and more difficult for the EU to have an impact, to meet its objectives, protect its interests and promote its values. Unity alone is not enough.

1.3 Theory and EU foreign policy-making: The potential for a common EU foreign policy

Other observers would point out that these obstacles have not stopped the member states from developing the mechanisms for foreign-policy cooperation, or declaring that they do share some common interests and objectives and desire to pursue them collectively – or even that they share a European identity. There are pressures for collective action, which can result in common foreign policies. These pressures are both external and internal.

External stimuli include concrete demands on the EU for action, as well as the more diffuse effects of international interdependence or globalization, and the awareness that in a world of rising powers, EU member states need to stick together to protect and promote their interests. Interdependence implies more than interconnectedness; it characterizes an international system in which states are not the only important actors (non-state actors such as multi-national corporations and international organizations can have an impact), and military security is not the primary goal of governments (other goals such as economic wealth or environmental protection can top the foreign-policy agenda).[28]

Interdependence could, of course, impede collective action: the member states could react differently to international developments, because they are affected differently by them (the logic of diversity). The cross-national ties of non-state actors, and the transnational nature of key problems facing governments, can also make *state* action ineffective, injudicious, or irrelevant. These ties and issues may extend well beyond the EU, making action at the EU level equally difficult, especially if only some of the member states are affected or involved.

But interdependence could also encourage collective action by the EU in at least three ways. First, there is awareness that unilateral action is often either ineffective or impossible in an interdependent world. The EU member states would be much better off trying to act collectively. They recognize that there is a 'politics of scale': they will 'carry more weight in certain areas when they act together as a bloc than when they act separately'.[29] In a world in which power is more diffuse and more actors (specifically the rising powers) can exercise influence, presumably the benefits of the politics of scale should be particularly noticeable. Secondly, interdependence creates opportunities for EU action. There is more room for the EU to act autonomously: its civilian instruments could have more influence in a world in which economic clout is just as or even more important than military prowess. In addition, interdependence is not necessarily symmetrical: there are variations in states' sensitivity and vulnerability to changes in transaction flows. This gives the EU leverage: it could influence the domestic and external policies of third countries if they depend on the EU for trade, aid, or other benefits. (Conversely, of course, the extent of EU dependence on third countries for, say, material resources will affect EU policy-making.)

Thirdly, interdependence has shaped the 'policy agenda', in ways that can make collective action sensible and desirable. The EU's policy instruments (aid, trade, diplomacy) are suitable for dealing with new security threats, including (non-violent) ethnic disputes, violations of human rights, economic deprivation, and international crime – all of which would be difficult for the member states to handle separately. Furthermore, EU action may be considered to be more legitimate than unilateral action on issues such as the promotion of human rights and democratization, or humanitarian intervention.

There are also more concrete external factors encouraging common foreign-policy-making. The EU comes under considerable pressure to respond to the many demands on it for political dialogue, aid, trade agreements, association, membership, and so on. External demands grew particularly with the completion of the single European market between 1987 and 1993. Several writers have termed this 'externalization': development of the EC's internal market generates outsiders' pressure for compensation, to which the member states must respond collectively.[30] The Union's economic strength has generated expectations in the past that it will exercise political influence: for example, the Palestinian Authority frequently called on the Union to play a political role in the Middle East peace process that would be commensurate with the Union's status as the largest donor of aid to the Palestinians. Enlargement (the EU grew from six member states in 1957 to 28 in 2013) adds to the EU's 'global weight' and fuels higher expectations that the EU will act globally. Although the EU's economic 'glow' shines much less brightly in the wake of the eurozone crisis, many countries still look to the EU for political and economic ties, and there is still a long queue for EU membership even after the latest enlargements.[31] The EU may respond only partially or not at all to such demands, but they nonetheless create pressures for collective action.

Internal stimuli for EU foreign policy include both intra-EU and intra-member state factors. As even the intergovernmentalists argue, the member states can 'use' the EU to pursue strictly national economic or security interests. One or more member states (acting together) may lead a concerted push for EU action, because it will 'add value' to, or supplement, their own activities (and the EU may have more appropriate or even potentially more influential policy instruments). As the EU has enlarged, new member states have sought to influence the content and scope of its external relations. For example, the UK, Portugal and Spain wanted to incorporate relations with their former colonies; the Central and East European countries seek deeper relations with their eastern and south-eastern neighbours, but are wary of closer ties with Russia. Furthermore, collective action can conveniently provide a 'shield':[32] member states can hide behind the EU, citing the exigencies of going along with their partners when faced with unpalatable demands from outside (or domestic actors).

Pressures for EU action on international issues can also come 'from below', from domestic public opinion and domestic actors (parliaments, NGOs, and so on), as well as from transnationally organized actors such as NGOs based in Brussels, or 'epistemic communities', transnational networks of professional experts, who agree on certain beliefs and share common interests, and who supply knowledge to policy-makers.[33] Opinion polls have consistently shown high levels of support across member states for the general idea that the EU should cooperate in the field of foreign policy – while this may not necessarily translate into approval of specific foreign-policy actions, there is widespread support for the EU as a foreign-policy actor.

Neofunctionalism, a theory developed in the context of European integration in the 1950s and 1960s, points to several other pressures that could lead to common foreign-policy-making.[34] Neofunctionalists posit that integration proceeds gradually, via a process of spillover: sector integration, as in the coal and steel sectors, will beget its own impetus and extend to the entire economy, as a result of connections between sectors and the 'creative talents' of political elites who seize the opportunities to expand the tasks of the organization. Thus EU institutions – notably the Commission – may push for EU foreign-policy action. The Commission can help to articulate common European interests, suggest policy options, and encourage agreement among the member states on policies that represent more than the lowest common denominator. The European Parliament can also press for common foreign policies particularly by using its budgetary powers and its powers to approve external agreements. Spillover from economic integration could affect positively the prospects for common foreign-policy-making. The precursor of the CFSP, European Political Cooperation, was, after all, established in 1970 partly because the six member states felt the need to speak with a common political voice in international affairs, to match their growing economic voice. But spillover may be more diffuse, occurring through what Michael Smith has termed the politicization of the EC's external activities, for example, by setting political conditions for EC assistance.[35]

Incentives for common foreign-policy-making can also result from the very process of cooperation. Constructivists argue that through the process of cooperation, actors' interests and identities change. Institutions (stable sets of identities and interests) are created through reciprocal interaction; institutionalization is a process of internalizing new identities and interests. Collective identities and interests – feelings of solidarity, community and loyalty – could even be formed in this process.[36]

Many of the EU member states have worked together for at least three decades; processes of socialization and of 'engrenage' are at work here. Over 30 years ago, Philippe de Schoutheete pointed to the development of a 'coordination reflex' among EPC participants: they consulted each other before taking a stance on international developments.[37] Through these sorts of processes, member states become more likely to perceive common interests.[38] It is therefore possible, *pace* the sceptics, for common interests to develop even in the absence of a polity. Roy Ginsberg has called this a 'self-styled logic', in which common policies arise from the shared perception of European interests. Examples of such policies, reflecting an 'indigenous and unique European quality' are support for regional integration, EU membership conditionality, and aid for civil society.[39] The growth of 'we-feeling' among the EU member states could also help explain why they would choose to act through the EU, rather than through other organizations or unilaterally. As Ben Tonra argues, the continual reform of common foreign-policy-making procedures reflects a desire not only to improve the EU's problem-solving capacity, but also to strengthen collective identification and consequent action.[40]

This book considers the extent to which these various obstacles and pressures have played a role in the EU's selection and pursuit of the five foreign-policy objectives. Why do the member states push for common policies to pursue these objectives? What role do the EU institutions and other actors play in policy-making? Does a 'logic of diversity' predominate? Are EU decisions watered down to the lowest common denominator?

1.4 A distinctive international identity?

This book focuses on what the EU actually does in international relations, by examining how and why it pursues the five foreign-policy objectives. A related question is the extent to which the EU 'does' foreign policy differently: what is its 'international identity'?

Identity here is conceived as 'the images of individuality and distinctiveness ("self-hood") held and projected by an actor and formed (and modified over time), through relations with significant "others"'.[41] Although this definition comes from social psychology and applies to individuals, states – and organizations composed of states – also seek to project distinctive identities in the international arena. Of course, as noted in section 1.2, there could be objections to the notion that the EU even has an 'identity'. But there are '*EU* policies, activities and objectives', which have been decided in a complex policy-making environment in which no one state or institution determines outcomes, and in which all are bound – more or less – by the outcomes they produce together. The accumulation of EU decisions and activities distinguishes the EU not only from its constituent parts (perhaps uncomfortably so, for some member states, some of the time) but also from other international actors. Henrik Larsen has argued that the EU tries to present itself 'as a political unit with a role to play in world politics with its own interests. Europe is constructed as an international unit or identity, not just as the same as the West, in the same way as the USA also presents itself as a unit and not just the same as the West'.[42]

The question here is *how* distinctive an international actor is the EU, compared to other states and entities in the international system? To try to answer this question, this book asks two sets of further questions: (1) Why has the EU agreed on the five foreign-policy objectives? Are they the product of internal dynamics – and hence, arguably, unique? Or are they influenced more by external processes of normative globalization, such that the EU's distinctive identity is less obvious?; and (2) How does the EU pursue the five objectives? Are the instruments and the methods used by the EU to pursue these objectives those of a 'civilian power', or of a more assertive, almost state-like, 'power bloc'?

Whence the objectives: internal or global dynamics?

Two possible 'sources' of the EU's objectives are explored. On the one hand, there could be a link between the way EU policy is made and the content of the policy thus produced. On the other, the objectives and values of EU policy may reflect processes of what we can call 'normative globalization', meaning the ever-widening acceptance of norms, or standards of domestic and international conduct.[43] Thus the EU's foreign-policy activity simply mirrors and reproduces international norms. These two possibilities can be roughly categorized as the differing approaches of foreign-policy analysts, concerned with internal decision-making processes and outcomes, and of those constructivists concerned with the influence of socially constructed international norms on states (the EU, in our case).

With respect to the first source, the output of the EU foreign-policy-making process obviously reflects the values and interests of the main participants, the member states. It is they that primarily push for the EU to pursue particular objectives. But if the primary source of the EU's objectives is the member states, then the member states could also be pursuing those objectives in other international fora, and unilaterally. What may make the EU unique is the way in which national preferences can become EU policy, and the effects that EU membership may have had on the preferences themselves.

It can be argued that the EU's unique foreign-policy output derives from the very nature of the EU foreign-policy system. Richard Whitman defines the EU's international identity as 'EU operations explicitly directed outwards', conceived in terms of the instruments available to the Union as well as how 'elements of the Union that define its *sui generis* nature also contribute distinctive facets to its international identity'.[44] Such elements include its institutional structure and decision-making norms and procedures. In sum, the way that the Union makes and implements foreign policy is reflected in the content of the policy thus produced. To put it another way, the objectives and values that the EU promotes internationally are inherently linked to the internal dynamics of the Union itself.

For example, the EU very often establishes and develops relations based on law, through the conclusion of agreements with third countries and regional groupings.[45] We could interpret this emphasis on establishing contractual relations as a reflection of the Community's origins as an attempt to instil the rule of law in relations between its member states. As François Duchêne argued: 'The European Community's interest as a civilian group of countries long on economic power and relatively short on armed force is as far as possible to *domesticate* relations between states, including those of its own members and those with states outside its frontiers.'[46] Lily Gardner Feldman has argued that the legacy of reconciliation between former enemies (France and Germany in particular) 'provides European foreign policy with a distinctive content – a focus on peace and development, on the one hand, and the creation of cooperative institutional structures, on the other'.[47]

Thus the EU conducts foreign policy that derives from the way the EU itself developed. Christopher Hill and William Wallace have noted, 'European diplomacy has steadily become associated in the public mind with a distinctive set of principles', which include a preference for diplomacy over coercion, the use of mediation to resolve conflicts, a preference for long-term economic solutions to political problems, and the promotion of human rights.[48] For Stephan Keukeleire, this is 'structural diplomacy', and it is 'aimed at promoting a more favourable international environment, both in the internal situation of the countries concerned and in the inter-state relations and general situation of [other] regions'.[49]

There have been fears that the integration process could deprive the EU of this distinctiveness. Decades ago, Johann Galtung expressed the fear that the European Community would develop into a superpower, recreating the ills of sovereignty and power politics on a larger scale; David Mitrany opposed regional integration schemes for similar reasons.[50] But others argue that it is impossible for integration to be deepened along state-like lines given heterogeneity within the EU, which increases because of enlargement. Jan Zielonka argues that the EU will increasingly resemble a 'neo-medieval empire', with 'overlapping authorities, divided sovereignty, diversified institutional arrangements and multiple identities', not a Westphalian model, with its 'concentration of power, hierarchy, sovereignty and clear-cut identity'.[51]

In any event, the way foreign policy is made within the EU may not be the most important determinant of the content of that policy. The 'distinctive set of principles' associated with EU foreign policy may be less distinctive if we posit that the principles themselves are fairly universal. Once the overwhelming exigency of survival in a nuclear-armed bipolar confrontation passed, states – and non-state actors, including international organizations – have been freer to pursue milieu goals of the sort liberal internationalists would recognize: the export of democracy, promotion of human rights, promotion of free trade, and so on. The Union's foreign-policy output may thus reflect the *zeitgeist* of post-Cold War normative globalization.

Certainly the EU's objectives are shared with other states and organizations, as will become obvious in later chapters. Within Europe, a far-reaching normative framework has developed. As Gregory Flynn and Henry Farrell argue,

> [a] new hierarchy of norms, centred around an altered sense of sovereignty, nonintervention, and self-determination, has emerged. The quality of interstate order has been linked to the quality of states – to their ability to organize sovereignty along liberal democratic lines.[52]

But significantly, Flynn and Farrell argue that these developments were taken within the Conference on Security and Cooperation in Europe (CSCE). The EU is not the only framework in which liberal norms are developed and given expression. It exists in a dense institutional environment in Europe, and its member states are members of other organizations that have contributed to the spread of norms. These also include the Council of Europe, an organization older than the European Community, specifically dedicated to fostering democracy and the protection of human rights, and even NATO, which shifted in the 1990s from an emphasis on collective defence to conflict resolution and prevention.

The EU's member states may thus be converging on a set of goals that reflect international norms, and they may view the Union as an (or the most) appropriate forum in which they can pursue those goals. The values they share may be widespread, not EU-specific, and the EU may be seen as the framework within which such values can be articulated. In this case, the process of cooperation within the Union reproduces broader values, more than it generates unique foreign policy.

To try to establish the extent to which the EU's objectives reflect distinctively EU principles, or more universal principles, the history of the objective as an EU foreign-policy objective will be traced in each chapter. Why and when did the EU adopt it, and who was pushing for its adoption? Did the EU adopt the objective before other actors did, or did it follow them? Each chapter considers how the Union legitimizes its pursuit of the objectives. Does the Union – in its official declarations, policy statements and so on – refer to specifically EU principles as the justification for its actions? Or does it refer to more universal principles, that could be accepted as valid by other international actors? Some objectives may be more clearly delineated and unique EU objectives, others may reflect the influence of universal principles to a greater extent.

Civilian power, power bloc . . . or flop?

Even if the EU's objectives largely reflect normative globalization rather than EU-specific values, then the way that the EU pursues those objectives may still be considered a unique aspect of its international identity. What foreign-policy instruments does the EU use and how does it wield them? In other words, how does the Union 'behave' internationally?

The instruments that the EU can use are economic, diplomatic, and to some extent, military; Chapter 3 elaborates on the EU's 'arsenal' of policy instruments. The instruments that the EU uses are key, but so are the ways in which the EU uses them to try to achieve its ends. K. J. Holsti put forward six ways in which an international actor can influence other international actors: using persuasion (eliciting a favourable response without explicitly holding out the possibility of punishments); offering rewards; granting rewards; threatening punishment; inflicting non-violent punishment; or using force.[53] Persuasion is similar to Joseph Nye's conception of 'soft power', which co-opts rather than coerces people. 'A country may obtain the outcomes it wants in world politics because other countries – admiring its values, emulating its example, aspiring to its level of prosperity and openness – want to follow it'.[54] It is essentially the power of attraction, and Nye explicitly differentiates this from coercion or inducement, which he calls command power.[55]

Foreign-policy instruments can be used in these different ways: the 'stick' (punishment) is not just military, nor is 'the carrot' (rewards) solely economic. Economic instruments encompass the promise of aid, aid itself, sanctions, and so forth; likewise, military instruments range from the actual use of force to compel or deter an enemy to training and aiding militaries in other countries, to ensuring defence of the national territory against a military invasion. Civilian (non-military) instruments can be used quite coercively. Conditionality, for example, can be seen as both an inducement (aid or other benefits will be extended if certain economic and/or political conditions are met) and a tool of coercion (if those conditions are violated, the benefits will be cut off), though following Nye's argument, it is always an exercise of command power.

The chapters on the five foreign-policy objectives analyse which policy instruments the EU uses to pursue the objectives. They examine the resources that EU member states are willing to expend to try to achieve the objectives, and any constraints on the use of the instruments. Then the chapters consider how these instruments are wielded: does the EU prefer positive to negative measures? To what extent does the EU rely on command power (coercion or inducement) and to what extent on persuasion to achieve its objectives? Does it apply conditionality, and how consistently?

The findings regarding the objectives the EU pursues, the kinds of instruments the EU uses, and the way in which it uses them, feed back into academic debates over what kind of entity the EU is and whether a definite label can be pinned on the EU. For the sake of simplicity, three such labels are used here: civilian power, power bloc, or flop.[56] Grouped under 'civilian power' are the strikingly similar categories of civilian force, normative power, civilizing power, post-modern power, and quiet superpower. A civilian power can be defined according to three elements: means (policy instruments); ends (goals, objectives); and use of persuasion. It is 'an actor which uses civilian means for persuasion, to pursue civilian ends'.[57] 'Civilian means' are non-military: a civilian power eschews the use of coercive military force. 'Civilian ends', using a lowest common denominator definition, are international cooperation, solidarity, domestication of international relations (or strengthening the rule of law in international relations), responsibility for the global environment, and the diffusion of equality, justice and tolerance (all milieu goals, essentially).[58] The ways in which means are used can be placed along a spectrum from persuasion to coercion; civilian powers rely on persuasion, not coercion.

Civilian power is not completely unique in international relations: small states tend to rely on persuasion rather than coercion. But it is more unusual for states with considerable resources to choose to behave like civilian powers – Germany and Japan stood out because of this. Similarly, an entity like the EU with considerable resources and capabilities would stand out in international relations if it behaved (normally) like a civilian power.

A 'power bloc', in contrast, pursues more self-interested (possession) goals, and is not averse to using coercion (carrots and sticks) to achieve those goals. In this view, the EU can and does use its (considerable) economic and diplomatic (and even to some extent military) strength to promote and protect its interests. Those interests are more self-interested than other-regarding (for example, protection of commercial or political ties). The EU is the largest and richest trading bloc in the world, one of the largest aid donors, and its member states have some of the world's most capable military forces. It could thus exercise quite a lot of leverage in its relations with other countries.

The literature on the EU's international identity often refers to what is a hybrid of civilian power and power bloc. This captures cases where the EU uses (or could use) coercion, even military force, to pursue milieu goals. Some observers have called on the EU to display such hybrid behaviour: Stelios Stavridis argues that to be a civilian power, the EU *must* use military means, because force can be necessary to promote human rights and democratic principles.[59] Göran Therborn argues that 'without the backing of force and a willingness to use it, "Europe" is unlikely to become a normative power, telling other parts of the world what political, economic and social institutions they should have'.[60] For other observers, however, this sort of behaviour would come dangerously close to that of a pure power bloc, purporting to act in the name of milieu goals but actually intent on boosting its own power or protecting its own interests. In much of the literature on civilian power, normative power, post-modern power, and so on, the use of coercion (above all military force) tends to fall outside such categories. Despite its messiness, the hybrid might nonetheless capture EU foreign-policy behaviour.

Finally, of course, there is the possibility that the EU is a 'flop' – it could fail to reach and maintain a common policy at all, or it could be irrelevant, failing to have much of an influence on third countries or international developments.

1.5 Outline of the book

Chapters 2 and 3 provide the background for understanding the EU's foreign-policy system. Chapter 2 explains the evolution of that system and the expansion of the Union's foreign-policy role. Chapter 3 discusses the policy instruments the EU can wield. The five foreign-policy objectives are then analysed in Chapters 4–8. How the EU came to adopt each objective and how it seeks to achieve it are the two guiding questions for each chapter. For the first question, the balance of external and internal stimuli behind the adoption and development of each objective will be considered, in particular to uncover the extent to which it can be considered to be 'European', in the sense that it reflects internal dynamics of cooperation more than adaptation of international norms. Who was pushing for its adoption? What were the reasons given for its adoption? Do the EU's documents refer to universal values or international developments; does the EU encourage third states to adapt to universal standards or to EU ones? Is it an agent of normative globalization or structured by it? How important are milieu goals compared to possession goals? Addressing the second question, how the EU pursues the objectives, each chapter analyses the policy instruments that are used, and the tendency or not to use coercion with respect to third states. Each chapter also considers the role that obstacles such as the logic of diversity, bureaucratic politics and pressures such as the politics of scale or external demands, play in the decision-making process.

Questions for discussion

1. Consider the various lists of EU foreign-policy objectives. Why might 'milieu goals' be so prominent in those lists?

2. How constricting are the obstacles to common EU foreign-policy-making?

3. In your view, is the potential for common EU foreign-policy-making greater than the obstacles that could prevent it?

Suggestions for further reading

Ginsberg, Roy. 'Conceptualizing the European Union as an International Actor: Narrowing the Theoretical Capability-Expectations Gap', *Journal of Common Market Studies*, 37, 3 (1999).

Hill, Christopher. 'The Capability–Expectations Gap, or Conceptualizing Europe's International Role', *Journal of Common Market Studies*, 31, 3 (1993).

Krotz, Ulrich. 'Momentum and Impediments: Why Europe Won't Emerge as a Full Political Actor on the World Stage Soon', *Journal of Common Market Studies*, 47, 3 (2009).

Thomas, Daniel C. 'Still Punching below its Weight? Coherence and Effectiveness in European Union Foreign Policy', *Journal of Common Market Studies*, 50, 3 (2012).

The Evolution of the EU as an International Actor

The European Union has evolved considerably from its 1950s origins as a common market with six member states. The European Community of the 1950s and 1960s had some relations with third countries, namely former European colonies in Africa, and was beginning to assert a common stance in international trade negotiations. The European Union in 2013 had twenty-eight member states, had opened accession negotiations with three states (Iceland, Montenegro, and Turkey), and had promised accession to another four (or five, including Kosovo). It is the world's largest unified market and trading bloc, conducts economic and political relations with virtually every country on earth, and has sent thirty civilian and military missions to countries on three continents.

The EU has considerable 'presence' in international affairs: other international actors cannot fail to notice its resources, and its internal policies (such as its agricultural or monetary policies) affect other international actors. Presence is a consequence of the EU's internal development, not necessarily of any explicit externally directed EU policy.[1] But the EU is not always able to translate presence into 'actorness', that is, the ability to function actively and deliberately in relations to other actors in the international system.[2]

The articulation of policy objectives is one requirement of actorness, as noted in Chapter 1, but the pursuit of those objectives is even more so. The EU member states and institutions must be able to agree on external actions, maintain those positions, and mobilize the resources necessary to pursue them. They are not always able to do so – and have on occasion been very publicly divided over international issues (most spectacularly over the Iraq war in early 2003; more recently over intervention in Libya in 2011). But nonetheless, the member states have continually sought to improve the procedures that could allow agreement to be reached more easily, strengthen the institutions that could foster agreement and implement common policies, and increase the resources that could be wielded on behalf of a common policy. At the same time, however, the member states have sought to retain control over decision-making procedures, and have jealously guarded their own autonomy especially in the sphere of foreign and defence policy. The tension between the drive to act collectively on the world stage and the desire to retain national autonomy has shaped the institutions and procedures developed in the external relations field, as well as the outcomes produced by them. This chapter describes the evolution of the institutions and procedures relevant to the EU's international actorness; the next chapter analyses the EU's foreign-policy instruments.

2.1 Community external relations and EPC

The foundation of the original European Communities was, above all, a unique resolution of the 'German problem', or the preponderance of German power.[3] Although post-World War II Germany was divided – its western part allied to the western bloc, and its eastern part allied to the eastern bloc – West Germany was still viewed suspiciously. But instead of isolating and balancing West Germany, western states – led most forcefully by the USA – eventually agreed to integrate it into European and Atlantic cooperation frameworks.[4] The US views chimed with those of European federalists, who urged the creation of a 'United States of Europe' as a means to peace on the continent.

Of course, a bigger threat to post-war peace in Western Europe soon became obvious: the Soviet bloc. Without US help, Western Europe could not counter that threat: the 1948 Brussels Treaty alliance, between Belgium, France, Luxembourg, the Netherlands and the UK, could not possibly have resisted a Soviet invasion of Western Europe. Instead, with the North Atlantic Alliance, agreed in May 1949 by the USA, Canada and ten West European countries (excluding West Germany), Western Europe's defence rested largely in US hands.

US views of West Germany were not initially welcomed. But France, the state most reluctant to integrate West Germany into European cooperation frameworks, was eventually forced to formulate a plan to do so. In May 1950, French foreign minister Robert Schuman announced a radical plan, the pooling of French and German coal and steel production under a supranational authority. Economic integration was the means, peace was the end, as Schuman stated:

> By pooling basic production [in coal and steel] and by instituting a new higher authority, whose decisions will bind France, Germany, and other member countries, this proposal will lead to the realisation of the first concrete foundation of a European federation indispensable to the preservation of peace.[5]

The Schuman Plan was formalized in the Paris Treaty establishing the European Coal and Steel Community (ECSC) in 1952. Six states were founding members: France, West Germany, Italy, Belgium, Luxembourg and the Netherlands. The UK and other West European states stayed aloof, unwilling to accept the limits on sovereignty that the ECSC would pose. A High Authority, composed of independent experts, was responsible for formulating a common market in coal and steel, and for supervising pricing, wages, investment and competition. Its decisions were binding on the member states.

There were still strains when in 1950, the USA insisted on rearming West Germany. The North Korean invasion of South Korea in June served as a warning: the Atlantic Alliance had to be prepared to counter a Soviet invasion of Western Europe. It must thus become an integrated military organization, including a rearmed West Germany. This was a very sensitive issue, particularly for the French, invaded by Germany three times in the previous century. France's response to the US pressure was to propose a European Defence Community (EDC), which would create a European army; there would be no separate German army. In 1952, the six ECSC member states signed the EDC treaty. It proved a rash attempt to force the pace of integration in defence: in August 1954, the French National Assembly refused to ratify the EDC treaty, and the project died.

The USA still insisted on rearming and integrating Germany into NATO, and the British proposed the solution to French concerns. In October 1954, the 1948 Brussels Treaty became the Western European Union (WEU), and Italy and West Germany joined it. British troops were stationed in West Germany, and West Germany formally renounced the production, storage and use of atomic, biological and chemical weapons. West Germany also joined NATO. The WEU, however, never fulfilled its role as a defence organization. Until the UK joined the European Community in 1973, it served as a forum for consultations between 'the Six' and UK; it then hibernated until 1984.

The next steps in the West European integration process were gradual, limited to the economic field. European integration was 'relaunched' in 1955 at the conference of Messina, Italy, where the Six agreed to discuss further integration. Two years later, in Rome in March 1957, two treaties were signed, one creating a European Atomic Energy Community, and the other the European Economic Community (EEC). The most important is the EEC (the 'European Community' often meant the EEC only, and the other two communities are so limited in scope they will not be considered further in this book). It was to be a common market: goods, services, capital and labour would circulate freely between the member states, there would be a common external tariff, and common policies would be agreed in a host of economic areas including foreign trade and agriculture. Most significant was its supra-nationalism: after a transition period, common policies, proposed by an independent Commission composed of officials, would be decided by the Council of ministers from the member states by qualified majority voting (QMV).[6] Member states could thus be outvoted. The Council of Ministers was presided over by each member state, in turns, for six months; its formation changed according to the topic at hand (agricultural ministers discussed agricultural policy, and so on). A European Court of Justice (ECJ) was to interpret EC law, and its decisions are binding on the member states. An assembly (later called the European Parliament) of parliamentarians from the member states was to be consulted, but in the beginning had little formal role to play in decision-making.[7]

The Rome Treaty provisions were not always fulfilled according to plan. Although the customs union (internal tariffs removed, external tariff imposed) was set up rapidly, free trade in goods, services, capital and labour was blocked by non-tariff barriers until the single European market was completed in 1993 – and still some barriers remain. QMV was introduced considerably later than scheduled, as part of the single market initiative. The European Parliament also acquired more and more powers to revise and reject decisions. From the 1970s, the European Council – composed of the heads of state or government – assumed a prominent role in decision-making, endorsing or launching important initiatives and trying to overcome disagreements that could not be resolved at lower levels. By the end of the Cold War, the scope of economic integration had expanded progressively, and economic and social policy-making was increasingly occurring at the European level, through a supranational process (usually called the 'Community method'). In its first two decades, more European countries joined the Community: Denmark, Ireland and the UK in 1973, Greece in 1981 and Portugal and Spain in 1986.

The growth of the European Community as an economic power has not been accompanied by as profound a development of its internal or external political dimension. The EDC disaster cast a long shadow over the development of a political dimension: a supranational approach to foreign and defence policy was unacceptable to the member states. In the early 1960s, French President Charles de Gaulle attempted to relaunch discussion of political union, but the Fouchet Plans went nowhere: they would have subjected the supranational EC to the authority of an intergovernmental body, anathema to European federalists, while the exclusion of non-member UK from foreign and defence policy cooperation did not make sense to the other member states.

In 1969, with new French political leadership, and an international context – superpower détente – more conducive to a European political voice, the member states re-opened discussions on political union. At their summit in The Hague, the heads of state or government asked the foreign ministers to propose ways of achieving political union. They reported back in October 1970, and in the Luxembourg report, proposed cooperation on foreign-policy issues, within a framework to be known as European Political Cooperation (EPC).[8] Foreign-policy cooperation would respond to France's desires for a stronger European voice in international affairs, and would provide an acceptable 'cover' for a more assertive West German policy towards its eastern neighbours (*Ostpolitik*), East Germany first among them.

EPC was to be a separate framework from the Community, and based on intergovernmental principles (namely unanimous voting). This satisfied supranationalists, wary of any attempt to establish intergovernmental control over the EC, and intergovernmentalists, wary of encroachment by the Community on foreign policy. Foreign ministers were firmly in charge, supported by officials in their ministries (the Political Committee, composed of political directors; European Correspondents and working groups, composed of lower-level officials). The Commission was only associated with EPC, the European Parliament played a marginal advisory role, and the European Court of Justice could not review EPC decisions. The Council presidency managed EPC, and, often with the help of the past and future presidencies (thus composing the troika), presented EPC positions to third countries.

EPC's goals were modest: regular consultation, coordination of national positions, and, where possible, common action. Decisions were taken in meetings of the foreign ministers, officially by unanimity. Over time, the foreign ministers agreed a series of improvements to EPC (see Box 2.1). After initially refusing to bridge the EC-EPC divide, the member states increasingly used the Community's economic resources to back up EPC decisions (as in the imposition of sanctions), although most often EPC's 'output' was limited to a declaration.

EPC did not discuss defence issues at all; NATO was the organization responsible for defence. But in the early 1980s, some member states, concerned with the Reagan Administration's bellicosity towards the Soviet bloc, sought to cooperate in security and defence. This had to take place outside EPC, because Denmark, Greece and neutral Ireland opposed discussing defence within EPC,

Box 2.1 Chronology: The evolution of a common EU foreign, security and defence policy

March 1948: Belgium, France, Luxembourg, the Netherlands, and the UK sign the **Brussels Treaty** of mutual defence.

April 1949: The US, Canada and ten West European countries sign the **North Atlantic Treaty**.

May 1952: The **European Defence Community** treaty is agreed by the six ECSC member states. It would have created a common European army, and permitted West Germany's rearmament. In August 1954, the French National Assembly rejects the treaty.

October 1954: The **Western European Union (WEU)** is created on the basis of the Brussels Treaty, and expanded to include Italy and West Germany. West Germany joins NATO.

December 1969: At their **summit in The Hague**, the EC heads of state or government ask the foreign ministers to study ways to achieve progress in political unification.

October 1970: The foreign ministers approve the **Luxembourg Report**, setting up European Political Cooperation. They will meet every six months, to coordinate their positions on international problems and agree common actions. They will be aided by a committee of the directors of political affairs (the **Political Committee**).

July 1973: The foreign ministers agree to improve EPC procedures in the **Copenhagen Report**. They will meet at least four times a year; the Political Committee can meet as often as necessary. **European Correspondents** and **working groups** will help prepare the Political Committee's work. The Commission can contribute its views to proceedings.

October 1981: Measures approved in the **London Report** include the crisis consultation mechanism: any three foreign ministers can convene an emergency EPC meeting within 48 hours. In meetings with third country representatives, the presidency can be accompanied by the preceding and succeeding presidencies (the **troika**). The Commission is 'fully associated with EPC'.

October 1984: The **WEU is reactivated**, as WEU foreign and defence ministers agree to meet regularly.

February 1986: The **Single European Act** (SEA) is signed; contains Title III on EPC. EPC can discuss the 'political and economic aspects of security'. EPC and the EC's external relations must be consistent. A small EPC secretariat, based in Brussels, will help the presidency.

February 1992: The **Maastricht Treaty** is signed, replacing EPC with the Common Foreign and Security Policy. The Council of foreign ministers will decide **Common Positions** and **Joint Actions**, and QMV can be used to implement the latter. The Commission can initiate proposals. CFSP activities can be financed by the EC budget. The EU can request the WEU to implement decisions that have defence implications.

June 1992: The **Petersberg Declaration** states that the WEU will engage in humanitarian and rescue tasks, peacekeeping, and crisis management tasks, including peacemaking ('**Petersberg Tasks**'). Three forms of WEU membership (full, associate and observer) are created.

October 1997: The **Amsterdam Treaty** is signed; contains several reforms of CFSP. QMV can be used to implement the European Council's **Common Strategies**, and member states can abstain from decisions. A **High Representative for the CFSP** is created, and replaces the past presidency in the troika. The High Representative heads a new **Policy Planning and Early Warning Unit**. The EU can launch the **Petersberg Tasks**, which are to be implemented by the WEU.

December 1998: Franco-British declaration on EU military capability at **St Malo**.

December 1999: The **Helsinki European Council** sets the **headline goal** for the common European security and defence policy. By 2003, the EU will be able to deploy within 60 days and for at least one year, military forces of up to 50,000–60,000 persons capable of the full range of Petersberg Tasks. Helping to run the new policy will be a Political and Security Committee, Military Committee and Military Staff.

March 2002 – June 2003: Convention on the Future of Europe drafts a **constitutional treaty** creating a European 'foreign minister'; a European external action service (EEAS); a European armaments, research and military capabilities agency.

November 2003: EU foreign ministers reach agreement on permanent structured cooperation in defence (battle groups); a mutual assistance clause; creation of an EU civil and military planning cell within the EU military staff.

June 2004: The provisions agreed since 2002 are incorporated in the **constitutional treaty**, which is rejected in referenda in 2005 in France and the Netherlands.

December 2007: The member states sign the **Lisbon Treaty**, which retains most of the constitutional treaty's provisions on foreign relations.

largely on principled grounds. So in 1984, the other member states revived the WEU, as a forum in which they could discuss defence issues without a US presence. At the time, the WEU conveniently did not include Denmark, Greece or Ireland.

Also in the 1970s, the EC member states began to cooperate informally in the field of justice and home affairs. Again, they did so in an intergovernmental framework, separate from the Community. In 1975, they formed the Trevi Group, to try to coordinate responses to terrorism: by the mid 1970s, terrorist groups within Europe (such as the Red Brigades in Italy or the IRA in the UK) and from outside it (such as Palestinian groups) were operating across Community borders. National officials from justice and interior ministries participated in Trevi. Over time, Trevi's deliberations extended beyond terrorism, and several working or ad hoc groups in other areas were set up: Working Group I dealt with anti-terrorism, exchanges of information, and the security of air traffic, nuclear installations, and cross-border transport; Working Group II handled police tactics and equipment, and from 1985, issues of cross-border order, namely football hooliganism; and Working Group III dealt with serious international crime, including drug-trafficking, bank robbery, and arms trafficking. Ad hoc groups on organized crime and on immigration were also created. In 1990, Trevi ministers agreed to establish a European Drugs Intelligence Unit. Much of Trevi's activity involved exchanging information, exchanging experts and officials, and comparing member state practices. Sensitivities about national sovereignty prevented the member states from reaching substantial, binding agreements.

By the end of the Cold War in the late 1980s and early 1990s, EC member states were enmeshed in an increasingly dense network of intergovernmental cooperation on foreign policy and combating international crime. The European Community was in the midst of implementing a single European market, and had already doubled its size to twelve member states. And then the Berlin Wall was torn down and the era of bipolar confrontation, dominated by the ever-present threat of nuclear war between the USA and Soviet Union, came to a surprisingly peaceful end.

2.2 Reforms in the 1990s: Three pillars of the EU

The end of the Cold War had a profound impact on the process of European integration. In the short run, the early 1990s, the impact was felt principally in two ways. First, the 'German problem' re-appeared: German re-unification (on 3 October 1990) generated concerns about German domination of Europe. The solution again became 'more Europe', deeper political and economic integration. Second, reinforced by the dynamism of the single European market at the end of the 1980s, the end of the Cold War created internal and external expectations that the Community would take on a greater international role. EPC was no longer considered adequate for the 'new world order' and thus deeper integration would include the area of foreign policy. In the longer run, enlargement to the Central and East European countries has also affected the integration process – notably by prompting further institutional reform which also brought changes in the area of foreign and defence policy.[9]

In 1991, the Maastricht Treaty was negotiated; it entered into force on 1 November 1993. The Maastricht Treaty created a European Union composed of three pillars: the European Community, Common Foreign and Security Policy, and Justice and Home Affairs. The Community pillar contained amendments to the treaties of the three original European Communities. The second (CFSP) and third (JHA) pillars were rooted in the EPC and Trevi frameworks respectively. The Maastricht Treaty on European Union was revised once in the 1990s, with the Amsterdam Treaty (which entered into force on 1 May 1999). At the Helsinki European Council in December 1999, the member states took several important decisions about the CFSP, which were later codified in the Nice Treaty (which entered into force on 1 February 2003). This section describes each of the pillars in turn as they developed in the 1990s.

The European Community pillar

The Maastricht Treaty's most far-ranging innovation was to launch Economic and Monetary Union, culminating in a single European currency. The weaknesses of the single currency system became glaringly evident in the prolonged euro crisis from 2008 onwards, which has had a damaging impact on the EU's international image and foreign-policy capabilities, as will be seen throughout this book. The focus here, though, is on the changes that were made to the European Community's framework for 'external relations' (relations with the outside world).

The Rome Treaty contained only three important provisions regarding the Community's external relations:

(1) the Common Commercial Policy (CCP);
(2) the power to conclude association agreements with third countries and groups of states; and
(3) the possibility of cooperating with the United Nations, the Council of Europe, and the Organization of Economic Cooperation and Development (OECD).

The Common Commercial Policy is the most important basis for the Community's external activities. Because it is a customs union, there are common rules for imports into the Community, and only the Community can negotiate changes to them. Only the Community can offer trade agreements to third countries, in addition to cooperation and association agreements. The CCP also enables the Community to play a major role in international trade negotiations; the EC is a full member of the World Trade Organization (WTO, the 1995 successor to the General Agreement on Tariffs and Trade, or GATT).

The rules for making decisions on the CCP were supranational right from the start. The Council takes the decision to open and conclude agreements, and sets out a negotiating mandate; the Commission (either the directorate-generals for trade or external relations) negotiates the agreements with third countries, though the Council keeps a steady eye on the Commission as it does so, via special committees of national representatives. Council decisions on trade agreements are taken by qualified majority voting, but by unanimity on association agreements. These basic rules were not changed in the Maastricht Treaty. The European Parliament initially had no say in the CCP, but in the Single European Act and Maastricht Treaty, it gained the power to 'assent' to most trade and cooperation agreements and all association agreements.

When the EEC Treaty was negotiated, international trade was primarily trade in goods, and the CCP was thus designed to enable the Community to negotiate agreements to cover that sort of trade. But by the time GATT members were negotiating the Uruguay Round (1986–94), the trade agenda had expanded to include trade in services, intellectual property and invest-ment. EC member states did not want these matters to fall under Community jurisdiction, with the Commission negotiating on their behalf.[10] But this resistance hindered the Community's ability to negotiate with other actors. In the Amsterdam Treaty, the member states agreed that the Council could decide unanimously that the Community can conclude agreements on ser-vices and intellectual property. Under the Nice Treaty, such a decision can be taken by QMV, with some exceptions (cultural, audiovisual, educational and health services).

The extent of the Community's contractual relations with third countries became more wide-ranging: as the Community's remit grew (to encompass research and development, environmental protection, and so on), so too did the content of its international agreements, which included provisions for cooperation on such matters with third countries. Agreements also increas-ingly included matters which did not fall under the Community pillar, such as foreign-policy cooperation

The other major area of the Community's external relations is the provision of financial aid to third countries. The Rome Treaty made no explicit provi-sion for granting assistance to third countries, but very early on, the Community began granting aid to developing countries, mostly former European colonies in Africa. The Maastricht Treaty added a chapter on devel-opment cooperation which provided a firm legal basis for aid to developing countries; there was a different legal basis for assistance to countries 'in transition' (such as in Eastern Europe). The Commission managed the EU's aid programmes, using its network of over 100 delegations in third countries to do so. What neither the Maastricht Treaty nor any subsequent treaty has done is to merge all the funding for developing countries in the Community framework. Instead, money comes from two sources: the EC budget,[11] and a separate fund for African, Caribbean and Pacific (ACP) countries, the European Development Fund.[12] Decisions on the size and allocation of the aid budget are done through the supranational Community budgetary process; the EDF is agreed separately by the member states. This mixture of legal bases and budgetary sources reflects the incremental *ad hoc* development of the EU's relations with countries in need of aid. The member states also have their own aid programmes, and the Community and member states are supposed to ensure their complementarity, but this has proved difficult to do.[13]

The CFSP pillar and the launching of a common security and defence policy

The CFSP's institutional structure as set up by Maastricht was quite similar to that of EPC, but in the 1990s, a process of 'Brusselization' occurred (see Box 2.1). EPC was 'decentralized': foreign ministers and foreign ministry officials travelled to EPC meetings, which were chaired by the rotating Council presidency, and permanent Brussels-based institutions were not established.[14] In the 1990s, however, foreign-policy issues were more and more discussed, and decided, by institutions and people based in Brussels rather than in national capitals.[15] For one observer, Brusselization is 'diminishing the roles of the Member States and of intergovernmentalism', and represents a new form of governance of the CFSP.[16] The member states, however, remain wary of any unintended consequences that might result from Brusselization, and try to retain control over what happens in Brussels.

Under the Maastricht Treaty, the European Council set the broad guidelines for CFSP; the Council of foreign ministers implemented them. As with EPC, the Council's work with respect to CFSP items was prepared by the Political Committee, which in turn relied on the work of European Correspondents and working groups. The European Commission was fully 'associated' in discussions. The Parliament was informed of CFSP issues, and could make recommendations, but its views did not have to be incorporated into CFSP decisions. The CFSP did not fall under ECJ jurisdiction. Under the Maastricht Treaty, the CFSP was represented externally through the presidency and the troika, just as EPC had been.

This basic institutional framework was altered first by the Amsterdam Treaty and then by the decisions of the December 1999 Helsinki European Council. Amsterdam added two important institutions to the mix, both of which are based in Brussels: a policy unit, and a 'High Representative for the CFSP'. The policy planning and early warning unit was created in response to concerns that the EU was too reactive in the face of international crises, such as those that afflicted the Balkans throughout the 1990s. The small unit, set up within the Council secretariat, was staffed by Commission and national officials, and monitored developments in areas relevant to the CFSP, provided early warning of crises, and produced policy option papers.

The High Representative was to help formulate, prepare and implement CFSP decisions, and head the policy unit. The High Representative participated in a new troika, with the current and incoming presidencies, in association with the Commission. The intention was to give the CFSP more continuity in its international representation, but the High Representative was still only one voice in the system. Javier Solana, a former Spanish foreign minister and NATO Secretary-General, served as High Representative from October 1999 to December 2009.[17]

The 1999 Helsinki European Council took momentous decisions launching a European security and defence policy, or ESDP (on which, see further below). To provide political guidance and strategic direction to ESDP operations, new bodies were set up within the Council framework: a Political and Security Committee (PSC); a Military Committee; and a Military Staff. The PSC replaced the old Political Committee.[18] It consists of ambassadors from the member states, who reside permanently in Brussels, and meets at least twice a week. It helps to formulate and implement common EU external policies, coordinates CFSP working groups, and gives political direction to the development of EU military capabilities. It developed strong relations with other institutions in Brussels: the Commission, Coreper, High Representative, and policy unit. This is the most obvious sign of Brusselization: the core committee on common foreign and security policy is no longer composed of the top officials from national foreign ministries, who travelled to Brussels about once a month, but rather of officials based in Brussels who meet much more often.

The Military Committee consists of the member states' chiefs of defence or their military representatives. It provides military advice to the PSC. The Military Staff provides early warning and strategic planning, and is helping to identify gaps in the EU's military capabilities. Occasionally the defence ministers met informally, but defence policy was formally dealt with by the General Affairs and External Relations Council, composed of foreign ministers.

As for CFSP decision-making procedures, from Maastricht they have arguably been 'legalized', in that the rules have been clarified, codified and increasingly invested with the status of law.[19] The Maastricht Treaty's provisions were intended to improve on those of EPC in three ways. Firstly, the Commission could propose actions, alongside the member states, but the vast majority of proposals were still initiated by the member states, illustrating the extent to which the Commission was *not* a driving force in the CFSP, in contrast to the role it plays in the first pillar.[20] Because of the significance of the EU's economic tools, however, the Commissioners for External Relations (in particular) or for relations with developing countries were still important voices at the decision-making table. Secondly, two new procedures were added: the Council of foreign ministers could agree a *Common Position* or a *Joint Action*. A Joint Action signalled that the EU was actually doing something (spending money, for example). Member states' positions must conform to both types of decision. The Amsterdam Treaty added a third procedure: the European Council could agree a *Common Strategy*. Thirdly, in the Maastricht Treaty, QMV was slipped into decision-making: the Council could decide, by unanimity, that further decisions on a Joint Action would be taken by QMV. Under Amsterdam, unanimous voting was to become less the rule and more the exception, a perceived necessity if CFSP was to function as the EU enlarged. The Amsterdam Treaty provided for constructive abstention and the use of QMV when a Common Strategy was adopted (see Box 2.2). The Nice Treaty later extended QMV to decisions on appointing envoys. However, since some member states (such as the UK) still insist that consensus should always be

---

Box 2.2 CFSP decision-making procedures before and after the Lisbon Treaty

Until 1 December 2009:	After 1 December 2009:
The European Council agrees **Common Strategies**, by unanimity, in areas where the member states have interests in common. A Common Strategy sets out the EU's objectives, duration and means to be made available to carry it out.	The European Council can take **'decisions relating to the Union's strategic interests and objectives'**. They define the duration and means to be made available to carry it out.
The Council of foreign ministers implements Common Strategies by agreeing **Joint Actions** and **Common Positions**; in so doing, it votes by QMV.	The Foreign Affairs Council implements decisions relating to the Union's strategic interests and objectives by agreeing **'decisions on the actions to be undertaken by the Union'** and **'decisions on the positions to be taken by the Union'**. In so doing, it votes by QMV.
The Council may also approve Joint Actions and Common Positions separately, not as measures implementing a Common Strategy. In this case, the Council votes by unanimity, although it may decide unanimously to implement a Joint Action by QMV.	The Foreign Affairs Council may also approve decisions on 'actions' and on 'positions' separately. In this case, the Council generally votes by unanimity, with the following exceptions. It may use QMV:
Joint Actions address specific situations where operational action by the EU is considered to be required. **Common Positions** define the EU's approach to a particular matter of geographical or thematic nature.	• when adopting any decision implementing a decision defining a Union action or position; • when adopting a decision defining a Union action or position, on a proposal which the High Representative has presented following a specific request from the European Council, made on its own initiative or that of the High Representative

Until 1 December 2009:	After 1 December 2009:
The Council may use QMV to appoint special representatives.	The Council may use QMV to appoint special representatives.
A member state can oppose the use of qualified majority voting for reasons of important national interests (the **national interest brake**), and qualified majority voting does not apply to decisions having military implications.	A member state can oppose the use of qualified majority voting for reasons of important national interests (the **national interest brake**), and qualified majority voting does not apply to decisions having military implications.
One or more member states can abstain from voting on a decision, without blocking it (the **constructive abstention** clause). But they must accept that the decision commits the Union and agree not to take action likely to conflict with it. If the member states abstaining from a decision represent more than one-third of the weighted votes, then the decision cannot be adopted.	One or more member states can abstain from voting on a decision, without blocking it (**constructive abstention**). But they must accept that the decision commits the Union and agree not to take action likely to conflict with it. If the member states abstaining from a decision represent more than one-third of the member states representing one-third of the EU's population, then the decision cannot be adopted.
The Commission shares the right of initiative with the member states, but does not have a vote.	Any member state, the High Representative, or the High Representative with the Commission's support, may submit initiatives or proposals to the Council.

sought, QMV was never actually used – a sign that the member states will not easily relinquish control over foreign-policy issues.

With the intention of a proactive international role for the EU, money became an issue. EPC had no budget; if EPC decisions had financial implications, the member states split the costs. The Maastricht Treaty provided for CFSP activities to be funded through the Community budget – an opening for the European Parliament to use its budgetary powers to exercise influence over the CFSP. Who pays for CFSP actions was a matter of dispute between the member states, and between the Council and Parliament, until a July 1997 agreement on financing CFSP was reached. The CFSP's budget, however, has always been tiny compared to the Community's aid budget though it has grown over time: in 1994, only €1 million was devoted to CFSP, 0.02 per cent of the €4.2 billion for 'external action'; in 2011, €303 million was spent on CFSP, four per cent of the €6.9 billion devoted to the 'EU as a global partner'.[21] (The financial crisis, however, has had an impact on this budget too – with only €296.3 million budgeted for 2014; see Table 3.2).

The CFSP's record after the Maastricht Treaty entered into force was mixed. Election observers were sent to places such as Russia and South Africa, and special representatives contributed to peace processes in the Middle East and the Great Lakes region of Africa. But there was a feeling that the EU was not matching its economic weight with political clout. Despite a continuous output of CFSP decisions, the EU was ineffective in the Bosnian war, and early on, was sidelined from international efforts to resolve the crisis. Its record in the other major crises of the 1990s, such as the genocide in Rwanda, was even less admirable in that there was often no substantive policy at all. This disappointment contributed to a revision of the CFSP provisions in the Amsterdam Treaty – with the addition of the High Representative and policy unit, and changes to decision-making procedures. But the dissatisfaction with the arrangements for using military force eventually resulted in the most far-reaching reforms of the CFSP. There has been a prevailing feeling that the EU needs to be able to use force to contribute to international peace and security and to further its own interests.

At the end of the Cold War, several member states argued that the CFSP needed a military dimension: the USA was withdrawing its troops from Europe, and the Europeans were expected to contribute to international peacekeeping missions. But the member states were (and still are) divided over issues such as the relationship of a European defence structure to NATO (several do not wish to jeopardize NATO's pre-eminent role in European security), and to the EU (several member states oppose any moves to turn the EU into an alliance). But they could agree to discuss defence, and that the recently revived WEU should be the EU's defence arm. Under the Maastricht Treaty, the Union can request the WEU 'to elaborate and implement decisions and actions of the Union which have defence implications'.

This was still controversial. The neutrals (Ireland was joined by Austria, Finland and Sweden in 1995) could take some comfort in the Treaty's pledge that the Union's policy 'shall not prejudice the specific character of the security and defence policy of certain Member States'. But it was all a step too far for Danish public opinion: after the Danes rejected (initially) the Maastricht Treaty in a referendum in June 1992, Denmark was granted an opt-out from the defence (and other) provisions.

There were two further problems with using the WEU as the EU's defence arm. Firstly, when the Maastricht Treaty entered into force, the WEU was not capable of implementing decisions with defence implications. So the WEU Council of Ministers first limited the WEU's potential activity. In June 1992, in the Petersberg Declaration, they declared that the WEU would engage in humanitarian and rescue, peacekeeping and crisis management tasks (the Petersberg Tasks), not common defence. The WEU member states pledged forces and resources that would be made available for carrying out the Petersberg Tasks, but these were not considered sufficient. So in June 1996, NATO approved the concept of Combined Joint Task Forces (CJTFs): the WEU could lead a CJTF, using NATO facilities and resources. But this arrangement was far too unwieldy to be of much use, and EU/WEU action still depended on member state agreement. When faced with a breakdown of order in Albania in early 1997, for example, the member states could not agree to send a WEU force. Instead, Italy assembled a 'coalition of the willing', acting under a UN mandate, to restore calm in the country.

The second problem was the differing memberships in the EU, WEU and NATO. In an attempt to simplify matters, the WEU created several types of membership. Observers (the neutral states and Denmark), associates (non-EU NATO members such as Turkey) and associate partners (Central and East European countries) could attend some WEU Council meetings, and participate in WEU missions.

The Amsterdam Treaty did not reform substantially the Maastricht provisions because the neutral states and the UK opposed merging the EU and WEU. But in late 1998, a new British government changed its stance on this. In a summit in St Malo, France, British Prime Minister Tony Blair and French President Jacques Chirac declared that the EU must be willing and able to respond to international crises by undertaking autonomous action, backed up by credible military forces. There are clearly differences in the British and French visions: for Britain, the EU can act when NATO does not wish to do so; for France, NATO does not have such a primary role. But the two countries could at least agree to develop the EU's military capacities.[22]

Surprisingly, even the neutral EU member states were willing to develop the initiative, reflecting widespread dissatisfaction with the fact that NATO was still the primary actor in the 1999 Kosovo crisis. In December 1999, the Helsinki European Council launched what is now known at the Common Security and Defence Policy (CSDP, formerly ESDP) by setting a headline goal: by 2003, the EU must be able to deploy within sixty days and sustain for at least one year military forces of up to 50,000–60,000 persons capable of the full range of Petersberg Tasks. The member states have since made commitments to attain the headline goal but there are still numerous gaps in resources. In the same period, the member states have agreed to devote resources to 'civilian crisis management', or sending non-military experts to assist countries in crisis.

The EU–WEU–NATO triangle became a bilateral EU–NATO relationship. This has been problematic, because the EU's relationship with non-EU European NATO member states, particularly Turkey, is contentious. After a lengthy period of haggling, 'Berlin-plus' arrangements on cooperation between EU and NATO were finally agreed in December 2002, allowing the EU to launch its first CSDP missions. But the 2004 accession to the EU of non-aligned Cyprus, with its own concerns vis-à-vis Turkey, led to considerable difficulties in the EU–NATO relationship. Turkey will not let NATO exchange information with the EU (lest it go to Cyprus), while Cyprus will not let the EU engage in most discussions with NATO.[23] The WEU finally disappeared as an organization on 30 June 2011.

The JHA pillar

The combined effects of the completion of the single European market, the collapse of communism in Central and Eastern Europe, and the wars in the former Yugoslavia, intensified the need for cooperation to combat international crime. Germany, now on a much more open frontier between west and east, pushed strongly for collective action.[24] Larger movements of people across internal EC borders, and from outside, plus an apparent increase in transnational crime as a result (certainly as perceived by European publics), created exactly the sort of demand for cooperation that interdependence theorists recognize. As a result, Trevi, more of a network than a policy-making framework, was institutionalized and codified as part of the Justice and Home Affairs (JHA) pillar in the Maastricht Treaty, under which a large number of topics fell (see Box 2.3).

The JHA pillar was intergovernmental: the Council of Justice and Interior Ministers took decisions, almost always by unanimity. The Commission (DG Justice, Freedom and Security) participated in JHA meetings at all levels, and shared the right of initiative in most areas. The European Parliament was to be regularly informed of JHA discussions and consulted on JHA measures. The ECJ could be asked to interpret the provisions of conventions, provided that the member states had accepted ECJ jurisdiction.

Box 2.3 Areas for cooperation in the Justice and Home Affairs pillar (Maastricht Treaty)

(1) asylum policy;
(2) rules governing the crossing by persons of the external borders of the member states;
(3) immigration policy and policy regarding nationals of third countries:
   (a) conditions of entry and movement by nationals of third countries on the territory of member states;
   (b) conditions of residence by nationals of third countries on the territory of member states, including family reunion and access to employment;
   (c) combating unauthorized immigration, residence and work by nationals of third countries on the territory of member states;
(4) combating drug addiction in so far as this is not covered by 7) to 9);
(5) combating fraud on an international scale in so far as this is not covered by 7) to 9);
(6) judicial cooperation in civil matters;
(7) customs cooperation;
(8) judicial cooperation in criminal matters; and
(9) police cooperation for the purposes of preventing and combating terrorism, unlawful drug trafficking and other serious forms of international crime, including if necessary certain aspects of customs cooperation, in connection with the organisation of a Union-wide system for exchanging information within a European Police Office (Europol).

Following Maastricht, progress in reaching and implementing binding agreements remained slow. For example, three years of negotiations were needed to conclude an agreement to create a European police office (Europol), which then took an additional two years to ratify. The Europol convention finally entered into force in October 1998, and Europol became operational in July 1999. The JHA pillar mostly produced non-binding recommendations and conclusions. Cooperation on legal and judicial matters, after all, requires states to reach agreements – and compromises – on highly sensitive matters. The logic of diversity works not just in foreign and defence policy, and can even be stronger when it comes to national legal systems.

The Amsterdam Treaty created a new goal for the integration process: to provide EU citizens 'with a high level of safety within an area of freedom, security and justice' (Article 29). The treaty substantially revised the JHA pillar, and items 1 to 7 in Box 2.3 were moved into the first pillar (thus 'communitarizing' them). Since 2004, a supranational decision-making procedure on these issues is used: the Commission has the sole right to initiate legislation, on which the Council votes by QMV and the European Parliament has co-decision powers. But flexibility had to be introduced: Denmark, Ireland and the UK have opt-outs from the new first pillar provisions on asylum, immigration, external border controls and judicial cooperation in civil matters, though they can decide to adopt any measure proposed under them. The Amsterdam Treaty also incorporated the Schengen agreement on the free movement of people (with British, Irish and some Danish opt-outs).[25]

Following the Amsterdam Treaty, the large member states (in particular France and the UK) increasingly saw the utility of cooperation on justice and home affairs issues. The October 1999 Tampere European Council agreed several ambitious priorities, including the development of a common asylum system and common management of migration flows; a fast-track extradition system; and setting up a unit of national prosecutors, magistrates or police offices, called Eurojust, to help coordinate and support investigations into organized crime.

2.3 The torturous history of the Lisbon Treaty

The intergovernmental conference (IGC) which led to the Nice Treaty was infamous for being bad-tempered, as heads of state or government fought over reforms. Dissatisfaction with both the Nice Treaty and the IGC itself led the EU to try something different in the (inevitable) next round of treaty revision. In December 2001, the Laeken European Council declared that

> The Union needs to become more democratic, more transparent and more efficient. It also has to resolve three basic challenges: how to bring citizens, and primarily the young, closer to the European design and the European institutions, how to organize politics and the European political area in an enlarged Union and how to develop the Union into a stabilising factor and a model in the new, multipolar world.[26]

The European Council decided that the next intergovernmental conference would be preceded by a 'Convention on the Future of Europe', which would debate the challenges to the EU's development and possible responses. The Convention convened in 2002–3, and consisted of delegates from the member states, candidate countries, national parliaments, European Parliament, and European Commission. In summer 2003, the Convention agreed a draft 'constitution'. The member states then fiddled with the text until June 2004, when they finally agreed on a 'Treaty establishing a Constitution for Europe'. A year after that, the French and Dutch electorates rejected the constitutional treaty in referenda, and three years of disarray in the EU followed. In June 2007, the member states agreed to include most of the constitutional treaty's provisions in a new treaty and in December 2007, they signed it in Lisbon, so it is known as the Lisbon Treaty. Ireland was the only country to hold a referendum on the Lisbon Treaty, in June 2008, and a majority of voters rejected the treaty. Again, there was disarray in the EU, and Ireland was pressed to hold another referendum. This took place in October 2009 and approved the treaty. The Lisbon Treaty finally entered into force on 1 December 2009, eight years after the Laeken Declaration – and amid considerable doubts that citizens felt closer to the EU.

The Lisbon Treaty simplifies the EU's structure by eliminating the third pillar, folding what remained of the JHA pillar into the supranational first pillar, with only a few matters subject to unanimous voting in the Council.[27] But it retains most of the fundamental differences between the first and second pillars. The 'EU' and not the European Community is now the institution with international legal personality: the EU concludes agreements, and EC delegations were transformed into EU delegations. As will be seen throughout this book, there are still institutional turf wars with respect to intergovernmental and supranational policy-making in foreign policy and in the 'external dimension' of justice and home affairs, so this partial simplification of the EU's structure has not (yet) improved policy coherence.

Under the treaty, new institutions were created and old ones reformed. Firstly, the treaty radically altered the role of the Council presidency. This reflected years of debates. On the one hand, many member states, especially the smaller ones, took the opportunities posed by the presidency very seriously, and insisted on the equal right of all member states to hold the presidency.[28] Holding the presidency allowed a member state to push specific priorities (through agenda setting, for example). On the other hand, there were calls to abolish or radically reform the rotating presidency, as EU enlargements increased the number of small member states less able to handle the demands of the presidency, and lengthened the amount of time between any member state's presidencies (in an EU of 28 countries, a member state will hold the presidency only once every fourteen years). There were also criticisms of the impact the rotating presidency had on the external representation of the EU, in that the EU's 'voice' changed every six months and was confusing to outsiders – Solana's position had been created in the Amsterdam Treaty to try to address those criticisms.

The Lisbon Treaty created a 'permanent' (up to five years) president of the European Council, and a 'High Representative of the Union for Foreign Affairs and Security Policy' who chairs the Foreign Affairs Council (the renamed Council of foreign ministers). Otherwise, the presidency system continues, but it now operates on issues outside the remit of the Foreign Affairs Council, and below the level of the heads of state or government. Council presidencies can assist the High Representative – the Polish foreign minister, Radoslaw Sikorski, represented the EU a few times during Poland's presidency in 2011 – but they are deputizing for, not replacing, the High Representative.[29] The presidency system also continues at several international organizations: where the European Community already had a seat (such as the World Trade Organization), the EU has inherited that, but elsewhere it has proved more difficult to fit the Lisbon Treaty arrangements into a world of international organizations whose members are states. Although the EU was granted a special observer status in the General Assembly in May 2011, allowing it to speak on behalf of the EU there, elsewhere – such as the UN Human Rights Council – the rotating presidency speaks for the EU member states (often in tandem with the EU delegation representative).[30]

While the Lisbon Treaty reforms have (generally) introduced more continuity of leadership at the top of the EU, they have not necessarily reduced the potential for incoherence: there are still several voices 'speaking for Europe', as the European Council presidency, High Representative and European Commission president all have a role to play in representing the EU in international affairs. Furthermore, the disappearance of the presidency system may have some negative consequences if member states feel less involved in the EU foreign-policy-making system, less able to push for their priorities or protect their interests, and less inclined to try to drive or lead EU foreign-policy initiatives. There have been suggestions to involve presidencies more in agenda and priority setting.[31]

The new-fangled High Representative is an attempt to reduce problems caused by the division between the Community and CFSP pillars. In addition to chairing the Foreign Affairs Council (and therefore assuming the responsibilities of the old presidency), the new High Representative will do the job of the old High Representative *and* that of the old External Relations Commissioner (serving also as Vice-President of the European Commission), and therefore presumably will be better able to unite the EU's diplomatic, economic and military capabilities in pursuit of more coherent policy. In addition, the High Representative heads up an entirely new body, the European External Action Service (EEAS) – and was responsible for creating it from scratch. This is quite a demanding job description, and it would have been a challenge for anyone to handle well.

In November 2009, the European Council chose Baroness Catherine Ashton to be the new High Representative and Herman van Rompuy to be the European Council President. At the time of their appointments, Ashton had been serving as European Commissioner for Trade and Van Rompuy had been the Belgian prime minister, each for about a year. Both were relatively unknown – certainly compared to the possible post-holders that had been discussed in the media and policy circles beforehand, Tony Blair (former British prime minister) and Carl Bildt (former Swedish prime minister). This led to the assumption that EU member states were not willing to appoint to those posts charismatic, powerful figures who could potentially outshine national politicians.

Ashton has faced constant and considerable criticism of her handling of the job – much of which fails to take into account that the demands on her are unreasonable.[32] She had to spend much of her first year as High Representative setting up the EEAS, and found it difficult to navigate amongst all of the competing interests (from the Commission to European Parliament to the member states). She was subjected to much sniping from the sidelines. In December 2011, the foreign ministers of twelve EU member states made several 'suggestions' to Ashton, implying that she had not done enough to set priorities, or foster cooperation between the EEAS and, on the one hand, the Commission, and on the other, the member states.[33] But over time, she racked up several accomplishments, in addition to creating the EEAS. She established a close working relationship with Hilary Clinton, the US Secretary of State until early 2013. She led negotiations with Iran over the nuclear issue. And in April 2013, she and her special adviser Robert Cooper convinced Serbia and Kosovo to reach a deal normalizing their relations.

A more fundamental problem is that while the new High Representative gives EU foreign policy more continuity and visibility, over sensitive matters she will always play second fiddle to the 'Big Three' (France, Germany, the UK). If these three countries are deeply divided, there is probably little that the High Representative can do to bridge the divide; if they are united, then she could be sidelined. Ashton experienced on several occasions the extent to which the Big Three can undermine collective EU action: as the 'Arab spring' unfolded in January 2011, the British foreign secretary arrived in Tunisia to meet the new government even before Ashton could finish planning her own trip; on 29 January 2011 France, Germany and the UK issued a declaration on Egypt two days before EU foreign ministers met, as Ashton was trying to build a consensus; the UK blocked dozens of EU statements at the UN in 2011 because it objected to the wording (preferring 'EU and its member states' to 'EU').[34] One observer, however, argues that Ashton and her officials regularly 'blame all the problems with EU foreign policy on the member states themselves', but that instead of complaining, she 'should instead try to get ahead of the member states by taking initiatives and by showing leadership'.[35]

As for the EEAS, the Lisbon Treaty indicated only that it will support the work of the High Representative and that it is to be composed of officials from the Commission and Council secretariat, and seconded national diplomats. All decisions on its organization and functioning were to be taken after the treaty entered into force – and preparatory work on this was halted after the first Irish referendum rejected the Lisbon Treaty. So only after the Treaty entered into force did work really begin – and so did the bureaucratic infighting. The European Parliament was highly critical of early ideas, as it pushed for the Service to be part of the Commission (where the EP could oversee it). Commission President Barroso took steps that constrained Ashton right from the start: for example, he incorporated neighbourhood policy within the Commission directorate-general for enlargement, thus keeping that important portfolio out of the EEAS.[36] (In the mid-term review of the EEAS, released in July 2013, Ashton described the early days of setting up the EEAS as 'in a word, tough'.[37])

Ashton still managed to push a proposal through, and the Council decision establishing the EEAS was agreed on 26 July 2010 – only eight months after the Lisbon Treaty entered into force. As of July 2013, 3,417 people worked for the EEAS (with an additional 3,000 Commission staff in the EU's 139 delegations), but morale was low, and turnover high.[38] Eventually, one-third of EEAS staff will be diplomats from the member states, and the current proportion is just below that, 32.9 per cent. The EEAS has responsibilities ranging from managing the EU's delegations abroad, to contributing to development aid programming and running civilian and military missions.

Forging a 'European diplomatic service' is bound to be a long-term process, but the EEAS could eventually build a *real* bridge over both the pillar divide and the divide between the EU and national levels of foreign-policy-making.[39] The failure to agree on EU policy can reflect failure to agree on what is actually happening and what therefore needs to be done; long-term cooperation in the EEAS may help foster agreement on analyses of situations and therefore on what the EU should do.

The Lisbon Treaty reformed decision-making procedures, somewhat (see Box 2.2). It rather clumsily renamed CFSP decisions (Common Strategies are now 'decisions of the European Council on the strategic interests and objectives of the Union', for example). The European Commission has lost the power to make foreign-policy proposals, which it had gained under the Maastricht Treaty. Instead, the High Representative (also a Vice-President of the Commission) – alongside the member states – may submit initiatives or proposals. The High Representative can do this on his/her own or with the Commission's support. All of these decisions are to be taken by unanimity, but the Council can use QMV in some limited (and somewhat complicated) situations. As was the case before the Lisbon Treaty entered into force, perhaps half of all foreign-policy decisions are actually agreed at the level of Council working groups and socialization processes lead to a more 'co-operative style of negotiations' which facilitates compromises.[40] What this indicates is that there are still competing dynamics at play in EU foreign-policy-making: intergovernmentalism and a strong desire by member states to control the process while still taking advantage of the politics of scale, combined with Brusselization and socialization that point to a more cooperative and consensual process.

With respect to the Common Security and Defence Policy (CSDP), the Treaty introduced two new clauses that resemble a mutual defence guarantee. A 'solidarity clause' states that the EU and member states will assist a fellow member state if it is the object of a terrorist attack or the victim of a natural or man-made disaster. Even more strikingly, the treaty declares that if a member state is the victim of armed aggression on its territory, the other member states have an obligation of assistance towards it. However, this is 'in accordance with Article 51 of the United Nations Charter', 'shall not prejudice the specific character of the security and defence policy of certain Member States' (read the neutrals), and is 'consistent' with NATO commitments (Article 42 (7), Treaty on European Union). The Petersberg tasks are to be expanded to include joint disarmament operations, military advice and assistance tasks, conflict prevention and post-conflict stabilization, and assistance to third countries in combating terrorism on their territories. The Lisbon Treaty introduced a reform that was implemented even before the treaty entered into force: a European Defence Agency, which was actually created in 2004 to coordinate procurement policy and research and development.

The Lisbon Treaty introduced 'enhanced cooperation', to allow closer cooperation amongst member states willing to increase their defence capabilities. Member states wishing to participate in permanent structured cooperation should have the capacity to supply 'battle groups' (combat units of about 1,500 soldiers which could be deployed rapidly to undertake Petersberg tasks, particularly in response to a request from the UN). Even before 2009, battle groups were set up, some by small groups of member states together, others by France, Italy, Spain and the UK separately. However, the EU has yet to deploy a single battle group.

Finally, with respect to external trade, the Lisbon Treaty altered decision-making by giving the European Parliament the power to approve trade measures such as anti-dumping duties, to give its consent to *all* trade agreements, and to receive reports on the progress of trade negotiations.

Conclusion

The institutions and procedures that have developed in the broad field of external relations have been under constant revision as the member states have sought to balance their collective economic strength with a political voice in international affairs. They have also tried to address the implications of international change – including the rise in international crime, and the expectations that the EU will assume more responsibilities for ensuring peace and security especially in its periphery. But they have not agreed to establish supranational procedures and institutions in sensitive issues such as foreign and defence policy. We are nowhere near the establishment of a *single* European foreign policy. But there is still a push to improve and strengthen the EU's international role, which occurs in spite of – and perhaps because of – disagreements which may divide the member states over particular international issues. The member states have never turned away from foreign-policy cooperation – in fact, arguably, quite the opposite occurs. A 'logic of integration', the politics of scale, the pressures of outsiders, and so on, all seem to prompt the member states into strengthening the EU's international actorness, while not eliminating their own. (Whether these same factors contribute to common foreign-policy output is another matter.)

The effects of enlargement on the EU's external relations have thus far been broadly positive: new member states bring with them their own links to different third countries, and this has expanded the extent of the EU's network of relations. Enlargement has not made it more difficult to reach agreement among the member states on strengthening institutions and procedures (albeit within limits), though more member states has complicated decision-making in particular cases (such as EU–NATO relations) The next chapter takes a closer look at the kinds of output that can be produced by the EU's institutions and procedures.

Questions for discussion

1. To what extent was the Common Foreign and Security Policy as introduced by the Maastricht Treaty an 'improvement' on European Political Cooperation?

2. How radical were the reforms to the EU's foreign-policy system in the Lisbon Treaty?

3. Why did the High Representative of the Union for Foreign Affairs and Security Policy describe the period since the entry into force of the Lisbon Treaty as 'tough'?

Suggestions for further reading

Müller-Brandeck-Bocquet, Gisela and Carolin Rüger, eds. *The High Representative for the EU Foreign and Security Policy – Review and Prospects*. Baden-Baden: Nomos, 2011.
Nuttall, Simon. *European Political Co-operation*. Oxford: Clarendon Press, 1992.
Vanhoonacker, Sophie, Petar Petrov and Karolina Pomorska, eds. Special Issue on 'The Emerging EU Diplomatic System', *The Hague Journal of Diplomacy*, 7, 1 (2012).

CHAPTER THREE

The EU's Foreign-Policy Instruments

The EU is one of the largest, wealthiest regions on earth and, as will be described in this chapter, can wield a wide range of policy instruments. If it is to exercise influence, however, the EU member states must agree to use these considerable resources collectively in pursuit of common foreign-policy objectives, which is a well-known challenge. A newer challenge is that power in the international system is considerably more diffuse than it was at the end of the Cold War and so even if it is united, the EU may struggle to exercise influence. Although the EU still clearly has considerable clout, compared to other 'powers' (see Table 3.1), international relations is becoming more multipolar, and Europe less 'over-represented' in major multilateral fora. For example, in 2008, the G-7 group of rich (North American and European) countries was superseded by the creation of the G20 major economies (including Brazil, China, India and Russia, among others), which has become an important forum for consultation on a number of international issues. And there have been repeated attempts to expand the permanent membership of the UN Security Council to include countries such as India or Brazil: a move which would dilute the European (France and the UK) presence there. The euro crisis has exacerbated this trend – at least in the medium term. The diffusion of power in international relations affects the EU's potential influence: it means, for example, that conditions on EU aid may have less of an impact if the recipient can simply turn to other donors or investors that are less scrupulous.

If the EU member states agree to act collectively towards a particular 'third' (non-EU) country or on a particular international issue, what sorts of policy instruments can the EU wield? Foreign-policy instruments are those means used by policy-makers in their attempts to get other international actors to do what they would not otherwise do.[1] David Baldwin has specified four types of instruments used in national foreign policy:

- propaganda, or the deliberate manipulation of verbal symbols;
- diplomacy, or the reliance on negotiation;
- economic, or resources which have a reasonable semblance of a market price in terms of money; and
- military, or the reliance on violence, weapons or force.[2]

Table 3.1 Comparison of EU and other 'powers'

	Population (2013 estimate)	GDP 2012 estimate (in trillion US $)	GDP per capita, 2012 estimate (in US $)	GDP growth (2012 estimate)	Exports as percentage of world total, 2011	Imports as percentage of world total, 2011
EU	503,890,016	15.970	35,100	−0.3	15.08	16.43
US	316,668,567	15.940	50,700	2.2	8.09	12.26
China	1,349,585,838	12,610	9,300	7.8	4.26	5.89
India	1,220,880,359	4.761	3,900	6.8	1.66	2.51
Brazil	201,009,662	2.394	12,100	0.9	1.40	1.28
Russia	142,500,482	2.555	18,000	3.4	2.85	1.75

Sources: first four columns: CIA, The World Factbook 2013 (https://www.cia.gov/library/publications/the-world-factbook/index.html); fifth and sixth columns: World Trade Organization, Statistics Database (http://stat.wto.org/Home/WSDBHome.aspx) (last accessed 3 September 2013).

For the most part, the EU wields diplomatic and economic instruments, but in the last ten years, has increasingly used military instruments as well, though mostly of a decidedly soft type (light peacekeeping, training missions, and the like). Propaganda is difficult for the EU to produce: its declarations are not only often the result of careful compromise among the member states, but can be interpreted differently by them when they communicate with other states. Under these circumstances, deliberately manipulating words for audiences in third countries is virtually impossible. The EU's 'message' is generally expressed through diplomatic channels.

The use of foreign-policy instruments is a rather complicated affair, as the rules and procedures for using economic, diplomatic and military instruments differ. Before the Lisbon Treaty entered into force, the pillar structure could be a hindrance – also because there was competition between the intergovernmental and supranational bodies over control of some instruments (such as election observation missions). In the Lisbon Treaty, the member states tried to resolve some of the problems by creating the EEAS and the new High Representative post, but there are still different decision-making rules for different instruments, and bureaucratic politics can still hinder policymaking. This chapter outlines the EU's economic, diplomatic and military instruments, and then discusses the challenge of 'consistency', or the making of policy which involves multiple instruments.

3.1 Economic instruments

Two of the EU's most powerful foreign-policy instruments are economic: the capacity to enter into international agreements, and the provision of financial assistance to third countries. There is a huge demand for agreements with the EU, the largest trading bloc in the world. The EU is also one of the world's largest aid donors. These primarily economic instruments give the EU the potential to exercise considerable influence in international affairs.

Until the Lisbon Treaty entered into force, these were instruments that fell under the European Community pillar – and the 'European Community' was the formal name of the institution concluding agreements and offering aid, as only it had been endowed under the treaties with the capacity to do so. The Lisbon Treaty gave the European Union international legal personality so the institution concluding agreements and offering aid is now the EU (which makes things considerably less confusing for anyone not an expert on the EU!). In addition, trade and development policies were explicitly listed under the section on the EU's 'external action' and are to be conducted in pursuit of those general principles and objectives. Although this implies that trade agreements will thus be used to further the EU's foreign-policy aims, in practice trade policy is increasingly being conducted for 'economic', not foreign policy, reasons. Indeed, as will be seen below, a striking development of the last decade is an increasing distinction between foreign economic policy and foreign policy – ironic, considering the efforts made to increase coherence in the EU's foreign relations.

Agreements with third countries

The EU can offer three main types of agreements to third countries: trade; cooperation; and association. The Common Commercial Policy provides the basis for concluding trade agreements; cooperation and association agreements are based on other treaty provisions. Only two EU institutions are responsible for negotiating and concluding international agreements, the Commission and the Council, but the European Parliament can approve or reject agreements.

Trade agreements provide a schedule for lifting trade restrictions on imports into the EU and used to be offered on a non-reciprocal basis thus favouring the third country. However, since the Doha round of negotiations on a new world trade agreement have been moribund since 2001, the EU has been busy negotiating 'free trade agreements', which are reciprocal and aim to open up markets to EU businesses. Negotiations on free trade agreements (FTAs) have been launched with key trading partners such as the USA, Japan and Canada, and have been concluded with Chile, Colombia, Mexico, Peru, Singapore, South Africa and South Korea, among others.[3] The motivation behind the drive to conclude FTAs with established and rising economic powers is clearly economic. In 2006, the European Commission argued that trade policy had to help create jobs and drive growth in Europe, and thus 'economic factors must play a primary role in the choice of future FTAs. The key economic *criteria* for new FTA partners should be market potential (economic size and growth) and the level of protection against EU export interests (tariffs and non tariff barriers).'[4] As the Commission stated in 2010, the focus was to be on delivering '*balanced* free-trade agreements' (my emphasis), or, in other words, ensuring that Europe has access to overseas markets on a reciprocal basis.[5]

The EU also concludes more extensive agreements. Cooperation agreements include measures for cooperation on economic and commercial matters, as well as for liberalizing trade. They also usually set up a framework for dialogue with the third country, including on foreign policy and justice and home affairs issues. A cooperation council, composed of ministers, and a cooperation committee, composed of officials, will meet regularly, as will members of the European Parliament and parliamentarians from the partner country. Agreements concluded with developing countries also provide development aid.

Association agreements set up a closer relationship with a third country or grouping of states. In addition to trade measures, they provide for cooperation in a wide variety of sectors, and often include protocols that specify a package of EU aid and European Investment Bank (EIB) loans. Association agreements can even extend the customs union (as with Turkey) or the internal market (as in the European Economic Area with Iceland, Liechtenstein and Norway). An association council, consisting of ministers from both sides, will meet regularly to discuss issues including foreign-policy matters. Parliamentarians from the European Parliament and the associated country will also meet regularly.

Provisions on 'political' issues have been included in cooperation and association agreements. Since 1992, with respect to other European countries, and 1995, with respect to all third countries, agreements include the 'human rights clause', a unique and innovative instrument (see Chapters 5 and 6).[6] It allows the EU to suspend or denounce an agreement if the third country has violated human rights or democratic principles. From the late 1990s, agreements have also included a clause on cooperating against illegal immigration; since 2002, several agreements have included a clause in which both sides agree to cooperate in the fight against terrorism; a clause on the non-proliferation of weapons of mass destruction is also now supposed to be mandatory. In none of those cases has the EU gone so far as to make cooperation on such issues a condition of the agreement – and indeed, more recently, the EU has backed down from its insistence that agreements include such 'political clauses' as they are not much liked by third countries and there is much reluctance to jeopardize important trading relationships by insisting on their inclusion. Agreements with India and ASEAN countries are likely not to include the non-proliferation clause (and India is objecting strongly to the inclusion of the human rights clause as well).[7]

Virtually every country on earth is linked to the EU through a formal agreement, with a few exceptions. Several regional groupings also have formal agreements with the EU (see Chapter 4). The extent of the network of partners illustrates the influence of law on the EU's external relations: a great deal of what the EU does in international relations is to develop relations that are based on law, that is, on legal agreements.[8]

Although economic motivations are driving the EU's moves to conclude FTAs with numerous third countries, the EU does still wield its trade instruments for political purposes. Decisions to conclude an agreement with a third country or regional grouping can be political: for example, in 1997, the European Community concluded an interim association agreement with the Palestinian Liberation Organization for the benefit of the Palestinian Authority, clearly a political act. Secondly, the kind of agreement concluded with a country is an important political decision: association agreements signal a privileged partnership. Thirdly, the content of agreements also differs between partners: some provide for extensive economic and political cooperation, others less so. This, too, reflects political considerations.

With its cooperation and association agreements, the EU gradually created a hierarchy of partners: its closest partners (Turkey; south-east European countries; the Cotonou convention partners; the Euro-Mediterranean partners; the European Economic Area countries) are linked by association agreements; other countries (the former Soviet republics; several Latin American countries; Asian countries) only by cooperation or by less extensive association agreements. The 'pyramid of privileges'[9] shifted over time: in the 1980s, the ACP partners were unquestionably at the top; now the EU's neighbours crowd the top spot. The emphasis on the neighbourhood reflected the new post-Cold War priorities of stabilizing eastern and south-eastern Europe, and spreading security to the southern shore of the Mediterranean. But the new FTAs disrupt this hierarchy – FTAs are being negotiated or concluded with neighbours and far-flung countries alike.

In addition to agreements, there are other important economic instruments. The EU's Generalized System of Preferences (GSP) provides poor countries with tariff-free access for some exports to the EU. In 2014, the scheme will change: the number of beneficiaries will be reduced from 176 to 89, principally by excluding high and upper middle-income countries (such as Argentina, Brazil, Malaysia, Russia and Saudi Arabia).[10] Thus the scheme should better benefit poorer countries. In addition, under the GSP+ arrangement, developing countries can gain additional preferences if they implement certain international conventions on human and labour rights, the environment and good governance (see Chapters 5 and 6). The Everything But Arms initiative offers even more generous access – duty-free and quota-free for all exports except arms – to the world's 49 poorest countries.

All of the economic instruments listed above can be used as incentives, as positive measures to encourage countries to undertake reforms or comply with EU standards or values. This is 'positive conditionality', which entails promising a benefit to a state if it fulfils specified political and/or economic conditions. The instruments can also be used as negative measures:

agreements can be suspended or renounced, trade can be disrupted, and trading preferences can be withdrawn. This is 'negative conditionality' – reducing, suspending, or terminating benefits if the state in question violates the conditions. As will be discussed in Chapters 4 to 8, the use of conditionality is a major element in the EU's pursuit of the five policy objectives considered in this book.

Sanctions can also be imposed to conform to UN Security Council decisions. Sanctions are imposed first by a unanimous decision taken in the CFSP framework, and then the Council implements the sanctions with decisions taken by QMV. The EU prefers 'smart' sanctions, which are targeted at particular individuals (freezing their assets, for example) or goods (such as 'conflict diamonds', or timber), and thus avoid doing harm to the wider population. The use of sanctions has increased dramatically in the last few years, from 20 or so decisions a year between 2007 and 2010 to almost 70 in 2011. Much of the growth was due to the imposition of new sanctions on Iran, Syria and Libya – in the last two cases because of the use of force by the Assad and Ghaddafi regimes against civilians.[11]

Aid to third countries and regional groupings

The resources available to the EU for assistance to third countries have increased from a mere 0.2 per cent of the EC's budget in 1966 to 6.4 per cent in 2012 (not including the EDF).[12] Although the Union's budget is relatively small (just over 1 per cent of the EU's GNI), it still spends a considerable amount of money on external action (see Table 3.2). The European economic crisis has, however, affected the member states' willingness to increase the EU budget, and the 2014–20 total budget is smaller than the 2007–13 budget – though in the area of external action, there has actually been a small increase. What is more notable is the difference between the 2013 and 2014 budgets: several programmes are conspicuously smaller in 2014, including for areas considered to be strategically important, such as the European neighbourhood (see Table 3.2).

The Union (excluding aid given by the member states) is one of the largest donors in the world: since 1986, it has been at least the world's sixth largest aid donor, and distributes aid to about 130 recipient countries, the largest spread of any donor.[13] More recently, the EU has moved towards a more focused approach in its development policy. In May 2012, the Council approved a Commission proposal (entitled 'An Agenda for Change') which states that to achieve 'maximum impact and value for money', the EU must target its resources where they will have the most impact; this 'may result in less or no EU development grant aid' for some countries, while others – especially in the European neighbourhood and Africa – may receive more aid.[14]

The Commission tries to coordinate the aid policies of all the EU member states, to try to ensure that the EU and the member states have more of an

Table 3.2 The EU's external relations budget

Commitments (not payments forecast) All figures in euros; 2011 prices for 2007–13 figures; 2013 prices for 2014–20 figures Only programmes relevant to this book are included					
Financial Instrument	Countries covered/ purpose	2007– 2013 budget	2013 budget	2014– 2020 budget	2014 budget
European Instrument for Democracy and Human Rights	Any third country, though there are priority areas	1.104 billion	177.1 million	1.332 billion	179.3 million
Instrument for Stability	Any non-EU country	2.062 billion	325.4 million	2.338 billion	314.5 million
Common Foreign and Security Policy		1.981 billion	396.3 million	2.338 billion	314.5 million
Development Cooperation Instrument (DCI)	47 countries mainly in Asia, Latin America; thematic programmes cover all developing countries	10.057 billion	2.641 billion	19.661 billion	2.309 billion
European Neighbourhood Instrument (ENI) (This was called the European Neighbourhood and Partnership Instrument, ENPI, 2007–13)	Countries in Eastern Europe and around the southern Mediterranean (2007–13: including Russia)[1]	11.181 billion	2.470 billion	15.432 billion	2.113 billion
Instrument for Pre-accession (IPA)	Countries that are either current or potential candidates for EU membership (including Turkey and the Western Balkans countries)	11.5 billion	1.898 billion	11.698 billion	1.573 billion
European Development Fund (EDF) (Cotonou agreement) – separate from the EU budget	79 African, Caribbean and Pacific (ACP) countries	22.7 billion	3.058 billion	26.984 billion	2.951 billion

Table 3.2 *Continued*

Financial Instrument	Countries covered/ purpose	2007– 2013 budget	2013 budget	2014– 2020 budget	2014 budget
Humanitarian aid		5.6 billion	865.3 million	6.621 billion	905.3 million
Macro-financial assistance	To meet exceptional balance of payments problems	791 million	94.6 million	564 million	76.3 million
Total for Heading 4 (External Action), excluding EDF but including other programmes not listed above		56 billion	9.341 billion	66.2 billion	8.335 billion

[1] A separate programme for 'Partnerships' has been set up for 2014–20, with a budget of €106 million in 2014, and €844 million for 2014–20.
Source: European Commission, 'Draft General Budget of the European Commission for the Financial Year 2014: Working Document Part VIII, Expenditure related to the external action of the EU', COM (2013) 450, June 2013, p. 50; Council of the EU, 'Multiannual Financial Framework 2014–20 – List of Programmes', document no. 8288/13, 9 April 2013; EuropeAid website: http://ec.europa.eu/europeaid/how/finance/index_en.htm (last accessed 25 November 2013).

impact on target countries. The Commission's 'federator role' was agreed in the 2005 European Consensus on Development, by the Council and member states' governments, the Commission and the European Parliament.[15] But as two observers note, 'most EU member states are not overly enthusiastic about a common EU development policy' because it competes with their own identity and visibility as donors.[16] Furthermore, in the European Consensus, the member states agreed that collectively they would give 0.7 percent of GNI as official development assistance in 2015, with an intermediate target of 0.56 percent in 2010. They did not achieve the intermediate target – reaching only 0.44 percent in 2010, and, given the pressures on national budgets caused by the general financial crisis, look unlikely to meet the 2015 target either.[17]

Coordination within the EU is also not a straightforward matter. Firstly, although the Lisbon Treaty makes it clear that the EU should aim for 'policy coherence' in its policies towards developing countries, NGOs have repeatedly pointed to incoherence. Internal policies such as the common agricultural policy or common fisheries policy can undermine the overall objective of promoting sustainable development, while the links between migration and development have not been fully addressed, for example by encouraging 'circular migration' (migrants coming in and leaving on a regular basis).[18]

Secondly, within the institutions coordination is challenging. The entry into force of the Lisbon Treaty fostered yet another major re-organization of the institutions and their responsibilities in the area of aid policy. Those responsibilities are now split between the European External Action Service and the Commission. The Commission merged parts of the former External Relations Directorate-General and the former EuropeAid Cooperation Office into a new DG for Development and Cooperation, known as DG DEVCO. Both institutions have a say in planning aid (DG DEVCO takes the lead on thematic programming, EEAS on development policy including the EDF), but DG DEVCO has sole responsibility for implementation. These arrangements have caused some confusion 'in the field' (amongst aid workers) though this may diminish as the system is still very new, but there are still tensions – alongside cooperation – between DEVCO and the EEAS.[19]

In addition, a new Commission service, for Foreign-policy Instruments (FPI), was created to manage the EU's funding for the CFSP, Instrument for Stability, cooperation with industrialized countries, and election observation missions. It is to work together with the EEAS and other Commission directorate-generals. The preparation of the thematic programme on cooperation on migration and asylum with third countries is carried out by DG Home Affairs – not DEVCO or the EEAS. The fragmentation of the decision-making process regarding aid for third countries does not help to foster coherent foreign-policy-making.

Decisions to grant aid are politicized, though not necessarily in accordance with a prior CFSP decision.[20] Virtually all of the Community's aid to third countries is now supposed to be conditional on respect for human rights and democratic principles. In addition, a small amount of aid has been targeted for the promotion of democracy and human rights (the Instrument for Democracy and Human Rights, see Chapters 5 and 6), and to try to reduce illegal immigration and drug trafficking (see Chapter 8). More controversially, development aid is increasingly used for 'security' issues, such as demobilization, disarmament and reintegration programmes for fighters in war-torn developing countries.

The changing distribution of the Community's aid since the 1970s again reveals shifts in the hierarchy of its preferred partners. African countries were once the largest recipients; but by the mid 1990s, Africa was clearly no longer so privileged. In 1970–4, thirteen of the top fifteen aid recipients were ACP countries; in 1996–7, only two were – having been replaced by countries in Europe and around the Mediterranean.[21] The list of the top ten recipients of EC development aid in 2009–10 clearly reflects political priorities: Turkey, West Bank and Gaza Strip, Afghanistan, Democratic Republic of Congo (DRC), Kosovo, Serbia, Sudan, Morocco, Ethiopia and Mozambique.[22] Most are neighbours; some are countries where member states have deployed troops (Afghanistan, DRC); only four are in sub-Saharan Africa. Development NGOs have decried this shift, arguing that the EU's objective of reducing poverty is thereby undermined.[23] It remains to be seen whether the implementation of the 2012 'Agenda for Change' will shift this hierarchy.

The Community also offers grants and loans (macroeconomic assistance) to third countries experiencing balance of payments problems (now mostly in the Western Balkans or Eastern Europe): in 2011, €181 million of such assistance was disbursed.[24] The budget for this has been decreasing (see Table 3.2). The European Investment Bank, an arm of the Community, lends to third countries, on a limited basis. In 2012, the EIB loaned €7.4 billion to numerous third countries, of which €3.1 billion was for pre-accession countries.[25]

As with trade, the EU can also suspend or reduce aid as part of a sanctions package – though it usually avoids doing so if this will harm the population of a third country. Under the human rights clause, if recipient countries violate human rights and democratic principles, the EU can also reduce or suspend aid or, as is more often the case, redirect aid to political reform projects or the provision of basic needs.

The EU can thus wield quite influential economic instruments, as summarized in Table 3.3. But it should be noted that several economic instruments are not controlled exclusively by the Union, though the member states can also wield these instruments on behalf of an EU policy. The member states can grant export credits,[26] promote investment, and conclude economic cooperation agreements with third countries, as long as the provisions of their agreements do not violate the CCP. They can tax, and freeze, foreign assets. Member states can provide debt relief, which was, for example, a major part of the West's efforts to assist Central and Eastern Europe, post-war Iraq and Nigeria.

Table 3.3 The EU's economic instruments

Positive measures	Negative measures
Conclusion of trade agreement	Embargo (ban on exports)
Conclusion of cooperation agreement	Boycott (ban on imports)
Conclusion of association agreement	Delaying conclusion of agreements
(all of the above on more or less favourable terms)	Suspending or denouncing agreements
Tariff reduction	Tariff increase
Quota increase	Quota decrease
Granting inclusion in the GSP (GSP+)	Withdrawing GSP (GSP+)
Providing aid	Reducing or suspending aid
Extending loans	Delaying granting of successive loan tranches
	Freezing financial assets

3.2 Diplomatic instruments

Primarily through the CFSP, the Union can wield a wide variety of diplomatic instruments, listed in Box 3.1. For most of the EU's diplomatic instruments (all but offering EU membership, sending election observers, sending civilian experts and negotiating international agreements), decisions to use these instruments are taken solely within the CFSP framework, which usually entails a unanimous decision by the member states. It should be stressed that the EU does not have exclusive competence to wield these instruments; most of them could be used unilaterally by the member states. Table 3.4 illustrates the geographical spread of CFSP decisions (which includes decisions on sanctions): as can be seen, Africa and neighbouring regions are the subject of the most CFSP decisions.

'Strategic partnerships' are a relatively new addition to the EU's 'armoury' of diplomatic instruments. These emerged in the first decade of the twenty-first century, and although they are not well defined by the EU, they essentially comprise a political declaration with a 'strategic partner' which aims to deepen the partnership through more intensive dialogue, the negotiation of new agreements, cooperation in many areas, and so on. There is no procedure for deciding which countries are to be strategic partners, and a European Council discussion on the issue in September 2010 did not reach any firm conclusions. In a variety of different documents, the EU has declared that the following are strategic partners: the USA, China, Japan, Brazil, Russia, India,

---

Box 3.1 The EU's diplomatic instruments

Strategic partnerships
Démarches
Declarations/Statements
High-level visits
Supporting action by other international organizations
Diplomatic sanctions
Travel/visa bans on particular individuals
Diplomatic recognition
Agreements on CFSP or JHA matters
Political dialogue
Making peace proposals
Sending special envoys
Sponsoring peace conferences
Sending cease-fire monitors
Administering foreign city
Sending election observers
Sending civilian experts
Imposing arms embargoes
Offering EU membership

Table 3.4 CFSP decisions, 2007–2010

	2007	2008	2009	2010
Total CFSP decisions	96	117	90	94
(Of which: sanctions)	25	27	29	20
(Of which: special representatives)	15	18	16	25
By topic:				
Africa	27	35	29	36
Europe	31	33	24	26
Asia including Central Asia	13	14	12	11
Middle East including Iran and Iraq	10	15	13	13
Terrorism	5	7	5	1
Security institutions	3	4	4	0
Non-proliferation	7	9	3	7

Sources: 'Actes Juridiques PESC 2007', Annex 1 in Council of the European Union, 'Annual Report on Main Aspects and Basic Choices of the CFSP – 2007', doc 8617/08, 25 April 2008; 'Legal Acts in the CFSP area', Annex 1 in Council of the European Union, 'Annual Report on Main Aspects and Basic Choices of the CFSP – 2008', doc 10477/09, 2 June 2009; 'Legal Acts in the CFSP area', Annex 1 in Council of the European Union, 'Annual Report from the High Representative of the Union for Foreign Affairs and Security Policy to the European Parliament on the Main Aspects and Basic Choices of the CFSP – 2009'; 'Actes Juridiques PESC 2010', Annex 1 in Council of the European Union, 'Annual Report on Main Aspects and Basic Choices of the CFSP – 2010', doc 12562//11, 6 July 2011.

Canada, Mexico, South Korea and South Africa. What unites them is that these are all rich and/or large, emerging or already developed 'powers'. As will be discussed in Chapter 4, the focus has been on bilateral relationships, though the EU also has declared it has or wants a strategic partnership with regional organizations such as the African Union.

Démarches are generally confidential messages to other governments, delivered by the ambassadors of the troika or just the presidency. They request further information on policies or express concern about developments (often relating to particular human rights issues, or requests to support EU positions at the UN or in other international conferences). Declarations or statements are used to express the EU's position (condemnation, concern, or support) on a particular situation. In 2003, the EU sent 606 démarches; in 2005, though, only 292. The annual reports on the CFSP published since then do not indicate how many demarches have been issued. In 2005, the EU made 153 declarations.[27] Interestingly, since the entry into force of the Lisbon Treaty, CFSP statements have plummeted, with only 58 in 2010, 84 in 2011, and 60 in 2012.[28] These have been supplanted by High Representative statements, of which there have been hundreds since 2010.[29] These are issued on the High Representative's behalf, without extensive consultation with the member states, so they can be issued quickly in response to events, and more strongly worded (member state agreement could result in watering down the statement). But there are risks here, in that member states could feel less 'ownership' of EU foreign policy and distance themselves from the EU level.[30] Furthermore, the EU's credibility will suffer if the rhetoric of its statements is not matched by the determination to follow through if there no internal consensus among the member states to do so.

In the past (until the Lisbon Treaty entered into force), the EU's position was transmitted by the troika, presidency, or CFSP High Representative 'in person', on a visit to the third country or via the ambassadors in the country concerned. Now the presidency has virtually no role to play in transmitting CFSP positions; this is usually carried out by the High Representative or EEAS officials.

The member states have also jointly supported action by international organizations, such as sponsoring resolutions in the UN General Assembly. The member states can jointly impose diplomatic sanctions on a third country, such as withdrawing their ambassadors, expelling military personnel in third country representations in their countries, and suspending high-level contacts. They can impose travel or visa bans on particular individuals from third countries.

Concerted diplomatic recognition has also been attempted – though not very successfully. Infamously, the Yugoslav republics and the former Soviet republics were to have been recognized jointly, according to a series of criteria set out in December 1991.[31] While the recognition of former Soviet republics posed no problems, both Germany and Greece broke ranks with the common policy regarding Yugoslavia: Germany recognized Croatia and Slovenia early, while Greece blocked recognition of the Former Yugoslav Republic of Macedonia (FYROM). More recently, since 2008, EU member states have failed to agree on recognizing Kosovo as an independent state: 23 member states have, but Cyprus, Greece, Romania, Slovakia and Spain have so far refused to do so. There have been other failures to agree joint recognition: post-colonial Angola in the 1970s, and North Korea in 2000.[32]

After the Amsterdam Treaty entered into force, the EU was able to conclude agreements with third countries on foreign policy and justice and home affairs matters. These usually make arrangements for cooperation between the EU and a third country in CSDP missions or on issues such as mutual assistance in criminal matters. Furthermore the Union has recently concluded several 're-admission agreements', in which a third country agrees to take back any illegal immigrants found in the EU which have come from or passed through its territory (see Chapter 8).

The EU is engaged in numerous 'political dialogues' with third countries and regional groupings, some of which have been provided for in cooperation or association agreements. Political dialogue meetings can cover all matters relating to foreign and security policy (including issues such as terrorism or immigration). Dialogues with important strategic partners, such as the United States and Russia, involve frequent meetings at several levels (from senior experts to heads of state or government); other dialogues take place less frequently, at lower levels, and used to involve only the troika or the presidency. The dialogues provide an opportunity for the EU to express support, concern or condemnation, and can also be used as a 'carrot' in and of themselves, given the great demand for dialogue with the EU by third countries. There are also separate human rights dialogues (see Chapter 5) and migration dialogues (see Chapter 8) with particular countries.

The Union has, on several occasions, tried to help resolve conflicts or potentially dangerous disputes, using a variety of instruments. Some of these are fairly low-key, such as advancing peace proposals or sending envoys to participate in the peacemaking process. In the mid 1990s, the EU sent envoys to the Great Lakes region and the Middle East, and various EU mediators tried to foster peace in the Balkans. At the time of writing, EU 'special representatives' (envoys) were contributing to peacemaking in the following regions/countries:

- African Union
- Horn of Africa
- Sahel
- Afghanistan
- Bosnia and Herzegovina
- Kosovo
- South Caucasus and the crisis in Georgia
- Central Asia
- Southern Mediterranean region

Several of the special representatives are 'double hatted', serving also as the heads of the EU delegations, as in the case of Afghanistan, Kosovo, and Bosnia and Herzegovina. There is also now an EU Special Representative for human rights (see Chapter 5). Ashton discontinued the mandates of several special representatives (for the African Great Lakes region, the former Yugoslav Republic of Macedonia, Moldova, Sudan, South Sudan, and the Middle East Peace Process) – often in the face of considerable opposition from member states. Instead, the EEAS is to assume more responsibility for relations with those areas, and less money is to be spent on expensive special representatives.

The EU has taken high-profile initiatives to foster peace and prevent conflict, namely in the former Yugoslavia. In 1991–2, it tried to broker cease-fires, dispatched cease-fire monitors (the European Community Monitoring Mission), ran a peace conference in The Hague, and submitted peace plans. The EU administered the city of Mostar in Bosnia and Herzegovina between 1994 and 1996. The EU's mission was to create the conditions that would permit the reunification of the city, by overcoming the division between Muslims and Croats. An EU administrator was placed in charge, and the EU funded infrastructure repair and development and social services. The WEU supplied a team of policemen who tried to establish a unified police force. The EU and WEU did not, however, succeed in reconciling the two communities.

The EU has sponsored multilateral conferences to try to prevent conflicts, including two 'Pacts for Stability', one for Central and East European countries (in 1994–95) and one for South-East European countries (2000–8). In these, countries were urged to identify projects that would facilitate good-neighbourly relations, and to reach agreements among themselves settling borders and ensuring protection of minorities.

To try to ensure peaceful transitions to democracy, the EU has sent election observers to various third countries (at least three a year since 1996). And since 2001, the EU can fund the sending of other civilian experts (such as customs officials, border guards and other such personnel) to help in crisis situations, using the funding programme that is now called the Instrument for Stability.

The EU has also worked to develop 'civilian crisis management' capabilities in the areas of police, rule of law, civilian administration and civil protection. In June 2000, the European Council set a 'headline goal' for police missions, and in June 2002 the Council agreed a goal for 'rule of law' missions. The aim was for the EU be able to send over 5,000 police officers to strengthen local police forces in third countries, and up to 282 lawyers, prosecutors, judges, and prison offices to help train local personnel and provide expertise. Finding competent people to deploy is not always easy or uncontroversial – sending police abroad, for example, may be seen as damaging police efforts at home. There have been two additional 'headline goals' set, in 2008 and 2010, which aim to further improve civilian capabilities (in areas such as security sector reform, mediation, disarmament, demobilization and rehabilitation, and border control). In 2006, rapidly deployable 'civilian response teams' became operational, with 83 experts trained in various aspects of civilian crisis management. In 2004, five EU member states (France, Italy, Spain, the Netherlands and Portugal) created a 'European gendarmerie force' (EGF), composed of specialized police forces; the EGF can be used for civilian operations.

The headline goals have not, however, been met, even though several civilian missions have since been launched (see Table 3.5). Member states have to volunteer civilian experts for each mission, on a case by case basis. As two experts reported in 2009: 'Two months after the EU's police mission to Macedonia deployed in late 2003, for example, it still faced a personnel shortfall of 30%. More recently, the EU's police mission in Afghanistan remains at just half its authorized strength.'[33] These persistent shortfalls jar with a common image of the EU as a leader in 'civilian crisis management' – which even NATO has recently sought to follow (in NATO's 2010 Strategic Concept,

NATO members pledged to build a 'modest' civilian crisis management capability).[34] Civilian missions have been funded by the CFSP budget, the EDF and other EU funds as well as member state contributions.[35]

The EU has also taken steps on arms control policy, including a 1995 moratorium on the export of anti-personnel land mines. Arms embargoes have been imposed on third countries. The EU has taken initiatives to limit the spread of arms, establishing norms regarding arms exports (see Chapter 7).

Finally, one diplomatic instrument that the EU can wield is not a CFSP instrument, it is cross-pillar: the offer of EU membership. Candidate countries are supposed to meet the requisite conditions: democratic institutions and respect for human and minority rights; a fully functioning market economy; implementation of the *acquis communautaire* (the body of EU law); and willingness to resolve disputes with neighbouring countries.[36] The prospect of EU membership for the Central and East European countries proved to be the EU's most powerful instrument to encourage them to undertake major economic and political reforms, and behave as good neighbours. The prospect of membership for Cyprus was also held out partly in the hopes that it would unblock the stalemate there, but did not (perhaps because the EU did not insist on a resolution of the conflict before it agreed to enlarge to the country). The lure of EU accession – and the consequent willingness to comply with the membership conditions – may be diminishing, in part because of the current lack of enthusiasm within the EU to enlarge further in the near future. Nonetheless, the EU still wields membership conditionality to try to influence developments in the Western Balkans and Turkey.

3.3 Military instruments

Since the 1999 Helsinki European Council decisions on the CSDP (and the subsequent Berlin-plus arrangements with NATO), the EU has launched a few military missions (see Table 3.5). It has long been the case, however, that the EU member states are not providing capabilities as envisaged in 1999. The EU has tried to increase its military capabilities, to be able to undertake larger and/or more demanding missions. In addition to the battle groups, the 1999 Helsinki headline goal has also been revised: in May 2004, the Council agreed a new 'Headline Goal 2010', which set new targets, principally to enable the EU to act more rapidly (within 10 days of a decision to launch an operation). The 'HG2010' emphasizes improving the 'interoperability' of member states' military forces and adding 'lift' capacities to increase the 'deployability' of EU troops (transporting troops and equipment to the site of the mission). Yet shortfalls in capabilities remain. Not a single battle group has ever been deployed – and even more strikingly, member states are not even volunteering battle groups for the roster, which means that in 2013, for example, only one battle group was on standby in each semester, as opposed to the two that were originally supposed to have been pledged.[37]

Table 3.5 EU civilian and military missions 2003–2013

Dates	Country	Type of Mission	Mission Objectives	Size (approximate numbers of international personnel)
Missions in Europe				
January 2003–June 2012	Bosnia and Herzegovina	EU Police Mission (EUPM) – civilian	Establish a sustainable, professional and multi-ethnic police service	774 in 2003; 80 in 2012
March–December 2003	Former Yugoslav Republic of Macedonia (FYROM)	Operation Concordia replaced NATO operation to support peace efforts – military	Contribute to a secure environment and allow implementation of peace agreement	400
December 2003–December 2005	FYROM	EUPOL Proxima, EU police mission – civilian	Monitor, mentor and advise police, thus helping to fight organized crime	200
July 2004–July 2005	Georgia	EUJUST Themis rule of law mission – civilian	Support reform of criminal justice system	27
December 2004–	Bosnia and Herzegovina	EUFOR/Operation Althea replaced NATO peacekeeping force – military	Help BiH make progress in the context of the SAP; ensure compliance with peace agreement; contribute to secure environment	600
October 2005–	Moldova/Ukraine	EU BAM border assistance mission – civilian	Prevent smuggling, trafficking, and customs fraud, by providing advice and training to border and customs services	220
December 2005–June 2006	FRYROM	EU Policy Advisory Team (EUPAT) – civilian	Monitor and mentor police on border control, public peace and order, fight against corruption and organized crime	30

Table 3.5 *Continued*

Dates	Country	Type of Mission	Mission Objectives	Size (approximate numbers of international personnel)
October 2008–	Georgia	EU monitoring mission (EUMM) – civilian	Monitor ceasefire	300
December 2008–	Kosovo	EU rule of law mission (EULEX) – civilian	Rule of law	2250
Missions in Africa				
June–September 2003	Democratic Republic of Congo (DRC)	Operation Artemis to stabilize the Bunia region before UN troops arrived – military	Help stabilize security conditions and improve humanitarian situation in Bunia	1800
December 2004–June 2007	DRC	EUPOL Kinshasa police mission – civilian	Monitor, mentor and advise the Integrated Police Unit	30
June 2005–	DRC	EUSEC DRC: mission to assist security sector reform – civilian	Advise and assist authorities in charge of security	50
July 2005–December 2007	Darfur, Sudan	EU assistance to AMIS African Union mission – civilian and military	Support AU political, military and police efforts to address crisis in Darfur	47
July–November 2006	DRC	EUFOR DRC: assist UN to supervise elections – military	Help UN peacekeeping force secure the region during elections	2300
July 2007–	DRC	EUPOL DRC Police mission: assist reform of Congolese national police – civilian	Assist police authorities in field of security sector reform	50

Continued

Table 3.5 *Continued*

Dates	Country	Type of Mission	Mission Objectives	Size (approximate numbers of international personnel)
March 2008–March 2009	Chad, Central African Republic	EUFOR Tchad/RCA: policing mission and military security mission to protect Darfur refugees – civilian and military	Protect civilians in danger and UN personnel; facilitate delivery of aid	3700
June 2008–September 2010	Guinea–Bissau	EU SSR Security Sector Reform mission – civilian	Advise and assist security sector reform	24
December 2008–	Off the coast of Somalia	Operation Atalanta: EU naval force against piracy – military	Protect merchant and vessels of the World Food Programme; deter, prevent and bring to an end acts of piracy	1200
April 2010–	Somalia/Uganda	EUTM Somalia: mission to train security forces – military	Train Somali security forces	100
April 2011	Libya	EUFOR Libya: deliver humanitarian aid – military	Mission was to supply aid, but only if UN requested assistance. The mission was never launched.	n/a
June 2012–	South Sudan	EUAVSEC South Sudan: aviation security mission– civilian	Strengthen aviation security at Juba International Airport in response to invitation by South Sudan	44
July 2012–	Somalia, Djibouti, Kenya, the Seychelles, Tanzania, and Western Indian Ocean	EUCAP NESTOR: maritime training mission – civilian	Enhance maritime capacities of 5 countries. To complement Operation Atalanta and EUTM Somalia	40
August 2012–	Niger	EUCAP SAHEL: security forces training – civilian	Provide Nigerien Forces with counter-terrorism and anti-organized crime training and support	50

Table 3.5 *Continued*

Dates	Country	Type of Mission	Mission Objectives	Size (approximate numbers of international personnel)
February 2013–	Mali	EUTM Mali: security sector forces training mission – military	Help re-establish democratic order and state authority; neutralize organized crime and terrorist threat	500
May 2013–	Libya	EUBAM Libya: border assistance mission – civilian	Help authorities enhance security of borders	100
Missions in the Middle East				
February 2005–December 2013	Iraq	EUJUST Lex: rule of law – civilian	Train officials in criminal investigation	55
January 2006–	Palestinian Territories	EUPOL COPPS: police mission – civilian	Provide support for sustainable and effective policing arrangements	71
November 2005–(suspended since June 2007)	Palestinian Territories	EUBAM Rafah: mission on border between Gaza Strip and Egypt – civilian	Monitor operation of Rafah Crossing Point	4
Missions in Asia				
September 2005–December 2006	Aceh, Indonesia	Aceh Monitoring Mission: help implement peace agreement – civilian	Monitor implementation of peace agreement	80 initially; 36 from September 2006
June 2007–	Afghanistan	EUPOL Afghanistan: police sector reform – civilian	Monitor, advise and train officials to help establish effective civilian policing arrangements	350

Military missions are funded by the 'Athena mechanism' that divides costs up among the member states according to their relative GDP, or by the 'costs lie where they fall' principle (member states fund what they contribute) – which may make some member states reluctant to contribute forces, in an age of austerity and tight budgets. Third countries can take part in EU missions, and many have done so. In 2012, fourteen non-EU countries contributed 546 personnel to CSDP missions; Turkey alone contributed about half of that total, but the USA, Switzerland and Chile were among other notable contributors.[38] But third countries cannot make up for EU shortfalls in capabilities.

The development of the EU's military dimension means that it no longer fully conforms to one element of the 'civilian power' identity: while the EU is certainly not barging around the world using its military instruments coercively, it is still quite clearly now in possession of military instruments and is using them.

3.4 Consistency and coherence

'Consistency' has several meanings. One refers to the external dimension of EU policy. Consistency in this sense means that the EU treats third countries similarly: the EU's reaction to human rights violations, for example, would be similar regardless of which country they take place in.

Consistency also has an internal EU dimension, when it is often referred to as coherence. A major issue in the pursuit of the EU's objectives is the coherence of EU action, at all levels – between the different decision-making frameworks (the former pillars), and between national and EU policy. Horizontal coherence is usually understood to mean that external measures and actions taken in each policy-making framework must be compatible and, ideally, mutually reinforcing. This is challenging: implementation of protectionist policies such as the Common Agricultural or Fisheries Policy can, and does, directly conflict with the objectives of other policies, such as development policy. Vertical coherence means that member states try to agree common policies, respect the overall EU consensus, and do not take action that contradicts, or undermines, EU policy. Again, this is challenging. Internal coherence refers to how well the institutions in each framework coordinate with each other.[39]

Initially, the member states resisted overlap between the pillars. For example, the practice of imposing EC trade sanctions was controversial through the early 1980s, because some member states objected to the use of Community instruments for overt political purposes. Community sanctions were imposed for the first time against the Soviet Union in 1982, following an EPC decision condemning the imposition of martial law in Poland. It then became a normal practice for a political orientation regarding sanctions to be defined in EPC (now CFSP) and implemented through EC instruments.

Ever since the Maastricht Treaty, the Union has declared that its external activities must be 'consistent'. The decision to merge the positions of High Representative for the CFSP, External Relations Commissioner, and rotating presidency into one new High Representative post is one example of attempts to improve consistency; the European External Action Service is another. But there are still problems – the new institutions have not necessarily resolved these, yet. Over time the Lisbon Treaty arrangements may lead to more cooperation across institutions in Brussels and with member states.

Conclusion

The EU has at its disposition many of the same traditional foreign-policy instruments used by states, as well as a few unique ones. Unique instruments include the emphasis on concluding agreements with third countries and regional organizations, the inclusion of the human rights clause in agreements, the conditional offer of EU membership, and political dialogue with regional groupings. In comparison to other international organizations (even the UN), it can certainly wield more foreign-policy instruments. But the EU lacks several instruments, even in economic areas, and its use of instruments can be hindered because the division of competences between EU institutions, and between the national and European levels, is still contested. The member states must agree unanimously to use many of the instruments that the EU does have. Reaching agreement among the member states can entail compromising on the 'strength' of the measures taken, which could thus reduce the EU's potential influence. Resources are also necessarily limited and choices must be made about where and when to utilize them. The next five chapters analyse how the EU wields its instruments to try to achieve the five foreign-policy objectives.

Questions for discussion

1. Is there still a 'capability-expectations gap' in European Union foreign policy?

2. Is the EU's economic power the most important source of its influence in international relations?

3. To what extent did the Lisbon Treaty foster 'horizontal coherence'?

Suggestions for further reading

Helwig, Niklas, Paul Ivan and Hrant Kostanyan. *The New EU Foreign Policy Architecture: Reviewing the First Two Years of the EEAS*. Brussels: Centre for European Policy Studies, 2013.

Gänzle, Stefan, Sven Grimm and Davina Makhan, eds. *The European Union and Global Development*. Houndmills: Palgrave Macmillan, 2012.

Lehne, Stefan. 'The Role of Sanctions in EU Foreign Policy', Carnegie Endowment for International Peace, 14 December 2012.

Portela, Clara. *European Union Sanctions and Foreign Policy: When and Why Do They Work?* London: Routledge, 2010.

CHAPTER FOUR

Regional Cooperation

Fostering regional cooperation is the oldest of the foreign-policy objectives considered in this book. It is also the one objective which clearly derives from the nature of the EU itself: internal practice, values and experiences have patently produced this particular foreign-policy objective. The newly formed European Community quite quickly advocated regional cooperation and the creation of regional organizations elsewhere: the first relationship it established with non-European states was with the African countries *grouped together*, in the 1960s. Since then, the EU has continued to build relations with many regional groupings across the globe. The end of the Cold War sparked a new wave of regionalism, further increasing the Union's activity in support of regional cooperation.[1] However, in the last decade or so, the EU has tempered this goal by fostering bilateral relationships – especially with strategic partners. At the same time, the EU's attractiveness as a model of regional integration has declined, due in large part to the continuing euro crisis. In sum, the relative importance of this particular objective has been declining. This chapter tracks and assesses the EU's promotion of regional cooperation.

Regional cooperation is defined here, in line with EU lingo, as 'all efforts on the part of (usually) neighbouring countries to address issues of common interest'.[2] The EU's promotion of regional cooperation encompasses two practices: classifying neighbouring countries together under regional strategies, and supporting regional groupings.

The extent to which the EU groups countries together on a regional basis has been a striking and unusual feature of its foreign relations; no other international actor does this to the same extent. The EU has usually preferred to deal with third countries collectively: it lays out regional 'strategies', sets up aid programmes on a regional basis, and concludes specific kinds of agreements with countries in a particular region, though this last trend has been countered by the drive to conclude bilateral free trade agreements with a number of key trading partners around the world. The EU encourages the countries grouped regionally to cooperate with each other: neighbouring countries are usually highly interdependent and they are likely to share transnational problems, such as environmental pollution or drug trafficking, so that any policy designed to address such problems must necessarily be regional in scope. Where regional groupings (whether formal organizations or looser frameworks for cooperation) have formed, or where countries are considering forming a regional grouping, the Union usually supports them actively. Such bloc-to-bloc relations have been termed 'inter-regionalism'.

How the EU's regional cooperation objective fits with the contemporaneous development of important bilateral relationships is, however, an important question. As Annegret Bendiek and Heinz Kramer note:

> The EU's strategy-based inter-regional relations and 'strategic partnerships' do not follow a clear paradigm. It is neither clear who the actual addressees of the different regional strategies are, nor what connections exist between inter-regional relations and bilateral 'strategic partnerships' with states of the said region.[3]

There are thus, as Bendiek and Kramer argue, many 'ambiguities' in the EU's labelling of 'strategic' partners and regions.

The first section of this chapter analyses how the EU's model of regional cooperation has influenced its external policy. Section 4.2 considers various explanations for the adoption of the objective, and then examines the EU's pursuit of the objective vis-à-vis specific regions of the world. Sections 4.3 and 4.4 discuss in more detail how the EU defines cooperation and tries to foster it. The final section evaluates the EU's promotion of regional cooperation.

4.1 Regional cooperation within the EU

The EU is undoubtedly the most integrated regional grouping in the world, and has served as a model – or at least a reference point – for many other regional groupings. This is not to deny that its own development has been at times characterized more by intergovernmental disagreements than integrationist harmony, but the achievements of integration remain impressive – despite the euro crisis or seemingly interminable debates about institutional reform. But how much of the 'EU model' can be exported elsewhere? A rather unique set of factors have favoured integration in Europe.

Firstly, the integration process within Western Europe was deliberately launched as a limited scheme to integrate only two economic sectors, coal and steel. Attempts to rush the process (the EDC treaty) failed, so a gradual approach to integration prevailed. Undeniably, the scope of integration has increased as more and more areas now fall under the EU's remit. The level of integration has also increased: QMV is the formal rule for all but a few issue areas (most importantly foreign and defence policy), and the EP has a larger say in decision-making. What set the process off, however, was sectoral economic integration between advanced industrialized countries, monitored and spurred on by common institutions.

Secondly, the domestic context of the participating states matters. The EU member states are all democracies (though some may have been fragile democracies when they joined). The trauma of World War II has also had a lasting impact, driving the conviction that another such catastrophe must be prevented. There is a propensity to diminish the importance of sovereignty, in favour of the greater collective good.

Thirdly, the West European integration process has been driven at least partially by security concerns, namely dealing with the 'German problem' and fostering Franco-German reconciliation. Economic integration was the means for achieving reconciliation and peace, and this was, crucially, agreed to willingly by both France and West Germany.

Fourthly, the US role was important especially in the early decades; the USA steadfastly encouraged and supported European integration. In 1947, the USA set conditions for Marshall Plan aid: the Europeans had to agree a joint plan for economic cooperation. The European response, to create the Committee of European Economic Cooperation, was a disappointment in Washington, which was urging the Europeans to set up a customs union.[4] The USA strongly supported the creation of the European Communities a few years later.

Finally, of course, European integration has taken place within a security framework provided by NATO and the US defence guarantee. Although not all of the EU's member states are in NATO, many theorists (particularly neo-realists) have argued that the security provided by NATO was crucial: integration among West European countries could only occur if they felt safe, vis-à-vis both external threats and the threats each might pose to the other. NATO provided such reassurances.[5]

All of this contributes to doubts about whether the EU model can be exported. In 1995, the European Commission listed several necessary factors for the success of regional economic integration schemes: the existence of genuine common interests; compatible historic, cultural and political patterns; political commitment; peace and security; the rule of law, democracy and good governance; and economic stability. These were not present in many developing countries. The Commission thus concluded, 'It should be recognized that the European model, shaped by the continent's history, is not easily transferable nor necessarily appropriate for other regions'.[6]

However, particularly since the end of the Cold War, regional groupings have been created or relaunched around the world, quite often to enhance regional security or address political matters; economic cooperation or integration is not necessarily the primary focus of the grouping. Several regional groupings are, however, experiencing problems; some of these – intergovernmental tensions over economic interests, for example – are familiar to observers of the European integration process; others indicate the absence or weakness of the European Commission's 'necessary factors' listed above.

Thus, rather than serving as a model for other regional groupings, the EU may function as a 'template' or a 'reference point'.[7] The EU has promoted general lessons stemming from its experience: regional institutions are a means of overcoming historical grievances and guaranteeing security and peace; and regional economic agreements that liberalize trade help foster economic growth and development, as well as achieve peace and security.

4.2 Regional cooperation as an EU foreign-policy objective

This section first considers why the EU promotes regional cooperation, and why it is apparently less focused on doing so now. It then analyses the development of the EU's support for regional cooperation on a region-by-region basis, beginning with Africa (its earliest external relationship).

Why does the EU promote regional cooperation?

The EU's promotion of regional cooperation has been a mixture of far-sighted strategy and ad hoc responses to external demands. The EU has encouraged regional cooperation where few efforts have been made in that direction by the putative regional partners, and has reached out unprompted to new regional groupings. But it has also extended support to regional groupings in response to demands for support by the groupings themselves. Regional groupings often demand stronger ties with, and support from, the EU: many of the EU's bloc-to-bloc dialogues were initially a reaction to such requests.[8]

The promotion of regional cooperation is an objective shared by all the EU member states and institutions (above all the European Commission). As seen below, German Foreign Minister Hans-Dietrich Genscher's active role in the 1970s and 1980s does stand out. But all member states support this objective. They do so through the EU for fairly obvious reasons: their own experiences of regional integration are EU-based, and the EU has the instruments and, more importantly, the authority, to best encourage regional cooperation.

There are several reasons why the EU may promote regional cooperation in a particular case; these can be divided roughly into 'self-interested' reasons and more 'altruistic' reasons. Usually a combination of these is at work. The diminishing force of these reasons has contributed to the shift towards strengthening bilateral relations. The reasons why the EU does *not* support regionalism in other cases also bear consideration, and here too there is a mix of motives.

The 'self-interested' reasons for promoting regional cooperation can be further divided into materialist and idealist considerations. Following Fredrik Söderbaum et al., on the materialist side, we could cite 'strengthening the EU's power', and on a more idealist side, 'building the EU's identity as a global actor'.[9] Strengthening or protecting the EU's economic power is clearly one motivation for pursuing regional cooperation. Although countries acting together in regional groupings can increase their bargaining leverage vis-à-vis the EU, the extent to which and the way in which the EU responds to such external demands still reflects power, as Elfriede Regelsberger argues, and it is the EU which bestows the benefits, or not.[10] Fostering regional cooperation tends to go hand in hand with facilitating trade and investment by EU economic actors. There has been rivalry with the USA to sponsor regional initiatives in Asia and Latin America, driven by competition for markets and influence in both regions, and a fear of exclusion from them. Similar motives (competition for energy resources) are prompting greater EU involvement with Central Asia. However (and complicating matters), EU economic interests are not sacrificed for the sake of fostering deeper inter-regional cooperation – so, for example, it has been difficult to reach an EU–Mercosur free trade agreement partly because the EU member states have been unwilling to liberalize trade in agricultural products.

But just as the drive to support regional integration was at least partly driven by a search for markets and in competition with the USA, the more recent drive to conclude free trade agreements on a bilateral basis (arguably again in competition with the USA, and now other powers too) reflects a desire to 'open' markets. Negotiations with regional groupings have been difficult and slow; negotiating bilateral free trade agreements can be a quicker and/or more effective way of improving market access.[11]

On the idealist side, the EU's promotion of regional cooperation is clearly one area where the EU stands out, internationally. Although the EU is by no means the only actor promoting regional cooperation, it is the only collective, regional organization that does so to such an extent. As Söderbaum et al. point out:

> Interregionalism not only justifies and promotes the EU's 'actorness' (both within EU itself and to the rest of the world), but also strengthens the legitimacy of other regions which, in turn, promotes further region-building and cross-cutting patterns of interregionalism. Thus, the EU's preference for region-building and interregionalism has implications not only for the foreign policy of the EU, but also for the organisation of the world polity where regional actors such as the EU gain legitimacy.[12]

As for 'altruistic' reasons, the Union's support for regional cooperation stems from the belief, born of its own experience, that it provides the basis for peace, economic development, and prosperity. The 2003 European Security Strategy asserts that 'regional organizations also strengthen global governance' and 'make an important contribution to a more orderly world'.[13] For the Commission, 'underlying this regional co-operation . . . is the EU's own philosophy that deeper co-operation with neighbouring countries is a route to national as well as regional stability and growth and that such co-operation serves their mutual interests'.[14] Regional integration fosters the integration of developing countries into the world economy, because it permits them to gradually increase their competitiveness, first in the regional context and then more widely: the regional integration process will 'help to insert [the] region in the world economy by developing larger and more stable economies able to attract investment'.[15] Mary Farrell, however, has countered that the

EU's model of regional integration in Africa is based on the promotion of liberalization and privatization, which fits well with EU interests, but not so well with African interests: 'European policy is much less active in addressing the real problems of poverty and instability that are likely to place severe limitations on either achieving economic liberalization or securing broad-based benefits in the long term.'[16]

This belief in the intrinsic value of regional cooperation does not, however, hold everywhere. The EU does not always promote regional cooperation enthusiastically or at all – even where a regional grouping may exist. Regional groupings that have been largely ignored by the EU include the Council for Mutual Economic Assistance (CMEA or Comecon) during the Cold War, the Commonwealth of Independent States (CIS), the North American Free Trade Area (NAFTA), the Organization of American States (OAS), and the Shanghai Cooperation Organization (SCO). In all of these groupings there is a powerful hegemon (or two, in the case of the SCO, as China and Russia are members), and the EU is either not keen on strengthening the hegemon's influence over the other members of the grouping (the case with respect to Comecon, the CIS, and SCO, and possibly with respect to the OAS), or does not see it necessary to deal with the regional grouping at all (NAFTA, for example, cannot negotiate agreements with other regional groupings).

Furthermore, the EU has reasons for preferring to develop bilateral relationships. This goes beyond the current tendency to conclude strategic partnerships with rising and established powers. To determine whether the Central and East European countries (CEECs) met the conditions for EU accession, the EU had to differentiate between them; this tended to inhibit regional cooperation because it emphasized 'bilateralism', relations between each individual CEEC and the EU. Differentiation is also evident in the Western Balkans, Eastern Europe and the Mediterranean – indeed, the 'new' European Neighbourhood Policy (devised after the 2011 'Arab Spring') emphases differentiation. To foster its values and interests, the EU has shifted towards a predominantly 'bilateral' strategy. In sum, the new emphasis on bilateral relations lessens the relative significance of inter-regionalism in EU foreign relations.

Africa

From the early 1960s, the Community grouped the (primarily French) former colonies in Africa together, under the 1963 and 1969 Yaoundé conventions. This African emphasis was unsuccessfully opposed by 'globalist' member states (Germany and the Netherlands), which supported a geographically wider network of development cooperation centred on the poorest countries.[17] The Yaoundé conventions were replaced by the Lomé conventions from 1975 (and the Cotonou convention from 2000), which embraced the former colonies of new member states (the UK and later Portugal), in Africa, the Caribbean and the Pacific, thus stretching the network considerably. Collective relations with the African and then ACP states, a sort of large 'regional grouping', formed the model for the Community's relations with other third countries.

Within the broad framework of 'Eur-Afrique' relations, the Community tried to encourage 'sub-regional' groupings, promising that these would receive EC aid, preferential duty-rates, and preferences when they bid for EC-financed contracts. But there were few initiatives around to support, because 'Africa's record of creating and sustaining regional frameworks is generally poor'.[18]

Only one attracted much interest, and that for political reasons. In 1986, EPC held an initial ministerial meeting with the Frontline States, a grouping of southern African countries designed to counter South Africa's armed incursions into their territory; the Community had already begun to provide some financial assistance to them. The ministerial meeting was intended to show support for the Frontline States, though few EC foreign ministers actually attended it.[19] Once the South African apartheid regime gave way to a multiracial democracy, the grouping was absorbed into the Southern African Development Community (SADC). In 1994, the EU and SADC initiated a regular dialogue, which continues today.

The Cotonou convention (articles 28–30) reiterates the EU's commitment to support regional and sub-regional cooperation. And there are now a dizzying array of regional groupings in Africa – though sustaining them is still difficult, given the absence or weakness of many significant factors (including peace and stability, but also state capacity).

The EU's attention, though, seems set on strengthening relations with the African Union (AU), which developed out of an emphasis on relations with Africa as a whole (separate from the ACP group). In 1994, a political dialogue between the EU and the Organization of African Unity (OAU, renamed the African Union in 2002) began. In April 2000, the EU held a summit with all of the African countries, which stressed 'the important interrelation between political stability, peace and security on one hand and regional integration on the other'.[20] In December 2005, the European Council proclaimed a 'strategic partnership' with Africa,[21] and in 2007, the 'Africa-EU Strategic Partnership' explicitly stated that 'the institutional architecture promoted by the Joint Strategy will, on the African side, be centred on the AU' because it is the 'natural interlocutor for the EU on continental issues'.[22] As is the case with other regions, the EU also has a 'strategic partnership' with the important regional power, in this case, South Africa, dating from 2007.

But EU–Africa relations at the highest level have been dogged by clashing policy objectives, for example with the promotion of democracy and human rights. The second EU–Africa summit, scheduled for April 2003, had to be postponed because several EU member states (led by the UK) refused to allow the Zimbabwean president, Robert Mugabe, to attend, while several African leaders declared that they would not attend if Mugabe could not. In 2002, the EU had imposed sanctions on Zimbabwe (including a visa ban on Mugabe) for violations of democratic principles (see Chapter 6). In 2007, the exact same issue arose again: the Portuguese presidency was quite keen on holding an EU–Africa summit in December 2007 and so invited Mugabe to enable the summit to take place; this time only the UK objected and Mugabe attended the summit. (The third EU–Africa summit was held in Libya in November 2010 – shortly before the Arab Spring led to destruction of the repressive Libyan regime.)

The EU professes support for sub-regional groupings in Africa. It has encouraged cooperation within 'regional economic communities' (RECs) such as SADC (and the smaller Southern African Customs Union), the Common Market for Eastern and Southern Africa (COMESA), East Africa Cooperation, Intergovernmental Authority on Development (IGAD), Indian Ocean Commission, the Central African Economic and Monetary Community, Economic Community of the States of Central Africa, Economic Community of West African States (ECOWAS), and the West African Economic and Monetary Union. Political dialogue with SADC dates from 1994, with ECOWAS from 1999, and with IGAD from 2003.

The profusion of regional communities – with overlapping memberships and similar aims – is problematic: for example, membership in more than one customs union is impossible unless the external tariffs are identical. The EU's own policy adds another, not entirely coherent, layer to this mix. Under the Cotonou convention, the ACP countries are to form regional sub-groupings, and a series of economic partnership agreements (EPAs), creating free trade areas, are to be negotiated with them – originally by the end of 2007. The new trading regime is designed to comply with WTO regulations on trading preferences, and reflects concerns that trading preferences have not improved the ACP countries' trade positions.

Initially, the EU was negotiating four EPAs with Southern, Central, West and East Africa regions: it divided countries up into those regions, and the EPA regions did not coincide with existing regional groupings.[23] In December 2007, the Africa–EU summit agreed that:

> The EU and AU will aim at integrating the RECs and the Sub-Regional Organisations (SROs) in the present institutional architecture and at minimizing overlap between, and conflicting mandates of, the entities concerned. The issue of the configuration of the EPA-related groupings is of particular importance in this context.[24]

Since then, the number and composition of regional EPAs has changed (see Table 4.1), but these groupings still do not match existing regional frameworks: SADC members, for example, are in three different EPA groupings.[25]

African countries (backed by many development NGOs and experts, as well as MEPs and even some member states) have been extremely critical of the EPAs, highlighting the costs of liberalizing trade with the EU. The Commission

Table 4.1 Progress in concluding EPAs in Africa

Regional EPA	Members of regional EPA	Status as of May 2013
Central Africa	Cameroon, the Central African Republic, Chad, Congo, the Democratic Republic of Congo, Equatorial Guinea, Gabon, Sao Tome and Principe	Cameroon signed the interim EPA for Central Africa as the only country in the region on 15 January 2009. The Agreement has not been ratified yet. Negotiations on regional EPA ongoing.
East African Community	Kenya, Uganda, Tanzania, Burundi and Rwanda	Burundi, Rwanda, Tanzania, Kenya and Uganda initialled a framework EPA (mainly dealing with trade in goods) on 28 November 2007, and are now negotiating a comprehensive regional EPA. The framework agreement has not been signed or ratified.
Eastern and Southern Africa	Djibouti, Eritrea, Ethiopia, Somalia and Sudan, Malawi, Zambia, Zimbabwe, Comoros, Mauritius, Madagascar and the Seychelles	In 2009 Mauritius, Seychelles, Zimbabwe and Madagascar signed the interim Economic Partnership Agreement (EPA). The Agreement is provisionally applied since 14 May 2012. The European Parliament gave its consent on 17 January 2013. Negotiations on comprehensive regional EPA ongoing.
Southern Africa Development Community	Botswana, Lesotho, Mozambique, Namibia, Swaziland and South Africa	An interim EPA was signed by the EU and by Botswana, Lesotho and Swaziland on 4 June 2009. Mozambique signed the agreement on 15 June 2009. Namibia has indicated it is not ready to sign. The agreement has not been ratified. Negotiations on comprehensive EPA (including South Africa) ongoing.
Western Africa	Benin, Burkina Faso, Cape Verde, Ivory Coast, Gambia, Ghana, Guinea, Guinea–Bissau, Liberia, Mali, Niger, Nigeria, Senegal, Sierra Leone, Togo and Mauritania	Two West African countries, Côte d'Ivoire and Ghana, initialled bilateral 'stepping stone' (or interim) EPAs with the EU at the end of 2007. The interim EPA with Côte d'Ivoire was signed on 26 November 2008. The interim EPA with Ghana has not been signed. Neither agreement has been ratified. Negotiations on regional EPA ongoing.

Source: European Commission, 'Overview of EPA', Updated 30 May 2013 (available at: http://trade.ec.europa.eu/doclib/docs/2009/september/tradoc_144912.pdf).

has tried to stress the 'development orientation' (fighting poverty, ensuring sustainable development) of the EPAs,[26] but the liberalization agenda remains firmly in place. The EU's approach, has not been particularly successful, as no regional EPA in Africa has yet been concluded, though interim EPAs have been, either with groups of countries or individual countries (see Table 4.1). The EU set yet another new deadline of 1 January 2014 for conclusion of EPAs, to coincide with the implementation of the new GSP regime, because this could put pressure on those countries that will not be GSP beneficiaries and thus would lose out without an EPA (such as Cote d'Ivoire, Gabon, Ghana and Namibia). But none was completed by the deadline and in any event, it remains to be seen whether the EU ends up fostering sub-regional economic integration in Africa or merely confuses the picture still further.

The EU's neighbourhood (I): The Middle East and the Mediterranean

The EU's attempts to encourage cooperation in the Middle East and Mediterranean have so far not been very successful – largely because such attempts do not fall on fertile ground. In December 1973, a delegation of Arab League foreign ministers showed up unannounced at a Community summit to propose cooperation. They were responding to a November 1973 EPC declaration which referred to the legitimate rights of Palestinians; this was seen as an indication of a collective pro-Arab stance. The Community agreed to discuss economic issues with the Arab League, but wanted to avoid discussion of the Arab–Israeli conflict, which would be internally divisive, and internationally explosive. The Euro-Arab dialogue fizzled out after Egypt was expelled from the Arab League in 1979 (for agreeing the Camp David accords with Israel). From 2011, however, the Arab League's prominence with respect to uprisings in Libya and Syria prompted the EU to strengthen its relationships with the regional body. A structured dialogue began that year, which was deepened in 2012 with ministerial and ambassadorial meetings.

In contrast, relations with the Gulf Cooperation Council (GCC) have not seen a similar improvement. In 1981, in the midst of regional instability (stemming largely from the Iran–Iraq war), the GCC was set up by six countries: Bahrain, Kuwait, Oman, Qatar, Saudi Arabia, and United Arab Emirates. With the Euro-Arab dialogue stalled, 'the Community saw that greater stability of oil supplies depended on placing EC-Gulf relations on a more direct and positive basis'.[27] The GCC countries are the most important source of European oil supplies. In 1988, at the behest of West German Foreign Minister Hans-Dietrich Genscher, the EC concluded a cooperation agreement with the GCC. This provided for yearly ministerial meetings, and included a commitment to negotiate a free trade agreement.

Developing relations has not been easy, however, and there is still no EU–GCC free trade agreement. In 1991, the Council stated that the GCC must first establish a customs union, which the GCC did only in 2003. The GCC then

suspended negotiations on the free trade agreement in 2010. Political dialogue continues, but the EU's environmental policies (such as support for the
Kyoto protocol) and its desire to put human rights and democracy issues on
the agenda have been obstacles to closer relations. Christian Koch notes that
'the EU–GCC relationship has still not reached priority status within the
EU . . . the political will is simply absent'.[28] Abdulla Baabood has pointed out
that the GCC is nowhere near as integrated as the EU and has had some
trouble speaking with one voice in negotiations with the EU, while on the EU
side, relations with the GCC countries, particularly in the security field, are
dominated by individual member states (the UK and France above all).[29]
Recently, the refusal by the GCC side to move to a 'union' or to enlarge its
membership have raised questions about its future.[30]

As for the Community's relations with Mediterranean countries, in the
1970s and 1980s, these were conducted bilaterally, though grouped under a
'Global Mediterranean Policy'.[31] The Mediterranean countries were 'at a level
clearly lower than the ACP countries in the "pyramid of privileges"', and the
bilateral agreements did not contribute much to the goal of free trade.[32] In
the early 1990s, southern EU member states began pushing for a new strategy
towards the Mediterranean, arguing that the region was being neglected
compared to Central and Eastern Europe and yet posed as much if not more
of a political and security challenge to the Union. The 'eastern dimension'
had to be balanced by a 'southern one'.[33] Crucial to the development of an
EU policy was French willingness to 'Europeanize' relations with the region,
rather than insist on an exclusive national policy.[34]

The EU's strategy initially centred on the Euro-Mediterranean partnership,
launched in Barcelona in November 1995, which brought together the EU
and twelve non-EU partners: Algeria, Cyprus, Egypt, Israel, Jordan, Lebanon,
Malta, Morocco, the Palestinian Authority, Syria, Tunisia and Turkey (Cyprus
and Malta have since joined the EU and Turkey is negotiating accession). The
Barcelona conference agreed a work programme based on regular political
dialogue, economic and financial cooperation, and social and cultural cooperation. The EU devised three instruments to implement it: the MEDA aid
programme (now the European Neighbourhood Instrument, ENI), Euro-Med
association agreements (similar for each partner), and intensive multilateral
dialogue.

The countries of the southern and eastern Mediterranean were grouped
together as a region by the EU; there was and still is no regional grouping
encompassing them all. The June 1994 Corfu European Council stressed 'the
value for all Mediterranean partners of jointly examining political, economic
and social problems to which solutions may be more effectively sought in
the context of regional cooperation'.[35] The EU was trying to construct a
Mediterranean regional identity 'from scratch', and attempting 'to apply the
Union model of functional cooperation to the construction of peaceful relations in the Mediterranean region'.[36] But as Claire Spencer points out, the

vision of a Mediterranean region 'is held more by European partners than by southern Mediterranean partners'.[37]

A shift in the EU's strategy became apparent several years after the Barcelona process was launched. The 2000 'EU Strategic Partnership with the Mediterranean and Middle East' emphasized both the need for 'differentiation' (not treating all partners the same) and the benefits of regional cooperation.[38] The European Neighbourhood Policy (ENP), launched in 2002, further recalibrated EU strategy. The ENP encompasses the southern Mediterranean countries, Armenia, Azerbaijan, Belarus, Georgia, Moldova and Ukraine. ENP countries are 'offered the prospect of a stake in the EU's Internal Market and further integration and liberalization to promote the free movement of persons, goods, services and capital'.[39] Increased economic integration and closer political cooperation are conditional, and clear benchmarks for each country are supposed to be set out. Action Plans have been agreed with each neighbour, listing the benchmarks and benefits on offer (though in practice, the benchmarks and benefits are not clear).[40]

What is particularly notable about the ENP is that it lacks a strong regional component: the emphasis is not on encouraging the countries to cooperate with each other, but on encouraging each to undertake economic and political reforms. Bilateralism predominates over regionalism. There is no overarching framework providing for regular meetings or contacts between all of the neighbours. Frustration with the large geographic scope of the ENP led eventually to the creation of two separate frameworks, the Eastern Partnership (for East European countries; see below) and the Union for the Mediterranean (UfM). The latter was pushed by the French, created in 2008, and mostly entailed an attempt to foster investment in technical projects in southern Mediterranean countries. But disputes over the Middle East peace process prevented summits from being held in 2009 and 2010, and the convulsions of the post-Arab Spring period have further stymied the UfM.[41]

ENP action plans do encourage cross-border cooperation (neighbour to neighbour, and neighbour to EU member state), encourage political dialogue (between the EU and each neighbour) on 'regional issues', and the need for Mediterranean countries to free up their trade with each other. But such priority actions are vastly outnumbered by the actions related to domestic reforms. The EU evidently concluded that the way to foster peace and prosperity in the neighbourhood is to foster reform in each neighbour first. The promotion of regional cooperation in the Mediterranean thus appears to have been superseded by an emphasis on bilateralism and differentiation. For Raffaella del Sarto and Tobias Schumacher, this approach fits both EU and Mediterranean interests: it allows the EU 'a far greater opportunity of exerting its political and (already strong) economic influence in the neighbourhood', and it corresponds to the preferences of the Mediterranean partners who 'never really appreciated being put into the group of "southern Mediterranean states", together with real or potential rivals or foes'.[42]

The problem, as is now obvious in the wake of the Arab Spring, is that the EU did not foster much reform at all in the Mediterranean countries (see Chapters 5 and 6); arguably it valued stability over reform and never really pressed authoritarian regimes to liberalize and democratize. The 'new' ENP, announced in the wake of the uprisings in various southern Mediterranean countries, however, reinforces the bilateralism of the 'old' ENP. The 2011 Partnership for Democracy and Shared Prosperity with the Southern Mediterranean

> is an incentive-based approach based on more differentiation (more for more): those that go further and faster with reforms will be able to count on greater support from the EU. Support will be reallocated or refocused for those who stall or retrench on agreed reform plans.[43]

Regional cooperation is less emphasized, though again the EU has stated that it supports 'projects which promote freer trade' in the region.[44] Thus regional *economic* integration is encouraged, but here again, the EU is pushing for free trade agreements with particular countries – in this case with Morocco: in early 2013, the two sides launched negotiations on a deep and comprehensive free trade agreement.

Asia

The EU's current preference for bilateralism over regionalism is also evident in other regions – notably Asia – though this was not the trend originally. In 1967, Indonesia, Malaysia, Philippines, Singapore and Thailand founded the Association of South-East Asian Nations (ASEAN). By the mid 1970s, ASEAN and the Community had initiated a dialogue. German Foreign Minister Genscher strongly pushed for formal EC–ASEAN ties, and the first joint ministerial meeting was held in November 1978.[45] An economic cooperation agreement was agreed in 1980. As Simon Nutall pointed out, '[a]lthough the agreement would not have been concluded had the Community not calculated that it was in its economic interest to do so, there was also a feeling that ASEAN was itself a factor of stability in the region and therefore of political interest to the Europeans'.[46] ASEAN has since widened (its membership has expanded to Brunei, Vietnam, Laos, Cambodia and Myanmar/Burma), and deepened (with a free trade area).

The EU–ASEAN relationship has not been problem-free. Human rights issues have caused problems. From 1988, the EU imposed sanctions on Myanmar (Burma) over its lack of democracy and respect for human rights. When Myanmar joined ASEAN in 1997, the EU refused to allow it to accede to the EC–ASEAN cooperation agreement, and the EC–ASEAN political dialogue was suspended. Furthermore, following the massacre of protesters in Dili, East Timor (Indonesia) in November 1991, Portugal (the former colonial power in East Timor) blocked the revision of the cooperation agreement. With a change of government in Indonesia in 1999, and East Timorese independence, the EU agreed to relaunch EU–ASEAN relations, resuming ministerial meetings even if they included Myanmar. More recently, the extraordinary political liberalization process in Myanmar, symbolized by the release of the opposition leader Aung San Suu Kyi from house arrest in late 2010, has paved the way still further for strengthened EU–ASEAN relations.

Over the past decade, EU–ASEAN relations have indeed improved – and cooperation in the Aceh Monitoring Mission in Indonesia in 2005–6 was an indication of this (see Table 3.5). The EU and ASEAN have formally endorsed the idea of an 'enhanced partnership', which entails cooperation in a wide range of areas (from crisis management to maritime security to people-to-people dialogue) and includes the goal of an EU–ASEAN free trade area.[47] Yet there is a parallel, and arguably more emphatic, push to conclude bilateral free trade agreements with individual ASEAN states (see also section 3.1). In December 2012, the EU and Singapore concluded negotiations on a free trade agreement; the EU has also launched negotiations on free trade agreements with Malaysia (in 2010), Vietnam (in 2012) and Thailand (in 2013). As Anja Jetschke and Clara Portela note, 'the emerging pattern of entering into free trade agreements . . . could undermine the EU's vision of promoting multilateral integration in the region'.[48]

Partly due to stasis in the EU–ASEAN relationship in the 1990s, the EU created another forum for relations with Asia, though it is not quite a bloc-to-bloc relationship and its membership has become ever more diffuse. In 1996, it launched the Asia–Europe meeting (ASEM), a clear answer to the US-sponsored Asia–Pacific Economic Cooperation (APEC) forum, which in 1994 adopted a plan for an interregional free trade area by 2020. ASEM initially included the EU member states, the ASEAN member states, Japan, China and South Korea; it now also includes India, Pakistan, Mongolia, Australia, Russia, New Zealand, Bangladesh, Norway and Switzerland. Every two years, a summit is held to discuss matters of foreign affairs and economic cooperation; foreign ministers and senior officials meet more often. ASEM is an attempt to draw Asian countries into a regional relationship with Europe. It reflects the perceived economic imperatives of assuring access to Asian markets, particularly given increased US involvement in pushing for trans-Pacific cooperation through APEC.

However, ASEM has not been free from tensions, initially echoing the EU–ASEAN tensions over the inclusion of Myanmar before the 'Burmese spring' (as the EU objected to including Myanmar in ASEM). The Asian side of ASEM is also not entirely coherent – primarily, but not solely, reflecting Chinese-Japanese tensions. In addition, the EU's attention to ASEM is 'balanced' by its desire to develop bilateral relations with important Asian powers.

China, Japan and South Korea have been singled out by the EU for 'strategic partnerships', which entail – among other things – regular summits at head of state level, as well as bilateral agreements. The bilateral relationship with

Japan began in 1991, with a joint declaration on relations – though for the most part that relationship is dominated by various economic, not political, issues. In 2013, the EU and Japan launched negotiations on a free trade agreement. Relations with China have developed rapidly though not without problems: summit meetings began in 1998 (lower-level political dialogue began in 1994), and in 2007 the two sides began negotiations on a partnership and cooperation agreement – which have not, however, yet been concluded. In 2010, the strategic partnership with South Korea was launched, and in 2011, the EU–South Korea free trade agreement, the first of the new generation of free trade agreements, entered into force.

In contrast to its relations with ASEAN, the EC has virtually ignored a much less successful grouping, the South Asian Association for Regional Cooperation (SAARC). This was formed in 1985 by Bangladesh, Bhutan, India, the Maldives, Nepal, Pakistan and Sri Lanka. Cooperation within SAARC is highly restricted, not least by animosity between India and Pakistan. In 1994, the EU began a low-key political dialogue with it, and the Commission offered technical assistance on economic cooperation from 1996. But the lack of cooperation within SAARC limits EU relations with it. Thus, the EU's relations with south Asian countries are predominantly bilateral. Annual summits with India began in 2000, and the EU has declared that it is one of its 'strategic partners'. Talks on a free trade agreement began in 2007, but have not yet concluded, due to differences over market accession, liberalization, and social, environment and human rights clauses.[49] Relations with other South Asian countries are considerably less developed, though the EU and Pakistan agreed in 2012 to intensify their dialogue in a number of areas. Human rights and related issues are currently disrupting the EU's relations with Sri Lanka.

As for Central Asia, it hardly figured in EU foreign relations until about 2005; increased concerns over energy supplies prompted the EU to pay more attention to the region, which is rich in energy resources. In July 2005, the Council appointed a special representative to Central Asia, one of whose tasks is to foster regional cooperation. In June 2007, the EU agreed a 'strategy for a new partnership' with Central Asia (Kazakhstan, Kyrgyz Republic, Tajikistan, Turkmenistan and Uzbekistan). The strategy 'aims at a balanced bilateral and regional approach': although 'bilateral cooperation will be of special importance', a 'regional approach is suitable for tackling common regional challenges'.[50] A regular political dialogue with Central Asia began in the same year. There is no regional grouping which links just the five countries, so this is another case in which the EU is trying to foster regionalism where so far it has been undeveloped – and again with little success. The 2012 review of the Central Asia Strategy noted that it remains 'true that relations between the Central Asian countries themselves are not always trouble-free and strained relations at times pose challenges in terms of finding solutions to shared problems', while the 2010 review acknowledged that 'regional cooperation between the countries of Central Asia has made little progress'. Despite this, the EU continues to encourage regional cooperation – while also differentiating its relations with the five countries according to their progress on reforms and other issues.[51]

Latin America

Until the 1990s, there was very little Community involvement with Latin America. Authoritarian regimes governed in many Latin American countries, the USA was the dominant external presence in the region, regional cooperation schemes were ineffective, and the Community had no security interests there.[52] The exception to this lack of involvement was Central America. In 1984, the Community launched the San José process to support Central and Latin American efforts to resolve conflicts in Nicaragua and El Salvador. French President François Mitterrand was pushing for Community involvement there, but all the EC member states were alarmed by US military support for armed rebels in Nicaragua and the authoritarian government in El Salvador, and felt that economic development and regional cooperation would better reduce instability in the region.

The EC and Central American foreign ministers held a conference in September 1984 in San José, Costa Rica, declaring that cooperation between the EC and Central America 'will reinforce the efforts of the countries of Central America themselves, with the support of the Contadora States, to bring an end to violence and instability in Central America and to promote social justice, economic development and respect for human rights and democratic liberties in that region'.[53] In November 1985, the Community signed a framework cooperation agreement with the Central American states and both sides began a regular political dialogue, the San José process. In 1999, an updated framework cooperation agreement with six Central American states entered into force, and in 2003, a political dialogue and cooperation agreement was signed with them. Under that agreement, the two groupings were to negotiate an association agreement once Central America had established a 'sufficient level of regional integration'. After Costa Rica, El Salvador, Guatemala, Honduras, Nicaragua and Panama began to establish a customs union, the EU launched negotiations on an association agreement with it in June 2007. The agreement was eventually signed in 2012 and has yet to enter into force. Note, however, that the agreement is not between two regional bodies, but between the EU and six Central American countries (which are part of the slightly larger Central American Integration System).[54]

As for the rest of the continent, as Latin American countries launched democratic and economic reforms in the 1980s, they also formed, or revitalized, regional groupings, drawing the Community's attention. In 1986, several Latin American countries set up the Rio Group, which was greeted positively by the EC/EPC.[55] In September 1987, informal meetings between the EC and Rio Group began, and were institutionalized in 1990.[56] The Rio Group was replaced by the Community of Latin America and Caribbean States (CELAC) in 2010; the EU's regular dialogue now takes place with CELAC, with summits every two years or so and meetings at lower levels more often.

The EU has supported the Caribbean Community (CARICOM) and the Caribbean Forum of ACP states (CARIFORUM). In 2006, the EU strengthened its political dialogue with CARIFORUM; in 2004, it began negotiating an EPA with the group.[57] The EPA was signed in 2008 but has yet to be ratified by all the countries involved.

In 1983, the Community concluded a regional framework agreement with the Andean Pact (now the Andean Community: Bolivia, Columbia, Ecuador and Peru).[58] In 1996 the EU began an ad hoc political dialogue with the Andean Community, and in 1998, concluded an updated regional framework agreement with it. The two sides intended to develop the relationship, signing a political dialogue and cooperation agreement in 2003, and beginning negotiations in 2007 on a comprehensive association agreement (leading to a free trade area). However, the political dialogue and cooperation agreement has not yet entered into force, and negotiations on the association agreement broke down in 2008. The Andean Community includes two countries – Bolivia and Ecuador – whose governments have rejected the proposed free trade area. Hence, once again the EU has turned to bilateralism, negotiating free trade agreements with Colombia (concluded in June 2012 but not yet in force) and Peru (in force from March 2013).

After Mercosur (Common Market of the South) was created in 1991 by Argentina, Brazil, Paraguay and Uruguay the EU responded with technical assistance from the Commission (from 1992) and formal links. Mercosur became the EU's priority negotiating partner in Latin America. In 1995, the EU and Mercosur concluded an interregional framework cooperation agreement, and agreed to negotiate an association agreement (including a free trade area). But economic cooperation has been slow to develop within Mercosur and it has not completed a promised customs union. Economic crises hit Brazil and then Argentina in the 1990s, and recovery since then has not led to deeper economic integration. Venezuela was accepted as a member in 2006, but relations between the Venezuelan government (then led by Hugo Chavez) and Brazil in particular were tense and Venezuela only formally acceded in 2012. Bolivia is in the process of joining, while Chile, Colombia, Ecuador and Peru are associated members.

Mercosur's various internal problems combined with the EU's reluctance to open up its market to agricultural imports and the stasis in the WTO Doha Round of international trade negotiations are among the most important reasons why the association agreement, under negotiation since 1999, has still not been concluded.[59] Similar to developments in Asia and elsewhere in Latin America, the EU has been strengthening its bilateral links with key countries in Mercosur. Brazil is a 'strategic partner', with whom the EU has held regular high-level summits since 2007. The EU has also concluded extensive bilateral agreements with Mercosur associates Chile (in force in 2003), Colombia and Peru.

At the regional level, in June 1999, the EU held its first high-profile summit with all the Latin American and Caribbean countries (including Cuba), and signalled its intent to develop links with the continent. EU–Latin American summits have been held regularly ever since. The EU has not, however, sought to develop relations with the Organization of American States (OAS), in which the USA is the dominant member. It has, though, been strengthening relations with the three North American countries in the OAS: all three are 'strategic partners'; the EU concluded an economic partnership, political coordination and cooperation agreement with Mexico back in 1997 and is currently negotiating free trade agreements with Canada and the USA.

The EU's support for regional groupings in Latin America must be seen in the light of US policy in Latin America, and its two-decades-old proposal for a Free Trade Agreement of the Americas (FTAA). Arguably, the EU's growing interest in Latin America was fuelled by competition with the USA. As Mahrukh Doctor notes, 'Peaks in EU negotiating seriousness [with Mercosur] tended to coincide with peaks in perceived US influence in the region.'[60] Both the US and EU approaches have been stymied: the FTAA idea virtually collapsed in 2003, while EU–Mercosur and EU–Andean Community negotiations have so far failed to produce an association agreement. And both have turned to bilateralism more recently. The USA too has concluded free trade agreements with exactly the same countries as the EU: Chile (2004), Colombia (2011) and Peru (2007).

The EU's neighbourhood (II): Eastern and South-eastern Europe

A high-profile exception to the Community's support for regional groupings was the Council for Mutual Economic Assistance (CMEA), the organization for 'economic cooperation' among communist countries. Through the early 1980s, the CMEA sought bloc-to-bloc relations with the Community, but the Community viewed it as an instrument of Soviet domination over Eastern Europe, and insisted on developing relations with the CMEA member countries separately. The ensuing stalemate was broken only after Mikhail Gorbachev assumed power in the Soviet Union and agreed to the Community's demands. From 1988, the Community concluded cooperation and then association (Europe) agreements with individual Central and East European countries.

In the early 1990s, the Community's approach to Central and Eastern Europe was still a regional one: the Europe agreements were tailored for each CEEC, but were similar in terms of conditionality and key provisions (such as political dialogue). The Community set up an aid programme, PHARE, for the CEECs. As part of this regional approach, the EU promoted regional cooperation, with aid for cross-border and regional projects and multilateral political dialogue.[61] Despite this, the EU's relations with the CEECs were predominantly bilateral. The CEECs viewed the EU's attempts to encourage multilateralism suspiciously: they did not want to recreate the CMEA, or encourage the EU to postpone consideration of enlargement. In response, the Union never forced the CEECs to cooperate with each other. Although almost all of the CEECs joined the EU in a 'big bang' enlargement in 2004, they did not form a cohesive grouping; all negotiated their accession separately.

However, as the prospect of enlargement grew closer, the extent to which the CEECs got along with each other and with their neighbours became more of a concern (see Chapter 7). The foremost attempt by the EU to encourage regional cooperation among the CEECs was the 1994/95 Pact for Stability. Not only were the CEECs strongly encouraged to reach agreements among themselves, but they were also to identify projects for regional cooperation, which could be funded by the EU.[62]

The EU also stepped up its support for European sub-regional groupings, such as the Visegrad group and Central European Free Trade Area (CEFTA), Council of Baltic Sea States (CBSS), Barents Euro-Arctic Council (BEAC), Black Sea Economic Cooperation (BSEC) and Central European Initiative (CEI). Many of these groupings were the fruit of EU member state initiatives; the Visegrad group (developed by Central European states) and BSEC (pushed initially by Turkey) are notable exceptions. All are strictly intergovernmental, weakly institutionalized, not well resourced, and depend fully on the will of their members to make something of them.[63] But support for sub-regional groupings is seen as a way to maintain links between an enlarging EU and those countries left out of successive rounds of enlargement, thus reducing the potential for tensions in the neighbourhood.

The EU's relations with other European countries are also based on regional strategies. The former Soviet republics, with the exception of the three Baltic republics, were initially grouped together, largely as a way of making it clear that they were not considered potential EU membership candidates. In early 1992, the Community decided to conclude special Partnership and Cooperation agreements with them, and devised a separate aid programme, TACIS (Technical Assistance to the Commonwealth of Independent States; now the ENI). But encouraging regional cooperation among the former Soviet republics – particularly within the context of the CIS – is difficult, because of the danger of legitimizing and strengthening Russian control over its 'near abroad', a particularly sensitive issue for Georgia, Moldova and Ukraine. Russia is not part of the ENP or the Eastern Partnership. In addition, there are still quite serious disputes between and within several CIS countries (including Armenia, Azerbaijan and Georgia). However, under the Eastern Partnership there are regular multilateral meetings at various levels (including summits), though they have not (yet) resulted in many concrete achievements.[64]

By far the EU's most active and coercive promotion of regional cooperation in Europe was in south-eastern Europe (or as it is often known, the 'Western Balkans'), from 1995. Although it seems counter-intuitive, given that many of the countries in the region once formed a single state, relations between the new states have obviously been exceptionally problematic. In December 1995, following the Dayton peace agreement, the EU launched the Royaumont Process, which was to encourage the normalization of relations between the countries concerned (Albania, Bosnia and Herzegovina, Croatia, the Former Yugoslav Republic of Macedonia, and the Federal Republic of Yugoslavia [Serbia and Montenegro]). The EU also devised a 'regional approach'. In April 1997, the General Affairs Council set political and economic conditions for trade relations, provision of assistance, and contractual relations with the five south-east European countries. The conditions include a readiness to engage in cross-border cooperation.[65] A special aid programme for reconstruction and rehabilitation funded regional cooperation and good-neighbourliness programmes.

The EU's strategy was revised during the 1999 Kosovo war. The Royamount Process was replaced by the Stability Pact for south-eastern Europe. Stabilization and Association Agreements (SAAs) are on offer, but with strict conditionality attached. Almost all of the countries of the region have negotiated an SAA with the EU, and most are in force (except for those with Bosnia and Herzegovina and Serbia), In July 2013, Kosovo began negotiations on an SAA. More importantly, the prospect of EU membership is held out for southeast European countries, if they meet the membership conditions. Such conditionality is meant to encourage reforms, but it means that the countries are judged and rewarded separately: the SAA and enlargement process effectively strengthens bilateral links between the EU and each country, although both the Stability Pact and the SAAs state that regional cooperation is necessary to solve the problems of the region.[66] In 2003, the Thessaloniki European Council reaffirmed the membership promise, and agreed to create the Western Balkans forum for regular dialogue between the EU and the region.

The regionalist strategy and the EU enlargement process fit uneasily together. The prospect of eventual EU accession was held out because it is considered to be the most powerful policy instrument the EU has to encourage the Western Balkan countries to undertake desired reforms. In response, Croatia applied for EU membership in February 2003, opened negotiations in October 2005, and joined the EU on 1 July 2013. Membership negotiations opened with Montenegro in June 2012. FYROM applied in March 2004 and was granted candidate status, but the opening of negotiations has been blocked principally by Greek objections. Serbia was granted candidate status in March 2012, and negotiations opened in early 2014. There are very large differences among the countries, so the option of a 'big-bang' enlargement is simply not feasible. So bilateralism and differentiation may hinder regional cooperation, a risky approach when politics in the region are still tinged with extreme nationalism and minority rights issues remain volatile. However, as Milica Delevic notes, there have been major steps forward in strengthening regional cooperation: at the end of 2006, all the countries signed the CEFTA agreement, which should create a free trade zone in the region, and a Regional Cooperation Council was created in February 2008 (evolving out of the Stability Pact).[67] But as countries join the EU they must leave CEFTA – which could have an impact on economic cooperation in the region. Furthermore, as countries join the EU they must strengthen their borders with non-EU countries, especially if they wish to enter the Schengen area quickly. Thus, Croatia dismantled its border posts with Slovenia and Hungary on 1 July 2013, but must strengthen its controls on the borders with Serbia, Bosnia and Herzegovina and Montenegro. Whether enlargement to the remaining south-east European countries will proceed quickly enough to make up for this remains to be seen.

4.3 How does the EU define regional cooperation?

In 1995, the Commission noted that 'there is no precise definition of regional cooperation and regional integration', but 'there is a broad agreement on what they mean in practice'. It defined regional cooperation as 'a general concept that refers to all efforts on the part of (usually) neighbouring countries to address issues of common interest'. It then differentiated between two kinds of 'efforts' with respect to the economic area: (1) regional *integration*, or those efforts whose objective is the elimination of policy-induced barriers to intra-group movement of goods, services, and factors of production; and (2) regional *cooperation*, those efforts aimed at reducing other barriers to the intra-group flows (such as the facilitation of transport and communication infrastructures), as well as any other activities leading to furthering the interdependence of the economies and to the better management of common resources.[68]

The EU supports both types of efforts, which are usually undertaken by a formal regional organization. It also supports efforts at what we can call regional political cooperation, which may or may not be institutionalized. This would include, for example, Central American efforts to mediate an end to the conflicts in El Salvador and Nicaragua. The EU's broad definition of regional cooperation fits with its tendency not to impose its own model on other regions, but rather to support such cooperative efforts as exist.

4.4 How does the EU encourage regional cooperation?

The EU uses several instruments to encourage regional cooperation: economic assistance for cross-border projects, regional cooperation and the operation of regional groupings; assistance to boost the conflict prevention and crisis management capacities of regional groupings; cooperation

Table 4.2 EU funding for regional cooperation

ACP (2008–13)	€2.7 billion (12% of the European Development Fund budget)
Asia (2007–13)	€775 million (16% of the overall funding for Asia)
Central Asia (2011–13)	€105 million (32% of overall funding for Central Asia)
Latin America (2007–13)	€556 million
Mediterranean countries (2011–13)	€343.3 million

Source: EuropeAid website, figures for regional cooperation under the headings for each region; see http://ec.europa.eu/europeaid/where/index_en.htm (last accessed 3 September 2013).

agreements with regional groupings; economic and political dialogue with groupings; and to a limited extent, conditionality.

Economic assistance

Particularly since the early 1990s, funding for regional cooperation has been included in most of the EU's aid programmes, including direct assistance to regional groupings.[69] Table 4.2 gives the amounts allocated for funding regional cooperation for several regions through 2013. The EU's support for regional cooperation distinguishes it from other donors. As the European Commission points out, in many regions, the EU is still the only donor which gives a significant volume of aid for regional programmes: for example, in the Mediterranean, none of the International Financial Institutions, no EU member state and not even the USA give substantial amounts of support for regional cooperation or to support regional organizations.[70]

The European Commission regularly produces regional indicative programmes and regional strategy papers, which set out the EU's priorities and plans for funding regional cooperation. High among the EU's priorities are usually: fostering regional economic integration; building and improving infrastructure links (transport and energy); improving the environment; promoting educational exchanges (and other people-to-people activities); and managing borders (to fight against organized crime and illegal immigration).

Assistance for conflict prevention and management

More recently, the EU has been giving aid to regional organizations – above all in Africa – to boost their capacity to prevent and manage conflicts in their region. The Peace Facility for Africa, €300 million for the three years from

2011 to 2013 (from the European Development Fund), supports the AU and sub-regional organizations in developing their ability to lead peacekeeping operations, based on the argument that 'without African leadership to end African conflicts there can be no lasting peace'.[71] The Peace Facility has supported the AU missions in Darfur, Sudan (AMIS) and in Somalia (AMISOM), a mission from the Central African Economic and Monetary Community in the Central African Republic, as well as institution-building.[72] In 2013, Ashton allocated €50 million from the peace facility to the International Support Mission to Mali (AFISMA), which followed on from French intervention in Mali in 2012.

Under the 2004 'Action Plan for ESDP support to peace and security in Africa', the EU pledged, *inter alia*, to provide technical advice to the AU and sub-regional organizations, send liaison officers and experts, and run training courses.[73] EU observers, police officers and military experts were deployed to assist AMIS, and the EU member states provided airlift. The peace facility supports African capacity building for preventing and managing conflicts.

Cooperation agreements

The EU has concluded cooperation agreements with several regional groupings (see Box 4.1).[74] According to the Commission, these agreements contribute to 'the reinforcement of regional identity and of the regional institutions.'[75] What is striking, however, is that most of the agreements with regional groupings are 'dated'. The only new agreements that have been successfully negotiated with regional groupings are the EPA with CARIFORUM, and the association agreement with Central America (though neither of these had entered into force at the time of writing). Instead, the notable successes for the EU lie in concluding bilateral free trade agreements – rather than reinforcing regional institutions.

Elsewhere, the lack of appropriate bloc partners means that most of the EU's external agreements are bilateral, but these have tended to be similar agreements for the countries of a particular region: Euro-Med agreements with the Mediterranean non-member countries; Partnership and Cooperation agreements with the former Soviet republics; Stabilization and Association agreements with the southeast European countries; and the previous Europe

---

Box 4.1 Cooperation agreements in force with regional groupings

ACP (Cotonou agreement, (2000), replacing the Lomé agreements)
Andean Community (1983, 1998, 2003)
ASEAN (1980)
Central American community (1985, 1999, 2003)
Gulf Cooperation Council (1988)
Mercosur (1995)

agreements with the Central and East European countries. The agreements encourage regional cooperation. In the case of the SAAs, countries must demonstrate a propensity to cooperate with their neighbours (among other conditions), and must conclude bilateral conventions on regional cooperation with other signatories. In the case of the Euro-Med agreements, the ultimate aim had been a Euro-Med free trade area by 2010 (not achieved). Note, however, that the more recent bilateral free trade agreements break with this pattern of 'regional' agreements: for example, Morocco is negotiating a deep and comprehensive free trade agreement with the EU.

Political dialogue

The EU engages in numerous political dialogues with regional groupings. A few political dialogues are based on cooperation agreements, others on a joint political declaration. The dialogues vary in intensity (how regularly they meet), format (the number of EU ministers/officials present), and level (ministerial, senior official, expert, and so on), according to the importance the EU accords them. Since the late 1990s, regular high-profile summits with African and Latin American countries have also been held. There are also EU special representatives (see section 3.2) to the African Union and to Central Asia.

The dialogues allow for discussion of issues of mutual interest – they may not primarily discuss the state of regional cooperation. They cover both political and economic issues, though it was not always thus: political and economic dialogues took place in different frameworks, and some covered only political or economic issues.[76]

The dialogues encourage cooperation in that they spur the regional grouping to collaborate and cooperate before, during, and after meetings. As Julie Gilson notes with respect to ASEM, 'East Asian participants meet in their collective capacity as "Asia", in order to frame a collective response prior to Asia–Europe meeting . . . the East Asian contingent has, to a large extent, to invent an "Asianness" upon which to build its regional position in the face of a definite counterpart (the EU)'.[77] They also, more broadly, communicate the EU's expectations that regions should cooperate peacefully.[78]

The EU has also set up multilateral political dialogues as a way to encourage regional cooperation, with states that do not (yet) form a regional grouping. The Euro-Med dialogue, the Western Balkans forum, and the dialogue with Central Asia are further examples of the EU's attempt to foster regional cooperation through dialogue where no regional grouping exists.

Conditionality

Regional cooperation, or the formation of a regional grouping, is generally not a formal condition for EU aid, dialogue or agreements. These instruments tend to be used positively, as support for groupings or to encourage regional cooperation. Where regional groupings are not considered strong enough (SAARC, for example), the EU does not try to coerce the member countries into further regional cooperation, by, say, refusing to conclude bilateral agreements or provide bilateral aid. Instead, it develops relations with regional groupings to the extent that they are cohesive.

There are exceptions to the reluctance to use pressure: several regional groupings have been told to deepen economic integration as a condition for further cooperation with the EU. The Cotonou agreement insists that sub-regional groupings be formed. Above all, in south-eastern Europe, the EU has been coercive: regional cooperation is a condition for a series of benefits. This condition clearly reflects the legacy of the wars in that region, and a determination to prevent future conflicts by re-building cooperative links.

4.5 Evaluation

The EU's promotion of regional cooperation is subject to the usual challenges of making consistent and coherent EU external policy. The inherently political objective of support for regional cooperation may prove difficult to implement, because of internal opposition to using the EU's economic instruments. The most obvious example is member state reluctance to open agricultural markets to outside competitors, which has complicated the negotiation of an EU–Mercosur free trade agreement.

Occasionally, one or more member states may oppose the development of relations with a regional grouping because of national concerns. This was the case, for example, with the Portuguese veto on a revised EU–ASEAN agreement. Member states may also downplay EU regionalism in favour of their own bilateral relations with countries in a particular region, as in the Persian Gulf.

What is obvious now, however, is that the instruments that the EU has traditionally used to foster regional cooperation are increasingly blunted by a preference for bilateralism. Usually this is because the EU is pursuing a free trade 'agenda', and has found it easier to do this bilaterally than on a region-to-region basis. In some areas, regionalism competes with the perceived benefits of bilateralism. In the ENP, the EU has chosen to emphasize bilateralism over regionalism, as a better way to encourage the sort of reforms and policies it wishes to see implemented in its neighbourhood. In Europe, the enlargement issue hangs over attempts to promote regional cooperation. The accession process is necessarily a matter for bilateral relations between the EU and the applicant country. This does not mean that the EU no longer promotes regional cooperation, but it does indicate an approach that mixes both (with bilateralism favoured).

The EU's promotion of regional cooperation depends also on the willingness and capacity of third countries to cooperate with each other. The attempts to create Mediterranean regionalism have so far come up against far too many regional divisions, and the GCC and Mercosur have been in crisis for some years now. The weakness or lack of 'necessary factors' for cooperation and integration, including peace and security, and economic stability, also inhibits regional cooperation – making the EU's promotion of regionalism very much a long-term goal.

A wider issue is the extent to which regionalism is compatible with multilateralism or 'globalism', despite the EU's persistent claims that it is. There are two concerns about this. The first is that regional trading blocs will hinder world-wide trade liberalization, or will lead to trade diversion rather than trade creation, thus harming non-members.[79] This is debated, and there are some who contend that regionalism could foster multilateralism and global free trade, though this optimistic view is increasingly challenged.[80] With the blockage of the WTO Doha round, the EU and others have moved to negotiate and conclude several bilateral – and some regional – agreements, and there are concerns this is damaging international free trade.

The second concern is that regionalism may hinder 'global order'. The issue, as Andrew Hurrell and Louise Fawcett point out, is how the regional and global levels can reinforce each other or come into conflict.[81] While the UN has urged regional groupings to assume greater responsibility for maintaining peace and security (thus alleviating the UN's burden), there are disadvantages to relying on regional groupings to do this. Regional organizations can lack the necessary internal cohesion to be able to undertake international responsibilities, and the necessary resources; and they may provide a cover for a regional 'bully' to exercise influence.[82] During the Bosnian war, for example, the relationships between the EU and UN, and NATO and the UN, were not always productive, but since then, there has been a much better relationship on the ground in south-eastern Europe, so a modus vivendi can be reached. Certainly, many commentators are optimistic that the EU's promotion of regional cooperation will contribute to a stable and peaceful world order. The new regionalism, with EU support, could represent an open 'postmodern' model of a 'renewed international system'.[83]

However, strong regional groupings may not necessarily share the EU's values or interests – and that the stronger they are, the more able they are to resist EU pressure or block EU policies. This has been evident in the UN context, where strong African and Arab groups have repeatedly stymied EU attempts to pass resolutions condemning human rights abuses in places such as Sri Lanka, Sudan and Zimbabwe.[84] ASEAN, the African Union and SADC have also resisted EU requests to back up its sanctions on Burma and Zimbabwe.[85] CARICOM and the Small Island Developing States (SIDS) group successfully led resistance in the UN General Assembly to the EU's request for 'enhanced observer status' (so that EEAS representatives – and not the EU presidency – could speak on behalf of the EU) in 2010; a somewhat watered-down version of the request eventually passed in 2011. In a world of strong regional blocs, the EU could be outmanoeuvred and outnumbered in multi-lateral fora.

Conclusion

The promotion of regional cooperation is clearly an EU foreign-policy objective that stems directly from its own internal identity. The EU stands out in international relations as a result of its efforts to promote regional cooperation – the most successful regional grouping in the world seeking to impart its own experiences to others. While other states may encourage regionalism (though none do to the same extent), their efforts simply cannot match the legitimacy and clear relevance of an EU strategy to do so. This is an area where the EU's 'soft power', the attractiveness of its model (as Nye would put it), reinforces its pursuit of the objective. The EU's promotion of regional cooperation is a classic example of what Stephan Keukeleire calls 'structural diplomacy' (see Chapter 1).[86] While such a policy clearly faces limits, it is nonetheless quite distinctive in international relations.

The way the EU promotes regional cooperation illustrates unique aspects of its foreign relations. It relies on legal frameworks (cooperation agreements and political dialogue commitments) and diplomacy to support regional groupings and encourage cooperation within regions that lack cohesive groupings. Although coercion is not entirely absent from the EU's strategy, generally speaking, the EU tries to persuade countries within a region to cooperate with each other, and regional groupings to proceed with further cooperative or integrative steps.

As Mario Teló reminds us, the EU's strategy will work to the extent that it chimes with the global *zeitgeist*. The EU's promotion of regionalism can succeed if it interacts with deep structural trends – if members of other regional groupings are autonomously pushing towards regional cooperation.[87] Regionalism is a promising trend for the EU, as long as it produces regional groupings willing to strengthen cooperation within the grouping, and with outsiders – and does not produce groups that challenge key tenets that the EU holds dear (such as protection of human rights).

What is also clear, though, is that the EU's promotion of regionalism is no longer as clear and prominent a foreign-policy objective as it was when the second edition of this book was published in 2008. There are various reasons why the EU has moderated its pursuit of this objective: the drive to open markets has led to the negotiation of bilateral free trade agreements with key trading partners around the world; the internal difficulties that some regional groupings have had discourages the development of region-to-region cooperation; and a policy of differentiation – devised to encourage and incentivize reform processes in third countries – sits uneasily with a policy of regionalism. This is not to say that the EU no longer promotes regional cooperation – it does. But it is to note that the EU is pursuing both regional and bilateral ties, and has no clear overall strategy regarding the optimum balance between the regional and the bilateral, nor regarding how to resolve the inevitable contradictions that such policies produce.

Questions for discussion

1. Why has the EU sought to strengthen other regional groupings?

2. How coherent are the EU's policies towards various regional groupings around the world?

3. Do you think that regionalism hinders or strengthens global order?

Suggestions for further reading

Edwards, Geoffrey and Elfriede Regelsberger, eds. *Europe's Global Links: The European Community and Inter-Regional Cooperation*. London: Pinter, 1990.
Special issue on the EU and Interregionalism, *Journal of European Integration*, 27, 3 (2005).

CHAPTER FIVE

Human Rights

The promotion of respect for human rights in third countries was one of the first topics on EPC's agenda in the 1970s, though explicit declaration of the objective did not occur until 1986. It precedes the EU's adoption of the democracy and good governance objective. Although human rights and democracy are often coupled together rhetorically, they are in fact quite distinct. Promoting democracy is a much more ambitious objective, given the extent to which it requires fundamental transformation of government and society. Furthermore, there is a considerable body of international law on human rights, which has been accepted widely by governments of all types; the same cannot be said of democracy or good governance. And, of course, democracies may not necessarily respect human rights.

Agreement among the EU member states on the importance of promoting human rights externally has been fairly uncontroversial. But agreement on *how* to do this, beyond declaratory diplomacy, has not been easy. The EU shares the 'principled belief' that human rights are a legitimate aim of foreign policy, but it has been divided over 'causal beliefs', or what sorts of policies promote human rights most effectively,[1] and over whether human rights should be prioritized in particular cases.

Philosophical and practical objections have been raised to the incorporation of human rights considerations into foreign policy. For realists, foreign policy must serve to further the national interest (above all the security of national citizens) and promoting the rights of citizens of other states would either distract from this crucial task or endanger it.[2] Other theorists highlight the clash of norms: promoting human rights in third countries could undermine fundamental norms of international society: sovereignty, inviolability and non-interference in the domestic affairs of other states.[3] Critics question the universality of human rights and view their promotion as the imposition of Western standards.[4] Some suspect that the underlying reason Westerners promote human rights (and democracy and good governance) in developing countries is to force them to undertake the reforms that are most conducive to the spread of neo-liberal capitalism.[5] Other observers point out that commercial and security interests usually 'trump' human rights considerations, leading inevitably to inconsistencies in external human rights policies.[6]

Yet the EU still promotes human rights in its foreign policy. To an extent, this is the result of thinking that human rights promotion is a security strategy: violations of human rights threaten security and stability within countries and between them. But it also reflects the belief, shared by the member states and EU institutions, that human rights *must* be promoted internationally, for their own sake. The EU insists on the universality of human rights, and rejects claims that promoting human rights is unwarranted interference in the domestic affairs of other states. However, considerations of human rights jostle along with other considerations in foreign-policy-making, and are not necessarily prioritized by policy-makers.

This chapter first reviews the development of the EU's internal human rights regime, and then traces the adoption of the foreign-policy objective (section 5.2). Section 5.3 considers how the EU has defined human rights, and sections 5.4 and 5.5 analyse how the EU pursues the human rights objective.

5.1 The protection of human rights within the EU

Europe stands out for having the strongest international framework for protecting human rights: the European Convention of Human Rights (ECHR), negotiated by the Council of Europe in 1950, lays down a number of mostly civil and political rights, including freedom from torture and slavery, and freedom of religion and expression. Under the ECHR, an individual can file a complaint against his or her own state, alleging violations of the Convention. Any resulting judgement of the European Court of Human Rights is then binding on the state. All EU member states except France ratified the ECHR before they joined the EU; France did so in 1974. This early consensus on the strong protection of human rights reflected the lessons of European experiences of Nazism and fascism: what happens within state boundaries must be subject to international scrutiny.

But this framework for protecting human rights within Europe is separate from the European Union. Even though its external human rights policy is quite prominent, the EU is still only a bit player in the protection of human rights within Europe, a deficiency that has been heavily criticized by NGOs and human rights experts.[7] The internal/external policy gap has negative implications for the legitimacy and effectiveness of the EU's promotion of human rights externally.[8]

Despite the persistence of what Andrew Williams calls the 'myth' that the EU was founded on respect for human rights, the founding treaties of the European Community did not actually refer to human rights, reflecting its origins as a common market, with integration limited to economic spheres.[9] The Rome Treaty established a few rights of EC citizens, but these relate to their roles as economic 'operators', as workers, business owners, and so on. The lack of guarantees regarding fundamental human rights became an issue after the European Court of Justice set out the doctrine of the supremacy of EC law over national law in 1964. This was resisted by the German and Italian constitutional courts, because EC law, in contrast to their national constitutions, did not protect human rights. In response, in a series of judgements from 1969, the ECJ asserted 'its jurisdiction over the review of Community provisions and action for conformity with human rights'.[10] Furthermore, the European Parliament, Council and Commission issued a brief declaration on human rights in 1977, proclaiming that 'in the exercise of their powers and in the pursuance of the aims of the European Communities they respect and will continue to respect [fundamental] rights'.[11] Yet no institutional framework for ensuring such respect was envisaged.

Twenty years later, the Amsterdam Treaty did strengthen the EU's internal human rights regime. It incorporated the social chapter, which allows for community decision-making in areas such as improving working conditions, freedom of association, and consultation of workers.[12] Article 13 allows the Council to take 'appropriate measures to combat discrimination based on sex, racial or ethnic origin, religion or belief, disability, age or sexual orientation'. The EU established a European Monitoring Centre on Racism and Xenophobia (from 2007 the EU Fundamental Rights Agency) but its remit is largely limited to research and analysis.[13]

The Amsterdam Treaty also included Article 6, which declares that 'the Union is founded on the principles of liberty, democracy, respect for human rights and fundamental freedoms and the rule of law, principles which are common to the Member States'. In the case of a 'serious and persistent breach' of these principles, a member state's rights could be suspended (Article 7). These provisions were introduced partly to guard against any backsliding by new member states. In the Nice Treaty, the provisions on suspending membership were modified, making it easier to investigate a member state where there was a risk of a violation of EU principles, and instituting a consultation process with it. The Council could then take a qualified majority vote to suspend certain rights of the member state. But as Andrew Williams points out, it is not clear what breach of human rights would prompt such action.[14] In 2011–13, Hungary's human rights and democracy situation was criticized by EU institutions, NGOs and others, but it is unlikely to be the first country to have its voting rights suspended, considering how radical a step that would be.

In December 2000, the Nice European Council proclaimed a non-binding Charter of Human Rights and Fundamental Freedoms, which includes rights guaranteed in the European Convention on Human Rights and the European Social Convention (a Council of Europe treaty on economic and social rights). The Charter does not extend EU competence: it applies to the actions of the EU institutions and is only addressed to the member states when they are implementing EU law.[15] Although the draft constitutional treaty incorporated the text of the Charter, objections principally from the UK meant that the Lisbon Treaty does not do so but instead states that the Charter has the same legal value as the EU treaties.[16] Furthermore, the Lisbon Treaty provides for EU accession to the European Convention on Human Rights. Agreement on EU accession was reached in April 2013. Once it is in force EU citizens will have protection vis-à-vis EU acts (just as they do vis-à-vis acts of the member states) and can therefore allege before the European Court of Human Rights that those acts have violated their fundamental rights. This will narrow the gap between the EU's internal human rights regime and external human rights policy.

Since 2010, the European Commission has produced an annual report on application of the EU Charter of Fundamental Rights, which focuses on EU law (thus mirroring the annual reports on EU human rights policy, which are now wholly focused on external policy).[17] There is thus scrutiny of what the EU does, though not much of what its member states do except when situations generate wider concern. The limits on EU competence mean that the EU institutions generally refrain from critiquing member states' records in human rights (the case of Hungary recently is a notable exception to this[18]).

For human rights NGOs, there are still double standards: the EU demands that third countries protect human rights yet ignores serious human rights problems within the EU. And such problems abound: in 2007, Amnesty International argued, the 'contrast deepened between the EU's stated values of democracy, human rights and the rule of law, and its own human rights performance'. The NGO's concerns about European domestic policy centred on 'dubious methods used to combat terrorism', 'abusive practices in the fight against irregular immigration', 'the ongoing discrimination towards Roma', and 'the current of homophobia that in some countries is present at the highest official level'. It lambasted the 'domestic human rights deficit' in the EU and argued that 'the attitude of complacency and denial [about the deficit] risks undermining the EU's global human rights effort'.[19] In 2012, Human Rights Watch expressed concern that civil liberties are perceived as conflicting with 'security' measures against terrorism, and that Muslims and Roma face discrimination across the EU.[20]

The internal/external gap is clear in the treatment of countries wishing to join the EU. In April 1978, the European Council declared that 'respect for and maintenance of representative democracy and human rights in each Member State are essential elements of membership of the European Communities'.[21] In June 1993, the Copenhagen European Council set firmer conditions for membership, one of which specifies that applicants must have achieved stability of institutions guaranteeing democracy, the rule of law, human rights and – going further than EU treaty provisions at the time – respect for and protection of minorities.[22] Applicant countries come under considerable scrutiny by the EU. Whether human rights conditionality is then applied consistently vis-à-vis applicant countries can be questioned, but the important issue here is that standards applied, level of scrutiny and enforcement potential differ depending on whether the country is an applicant or already a member state.

Another manifestation of the gap is the EU's relation to international human rights law. One of the sources of law which provide the basis for Community action are those international obligations which are 'common' to all the member states.[23] Yet, externally, the EU bases its human rights conditionality on international human rights treaties that not all of the member states have ratified. Furthermore the EU is not a party to any of the core international human rights treaties (though it is about to accede to the ECHR). While it projects human rights values internationally, the EU's human rights practices are not subject to international review. The EU isn't alone in this. The USA also refuses to ratify most international conventions but still insists on the universality of human rights in its own external human rights policy.[24] But this just means that both actors can be criticized for practising double standards – clouding their messages for human rights (see endnote 8).

The issues outlined in this section illustrate that the EU's promotion of human rights externally does not stem from the EU's experiences and practices, but from those of its member states. They are using the EU to promote human rights, but those principles were not developed within the EU context.

5.2 Human rights as an EU foreign-policy objective

Human rights promotion was an issue for foreign-policy cooperation almost right from the start. But during the first two decades of EPC, human rights were promoted primarily through declaratory diplomacy and dialogue. Only from the late 1980s were instruments with more 'teeth' used.

EPC's founding documents – the Luxembourg and Copenhagen reports – do not mention human rights. The 1973 Document on the European Identity mentions human rights once, but as principles that are elements of the European identity, not as objectives for EPC or the Community. The promotion of human rights, however, became a concrete objective in practice very early on.

At the first EPC meeting in November 1970, the foreign ministers chose to concentrate on two issues: the Middle East, and the upcoming Conference on Security and Cooperation in Europe (CSCE). This included 33 European states, the USA and Canada and resulted in the 1975 Helsinki Final Act. The EPC member states coordinated their negotiating position in the CSCE.

There, humanitarian issues, such as reuniting families divided between East and West, were important to West European states, in particular West Germany. 'For the West, respect for human rights and opening of human contacts were indispensable for the security of Europe; they were also essential if trust was to be built between East and West.'[25] On this issue, EPC, leading the West, was successful. The 'first basket' of the Final Act contains ten principles for relations, including the pledge that states will respect human rights and fundamental freedoms. The 'third basket' contains commitments favouring freer movement and contacts among people.

Human rights could be on EPC's collective agenda for the CSCE because, as Alfred Pijpers argued, 'there are no *fundamental* differences among the EC countries about such matters as the free flow of information, human rights, human contacts, or economic co-operation'. But, there were also no real conflicts between the USA and Western Europe on this either:

> this common perspective does not reflect specific West European interests, but rather general Western, not to say, universal values. . . . EPC has probably operated less as a diplomatic machine promoting the external interests of the European Community, than as a useful secretariat for the West at large.[26]

After Helsinki, however, there were transatlantic differences over human rights, and EPC functioned less and less like a 'Western secretariat'. The USA, beginning with the Carter Administration, used the CSCE forum to accuse the Soviet Union of human rights violations. West European countries were uncomfortable with the US approach, but increasingly they too stressed human rights, at least rhetorically.[27] The US emphasis on human rights violations 'tended to obscure and jeopardize the pursuit of humanitarian objectives in the Final Act relating to contact and communication *across the East–West divide*, issues that were of primary concern to the West Europeans, and the West Germans in particular'.[28] The Community preferred to encourage liberalization with low-key, persuasive diplomacy.

Outside the CSCE context, human rights issues occasionally came up on the EPC agenda (for example, the rights of Palestinians, apartheid in South Africa, or human rights as a basis for peace in Central America), but were usually addressed, in passing, only in common declarations. One exception was the 1977 Code of Conduct for EC firms operating in South Africa, a set of non-binding guidelines on working conditions for black workers. The member states could not agree on more negative measures, given the trading interests at stake, and a 'constructive engagement' policy helped to justify, for a while, the lack of EC sanctions.

The Community thus remained fairly immune from developments elsewhere in the 1970s. Starting in 1973, the US Congress passed legislation incorporating human rights into aid policies, and outlawing aid to countries committing gross human rights violations. In 1979 the promotion of human rights was declared to be an essential element of Dutch foreign policy. Development aid, however, would not be used as either a carrot or a stick, except in cases of gross and persistent violations of fundamental human rights.[29] In the 1970s, the Scandinavian countries also developed guidelines on incorporating human rights into foreign-policy-making.[30]

For the Community, using trade agreements or aid to punish human rights abuses was unacceptable. The Commission rebuffed the Parliament's proposals to draft agreements so that sanctions could be imposed if human rights were violated. The Community and its member states generally considered it more important to maintain trade ties with their neighbours in Eastern

Europe, than to threaten to cut off those links if improvements in human rights and political freedoms were not made (which was, broadly speaking, the US approach). The Community's development aid was supposed to be non-political, its relations with the 'Third World' free of the vestiges of colonialism and distinct from the superpowers.[31] The Community was thus distinguishing itself as a unique international actor, by maintaining a 'neutral' stance vis-à-vis the human rights records of third countries.

The first two Lomé conventions (1975–80 and 1980–85) did not refer at all to human rights, partly because the ACP countries opposed any attempt to provide aid with political conditions attached. But following the atrocities committed by Idi Amin's regime in Uganda in the mid 1970s, the Community agreed that measures should be taken if an ACP state systematically violated fundamental human rights.[32] At the Community's insistence, the Lomé III agreement (1985–90) contains a joint declaration reiterating that human dignity is an essential objective of development.[33] But beyond cases of atrocities, human rights considerations were largely excluded from relations with developing countries.

The situation began to change in the second half of the 1980s, partly because of strong criticism from the European Parliament. The EP has taken a keen interest in promoting human rights, declaring this as intrinsically related to its very identity as the only Community body elected by direct universal suffrage.[34] Despite (or perhaps because of) its limited powers in external policy, the EP has acted as a 'norm entrepreneur – an individual or organization that sets out to change the behavior of others'.[35] Since 1983, the EP has adopted an annual report and resolution on human rights in the world, in which it reviews Community activities. It requested that the Commission consider linking EC aid with minimum conditions of human rights protection, and build human rights considerations into development programmes and external agreements.[36] The EP used its assent power to press for consideration of human rights: in 1987 and 1988, it refused to assent to financial protocols with Turkey and Israel over human rights concerns. The EP became an active promoter of political conditionality.

The EP's pressure generated some response. In May 1986, the Dutch presidency submitted a memorandum to the EP on action taken in EPC in the field of human rights, since the last Dutch presidency in 1981.[37] (The Dutch initiative is not surprising given its 1979 human rights policy, as noted above.) The Presidency then submitted an annual written report to the EP (now it is the EEAS that prepares the report).

In July 1986, the foreign ministers approved a statement on human rights, declaring:

> The Twelve seek universal observance of human rights. The protection of human rights is the legitimate and continuous duty of the world community and of nations individually. Expressions of concern at violations of human rights cannot be considered interference in the domestic affairs of a State.[38]

It does not indicate how the Community/EPC would pursue this objective beyond declarations, and there was still widespread reluctance to use EC instruments to do so.[39]

Two cases, however, prompted a more active commitment. The Community imposed limited negative measures (a ban on new investments, and on the import of gold coins, iron and steel) on South Africa in 1985 and 1986, following the July 1985 declaration of a state of emergency there. It also imposed an arms embargo and some sanctions on China following the Tiananmen Square events of June 1989. Both cases would have been difficult to ignore, given public pressure for action. Beyond them, however, the importance of public opinion in shifting the EC's external human rights policy is unclear.

A more immediate motivation for strengthening the policy arose with the collapse of communism in Europe, and the desires of Central and East European countries (CEECs) to 'rejoin Europe', meaning accession to the Community (and NATO). In this context, the decision to use the Community's economic and political instruments on a conditional basis seems natural. With the end of the Cold War, the Community could insist on fulfilment of CSCE human rights principles, as they were no longer an instrument of bipolar confrontation. Furthermore, the end of the Cold War coincided with a very dynamic period in the Community's history: it was in the midst of completing the single European market and debating a single currency. There were high expectations, internal and external, that the Community could act effectively to assist the reform process in Central and Eastern Europe.

From 1988, the Community hoped to encourage its eastern neighbours to carry out political and economic reforms by making first trade and cooperation agreements, and then aid, association agreements, and EU membership conditional on satisfying certain criteria, including market economic principles, democracy, the rule of law, human rights and respect for and protection of minorities.[40] The EU considered political and economic reforms to be necessary to ensure security in Europe, but initially the focus was on providing aid for the economic transformation and using conditionality to encourage political reforms. Only in 1992, after the Yugoslav war broke out, did the EU set up a democracy aid programme. But it became increasingly willing to use carrots and sticks to foster political change to its east.

The policy towards Central and Eastern Europe both reflected and helped to prompt further changes in the *zeitgeist* regarding political conditionality. In 1990–91, EU member states also began to introduce political conditionality into their development policies. France (in June 1990), the UK (in June 1990), and Germany (in October 1991) announced that considerations of democracy and human rights would guide aid allocation. There were other reasons besides the Central and East European precedent for this shift: the end of the

Cold War meant that Western governments no longer had to support authoritarian governments in developing countries; findings by the World Bank in November 1989 that the failure of reforms in Sub-Saharan Africa was due partly to bad governance; and the need to raise public support for foreign assistance programmes. Aid would go to 'deserving' recipients, thus providing a rationale for continued giving.[41] The spread of democracy to several developing countries proved that democracy and the protection of human rights were universal trends and could and should be supported actively. The introduction of political conditionality in relations with developing countries thus reflects, to some extent, normative globalization, or what Ole Elgström calls 'ideational diffusion': the EC was following the international consensus on aid conditionality.[42] But the Community's experience in using conditionality to encourage reforms in Central and Eastern Europe reduced the reticence to use it elsewhere.

In June 1991, the Luxembourg European Council affirmed that '[t]he European Community and its Member States seek universal respect for human rights'. Furthermore, it indicated that human rights clauses in agreements were a way of promoting human rights.[43] On 28 November 1991, the Development Council agreed that considerations of human rights and democracy should be important elements in the Community's relations with developing countries, and that positive and negative measures could be taken.[44] The Maastricht Treaty reflects this: the development and consolidation of human rights and fundamental freedoms is an objective for both the CFSP and EC development cooperation.

Thus, by the time of the 50th anniversary of the Universal Declaration of Human Rights, in December 1998, the EU could declare that '[b]oth internally and externally, respect for human rights as proclaimed in the Universal Declaration is one of the essential components of the activities of the Union'.[45] Almost fourteen years later, in June 2012, the Council agreed an 'EU Strategic Framework and Action Plan on Human Rights and Democracy', which declared that 'the EU will promote human rights in all areas of its external action without exception'.[46] The promotion of human rights is clearly an important and well-established, cross-pillar foreign-policy objective.

Why has the EU reached agreement on this objective? As with regional cooperation, there is a mix of motives for adopting the objective, both self-interested (materialist and idealist) and altruistic. On the altruistic side, there is general agreement that human rights should be promoted for their own sake. As the EU declared with respect to the Universal Declaration of Human Rights: 'It constitutes the foundation for national, regional and global policies to advance and ensure human dignity world-wide.'[47]

On the self-interested side, security interests are an important motivation: the shared view is that states that protect human rights make better neighbours, that there is a virtuous link between human rights protection, democracy and conflict prevention, and that all of these also contribute to the fight against terrorism and illegal immigration. Of course, in some cases, security interests also block the promotion of human rights (see section 5.5), but the virtuous link permeates EU rhetoric, as these two quotes from key EU documents show:

> The best protection for our security is a world of well-governed democratic states. Spreading good governance, supporting social and political reform, dealing with corruption and abuse of power, establishing the rule of law and protecting human rights are the best means of strengthening the international order (European Security Strategy 2003).[48]

> Sustainable peace, development and prosperity are possible only when grounded upon respect for human rights, democracy and the rule of law (EU Strategic Framework on Human Rights 2012).[49]

Some critics allege a connection between (neo-liberal) economic motivations and the EU's promotion of human rights. As noted previously, the EU perceives a virtuous circle linking all sorts of policy objectives, from regional cooperation to human rights protection, from conflict resolution to economic growth. Certainly promotion of political *and* economic reform goes hand in hand in EU policies, and economic reform for the EU tends to imply liberalization. But it is a step too far to argue that human rights are promoted *because* they serve economic interests: economic interests (such as the preservation of trading links) can trump human rights considerations where there is a clash, while human rights considerations might prevail where economic interests are quite weak.

In a more idealist vein, the EU's promotion of human rights can be seen as an expression of its identity. 'The international human rights policies of most states are in significant measure identity based; that is, they reflect the extent to which (national and international) human rights values have shaped or re-shaped understandings of who they are and what they value.'[50] EU member states have ensured a high degree of human rights protection within their own states, and wish to promote these shared values through the EU (acknowledging the 'politics of scale').

Andrew Williams has argued that the European Community early on adopted human rights as an external objective in an attempt to boost its own legitimacy: 'Credibility and influence as an international actor were to be achieved, in part, through the display of an "appropriate" ethos, partially constructed through notions of liberty and freedom and the demonstration of that ethos in practice.'[51] Williams' argument is similar to one made by David Chandler, who asserts that Western governments pursue human rights foreign policies because taking the 'moral high ground' is a way to acquire domestic legitimacy: governments have to present themselves as having a sense of purpose.[52]

One problem raised by the idealist arguments is that presumably governments and the EU would lose legitimacy and credibility if their practices are found not to match their rhetoric. Declaring the commitment creates expectations – from NGOs, experts, policy-makers, legislators, and the public at large (within the EU and outside it) – that the EU will hold to it. Yet it is clear that there are inconsistencies in the EU's external human rights policy: arguably the greatest gap in EU human rights policy is not the internal/external one but that between rhetoric and practice. Some cases of human rights violations attract EU attention, others do not; in some cases the EU imposes negative measures, in other similar cases, it does not; in some cases the EU provides assistance for human rights reforms, in other similar cases, it does not.[53] The reasons for such inconsistencies will be explored later in this chapter, but their existence raises a question: why does the EU continue to declare a strong commitment to the human rights objective when in practice that commitment can be quite weak?

It is the assertion here that while there is a solid EU consensus on the desirability and/or need to promote human rights internationally, applying that consensus in particular cases is much more contentious. While there are cases in which other interests trump considerations of human rights, there are also genuine dilemmas: promoting human rights is not the EU's only policy objective, and other objectives or security imperatives can be prioritized in any particular instance; gauging the seriousness of violations in particular cases can be a matter of (subjective) judgement; whether to use negative or positive measures in any particular case is not a clear-cut issue; resources are finite and hard decisions have to be taken about how to deploy them. As Puetter and Wiener argue, 'norms offer neither stable guidance nor a specific template for policy design . . . They hence need to be operationalized and are, therefore, always subject to contestation.'[54] Such dilemmas combined with the usual compromises and flexibility that have to be expected in an intergovernmental policy-making entity such as the EU, result in inconsistencies.

While all of the member states and EU institutions agree on the importance of promoting human rights internationally, they do not do so to the same extent in every case. Northern states (such as Denmark, the Netherlands, Sweden and the UK) are usually more keen on vigorous action, including the use of negative measures. Southern states (France, Italy, Spain) tend to be more aware of competing interests and keener on 'engaging' with third countries – and less keen on prioritizing human rights. Under former Chancellor Gerhard Schroeder, Germany was often in the latter category (though Foreign Minister Joschka Fischer usually supported strong action).[55] The German government under Angela Merkel is inclined to a more 'northern line'.

As for the EU institutions, the EP, as noted above, clearly acts as a norm entrepreneur in this field, as did the Commission when Chris Patten was External Relations Commissioner. His successor, Benita Ferrero-Waldner, was not so active. CFSP High Representative Javier Solana was generally considered to be more comfortable with a realist approach to foreign policy than with promoting human rights and democracy.[56] At first, Ashton appeared to be uninterested in external human rights policy as well, with criticism that her initial draft of the EEAS did not mention human rights at all.[57] But in 2011 she led a review of the EU's human rights policy, and together with the European Commission produced a communication notably entitled 'Human Rights and Democracy at the Heart of EU External Action – Towards a More Effective Approach', which was followed by the 2012 Strategic Framework and the appointment of an EU Special Representative for Human Rights (see below).[58] But she prefers 'quiet diplomacy' while others, such as the German human rights commissioner, prefer to speak more forcefully to countries about protecting human rights.[59]

All of these internal differences result in the inconsistencies – smoothing them out inevitably requires compromises which will not be exactly the same solution in all cases. The problem is that with 'milieu' goals such as promoting human rights, the consequences of inconsistencies are serious. As R. J. Vincent noted:

> finding its place in the empire of circumstance is more damaging to human rights policy than it might be to other items of foreign policy, because it can be argued that it is on the substance and appearance of even-handedness that a successful human rights policy depends.[60]

5.3 How does the EU define human rights?

The EU's definitions of human rights in its foreign policy stem directly from international standards. For example, with respect to the ACP countries, the European Commission has defined human rights as those included in legal instruments such as the Universal Declaration of Human Rights, the 1969 American Convention on Human Rights, and the African Charter on Human and Peoples' Rights adopted in June 1981.[61] The EU also pushes actively for implementation of specific human rights treaties. For example, a CFSP Common Position, in June 2001, signalled EU support for the International Criminal Court (ICC).[62] For the most part, all the EU member states have ratified the relevant human rights treaties, with some exceptions: Malta has not ratified the Genocide Convention, while the Czech Republic ratified the ICC treaty only in 2009. Such exceptions illustrate a gap (albeit relatively small) between what the EU demands of others and what the EU member states do themselves.

The Union stresses the universality, indivisibility and interdependence of all human rights. In practice, though, there is more emphasis on civil and (to a much lesser extent) political rights. (Civil rights protect the individual's life and liberty, ban discrimination on the basis of race, gender and so forth, and guarantee certain freedoms such as freedom of thought, speech, religion and assembly. Political rights include the rights to participate in civil society and politics, such as the right to vote, and rights to a fair trial and due process.) Civil rights dominate the list of 'thematic issues' in the EU's annual human rights reports, with only one of twenty-one issues devoted to 'economic, social and cultural rights', and some attention paid to political rights such as freedom of association (see Chapter 6).

The emphasis on civil rights is also evident in the list of the EU's 'guidelines' on human rights, which have been adopted by the Council since 1998 and indicate how the EU will pursue particular human rights objectives:

- the death penalty
- torture and other cruel, inhuman or degrading treatment or punishment
- human rights dialogues
- children and armed conflict
- human rights defenders
- rights of the child
- violence against women and girls
- compliance with international humanitarian law
- rights of lesbian, gay, bisexual, transgender and intersex persons
- freedom of religion or belief.

For most of the guidelines, there is a firm basis in international law: for example, there are numerous international conventions outlawing torture; freedom of expression is included in the International Covenant on Civil and Political Rights; and the Convention on the Rights of the Child is the most widely ratified human rights treaty. Others are still developing areas in international human rights law: for example, dozens of states retain the death penalty, including the USA, and there are only a few international legal instruments on the abolition of the death penalty.[63]

The EU gives economic and social rights some emphasis. The protection of core human and labour rights has been a condition of the GSP since 1994, and the GSP can be withdrawn if a state violates them. In addition, a special incentive scheme (GSP+) provides additional trading preferences to countries that 'effectively implement' twenty-seven international treaties, including the core human rights conventions and International Labour Organization conventions on freedom of association, child labour, forced labour and non-discrimination. Preferences can be withdrawn if a state violates the principles listed in those conventions.[64] The Cotonou agreement also includes 'fundamental social rights' as human rights.

There are, however, EU-specific roots for the promotion of economic and social rights: the few rights in the Rome Treaty, after all, are economic and social. But pressing for social and economic rights is controversial: developing countries tend to view this as protectionism-in-disguise, with some sympathy in the EU. In practice, the Council has suspended GSP for only two countries,

Myanmar/Burma in 1997 over the use of forced labour, and Belarus in 2007 over violations of trade union rights. (In 2010 the EU withdrew GSP+ benefits from Sri Lanka because of violations of human rights – not labour or social rights).

The death penalty initiative and GSP conditionality are areas where the EU is promoting evolving international standards, and internal practice (of the member states) broadly but not entirely conforms to the international standards. In another area the EU's external policies have not been so in tune with internal practice: minority rights. In December 1991, EPC declared that a condition for recognizing new states in Eastern Europe and the Soviet Union was the provision of 'guarantees for the rights of ethnic and national groups and minorities'. EU membership conditions include 'respect for and protection of minorities'. Aid and agreements for Western Balkan countries are conditional on respect for minority rights. Both Pacts for Stability (for the CEECs, and for south-eastern Europe) emphasized the protection of minority rights. The EU's insistence on minority rights in applicant or potential applicant countries reflects lessons learned from the Yugoslav crisis: inadequate protection of minorities stokes conflicts, and the EU does not want to 'import' such problems. This was not its stance as late as June 1991, at the start of the Yugoslav war: the European Council declared that '[t]he protection of minorities is ensured in the first place by the effective establishment of democracy . . .. It stresses the need to protect human rights whether or not the persons concerned belong to minorities.'[65] By December 1991, the position had shifted.

There is, however, a distinct difference between what the EU promotes externally and what it promotes internally. The Lisbon Treaty states that the EU is founded on values which include the rights of persons belonging to minorities, but no previous EU treaty (including the Charter on Fundamental Rights) mentioned minority rights. There are European (but few international) standards. Minority rights were included in key OSCE documents, and the Council of Europe drafted a Convention on the Protection of National Minorities, which entered into force in 1998. The EU refers to these standards in relation to applicant countries. But not all EU member states accept them: Belgium, Greece and Luxembourg have not ratified the Convention, and France has not even signed it. As a result, the EU's policy has been contested by outsiders. Marika Lerch and Guido Schwellnus argue 'the lack of value consensus among EU member states . . . led to serious problems with providing coherent justifications for the policy'.[66]

In defining human rights, therefore, the EU's primary reference is (established or putative) international or European standards – whether accepted by all the member states or not, whether still evolving or not, whether universally accepted as general international law or not. This provides the EU's policy with *some* legitimacy – though greater conformity with those standards by all EU member states would bolster that.

5.4 How does the EU pursue the human rights objective?

The Union pursues the human rights objective with a number of instruments, but has long preferred positive to negative measures:

> The Community approach is geared to the principle that international cooperation must focus especially on positive measures providing incentives for the promotion of democracy and human rights; the use of sanctions should be considered only if all other means have failed.[67]

Positive measures are preferable to sanctions for several reasons. They help to establish the conditions under which democratic principles and human rights can be protected. Such measures seem to challenge sovereignty less than sanctions do. Negative measures do not necessarily address the causes of human rights violations, and can even worsen the situation. Governments may not be able to respond to outside pressure. Sanctions can antagonize states and hurt the population, or cause it to rally to the government's support.[68] But Margo Picken notes that 'constructive engagement' can substitute accountability with assistance: this 'allows business to continue as usual, while human rights violations are dealt with through quiet diplomacy, friendly advice and technical cooperation'.[69] So a reluctance to use negative measures may lead some observers to charge it with appeasement and complicity.

The ways in which the Union tries to promote human rights in third countries can be grouped in four categories: the use of conditionality, the provision of aid to improve or promote human rights, the use of diplomatic instruments, and the deployment of civilian and military missions. Coercive military measures are not, at least not yet, in this 'toolbox': military force has not been wielded by the EU to protect human rights (as in humanitarian interventions), and its use is controversial in general. In the case of Kosovo in 1999, EU member states were divided over whether NATO should intervene, although the EU did support NATO's coercive action against Serbia.[70] EU member states were again divided over whether to use coercion against Libya in 2011, when the Gheddafi regime violently repressed protesters, threatening to wipe them out in Benghazi; most infamously, Germany abstained in the UN Security Council vote authorizing NATO to use force. In the end, France and the UK led military action, with NATO joining the effort later, in which eleven EU member states (only) participated.[71] EU member states were again divided over whether to launch military strikes against the government of Syria in September 2013, after it allegedly used chemical weapons to kill over 1,000 civilians in a Damascus suburb. France was supportive of possible US air strikes, but Germany refused to participate and the UK stated it would not do so either after the parliament voted against participation. In sum, EU member states do not always agree on the use of military force to protect human rights.

Conditionality

Trade and association agreements, additional trade preferences under the GSP, technical and development assistance, diplomatic recognition, and other instruments are now supposed to be made conditional on respect for human rights: to receive such benefits, third countries are supposed to comply with that condition, and the benefits can be withdrawn if they later do not. Under CFSP Common Position on Arms Exports (see Box 7.1), member states should not issue export licenses if there is a clear risk that the arms could be used for internal repression, and should exercise caution in issuing export licenses to countries where serious violations of human rights have been ascertained.

The EU offers incentives, such as a cooperation or association agreement, to countries to press them to comply with human rights (and other) conditions or to reward them for improving their human rights records. However, there are actually very few non-OECD countries with whom the EU is not connected by an agreement (bilateral and/or regional) and they all have (or have had, until recently) extremely poor human rights records: Belarus, Myanmar/Burma, Iran, Libya, North Korea, Syria and Turkmenistan.[72] Regarding Belarus, Syria and Turkmenistan, agreements have been negotiated, but not yet concluded (in the case of Belarus, this is because of a specific EU decision not to proceed with ratification; in the case of Syria, because some member states are holding up its signature; and in the case of Turkmenistan, because the EP has refused its approval). If Iran were to comply with UN resolutions regarding its nuclear programme in exchange for incentives including an EU cooperation agreement, it is likely that human rights considerations would not prevent the EU from resuming negotiations on an agreement.[73] In 2007, the EU launched negotiations for a new agreement with China, and in 2008, it opened negotiations for a new agreement with Russia – both of whom have been heavily criticized over their human rights and democracy records.

The EP has stated 'that it is the responsibility of the Union to ensure, when signing an international agreement with a third country that includes a clause on human rights, that the third country in question respects international human rights standards when the agreement is signed'.[74] Yet the EU's preference is first and foremost to establish a framework for a dialogue and cooperation, to engage and not to isolate. This means that decisions to conclude agreements with some countries and not others are not necessarily based on human rights criteria.

Once an agreement has been concluded, the parties are then supposed to be bound by a 'human rights clause', an innovative and unique instrument, which since 1995 is to be included in all cooperation and association agreements.[75] This allows the EU to respond to human rights violations, while complying with the 1969 Vienna Convention rules on suspending and terminating treaties. If a party commits a material breach of a bilateral treaty, the other party can terminate the treaty or suspend its operation in whole or in part. Material breaches include the violation of a provision essential to the accomplishment of the objective or purpose of the treaty. Hence, the EU's human rights clause defines respect for human rights and democratic principles as an essential provision.[76] The provisions for implementing the clause state that the priority is to keep the agreement operational wherever possible, and a consultation procedure is to be followed before taking action. The human rights clause is also included in EC regulations on aid, allowing full or partial suspension of aid if the principles of democracy, rule of law, and respect for human rights and fundamental freedoms are not observed.

Because the EU's relations with third countries are predominantly conducted through the negotiation and implementation of legal agreements, the clause is important; it formalizes the EU's commitment to human rights in relations with most of its partners, and increases its margin of manoeuvre to respond to violations. The human rights clause could be invoked against the EU, but holding the EU to account requires establishing the EU's responsibility and competence, no easy task; in addition, receivers of aid are extremely unlikely to suspend an agreement under which the EU provides assistance.

The human rights clause is included in agreements with approximately 130 countries.[77] It is, however, controversial. Australia and New Zealand refused to sign cooperation agreements with the EU if they included the clause, so less formal political declarations were issued instead.[78] Other countries have complained about the inclusion of the clause – Mexico, Nicaragua (in the EU–Central America association agreement) – though they accepted it in the end.[79] Both Canada and India are currently objecting to the inclusion of the human rights clause in the free trade agreements they are negotiating with the EU.[80]

Application of the clause, however, is not a straightforward matter. There are no clear guidelines on when or how it should be invoked.[81] It is therefore hardly surprising that there is considerable variation in its use. In practice, no agreement has been suspended or denounced because of the human rights clause, although aid has been reduced or suspended in a few cases, many of which, however, involve coups d'état, conspicuous violations of democratic principles (see Appendix). Even where it imposes negative measures, the EU usually avoids penalizing the population: aid is channelled through NGOs rather than through the government, and humanitarian aid always continues. Curiously, in some cases, negative measures are imposed without invoking the human rights clause, as happened in Mali after a coup d' état in 2012. Between 1995 and 2009, the human rights clause was invoked on 15 occasions – all with respect to African, Caribbean or Pacific countries.[82] In 2010, 'appropriate measures' were applied vis-à-vis five ACP countries (Zimbabwe, Fiji, Guinea, Niger and Madagascar), and only one targeted dialogue on the human rights clause was opened, with Guinea-Bissau.[83] This despite serious problems in other countries (such as the Democratic Republic of Congo, Ethiopia, Eritrea and Sudan), as even acknowledged in the country sections of the EU's annual human rights reports in 2010 and 2011. The human rights clause was never invoked with respect to any Euro-Med association agreement: only after the leaders of Tunisia and Egypt were deposed in 2011 were their assets frozen. In 2012, the human rights clause was not used as a basis for imposing negative measures on any third country.[84]

The EU's preference is *not* to impose negative measures: the Council and Commission maintain that 'the principal role of the clause is to provide the EU with a basis for positive engagement on human rights and democracy issues with third countries'.[85] Instead dialogue should be used to press for change.

The reluctance to impose negative measures is clear even with respect to arms exports – member states still sell arms to countries even if there are human rights violations occurring. There is evidence that arms exports from the EU member states to countries in conflict or where human rights abuses were taking place have dropped.[86] But this is not a uniform trend: in the five years preceding the outbreak of the Arab Spring, for example, EU member states sold over €1 billion worth of arms to Algeria, Egypt and Libya each – despite the human rights (and democracy) records of their regimes.[87] In August 2013, after the military government of Egypt killed hundreds of protesters, EU member states agreed informally (not in a binding decision) to suspend export licenses to Egypt for equipment that could be used for internal repression – but the decision has numerous loopholes (it does not include missiles, tanks or military helicopters, for example).[88] And to cite recent evidence from just one member state (unlikely to be an isolated case): in 2013, the UK Parliament's Arms Export Controls Committee found that the UK government had approved export licences for £12 billion worth of arms and military equipment for 27 countries that the Foreign Office classified as countries of human rights concern.[89] Clearly, member states' arms exports could counteract any criticism of countries for human rights violations – and thus produce incoherence in the EU's human rights policy.

The EU has tried to increase incentives and reward countries with improving or good records in terms of protecting human rights, democracy and good governance. This goes beyond the targeted aid for political reform of the European Instrument for Democracy and Human Rights or mainstreaming human rights considerations into development aid (see the next section). In the late 1990s, the EU pledged to increase aid to countries where the human rights situation is improving.[90] The Cotonou agreement allowed for more aid to better-performing countries: if countries address an agreed set of 'governance issues' (including human rights protection), they can receive an additional tranche of up to 35 per cent of their initial aid allocation. Another initiative was the 'Governance Facility', in the European Neighbourhood Policy Instrument, which provided a maximum of €300 million between 2007 and 2012 for ENP partners who made progress in implementing reforms agreed in their Action Plans. The facility was used rarely, though some extra money was given to countries such as Morocco and Ukraine, and the sums involved were generally not considered high enough to prompt a government to make substantial changes.[91] The Governance incentive tranche for ACP countries was eventually abandoned because 'it quickly lost momentum, political traction, and leverage capacity', according to the Commission and High Representative.[92]

Studies of aid allocations have shown much variation in the practices of the EU and European states with respect to the impact of human rights considerations on aid allocations.[93] But one study did find that the 'European Commission gave more aid to countries that had substantially improved their human rights records' and that if a country had substantially improved its record and had not previously been receiving aid, then the Commission was likely to add it to the list of recipients.[94]

In the wake of the 'Arab Spring', the European Commission reviewed the European Neighbourhood Policy (see also section 4.2). It is now to be based on the principle of 'more for more': only countries that respect human rights, democracy and the rule of law will be offered the prospect of concluding a deep and comprehensive free trade agreement, mobility partnerships (enabling greater mobility between the neighbour and the EU), and more aid.[95] The Commission has also proposed to make considerations of human rights (and democracy and good governance) central to decisions on development aid. As noted in section 3.1, under the 2011 'Agenda for Change', the EU is to concentrate its development cooperation in support of two goals: human rights, democracy and good governance; and inclusive and sustainable growth. 'The mix and level of aid will depend on the country's situation, including its ability to conduct reforms'.[96] It is too soon to tell the extent to which this new approach will lead to a shift of funds towards better performing countries, but the direction has been signalled: more conditionality.

Aid for human rights

Starting in 1986, the EC gave small amounts of aid to some third countries (such as Chile and the Central and East European countries) to help them improve their human rights records and institute democratic reforms. In 1994, under EP pressure, the various funds were finally consolidated under one budget heading, the European Initiative (now Instrument) for Democracy and Human Rights (EIDHR). Funds for this increased from ECU 59.1 million in 1994 to €98 million in 1999; the budget for 1999–2004 was €410 million and more than double that for 2007–13, €1.104 billion. Funding for 2014–20 will increase slightly to €1.18 billion (see Table 3.2). Several EU member states also give political aid, but there is little or no coordination of these programmes with the EU's.

The EIDHR has five core objectives:

(1) Enhancing respect for human rights and fundamental freedoms in countries and regions where they are most at risk;
(2) Strengthening the role of civil society in promoting human rights and democratic reform, in supporting the peaceful conciliation of group interests and in consolidating political participation and representation;
(3) Supporting actions in areas covered by the EU Guidelines on human rights;
(4) Supporting and strengthening the international and regional framework for the protection of human rights, justice, the rule of law and the promotion of democracy;
(5) Building confidence in and enhancing the reliability and transparency of democratic electoral processes, in particular through monitoring electoral processes.[97]

The EIDHR operates largely by extending grants to NGOs (EU-based and non-EU-based) to carry out projects. This means that where NGOs find it difficult to operate (in countries with the worst human rights violations), the EIHDR is consequently limited. It essentially can do little where the need is greatest.

The promotion of human rights and democracy in all aid programmes is supposed to be 'mainstreamed'. In the early 2000s, the Commission began to do this by incorporating issues of human rights, democracy and good governance into its strategy papers, national indicative programmes and individual projects, but it proved challenging to 'establish a stronger link' between technical cooperation, development aid and promoting respect for human rights.[98] A 2009 study for the European Parliament found that 'there is little evidence of any human rights-based approach at the programming level across different sectors, including transport, energy, health, the rule of law and governance'. This is significant because, as the authors point out in the case of transport, 'the construction of roads in certain countries may have an impact on land and the rights of indigenous people'.[99]

The 2012 EU Strategic Framework and Action Plan on Human Rights and Democracy reaffirms the commitment to mainstreaming human rights considerations in all areas of EU external action. The EU will do so in various ways, including:

– Heads of EU delegations are to work closely with human rights NGOs in the countries of their posting;
– All staff (EEAS, Commission, EU delegations, CSDP missions) are to receive training on human rights and democracy;

– Human rights principles are to be integrated into EU development
  activities;
– Assessment of human rights is to be an element in decisions on deploying
  aid, including budget support;
– Human rights country strategies to be taken into account in all dialogues,
  and when programming and implementing aid.[100]

Diplomatic instruments

Every year, the EU, through the CFSP, makes numerous declarations about the
human rights situation in third countries, and delivers démarches expressing
concern about particular cases, including on the death penalty, torture and
human rights defenders. Martine Fouwels argues that these instruments can
be effective, especially in individual cases of human rights violations.[101]

In July 2012, an EU Special Representative for Human Rights was appointed,
Stavros Lambrinidis.[102] The Special Representative's job includes enhancing
dialogue with third countries and action within international organizations.
Previously, from 2005, the High Representative for CFSP had appointed a
'personal representative for human rights'. The personal representative participated in dialogues and consultations with third states, engaged in public
diplomacy, helped promote the EU's human rights policy in international
organizations, and fostered the mainstreaming of human rights throughout
EU activities and policies.[103] Lambrinidis occupies a higher-profile post – and
his appointment is indicative of the EU's new emphasis on human rights.

Dialogue with third countries is an increasingly important instrument: the
Council affirms 'the importance it attaches to dialogue as a key tool in promoting human rights worldwide'.[104] All of the EU's political dialogues, both
bilateral and regional, are supposed to cover issues relating to human rights
and democratization.[105] In some cases, a dedicated sub-committee on human
rights has been formed under the rubric of an agreement with the third
country, and dialogue is conducted in that framework.[106] Through dialogue,
the EU can try to persuade third countries of the value of protecting human
rights, and therefore engage them in a process of socialization. But the inclusion of human rights and democratic principles in dialogue is not always
accepted willingly: there were tough negotiations on the content of the political dialogue during the Cotonou negotiations, and with the Euro-Med partners. Third countries view dialogue as just another way for the EU to exercise
pressure and conditionality.[107]

The EU also conducts 'structured human rights dialogues' with countries
such as Belarus, China and Turkmenistan. These are supposed to 'enable
the EU to discuss human rights with certain partners at a greater level of
detail than would otherwise be possible'.[108] The new Special Representative
for Human Rights is to play a role in human rights dialogues with third
countries.

The EU repeatedly states that it 'raises' its concerns about human rights issues in these dialogues, but it is not clear what follows from this: the EU's own reports give no indication of the extent to which the third country responded to the EU's concerns, nor whether the EU took any further action as a result.[109] A human rights dialogue with China has been operative since 1997, but in March 2000, the Council announced that it would review the dialogue to try to achieve 'a more focused and result-oriented approach', and in January 2001, it set out a number of priority areas on which it would seek progress by China.[110] But almost seven years later, the Council acknowledged that it had 'serious concerns about the human rights situation in China and deplores the fact that there has been very little progress in a number of areas of concern'. Despite this, the Council pledged only to continue to monitor the situation and to work for 'positive change' through continued dialogue and cooperation.[111]

External assessments of the dialogues are not publicly available. The 2012 EU Strategic Framework and Action Plan on Human Rights and Democracy sets the following goal for 2014: 'establish priorities, objectives, indicators of progress for EU human rights dialogue and consultations, to facilitate their review'.[112] This is laudable, but also signals that priorities and indicators have not thus far been set.

Diplomatic sanctions and arms embargoes have been imposed on a few third countries over their human rights records (see Appendix). Unity in implementing diplomatic sanctions, however, can be difficult to maintain: in 2005 Germany allowed the Uzbek interior minister to travel to Germany for medical treatment, in contravention of an EU travel ban.[113] In October 2007, Germany successfully pushed for the suspension of the travel ban, despite little evidence of progress on human rights in Uzbekistan. In 2009, all the sanctions on Uzbekistan were lifted – although the Uzbek government had not met the EU's conditions, namely investigating and holding accountable those responsible for the 2005 Andijan massacre. Regarding Cuba, from 2005 Spain successfully pressed for the suspension of diplomatic sanctions, again despite little evidence that the human rights (and democracy) situation in that country had improved.[114] And the member states agreed to allow Zimbabwean President Robert Mugabe to attend an EU–Africa summit in Lisbon in December 2007, despite the EU's travel ban on him.

The EU is also active in international human rights bodies, notably the UN Human Rights Council (HRC) and the Third Committee of the UN General Assembly. EU action includes issuing statements, sponsoring resolutions, and voting together. The EU has issued a large number of statements on human rights at the UN (around 90 a year in the Human Rights Council), but EU voting cohesion on human rights resolutions can be difficult to achieve (especially on issues relating to Israeli violations of human rights). And since a heyday in the 1990s, the EU has put forward fewer and fewer proposals for resolutions – partly because it usually encounters considerable opposition when it does so. EU member states also tend to be quite isolated – often in the minority on votes on resolutions with which they disagree. Because 'bloc politics' is so pervasive at the HRC, moderate states in blocs opposing the EU often find it more attractive to go along with the Organization of the Islamic Conference, or the Africa Group, or the Non-Aligned Movement, than to vote with the EU. In addition, the time-consuming nature of the EU internal coordination process at the UN leaves the EU with little time to build support for its positions.[115] In 2011 and 2012, however, there was a noticeable increase in the EU's activity at the HRC, due to the combined effects of US membership in the HRC and the Arab Spring. The USA was absent from the Human Rights Council from 2006 to 2009, and US membership has coincided with a vigorous response to the extraordinary developments stemming from the Arab Spring.

Civilian and military missions

'Mainstreaming' human rights in CSDP operations has been challenging. One study found that only eight out of twenty-two CSFP Joint Actions establishing missions made a reference to human rights.[116] Some missions have at least some human rights-related components – particularly the case of the 'rule of law' mission in Georgia, and police missions in Afghanistan, Bosnia and Herzegovina, DRC, FYROM and the Palestinian territories (see Table 3.5). The mandate for the Aceh Monitoring Mission specifically included monitoring of the human rights situation; the mission to Chad was aimed at protecting refugees displaced by the conflict in Darfur. But promoting human rights is not a priority in CSDP missions.

There has been no question of the EU itself launching humanitarian intervention against the wishes of the host state, and this would certainly be beyond the current capabilities of the CSDP. As already noted, EU member states have not always been united in supporting the intervention of other actors (namely NATO) to protect civilians. Thus, the coercive use of force to protect human rights is not part of the panoply of foreign-policy instruments used by the EU.

5.5 Evaluation: Inconsistency in the EU's human rights policy

Two aspects of inconsistency are considered here. Firstly, are there intra-EU 'coordination problems'? As discussed above, human rights are supposed to be promoted in all areas of the EU's external action. In addition, the member states and the EU are supposed to coordinate their policies on human rights and democracy, and inform each other of changes made to those policies.[117] But there have been problems. For example, Nathalie Tocci notes that in fall 2004, the Commission continued negotiating an ENP action plan with Israel, while the Council criticized Israeli raids in Gaza and supported an International Court of Justice opinion on the illegality of the West Bank barrier.[118] And the priorities the EU pursues at UN human rights fora do not match the apparent priorities in its human rights policy outside the UN (for example, the list of countries that are subject to EU negative measures or expressions of concern does not match the rather short list of country-related resolutions the EU pursues in the Human Rights Council). Decisions by the EU member states and the EU to take negative measures vis-à-vis particular third countries are not coordinated – or even similar: in 2005, for example, the Netherlands and Sweden froze aid to Ethiopia, following election-related violence and the arrest of hundreds of opposition activists, but the EU did not.[119]

The 2012 Strategic Framework tries to address these issues. Traditionally the Council's working group on human rights (COHOM) is to ensure that consistent and coherent decisions are taken across issue and geographical areas. It used to meet only once a month, was composed of experts based in the EU member states' capitals, and was headed by the rotating presidency. From 2012, COHOM is based in Brussels and has a permanent chair. This could allow for better mediation of disagreements between member states over the implementation of the EU's human rights policy, and a better matching of priorities pursued in various frameworks (bilaterally and multilaterally). It is obviously too soon to tell whether the EU's human rights policy will be more consistent, but the intention to improve horizontal coherence is there.

Secondly, how consistently has the EU incorporated human rights considerations into its relations with third countries? Inconsistency raises doubts about the extent to which human rights are a genuine concern in foreign policy. And an external human rights policy will have little impact if it is glaringly inconsistent: why should third countries try to meet the EU's demands if others do not face the same pressures?

As already seen, the EU is most certainly guilty of inconsistency, since third countries are treated differently, even though their human rights (and democratic) records are similar. This is most evident in the use of negative measures. But compared to other donors, the EU's practices are quite similar. For example, Gordon Crawford found considerable similarities in the practices of imposing (or not imposing) negative measures for violations of human rights and democracy of the EU, USA, UK and Sweden.[120]

The inconsistency allows us to reject one of the supposed reasons for promoting human rights abroad. If political conditionality is usually applied with respect to poor, marginal states, then the real reason for applying it cannot be to force third countries to adopt market economic reforms. Western investors and companies are unlikely to be keen about investing in or trading with marginal countries, so there would be little pressure to apply conditionality.

There are three reasons for the inconsistencies: one or more member states blocks the use of negative measures on certain third countries because they would harm their commercial interests; one or more member states blocks the use of negative measures because the country is politically or strategically too important to antagonize; and doubts about the effectiveness of negative measures in general affect policy-making. These dilemmas also affect national policy-making but they are compounded by the nature of the EU. Implementing negative measures (imposing sanctions, or suspending mixed agreements) requires consensus among the member states, and it is difficult to overcome the logic of diversity. Even where QMV can be used (to suspend aid or a Community agreement), it is difficult in practice to take measures if a member state is strongly opposed. And even where agreement can be reached, it may only result in a decision based on the 'lowest common denominator', which could entail the watering down of negative measures. Of course, there are advantages to collective action, in that member states can 'hide behind' it, disclaiming responsibility and citing the exigencies of going along with everyone else. But in cases where a member state strongly opposes the use of negative measures, it would be next to impossible for the EU to act. The north–south split on the use of conditionality means that the EU's position ends up being softer than northern member states would prefer.[121]

Illustrations of the role of security and economic considerations abound – and what follows are only a few examples. Although the EU has criticized the use of the death penalty in the USA, the Guantánamo prison, and the USA's rejection of the ICC, these issues are simply never going to be allowed to disrupt relations with such a major trading and security partner.[122] Commercial and strategic interests are also at play in limiting EU criticism of China and Russia, both permanent members of the UN Security Council. Not only are they important trading partners (and Russia a major source of energy), their cooperation is needed on a range of issues of importance to the EU, such as measures against Iran and North Korea for violating nuclear non-proliferation norms.[123] There has been little support in the EU to follow the USA and impose travel bans on Russian officials whose corruption was exposed by Sergei Magnitsky (who was then imprisoned, mistreated, and died while incarcerated in 2009). As one EU source reportedly said,

> Unfortunately, Magnitsky is just one of many such cases in Russia. If we imposed sanctions every time we found evidence of human rights absuses, it would make relations completely unworkable.[124]

Concerns about securing energy supplies and cooperation in the fight against terrorism have also led to stronger relations with Central Asia, despite protests from MEPs and human rights activists that doing so would send the wrong signal to states where human rights violations were still a regular occurrence.[125] And criticism of Israeli violations of human rights and international humanitarian law by Israel in the occupied territories has never resulted in negative measures being taken.[126]

There are also genuine doubts that negative measures *should* be taken in any particular case. It could be more effective to strengthen economic and political links with the country concerned, thus engendering a process of internal change. The EU generally recoils from cutting off aid to poor countries, which would not address the root causes of violations and would generate instability. There is also opposition within the EU even to smart sanctions because it could reduce EU influence by cutting off ties to the leadership. Such considerations have led to the EU's clear preference for engagement and dialogue.

Jack Donnelly believes that the problem of inconsistency can be overstated: if the causes of human rights violations differ, then so must policy. But, he maintains that 'if variations in the treatment of human rights violators are to be part of a consistent policy, human rights concerns need to be explicitly and coherently integrated into the broader framework of foreign policy'. This requires ordering foreign-policy goals and values, which could justify principled trade-offs.[127] But the EU has difficulty in setting priorities, and thus in justifying the trade-offs it makes on principled grounds. It is working to rectify this – and again the 2012 Strategic Framework on Human Rights is an indication of this.

Conclusion

External pressures on the EU to pursue human rights have been and are weak; it is not subject to specific demands for action from outside actors (including international organizations). The end of the Cold War provided the EU and other actors with a greater opportunity to promote human rights without the political overtones of the bipolar confrontation. But the EU need not have taken advantage of this opportunity, especially with as innovative and far-reaching human rights policy as has evolved.

The internal pressures to pursue an external human rights policy are much stronger. Initially a few actors pushed the issue: West Germany in the context of the CSCE; the European Parliament and the Netherlands in the 1980s in particular. There is now a consensus among the EU member states and institutions that human rights should be pursued with the EU's instruments. This reflects the widespread (Western) consensus that human rights violations are a source of insecurity, as well as the view that the protection of human rights is a valuable objective in and of itself. That the EU promotes human rights is clearly now a significant element of the EU's international image, one which the member states have generally been keen to maintain.

The EU was by no means the first actor to incorporate human rights considerations into external relations, but it has been a leading actor in the promotion of human rights since the end of the Cold War. In so far as the EU is one actor among many promoting universal human rights, it is not so unique. But the way the EU pursues the human rights objective is more unique. During the Cold War, the Community's preference for persuasion and 'neutrality' distinguished it from other actors. With the end of the Cold War, the preference for persuasion through dialogue remained, as did the reticence to use negative measures (for familiar security and commercial reasons, as well as a general scepticism about the efficacy of negative measures). The EU's approach is also uniquely based on legal texts, the human rights clauses in (legal) agreements and regulations on aid.

This is not, however, to downplay the problems illustrated by the internal/external policy gap and the rhetoric/practice gap. Arguably the EU is no different to other donors in not living up to its rhetoric, but then in this it too is subject to the general perception of the 'global south' that the 'global north' practises double standards, and punishes or rewards countries based on commercial or strategic interests and not actual human rights records. The legitimacy, credibility and effectiveness of EU policies to promote human rights will inevitably continue to suffer if the gaps are not closed.

Questions for discussion

1. Consider the reasons why there is a difference between the EU's internal human rights policies and its external human rights policies.

2. Why is the promotion of human rights such a prominent foreign-policy objective of the EU?

3. Evaluate the various instruments the EU has used to promote human rights in third countries: which do you think could be the most effective?

4. How great a problem is inconsistency in the EU's external human rights policies?

Suggestions for further reading

Brummer, Klaus. 'Imposing Sanctions: The Not So "Normative Power Europe"', *European Foreign Affairs Review*, 14, 2 (2009).

Manners, Ian. 'Normative Power Europe: A Contradiction in Terms?', *Journal of Common Market Studies*, 40, 2 (2002).

Williams, Andrew. *EU Human Rights Policies: A Study in Irony*. Oxford: Oxford University Press, 2004.

CHAPTER SIX

Democracy and Good Governance

Compared with other international actors, the Union adopted the objectives of promoting democracy and good governance relatively late, at the start of the 1990s. Some West European countries and the USA have long tried to export democracy to third countries,[1] but the Community/Union did not proclaim that it would do so until 1986, and then it appeared to have been tacked on to the human rights objective. Since 1991, promoting democracy has become somewhat more prominent and distinct as an objective – though it still is often unreflectively attached to the promotion of human rights: for example, the 2012 EU Strategic Framework and Action Plan on Human Rights and Democracy actually contains very little on democracy promotion.[2] The encouragement of good governance was proclaimed an objective in 1991, only after other international actors, namely the World Bank and several EU member states, had done so. The EU often links democracy with good governance, and the two concepts clearly overlap, so they are treated together in this chapter.

Promoting democracy and good governance involves helping to build institutions and foster a democratic culture, an inherently difficult if not impossible task to do from outside, and may even undermine democracy itself if outsiders end up limiting the freedom of choice of domestic actors. Legitimizing democracy promotion is also difficult because of the absence of any agreed definitions of the terms 'democracy' and 'good governance', much less any international treaties specifically protecting and promoting democracy and good governance. This contrasts with human rights. Karin Arts notes that 'there is neither a well-established rule or general principle of international law prescribing an individual or collective right to democracy nor an absolute duty of states or governments to be democratic', although the essentials of democracy (freedom of expression and the right to free and open elections) have been incorporated into human rights law.[3] Academics have asserted that democracy is an 'essentially contested concept', with little agreement among policy-makers or academics as to what it entails. This means that the objections raised to the incorporation of human rights into foreign policy are even more germane with respect to democracy. Good governance is still more nebulous: 'the notion of good governance is defined very differently by different actors and seems rather changeable'.[4] The lack of an international consensus on what democracy and good governance mean, much less on any 'right' to enjoy them, makes it difficult to design and legitimize coherent policies to bring them about.

Such considerations have long plagued democracy promotion, but they are currently dwarfed by a hostile environment for the policy objective. The 1990s seemed, for a time, a more hopeful era, in which more and more countries 'democratized'. And in the wake of the 11 September 2001 attacks, the USA (and to some extent the EU) emphasized a connection between the lack of democracy in the Middle East and international terrorism, and set out to foster political reform in that region and globally (though the extent to which reform was actually promoted is questionable – certainly it was not enough to jeopardize the hold on power of authoritarian regimes in North Africa and the Middle East). Despite some movement in the right direction, limits to what the former US President George W. Bush called the 'freedom agenda' have become increasingly apparent. The 2013 Freedom House index showed the seventh successive year of decline in 'global freedom': in 2012 more countries registered declines in freedom than registered gains.[5] Granted, 2011 was an astonishing year, with the Arab Spring, the first signs of reform in Myanmar and anti-government protests in Russia. Yet there have since been a coup d'état and violence in Mali, repression in Bahrain, fining and jailing of pro-democracy activists in Russia, troubled 'transitions' in Tunisia and Libya, war in Syria and a coup d'état in Egypt – indicating decisively that there is no smooth path towards democracy.

For some commentators, a backlash against democracy promotion (and even democracy itself) was spawned by the US invasion of Iraq in 2003 (and to some extent the intervention in Afghanistan).[6] 'Regime change' was quite openly the USA's principal war aim in Iraq – prompting a sustained backlash against not only 'coercive' democratization, but democracy promotion in general.[7] As a result, Thomas Carothers argues, authoritarian regimes around the world have been able to garner popular support for resisting any form of democracy promotion by outsiders in the name of protecting sovereignty.[8] Polling does show considerable support for democracy around the world, so the issue is less the idea of democracy than the promotion of democracy by external actors, which can be portrayed as foreign interference – and prohibited – by authoritarian and partially democratic regimes.[9] In addition, the EU (and other western countries) long tolerated authoritarian regimes in the Middle East/North Africa – prioritizing 'stability' over political processes that could lead to Islamic governments, the end of the Middle East peace process, and other perceived negative outcomes. Štefan Füle, the Enlargement and Neighbourhood Commissioner, admitted in February 2011 that 'Europe was not vocal enough in defending human rights and local democratic forces in the region. Too many of us fell prey to the assumption that authoritarian regimes were a guarantee of stability in the region.'[10] Yet there are still doubts that external actors, including the EU, have been doing enough to support democratization in North Africa and the Middle East: indeed, there has been much confusion in European responses to the initial Arab Spring and subsequent events such as the 2013 coup d'état in Egypt.[11]

The EU faces additional challenges that could limit the legitimacy and effectiveness of its policies in pursuit of this objective. The first is the by-now familiar internal/external policy gap. The Union is widely perceived as suffering from a 'democratic deficit', despite reforms in the Lisbon Treaty that address such issues – as illustrated in the widespread protests against eurozone policies and the EU in the wake of the financial crisis. The gap between internal Union practice and external policy objectives helps neither to adopt a clear strategy for achieving the objectives nor to foster external perceptions that the Union can legitimately demand that third countries improve their democratic and governance records. The second challenge, as was also the case of the human rights objective, is that the EU member states and institutions agree on the general idea of promoting democracy and good governance, but tend to be divided over the specifics of how (and whether) to do so in particular cases.[12] Again, the result is often a rhetoric/practice gap.

The rest of this chapter looks at how the EU pursues the objective. Section 6.1 looks at the internal EU practice of democracy and good governance. The following section analyses why the EU adopted the objectives of promoting democracy and good governance. Section 6.3 examines how the EU defines democracy and good governance, and section 6.4 the instruments it uses to promote them. The last section analyses critically the EU's policy.

6.1 Democracy and good governance within the EU

David Beetham has defined the 'basic core' of democracy as encompassing two principles: popular control over decision-making or decision-makers, and political equality of the people.[13] At first glance, the EU institutions resemble national democratic institutions: a directly elected parliament, an executive branch (the Commission), and a judicial branch (the European Court of Justice). The Parliament, which originally exercised only supervisory and advisory powers, has steadily increased its legislative powers. But to what extent are the basic principles of democracy incorporated in the EU? Firstly, EU decision-making necessarily involves compromises by member states, and some member states could oppose legislation that is nonetheless approved by qualified majority voting. National parliaments cannot block laws once they have been agreed by the Council, though under the Lisbon Treaty they can examine draft laws and contest them if they are seen as incompatible with the principle of subsidiarity (that is, the EU should take action only if the objectives of the action can be better achieved at the EU and not member state level). The EP and the Council now share 'co-decision' powers in many areas, but the EP cannot block all legislation (especially in the areas of foreign, security and defence policy). Hence, popular control over EU decision-making or decision-makers is not assured. Yet, the Council has declared that 'The EU and its Member States act in support of democracy drawing on strong parliamentary traditions, based on the role of national Parliaments and regional and local assemblies in Member States and that of the European Parliament.'[14] It is thus to be expected that an external/internal gap appears.

Secondly, the political equality of the people in the EU context is problematic. The Lisbon Treaty introduces a new double majority voting system. Until 2014, the voting weights of states are (more or less) related to the size of their populations, with large states having more votes, although still not on a proportional basis, and 255 out of the total 345 votes are needed to approve a decision. From 1 November 2014, as a result of the Lisbon Treaty, a qualified majority within the Council must consist of 55 per cent of member states representing 65 per cent of the EU's population.[15] The size of the member state thus matters more than its sovereign status (which would be the case if each member state had equal votes). This would be acceptable if the populations of small states (in particular) accept majority rule on an EU-wide basis, but this cannot be assumed, particularly as the Union enlarges and the 'community' grows larger and more diverse. In practice, though, the Council rarely votes and usually seeks a consensus.

In addition, ever since 1979, the percentage of the EU electorate that turns out to vote in European Parliament elections has dropped. Turnout in the first direct elections in 1979 was 62 per cent; this has steadily diminished to 43 per cent in 2009.[16] There are various reasons for this (including apathy, lack of awareness of the EP, and a lack of popular identification with the EU), but certainly EP elections are seen as 'second-order' elections, because they do not contribute directly to any change in national government or policy-making, much less a change of EU 'government'.[17] The rejection of EU treaties in referenda in various member states can be seen, at least partly, as an indication of public antipathy towards what is perceived as a remote, elite-driven integration process. And since the start of the eurozone crisis (with accompanying austerity policies, rising unemployment and negative or low growth – and public protests against EU economic orthodoxy), Eurobarometer polls have shown quite low levels of trust in the EU: in 2012 only a third of those questioned trust the EU – a drop of about ten percentage points since 2010.[18] An EU that appears to be so contested by its own citizens is not best placed to give lessons on democracy to third countries.

The convention method of drafting the Charter of Fundamental Rights and the constitutional treaty, and some of the provisions of the Lisbon Treaty itself show that the Union is capable of reforming itself along more democratic lines. The Commission asserts that the 'European Union is well placed to promote democracy and human rights. It is continually seeking to improve its own democratic governance . . . This gives the EU substantial political and moral weight.'[19] The gap between internal practice and the demands made of some third countries in the area of democracy and good governance is diminishing, but still exists. This indicates that the origins of the democracy and good governance objective do not lie with EU practice and experience.

6.2 Democracy and good governance as EU foreign-policy objectives

In December 1998, the EU declared:

> The universality and indivisibility of human rights and the responsibility for their protection and promotion, together with the promotion of pluralistic democracy and effective guarantees for the rule of law, constitute essential objectives for the European Union as a union of shared values and serve as a fundamental basis for action.[20]

But the promotion of democracy has not always been such an 'essential objective'. In 1973, the 'principles of representative democracy' were asserted to be a fundamental element of European identity, but not an objective for foreign-policy cooperation. Promotion of democracy made a brief appearance in the 1986 Statement on Human Rights: the foreign ministers reaffirmed 'their commitment to promote and protect human rights and fundamental freedoms and emphasize the importance in this context of the principles of parliamentary democracy and the rule of law'.[21] In practice, promoting democracy was not a prominent issue for the Community or EPC until the mid 1980s.

Why was democracy adopted relatively late as a foreign-policy objective? It could not be claimed that 'democracy' was a universal aspiration during the Cold War. 'Democracy' was used to define a wide variety of forms of government, as in the 'peoples' democracies' in Eastern Europe, or 'one-party democracies' in Africa. Despite this, until the 1980s, democracy really was a mode of government confined to a few, mostly Western, states, which gave it even more of a Western label than human rights.

In addition, urging governments to protect human rights is quite a different level of involvement than urging them to democratize, which could entail the overthrow of the very same governments. In the context of relations with communist countries in Eastern Europe, promoting democracy was not only unrealistic and impractical (witness the crushing of the 1968 Prague Spring), but also too antagonistic as it meant advocating the overthrow of the communist system itself. The Community/EPC preferred to encourage a gradual liberalization of the communist regimes, although it also supported totalitarian Romania, because of its anti-Soviet tendencies.[22] In relations with developing countries, promoting democracy was too intrusive, given that the Community prided itself on its 'neutrality' vis-à-vis the domestic arrangements of its development partners. The Community took negative steps only against regimes that committed very gross violations of human rights; coups d'état in the ACP countries were tolerated. While there was support for 'self-determination', particularly in southern Africa (in opposition to South

African control of Namibia, or Ian Smith's white regime in Rhodesia), this was not 'in the name of democracy'.

When people began to overthrow undemocratic regimes, the hands-off approach no longer seemed desirable. Democratization swept through Southern Europe in the 1970s, South America and the Philippines in the 1980s, Eastern Europe in the late 1980s and parts of Africa in the early 1990s, proving that democracy was not merely a Western phenomenon. With the end of the Cold War, strategic considerations could also make way for milieu goals such as promotion of democracy. In addition, in line with other donors, the EU was guided by a new orthodoxy: there is a virtuous link between democracy, good governance and development; and between democracy, human rights and conflict prevention. The promotion of democracy can also be seen as a response to public opinion and interest group pressure. No longer able to justify aid expenditure as necessary for geo-strategic objectives, donors have to justify it on other grounds, which resonate with domestic publics. Thus, they assert that aid should go to democracies rather than corrupt and autocratic regimes.

Following the Community's support for the democratic transitions in Greece, Spain and Portugal in the mid 1970s (by enlarging to those countries), promoting democracy became an issue in relations with Latin America by the mid 1980s, as countries across the region embarked on democratic paths. Before then, only Pinochet's Chile had occasionally received diplomatic démarches regarding human rights abuses.[23] In 1984, at the San José conference, the EC made it clear that democracy – among other more prominent factors, including equitable economic development – was a necessary basis for peace in Central America. From 1986, on the EP's initiative, the Community provided aid to democratic groups in Chile (ECU 22 million for 1986–91). In 1990, the first EC budget line specifically devoted to human rights and democracy was created, 'Democratization in Latin America'.

The transformation of Eastern Europe in 1989 in particular raised the issue of democracy on the agenda. The transition in Eastern Europe was a dual one, of both political and economic systems. The unprecedented economic transition received by far the most attention; it was more or less assumed that democracy would naturally accompany the switch to the market economy. The new regimes were also willing to pursue democratic reforms (at least to some extent). Respect for democratic principles and the rule of law was an early condition for agreements and assistance, but the Community's policy assumed that conditionality would suffice to encourage the new regimes to stay on a democratic path. The PHARE aid programme, established in 1989, initially focused solely on providing technical assistance for market economic reforms. Only in 1992 – after the sobering experience of Yugoslavia, where a democratic transition went badly wrong – was a democracy assistance programme incorporated under the PHARE umbrella (with an initial budget of ECU 10 million a year).

The promotion of democracy in developing countries became an issue for all donors in 1989, with the publication of a ground-breaking World Bank report on the sub-Saharan African economic crisis. The World Bank concluded that economic decline in Africa was the result of 'the deteriorating quality of government', and that 'Africa needs not just less government but better government'.[24] While the report did not specifically recommend democracy, it noted that the countries with the best economic performances in Africa were Botswana and Mauritius, both of which have parliamentary democracies and a free press. The World Bank thus established a link between democracy, good governance, and development, and led the way to a consensus among donors. Soon afterwards, other Western donors, including key EC member states such as France, Germany and the UK, adopted democracy and good governance (along with human rights) as considerations in allocating aid.[25]

These international and national developments were reflected in a change of Community policy. In its declaration on human rights, the June 1991 Luxembourg European Council also declared:

> Democracy, pluralism, respect for human rights, institutions working within a constitutional framework, and responsible governments appointed following periodic, fair elections, as well as the recognition of the legitimate importance of the individual in a society, are essential prerequisites of sustained social and economic development.[26]

In November 1991, the Development Council explicitly linked democracy, human rights and development: 'human rights and democracy form part of a larger set of requirements in order to achieve balanced and sustainable development. In this context, account should be taken of the issue of good governance as well as of military spending'. This is the first time 'good governance' appears in a Community declaration aimed at third countries, and certainly follows on from developments elsewhere. The Council suggested various positive initiatives for supporting democracy in third countries, and warned that appropriate measures would be taken if there were serious interruptions of democratic processes. The Community would also 'support efforts of developing countries to advance good governance', but there was no threat to impose negative measures for 'bad governance'.

The Maastricht Treaty, agreed in December 1991, included 'developing and consolidating democracy and the rule of law' as an objective both of development cooperation policy and of the CFSP. Three of the first five CFSP Joint Actions supported democracy by sending election observers to Russia, South Africa and West Bank/Gaza Strip. These positive actions were accompanied by an increasing use of conditionality, as respect for democratic principles became a condition for aid, agreements, and some other benefits, such as diplomatic recognition. The human rights clause includes respect for democratic principles as an essential element with third countries. But democracy is not a criterion in the 1998 Code of Conduct on Arms Exports and its successor the 2008 CFSP Common Position on Arms Exports, nor in the GSP, though 'good governance' – in the form of compliance with a set of international conventions on illegal drugs and corruption – is to be rewarded under the special incentives scheme of the GSP.[27]

As for good governance, it was an objective in the revised Lomé convention of 1995, but was not included as an 'essential element'. Aid could help democratization, strengthen the rule of law, and institute good governance. During the Cotonou convention negotiations, the EU pressed for the inclusion of good governance as an essential element, allowing the Union to take negative measures if the element was violated. This was strongly contested by the ACP countries, which argued that the concept was far too vague and could not be applied clearly and equitably.[28] But the Union succeeded in including a commitment to good governance as a 'fundamental' (not essential) element of the partnership, and violations were defined strictly as serious corruption. The 2006 European Consensus on Development (paragraph 42) states that Community development policy aims to eradicate poverty but also to promote 'democracy, good governance and respect for human rights'.

Why is the EU promoting democracy and good governance? Just as with the other policy objectives, there is a mixture of motives. First, there is a belief that they are desirable ends in and of themselves. Former External Relations Commissioner Chris Patten declared, 'it must be right for this European Union, increasingly and rightly seen as one of the bastions of democracy in the world, to devote a much greater effort to promoting free and fair elections beyond its borders, in countries where the rights which we are too often inclined to take for granted are still fragile or under threat'.[29] Certainly, this belief in the desirability of democracy and good governance permeates the EU's foreign policy, but it is by no means the only motive.

The second reason is that promotion of democracy and good governance will further the protection of human rights, even though established democracies may not fully protect human rights and can be subject to policies promoting human rights (the USA over the death penalty, for example). Back in 1995, the Commission argued:

> if human rights are a necessary condition for the full development of the individual, democratic society is a necessary condition for the exercise of those rights, providing the framework for individual development; again, human rights are a prerequisite for a democratic society, in that such a society is based on individuals' voluntary support for the life of the community.[30]

Thirdly, EU policy broadly accords with the democratic peace proposition: democracies don't fight each other, therefore promoting democracy is a peace strategy. Although the proposition has been debated in the academic literature, it has influenced EU policy-making. The Commission has argued that '[d]emocratic, pluralist governments which respect the rights of minorities are less likely to resort to nationalism, violence or aggression, either internally, against their neighbours or further afield'.[31] The Union's efforts to prevent conflicts in *and* between third countries are based in part on the belief that lack of good governance and respect for human rights are causes of conflicts, and support for democracy should help prevent conflicts (see Chapter 7). This guides other actors as well: many UN missions set up in countries ravaged by war since the late 1980s have entailed restoring or cultivating democracy. This is explicitly seen as contributing to lasting peace.[32] Related to the belief in the democratic peace proposition is the new argument that a lack of democracy and human rights is a cause of terrorism, so therefore promoting both is part of the fight against terrorism. While there are doubts about the link (if it holds, for example, why are there 'home-grown' terrorists in European countries?), as will be seen in Chapter 8, the EU does connect the two objectives.

A fourth reason for promoting democracy and good governance, particularly in developing countries, is that this will further social and economic development. As Gordon Crawford noted, 'the shift to promoting democratization represented an increasingly widespread presumption amongst governments and international organizations of a synergistic relationship between democracy and development'.[33] Although the presumption that political and economic liberalization are mutually reinforcing has not been proven, and is indeed questioned by academics,[34] the EU repeatedly emphasizes that democracy and good governance are the bases for 'equitable and sustainable development'. The European Consensus on Development declares that 'progress in the protection of human rights, good governance and democratization is fundamental for poverty reduction and sustainable development'.[35] In 2009, the Council of the EU repeated this, while the new Agenda for Change reiterates that 'good governance, in its political, economic, social and environmental terms, is vital for inclusive and sustainable development'.[36] However, the belief in the democracy–development link can sometimes manifest itself as a belief that economic development will lead to democracy: this was the case (as noted above) in Central and Eastern Europe after the end of the Cold War, and is still the case in the EU's approach to some African countries (for example, for years rapidly growing Rwanda was an aid 'darling' despite its questionable progress towards democracy).[37]

Despite these developments, the EU lacks a strategy for democracy promotion, while its promotion of good governance often equates to a desire for countries to spend aid effectively and comply with certain EU demands (such as controlling migration).[38] Rosa Balfour cites one Council official admitting that 'the EU does not have a real human rights and democracy policy. It has some bullet points'.[39] Firstly, there is 'an absence of a clear understanding of what should be the aim of and what should be promoted through EU democracy promotion policies'.[40] Many member states are blocking agreement on a 'European Consensus on Democracy', and it has also proved difficult to agree on a definition of democracy in the proposed document.[41] Secondly, it tends to support democratization only once it has been launched in third countries;

a case of 'democratization producing democracy aid'.[42] The EU has never been active in supporting democracy in completely undemocratic countries.

Thirdly, the EU lacks a clear vision of how the various elements of a possible democracy promotion strategy fit together. The EU has agreed procedures on observing elections, but no overall strategy regarding supporting election processes in general much less a view of how these fit with democratization.[43] Related to this, the EU places more emphasis on social issues, on civil rights, on women's rights, on governance – than on democracy itself.[44] It emphasizes 'democratic governance' in African countries, for example, which leads to a focus not on making 'the government more democratic but to enable it to successfully implement development programmes'.[45] Although the EU does take action in response to interruptions to democratic processes (such as coups d'état), for the most part its democracy promotion activities are rather technocratic and 'indirect' (in that they address only some elements linked to building democratic societies) – and eschew building institutions and fostering political competition.

Finally, as will be seen below, the lack of a strategy is clear in that there has been much inconsistency and incoherence particularly in how the EU has responded to events in different third countries. As was evident in the case of the human rights policy objective, the member states and EU institutions agree on the basic importance of promoting democracy and good governance (for the reasons above), but they are less than united when it comes to deciding on what sorts of actions should be taken (if at all) in particular cases. The north–south divisions are, if anything, more pronounced in the case of democracy promotion.[46] Differences of approach between the member states affect the type and strength of measures that the EU can take to promote democracy and good governance. This leads to glaring inconsistencies, as discussed in sections 6.4 and 6.5.

In 2009, the Council agreed an 'Agenda for Action on Democracy Support', whose aim is to improve the coherence and effectiveness of EU democracy support – an acknowledgement that such coherence was hitherto lacking. Ironically, little more than a year later, the EU's rather shallow support for democracy was illustrated with the outbreak of the Arab Spring in countries where the EU had not seriously promoted democracy before. But those events have led to much deeper consideration of how to promote human rights and democracy – seen not only in the 2012 EU Strategic Framework on Human Rights and Democracy but also in the revised European Neighbourhood and development policies.

6.3 How does the EU define democracy and good governance?

Given that definitions of both concepts – democracy and good governance – are neither codified in international agreements nor widely agreed, EU policy is difficult to legitimize with reference to international standards. The benchmark is Article 21 of the Universal Declaration of Human Rights:

> Everyone has the right to take part in the government of his country, directly or through freely chosen representatives . . . The will of the people shall be the basis of the authority of government; this will shall be expressed in periodic and genuine elections which shall be by universal and equal suffrage and shall be held by secret vote or by equivalent free voting procedures.

Article 19 also states: 'everyone has the right to freedom of opinion and expression'. These two rights offer a basic, albeit limited, democratic standard, but donors, including the EU, go well beyond this in their demands of compliance with democratic principles.

Progress has been made in setting democratic standards in post-Cold War Europe, specifically within the CSCE. In June 1990, CSCE states agreed to respect certain democratic principles, such as the holding of elections at reasonable intervals. In the November 1990 Charter of Paris for a New Europe, the heads of state or government of all of the CSCE participating states endorsed that document, and agreed to set up an Office of Free Elections (later the Office of Democratic Institutions and Human Rights, ODIHR) to implement it.[47] These standards are referred to by the Union in its relations with other European countries.

With respect to other countries, the Union has defined its own standards – not always to their satisfaction.[48] In 1998, a CFSP Common Position summarized democratic principles as the right to choose and change leaders in free and fair elections; separation of legislative, executive and judicial powers; and guarantees of freedom of expression, information, association and political organization.[49] In 2009, the EU set out what it considers to be the basic elements of democracy, while acknowledging that 'democratic systems may vary in forms and shape'. These are rather less prescriptive in terms of institutions and political rights than the definition of a decade earlier:

- for democracy to flourish, human rights (and especially the principle of non-discrimination, and minority rights) must be respected;
- men and women must participate on equal terms in political life and in decision-making;
- democratically elected citizens' representatives have an essential oversight role; and
- the accountability of leaders and public officials to citizens is an essential element of democracy.[50]

As for good governance, it is even less of an international standard. The World Bank defined governance as entailing three aspects: the form of political regime; the processes by which authority is exercised in the management of a country's economic and social resources; and the capacity of governments to design, formulate and implement policy, and to discharge functions. Initially it dealt with the second and third aspects; increasingly it takes the first into consideration.[51] Other donors have different conceptions of good governance, some are quite broad (and overlap with democracy), some are more restricted to accountability.[52]

In November 1991, development ministers gave some indication of what good governance entailed: 'sensible economic and social policies, democratic decision-making, adequate governmental transparency and financial account-ability, creation of a market-friendly environment for development, measures to combat corruption, as well as respect for the rule of law, human rights, and freedom of the press and expression'.[53] On the basis of this definition, developing countries could rightly suspect that the EU was primarily inter-ested in promoting the market economy. But in a March 1998 communica-tion, the Commission dropped the neo-liberal overtones (thus responding in part to ACP concerns), and emphasized the need to *democratize* the state.[54] Good governance is 'the transparent and accountable management of all a country's resources for its equitable and sustainable economic and social development'. It requires an independent and accessible judicial system, transparency, and public participation in the decision-making processes con-cerning resource management and allocation.[55]

However, in 2006, the Commission once again addressed the issue of 'gov-ernance', fusing good governance and democracy. 'Democratic governance' amounts to a *very* long list of 'principles' and 'dimensions', which includes the neo-liberal overtones previously dropped:

> Respect of human rights and fundamental freedoms (including freedom of expression, information and association); support for democratisation processes and the involvement of citizens in choosing and overseeing those who govern them; respect for the rule of law and access for all to an independent justice system; access to information; a government that governs transparently and is accountable to the relevant institutions and to the electorate; human security; *management of migration flows*; effective institutions, access to basic social services, sustainable management of natural and energy resources and of the environment, and the *promotion of sustainable economic growth and social cohesion in a climate conducive to private investment*.[56]

No priorities are indicated; in fact, the Commission argues that 'democratic governance is to be approached holistically', a 'compartmentalized approach . . . must be avoided'. [57] Documents published since then do not elaborate any further on a definition of governance.[58]

The EU has thus attempted to define democracy and good governance, the first more or less in line with such international standards as there are, the second more uniquely, though not in line with any internal codified practice, and extremely broadly. Nonetheless, its definitions are quite vague – which means that the EU is open to accusations that it is ready to 'adjust its promo-tion agenda to fit its own commercial and security interests', and this harms its credibility in this area.[59]

6.4 How does the EU pursue the objectives?

The tools that the EU uses to promote democracy and good governance are similar to those it uses to promote human rights: conditionality; aid; diplomatic instruments; and civilian and military missions. It also observes elections in third countries. As indicated above, the fact that the EU has not had a strategy for promoting democracy and good governance means that there has been a lack of coherence and consistency in the use of policy instruments. Since the 2009 Agenda for Action on Democracy Support, the EU has conducted a pilot exercise in nine countries, in which EU delegations identify all democracy support activities ongoing, establish a democracy profile, and analyse areas that need improvement. The next generation of pilot countries was to be chosen in 2013. In 2014, the EU is supposed to develop comprehensive 'democracy support plans' on the basis of the outcomes of the pilot exercises. This should improve the coherence and effectiveness of the EU's support for democracy in the pilot countries at least.[60]

Conditionality

The use of political conditionality is a top-down approach to promoting democracy: donors try to influence the governments of third countries. There is considerable debate about whether this is appropriate: can democracy be promoted from 'above' by outsiders? Or must it develop from within, and only political aid can help in this, by fostering civil society or helping to reform institutions? Doubts about whether conditionality can be used effectively to foster democracy have not, however, prevented the EU from using it – but it has had far from a consistent approach. In its 2009 Conclusions on Democracy Support, the Council declared that the 'EU does not intend to introduce new conditionality for EU development aid'.[61] Yet the experience of the Arab Spring just over a year later led to a different attitude: the EU had clearly been rather too tolerant of authoritarian regimes. So 'more for more' was to be the guiding philosophy of the new European Neighbourhood Policy, and political conditionality was strengthened in development aid (see the Agenda for Change).

As with human rights, the EU has long preferred a positive approach based on incentives and dialogue. Some countries embarking on a democratic transition have been promised benefits, including aid, association agreements, and even eventual EU membership (for European countries). In 2012, for example, the EU committed €150 million for development and democracy in Myanmar over two years (notably only €10 million of this was allocated to civil society and 'capacity building' in 2012; the rest went on health, education and other development goals).[62]

In the immediate neighbourhood, the EU's policy has arguably been successful. As Milada Vachudova illustrates, the EU's membership conditionality helped to create a coherent opposition and an open and pluralistic political arena in three CEECs that initially underwent an 'illiberal pattern of political change': Bulgaria, Romania, Slovakia.[63] But the credibility of the EU's promises is crucial. The more the EU's membership promise to Turkey became concrete (though 2005), the more the EU was able to influence the process of political reforms; but as EU actors (including governments in Austria, France and Germany) question whether Turkey should indeed be allowed to join the Union, the reform process has arguably been negatively affected.[64]

In areas beyond the candidate countries, it has not been easy to fulfil promises if they affect EU economic interests. The eurozone crisis has had a damaging impact on the generosity of the EU's response to the Arab Spring: although the EU initially pledged (and delivered) more aid, aid to the neighbourhood will *decrease* between 2013 and 2014, although funding for the European Neighbourhood Instrument increases in 2014–20 compared to 2007–13 (see Table 3.2). A promised 'mobility partnership' with Tunisia has not materialized, though one was concluded with Morocco in June 2013; crucially, though, these partnerships merely set objectives for cooperation, and visa facilitation is linked to readiness to sign a re-admission agreement (to take back illegal immigrants). Southern EU member states object to liberalizing agricultural trade with southern Mediterranean countries. Negotiations on new free trade agreements with Tunisia, Morocco, Jordan and Egypt are 'expected to get stuck quickly once they touch on the issue of liberalization of services . . . [as] no EU member state is interesting in opening up to the neighbourhood'.[65]

The use of conditionality in the eastern neighbourhood has also been stymied because Russia has vigorously opposed closer relations between the EU and its own neighbours. In 2013, it successfully pressed Armenia and Ukraine to refuse to sign new agreements with the EU. This prompted large protests in Ukraine, and the EU may yet help engender change in that country – but the episode illustrates the limits of EU influence when another power overrides the EU's conditional offer of new agreements.

The EU has also become much more careful about what it offers in the first place. Georgia (following the 'rose revolution' in 2003, which toppled a semi-authoritarian government) and Ukraine (following the 'orange revolution' of 2004 in which a flawed election result was reversed) both expected more from the EU than they received. Georgia was included in the European Neighbourhood Policy (along with Armenia and Azerbaijan, which are still quite undemocratic), but given no firm guarantees of eventual EU membership, and its ENP Action Plan did not promise much more than an earlier EU–Georgia partnership and cooperation agreement. The new Ukrainian government, under Victor Yuschenko, was dismayed not to be offered the prospect of EU membership, or even a more extensive ENP action plan than the one negotiated by the previous government.[66]

As noted in Chapter 5, the EU has begun to develop better mechanisms for redirecting assistance to democratizing and well-performing countries, though the governance facilities for the ACP and ENP countries were not considered successful. The 2011 Agenda for Change and the new European Neighbourhood Policy make it clear that development aid will be linked to partners' commitments to human rights, democracy and the rule of law. It remains to be seen how this will make a difference to the distribution of EU aid. In the past, some democratizing countries have not attracted any EU rewards, such as Thailand and Taiwan in the 1990s, while South Korea, then a consolidating democracy, found itself embroiled in commercial disputes with the EU and the new multiracial democracy in South Africa was engaged in rancorous trade negotiations with the EU.[67] The Agenda for Change implies that middle-income countries, even democratizing ones, will not receive additional aid (other than EIDHR funds).

Sometimes rewards are given to countries that are not democratizing, actions that Peter Burnell classifies as 'anti-democracy assistance' and 'counter-democracy promotion'.[68] Pakistan, under a military government from 1999 to 2008 (and originally the subject of EU sanctions), was granted an astonishing 72 per cent increase in aid for the period 2007–10 compared to 2002–6.[69] This apparently reflected a new 'strategic emphasis' on relations with Pakistan – whose stability is considered crucial for the fight against terrorism (a classic example of how security considerations can work *against* the promotion of democracy, instead of for it). The Central Asia strategy, with an increase in aid and strengthened dialogue, was initiated in 2007 despite a lack of democracy and violations of human rights in the Central Asian republics. In July 2007, the EU extended aid and cooperation to Libya after it released five Bulgarian nurses and a Palestinian doctor who had been bizarrely convicted of infecting Libyan children with HIV/AIDS – despite there being no evident progress on human rights and democracy in the country at the time. In 2010 the EU was preparing to grant Tunisia (then still ruled by the authoritarian Ben Ali) 'advanced status' because it was seen as 'an example for the region'.[70] The one country in the southern Mediterranean with whom the EU has been quickly developing much closer relations since 2011 is Morocco – yet while there have been some minor reforms there, the extent to which the country is embarked on a process of real democratic change is (so far) questionable.[71] Russia and China – neither of which can be classified as a democracy – are EU strategic partners.

Negative conditionality has been used to a limited extent. Thus Slovakia was initially excluded from the first round of EU membership negotiations in 1998 because of its shaky democratic credentials, and Turkey was excluded from membership negotiations until 2005 on the basis of its democratic and human rights record. Myanmar was excluded from the EU–ASEAN agreement (among other sanctions). The state of democracy has declined in Ukraine (it is now considered only a 'partly free' country) – to the extent to which the EU postponed the signing of a new association agreement in 2012–13 (although some member states would have preferred to strengthen relations with Ukraine to boost its autonomy from Russia).[72]

No negative measures were taken in the case of North Africa before 2011. Even since the Arab Spring, the EU still seems reluctant to take a tough stance on countries whose 'transition' to democracy is fragile (to say the least): conditionality did not play much of a part in the EU's response to the tumultuous events in Egypt through mid 2013, for example.

New aid has been suspended by applying the human rights clause for violations of democratic principles, such as coups d'état, which are highly visible violations (see Appendix).[73] In those cases, aid is usually redirected to projects to boost human rights and democracy standards or political stability. Yet the EU does not respond to all flawed elections: it did not do so in the cases of Kenya in 2007 (where contestation of the results led to widespread ethnic violence), or ever with respect to countries such as Rwanda, Egypt, Tunisia, Armenia and Azerbaijan (indeed the latter four countries still enjoyed increased benefits stemming from the ENP).[74] With respect to the ACP countries, no negative measures have been applied because of widespread corruption, though Liberia in 2001 was a slight exception to this.

The EU does not usually react to gradual declines into authoritarian practices: for example, aid to Zimbabwe continued as authoritarianism increased in the 1990s, and was only called into question when violence erupted over farm seizures.[75] Russia is probably the premier example of this tendency: as Sinkukka Saari shows, European organizations have found Russia's 'creeping challenge' to human rights and democracy norms hard to deal with or even recognize for what it is, and for a long time ignored negative developments there. One of the reasons, she argues, is that European organizations (the EU, Council of Europe, OSCE) hold a belief in a straightforward progression towards democracy (in line with much theorizing about democratization), and took Russian rhetoric about its commitment to democracy too much at face value.[76]

There is a notable exception to the EU's usual preference for positive measures. The EU (along with the USA, UN and Russia – fellow members of the 'quartet' involved in the Middle East peace process) cut off aid to the Palestinian Authority after the Islamist movement Hamas won elections in the Palestinian territories in January 2006 – elections which EU observers described as free and fair, and a 'milestone in the building of democratic institutions'.[77] Hamas, already designated a 'terrorist organization', was punished because it failed to meet three conditions: recognition of Israel, renunciation of violence, and acceptance of existing peace agreements. The decision was (and the continued boycott of Hamas, now only in control of the Gaza Strip, still is) controversial because it ignored some (very) cautious movement by Hamas towards meeting the conditions, and ignored the fact that several of the EU's partners elsewhere do not recognize Israel or necessarily 'accept' existing peace agreements.[78] The quartet's isolation of Hamas is now widely considered to be a failure, and alleged informal and back-channel contacts between European governments and Hamas in 2013 may be a first step away from the policy.[79]

Aid for democratization and good governance

The Community began giving democracy aid later than other donors, notably the USA: the US Agency for International Development (USAID) set up a major democracy initiative in 1990. Only in 1990 was a small programme, for Latin America, included in the EC budget (though some aid went to Chile from 1986); the PHARE democracy programme did not begin until 1992. The EIDHR budget has grown larger since then (see Table 3.2).

As noted in section 5.4, assistance has been given for a very wide variety of measures, including elections (only one phase of the democratic transition process) and on promoting civil and political liberties. The 2011–13 EIDHR Strategy Paper allocates 22.35 per cent of funding to election observation missions.[80] This is a higher percentage than the USA has given: between 1990 and 2005 about 14 per cent of democracy assistance supported electoral processes.[81]

To help build civil society in third countries, the EIDHR uniquely (compared to other donors) and extensively funds NGOs. The EU not only tries to boost the capacities of NGOs, but it provides democracy assistance largely *through* NGOs, who implement projects. The NGO focus has distinct advantages. EU policy-makers consider it a strength: it is non-prescriptive, grassroots, and focused on social development. The EU does not want to push political institutions on others.[82]

However, this approach has weaknesses. NGOs have to be well organized to receive funding, willing and able to commit time and resources to cope with the EU's long bureaucratic procedures; in fast-moving situations such as the Arab Spring, this is unlikely to happen, and in authoritarian countries, there are unlikely to be many such NGOs on the ground anyway. The EU's approach is essentially reactive, dependent on NGO responses to calls for tender, and on the quality of the projects that they propose. More NGOs does not necessarily mean more democratic government, and in countries undergoing a transition (such as Myanmar), the focus on building civil society to the virtual exclusion of helping to build democratic institutions does not seem appropriate.

The EU has also been reluctant to fund some types of civil society organizations, such as moderate Islamist groups in Mediterranean countries, even if this might isolate fundamentalist, anti-democratic elements.[83] And in the last decade or so, NGOs (particularly those receiving foreign funding) have been shut down, expelled or harassed in Belarus, China, Egypt, Kazakhstan, Russia, Uzbekistan, Zimbabwe, among other places – because the governments fear the NGOs will foment popular movements for democracy.[84] This makes a strategy based on funding NGOs quite risky – particularly because it could deprive the EU of one of its main instruments for promoting democracy. Normally, the EU does not aid 'exiles', and its activities in highly repressive countries are extremely limited.

The EU has begun to address such problems, giving some aid to Belarusian NGOs registered outside Belarus.[85] But the premier initiative to try to address such problems was launched by Poland. In February 2011, as protests spread in Egypt, Libya and Belarus, Poland argued for a European Endowment for Democracy (EED), which could provide more flexible and faster funding (as the US National Endowment for Democracy, or the German foundations, can). It would be independent of the EU but supported by voluntary donations from EU member states. In December 2011, the rest of the EU member states agreed, and set up a working group to help establish the EED. Yet enthusiasm for the initiative has varied widely, with some member states unwilling to contribute much to it at all, and various disagreements about its status (vis-à-vis the EU) and decision-making procedures.[86] The EED was established in October 2012 and began operating in 2013. It is not clear how well it will be funded in the medium term, nor how its activities will fit with EU activities to support democracy, but it could at least redress some of the weaknesses of the EIDHR identified above.

Election observation and assistance

As democracy spread to many countries in Asia, Latin America, Eastern Europe, and Africa, a new activity accompanied it: international election observation. Foreign observers, from individual (Western) states, NGOs, and international organizations, monitor election campaigns and voting to try to detect and deter fraud, in countries with little prior experience in conducting 'free and fair' elections.

The EU joined the election observation bandwagon fairly early on, as many initial CFSP Joint Actions involved election observation. But although in May 2001, the Council reserved the right to take decisions to support elections in the CFSP pillar,[87] since 2001, Election Observation Missions (EOMs) are funded by the EIDHR (the old Community pillar).[88] There were also initially problems coordinating all the actors on the ground: the Commission delegation, Council presidency, EU election observers, and MEPs did not always work well together, with a degree of rivalry evident.[89] This is less of a problem now, as the chief observer is an MEP, and European Parliament observer delegations are associated to EU EOMs.

The EU conducts several (sometimes more than ten) EOMs every year. There is an informal agreement between the EU and OSCE that the OSCE (not the EU) will observe elections in the OSCE area (North America, Europe, former Soviet Union), so the EU sends observation missions to countries further afield. In addition to election observation, the EU also gives technical and

material assistance, including providing voting equipment, helping to regis-
ter voters, training local observers, or providing support to NGOs involved in
civic education.

There are concerns that observers could legitimize electoral processes that
are fundamentally flawed, simply by being present. In June 1998, the Council
agreed EU guidelines on electoral observation. It set minimum conditions
that would have to be met before the EU sent observers, including genuine
universal franchise and access to the media by all contesting candidates and
parties. It also listed factors for assessing the validity of an election, including
the degree of impartiality shown by the election management body, and the
degree of freedom of political parties, alliances and candidates to organize
and express their views publicly.[90] The EU withdrew its election observer
mission to Zimbabwe in February 2002, because the government placed so
many limits on the mission that it would not have been able to judge whether
the presidential election was free and fair.[91]

The EU's approach to election observation, however, needs to be updated.
It is now developing guidelines on how to observe electronic voting, but
several events in recent years have shown that the problems with elections
often arise after voting has taken place: this was certainly the case in Kenya
in late 2007, where contestation of the results led to widespread ethnic violence, and in Ivory Coast in 2011, where the incumbent president refused to
acknowledge defeat in an election, leading to violence. The EU has not fully
acknowledged the need to extend its observation missions in case there is
post-election violence: for example, the EOM to the 2011 Ugandan general
elections issued its preliminary findings on 20 February 2011 and its final
report on 10 March 2011, even though the partial results of parliamentary
elections were not announced until 23 February and full results were published only on 4 March.[92] One observer recommends that the EU focus more
on the counting process, and have contingency plans in place to extend an
observer mission in a country where there is wide contestation of the results.[93]

In the end, the effectiveness of election observation depends on international actors, including the EU, condemning irregularities and following up
with other measures to try to raise the overall quality of democracy in the
particular country. In the past there were disagreements among observers
about whether to declare an election free and/or fair. In Nigeria in 1999, 'the
head of the European Union's observer team gave a ludicrously favourable
assessment of the poll within hours of its closing, apparently because he was
under pressure to raise the EU profile. His colleagues were furious that he
had not given them time to return to Lagos with details of numerous
violations'.[94]

Even where irregularities are noted, there may be little follow-up. Elections
in Nigeria in April 2007 were again marred by irregularities, but the EU
merely expressed its 'disappointment' in the process and reiterated its commitment to dialogue and engagement with Nigeria.[95] The EU observed four

elections in Sri Lanka over five years, and the observer missions all reported the same problems and made the same recommendations. But while the EU's country strategy paper for Sri Lanka 2007–13 mentioned following up on the observer missions' recommendations, it did not include a strategy for promoting election reform or democracy.[96] In future, the new democracy action plans may help the EU to draw together the results and recommendations of its election observation missions and its general approach to fostering democracy in third countries.

Diplomatic instruments

There are no political dialogues specifically focused on democracy, as opposed to those on human rights. The Commission has recommended, and the Council agreed, that all of the EU's political dialogues should cover issues relating to human rights and democratization if they do not do so already.[97] But given the EU's priorities (civil rights, civil society development), the dialogues are more human rights-focused than democracy-focused.

Richard Youngs notes that 'discursive socialization' has been touted by EU policy-makers as a significant contribution to the spread of democracy. By including the issue of democracy in institutionalized relationships – through the inclusion of the human rights clause in agreements – the EU puts the issue on the table. It can then try to involve a range of government and civil society representatives in a dialogue, 'unleashing a dynamic of socialization around democratic norms'.[98] The Commission has argued, 'The most effective way of achieving change is therefore a positive and constructive partnership with governments, based on dialogue, support and encouragement.'[99] The EU's dialogues are seen as a particularly unique contribution: the USA does not insist on dialogue, and only the EU, not the member states, forms the institutionalized relationships in which socialization can be actively fostered. However, in 'difficult' regions (such as the Mediterranean or Asia), democracy is less stressed than protection of basic human rights, and engagement with civil society is limited where opposition forces are ambivalent towards democracy (as in the Mediterranean).[100] Dialogue will only work if the third country is ready to cooperate, and is genuinely committed to pursuing change.

On the negative side, the EU has imposed diplomatic sanctions in several cases where third countries have violated democratic principles, as it did in the cases of Myanmar/Burma in 1990, Nigeria in 1995, Zimbabwe in 2002, and Belarus from 2002 to 2008 and then again since January 2011.[101]

Civilian and military missions

The few 'rule of law' and police missions that the EU has so far undertaken in several countries (see Table 3.5) are indirectly related to attempts to foster democratic reforms, though these have tended to be quite short in duration and small in size. For example, EUJUST Themis was launched in the aftermath of the 'rose revolution' in Georgia, but lasted less than a year. The EUFOR DRC mission, which helped secure the country during elections in 2006, was one of the largest CSDP missions but lasted only a few months. It is unlikely such short missions could have much of an impact of democratization.

However, the EU's involvement in Bosnia and Herzegovina, including essentially governing the country through the post of the High Representative (always an EU appointee and now also the EU's Special Representative to Bosnia and Herzegovina), has been a much longer affair – but has been criticized as actually undermining democracy. As of 2013, the High Representative can still dismiss elected officials if they obstruct the 1995 Dayton Agreement, which is now almost twenty years old. Many commentators think this undermines the potential for stable democracy in Bosnia.[102] This is perhaps an example of what Peter Burnell has called 'perverse democracy assistance and perverse democracy promotion' – a well-intentioned attempt to promote democracy which turns out to be counter-productive.[103]

One tool that the EU is certain not to use is the use of military force to impose or force democracy on a country. Not only does the EU lack the capabilities to do so, but its member states would simply not agree on another intervention along the lines of the 2003 Iraq war. For a time, the US willingness to use force in the name of spreading democracy distinguished it from Europe's approach (Mars vs. Venus), but the Obama Administration in the USA seems much less willing to even consider intervening militarily abroad to overthrow an autocratic regime.[104]

6.5 Evaluation: How consistent is the EU's policy?

The answer to the above question can only be 'not very', and inconsistency is most obvious in the imposition (or not) of negative measures for violations of democratic principles. The EU is not unusual in this. There is a discrepancy between donors' democracy-promotion rhetoric, which may be a response to public demands, and actual implementation of such policies, as visible in the paltry amount of aid dedicated to democracy promotion (the scale of which Burnell approximates to 'spitting in the wind'),[105] and the inconsistent use of pressure on violators of democratic principles.[106] As stated in Chapter 5, three broad reasons for the EU's inconsistency can be identified: commercial considerations; security and political considerations (including the desire of member states to protect important bilateral relationships); and doubts about the effectiveness of negative measures.

Some violations of democratic principles are tolerated, others are not; concerns for security and stability are often the reason for the discrepancy. The dominance of such considerations reflects the particular nature of the democratization process. Demanding that governments embark on a process of democratization is risky if it could entail their replacement with less acceptable alternatives. Democratization could also unleash considerable civil disorder, even civil war. The EU has played down undemocratic practices (such as less-than-free elections) in countries that are in post-conflict or post-authoritarian stages, precisely because of the risk of civil conflict.

An example of the dominance of security interests is the case of Pakistan. The EU initially threatened to impose sanctions on Pakistan, following the coup d'état by General Pervez Musharraf in October 1999, if a timetable for restoring elections was not set within one month. When the deadline passed, most member states were unwilling to do so: the new government was considered no worse than the previous administration of Nawaz Sharif, and Musharraf was promising to reduce tensions with India.[107] The foreign ministers suspended the signature of a cooperation agreement, and suspended regular political dialogue meetings, but agreed to continue with development aid.[108] After the 11 September 2001 terrorist attacks on the USA, the EU reversed even this soft negative stance, and sought to bolster the government of a crucial ally in the fight against international terrorism. The EU proceeded with signing the cooperation agreement, in November 2001, and extended additional assistance, including trading preferences (for textiles) under the GSP. In 2006, aid to Pakistan was increased substantially. When Musharraf imposed emergency rule in November 2007, the EU did not threaten to take negative measures, though it did express its deep concern with the move. (Pakistan has since held democratic elections and has an elected, civilian government now, but there are still considerable concerns about the state of democracy, human rights and general security in the country.)

The belief that a democratically elected government will be even worse – or at least not much better – than a military-led regime also lies behind the tolerance of the Algerian government's decision to cancel the 1992 parliamentary elections in the face of a possible victory by the Islamist movement. 'Radical Islam is seen as a threat to political stability in the region, with an Islamist victory in Algeria resulting in a domino effect in neighbouring countries and a wave of migration to southern Europe, especially France.'[109] Such concerns were reflected in the EU's long-running acquiescence in, and even acceptance of, undemocratic practices in North African and Middle Eastern countries such as Egypt, Jordan, Morocco and Tunisia. In the case of Egypt, there were other foreign-policy concerns, namely its role in the Arab–Israeli peace process, and the need for Egyptian support of Western policies in the Arab world.[110]

Unfortunately, such concerns later seemed highly relevant. The Arab Spring unleashed potential democratization dynamics – but also the ascendance of Islamic political movements (though this sparked a serious backlash against the Muslim Brotherhood in Egypt), and in the case of Libya and Syria, widespread violence and civil war. The EU's response has been inconsistent, and sometimes confused – as seen in its refusal to condemn the Egyptian coup d'état on 3 July 2013. High Representative Ashton did try to foster mediation between the deposed President Morsi and the military, and was the first foreign diplomat to meet Morsi after the coup, but her efforts could not prevent the military from launching severe repression of Morsi supporters. Some officials and diplomats may be ruing the day that democratization processes were unleashed.

Concerns for stability also prompted Western tolerance of (and even support for) authoritarian leaders in the Balkans (including Sali Berisha in Albania, Slobodan Milosevic in Serbia, from Dayton until 1998, and Franjo Tudjman in Croatia). Assisting political reforms is seen as a way to prevent conflicts, but in the long term; in the short term, the objective of stability has won out over encouraging democratization. Authoritarian leaders were considered necessary to implement the Dayton peace accord, or to keep a lid on civil disorder, with all of the cross-border effects that could have (for example, weapons smuggling). The EU and other actors thus sent inconsistent signals about their priorities.

The EU's relations with Russia are a prime example of how considerations of democracy have been downplayed, even as 'democratization' there has ground to a halt and gone into reverse.[111] It was far too inconvenient to notice such developments (much easier to trust democratization would continue there): Russian cooperation is needed for supporting UN Security Council resolutions on Kosovo, for disarmament initiatives, for nuclear non-proliferation, for the fight against terrorism, and so on. Russia supplies a very high proportion of the EU's energy needs. Many EU member states have simply been unwilling to put any pressure on Russia to conform to democracy and human rights standards. The EU lacks strategy for how it might try to reverse the authoritarian trend in Russia; Russia has also been adept at countering any possible openings for EU support – in prohibiting foreign funding of NGOs, for example.

It is, of course, difficult to calibrate the use of positive and negative measures – when should sanctions be lifted, when should they be imposed, what will really contribute to fostering reform in third countries? Thus some inconsistency is to be expected: different situations may require different responses, and judging what is appropriate or helpful is challenging. The EU has only recently begun to put together a more coherent strategy on support for democracy and good governance which could enable it to calibrate its support and negative measures more consistently – and this is still a work in progress.

Conclusion

The effectiveness of the EU's pursuit of the democracy and good governance objective is difficult to judge. As Thomas Carothers notes, democracy assistance may help deepen reforms in countries where democratization is advancing, but may only be able to help keep some activity going in countries where it is not. But 'democracy aid generally does not have major effects on the political direction of recipient countries'.[112] In fact, as noted in the introduction, trends seem to point to the rather depressing conclusion that democratization worldwide is stagnant.

Yet the EU continues to pursue the objectives of promoting democracy and good governance – and at least rhetorically its support for these objectives has grown since the Arab Spring. External factors seem to outweigh internal factors in this. Both objectives were declared and pursued relatively late, following the international spread of democracy and the development of an orthodoxy relating to democracy, good governance, development and peace. The Union was not at the forefront of efforts to foster democracy and good governance; its policies developed after many member states had already adopted these objectives. Internal pressure to adopt the objectives came from the member states, and to a limited extent from the EP. And the EU's promotion of democracy and good governance cannot be said to be the export of values and principles practised fully at the EU level. Generally speaking, then, the EU's adoption of these objectives has been reactive rather than proactive. Furthermore, the lack of international standards and the democratic deficit within the EU do not give the EU much solid ground on which to push other countries to implement democratic and good governance reforms.

The way in which the EU promotes democracy and good governance is not strikingly different from that of other actors, as it reflects an apparent consensus that both top-down and bottom-up measures must be used to promote democracy in particular, and that negative conditionality is not necessarily the best way to engender democratization. In contrast, the inclusion of democratic principles in the human rights clause, and the emphasis on dialogue, are more innovative and unusual, again reflecting the EU's preference for basing relations on legal agreements and persuasion. The inconsistent use of conditionality, is, however, a relatively common practice across donors.[113]

Of course, the extent to which the EU is committed to the objectives of democracy and good governance can be questioned. A modest amount of aid is provided for encouraging both objectives, and there is a lack of policy coherence (particularly between the encouragement of economic liberalization and the promotion of democracy). Negative and positive measures are applied inconsistently, especially where security interests are paramount. Nonetheless, the promotion of democracy, and to a lesser extent good governance, is seen to be an important part of the EU's international identity.

Questions for discussion

1. Analyse the differences between promoting human rights in third countries and promoting democracy.

2. Why is defining democracy and good governance so difficult?

3. Consider the policy instruments the EU uses to promote democracy in third countries: which do you consider to be most effective?

4. Why have critics said the EU lacks a democracy promotion strategy?

Suggestions for further reading

Balfour, Rosa. *Human Rights and Democracy in EU Foreign Policy: The Cases of Ukraine and Egypt*. London: Routledge, 2012.

Saari, Sinikukka. *Promoting Democracy and Human Rights in Russia*. London: Routledge, 2011.

Wetzel, Anne and Jan Orbie. 'With Map and Compass on Narrow Paths and through Shallow Waters: Discovering the Substance of EU Democracy Promotion', *European Foreign Affairs Review*, 16, 5 (2011).

Youngs, Richard, ed. *Survey of European Democracy Promotion Policies 2000–2006*. Madrid: FRIDE, 2006.

CHAPTER SEVEN

Conflict Prevention

Preventing violent conflict became a concern for the Union once it was clear that peace and security would not replace the balance of terror of the Cold War. The conflict in Yugoslavia in mid 1991 illustrated this most starkly, but by the end of 1992, violent conflicts also erupted in the former Soviet Union (Armenia and Azerbaijan, Georgia, Moldova, and so on) and northern Africa (Algeria), and there were tensions elsewhere (between Hungary and Romania, for example). These conflicts either were internal, though often with significant external consequences, or were largely attributable to the spillover of internal tensions (especially over minority rights).

Defence against a Soviet threat may no longer have been a concern, but the security of the EU and its member states was far from assured, though it was not actually militarily threatened by the spread of conflicts. Instead, such conflicts were costly for the EU in other ways (see section 7.2). But dealing with (or 'managing', in current parlance) violent conflicts through military intervention has not been a practical option for the EU, due to both institutional shortcomings and a lack of political will. Trying to prevent conflicts from breaking out in the first place has been a much more promising area for EU activity.

The EU's approach to conflict prevention incorporates both short-term measures to address the risk of imminent conflict and long-term measures to try to create the conditions for peace, for the most part within states (and on the assumption that this contributes to inter-state peace). The member states have agreed on basic causes of conflict (economic hardship; lack of respect for human and minority rights; political, economic and social inequality; and lack of democracy) and on appropriate long-term measures to address them (support for democratization, respect for human and minority rights, sustainable economic development, regional cooperation). These assumptions shape the EU's policies in various regions, but they do not add up to a coherent, overall strategy for preventing violent conflict.

A coherent strategy is necessary, firstly, because the EU's preferred measures – promotion of democracy, human rights, sustainable development, and regional integration – may contribute to conflict prevention, but they also may not. The EU has not really addressed how the root causes of conflict can be tackled, rather than just mitigated.[1] Democratization may permit the peaceful conciliation of group interests, but it can also unleash extreme nationalism and political instability, especially if new political parties reflect ethnic divisions. Hence, if the promotion of democracy is to prevent conflicts, programmes must be specifically designed to minimize the conditions that breed extremist political movements. As seen in Chapter 6, elections can trigger violence, but the EU's approach to election observation has not fully taken this possibility into account. Secondly, development or economic assistance, or trade concessions, must be used carefully to ensure that they do not create or exacerbate inequalities among different identity groups, a source of conflict. To some extent, these considerations have been incorporated into EU policies, but a coherent strategy is still more of an objective than a reality. Indeed, a 2007 Commission communication on an EU response to situations of fragility did not lead to an envisioned action plan because High Representative Ashton froze it.[2] Thirdly, regional integration – particularly in the form of EU enlargement – could have disintegrative effects because countries left out of enlargement could be destabilized, and there is a risk that new EU member states could take a hardline attitude towards outsiders.[3] Easing the insider-outsider distinction is one way to try to avoid such conflicts, but this is easier said than done.

Finally, without a coherent strategy – and the resources to back it up, crisis management (dealing with the crises that arise) crowds out conflict prevention. Indeed, the distinction between the two is even sometimes blurred in EU parlance.[4] Yet there is a difference between 'acting early' (conflict prevention) and 'reacting' (crisis management). Crisis management is inevitably more visible (in the media, in policy-making), requires more resources, and although the stakes are high, if successfully handled, bring greater rewards. Carving out the space for conflict prevention is crucial – but has been difficult to do in the EU's institutional setup. In 2011, Ashton halted a review of the 2001 Göteberg programme on conflict prevention because she wanted the EEAS to concentrate on on-going or impending crises – a prime example of the challenges of creating that space for conflict prevention.[5] Yet arguably it is in conflict prevention rather than crisis management that the EU could add considerable value to European policy-making – as quick decision-making is extremely difficult in an intergovernmental organization.

The Union's approach to conflict prevention is broadly shared by other actors, such as Canada or Norway, and international organizations, most notably the OSCE and UN. However, in contrast to these actors, the EU possesses a considerable toolbox of policy instruments, and, crucially, its own unique legacy as a successful exercise in conflict prevention.

This chapter first discusses the experience of preventing conflict within the EU. Section 7.2 analyses how and why the EU adopted conflict prevention as a foreign-policy objective. The following two sections discuss how the EU defines conflict prevention, and what instruments it uses to try to prevent conflicts. The EU's policies are evaluated in section 7.5.

7.1 Conflict prevention within the EU

Until the 1990s, the European Union was better known for preventing conflicts between its own member states than among or within third countries. A key reason, after all, for the creation of the European Coal and Steel Community was to prevent future conflicts in Western Europe, and specifically between France and Germany. The then EU High Representative for the CFSP, Javier Solana, asserted in 2001 that the EU

> came into existence as an exercise in conflict prevention. A half a century ago, we began the process of recovery from a global conflict of unprecedented dimensions. Today's European Union was borne (*sic*) from the determination of all our peoples that such a conflict should never happen again . . . Building stability and preventing conflict is at the heart of our endeavours.[6]

The route to peace via integration has been successful. While there has been violence in some parts of the EU (Northern Ireland, the Basque region, Corsica), these are or were contained conflicts, and violent conflict among EU member states is simply inconceivable. The EU is a 'security community': there are long-term, dependable expectations that members of the community will resolve their problems by a process of peaceful change.[7] This is an extraordinary achievement. As Maurice Keens-Soper argues:

> What is noteworthy from the standpoint of the present is how the assumption of peace, above all between France and Germany, has become so securely grounded as to be unworthy of comment. When expectations have taken such hold that their fulfilment goes unnoticed, it suggests that relations based upon them depend on more reliable material than the official undertakings of treaties. Habit has sealed what contract began.[8]

This does not mean the end of disputes among the member states; it does mean that expressing and resolving those disputes become the stuff of politics, comparable to the domestic political process. The success of the integration project bestows legitimacy and authority on the EU's pursuit of the conflict prevention objective.[9]

The EU's success as a peace project earned it the Nobel Peace Prize in 2012. The Nobel Committee justified this because 'the union and its forerunners have for over six decades contributed to the advancement of peace and reconciliation, democracy and human rights in Europe'. Reconciliation between France and Germany, and then between Western and Eastern Europe, had stabilized and transformed Europe from a 'continent of war to a continent of peace'.[10]

But while integration is undoubtedly an important factor in producing stable expectations of peace among European states, it is not the only factor. Traditional liberal theories of international relations also seem to fit here: democratic states do not fight one another, and EU member states are all democracies; violent conflict is incompatible with free trade and economic interdependence, and the EU member states are all 'trading states'.[11] In practice, it is the combination of all these factors that the EU promotes externally to prevent violent conflict, between *and* within states.

Realists, however, would argue that peace in Europe during the Cold War was the result of bipolarity and mutual deterrence. Western Europe benefited, and still benefits (now with much of Central and Eastern Europe too), from the American security guarantee, which guarantees peace.[12] In reaction to the awarding of the 2012 Nobel Peace Prize to the EU, some argued that NATO deserved it more (or at least as much as the EU did).[13] The 2003 European Security Strategy does admit that the USA 'has played a critical role in European integration and European security, in particular through NATO'.[14] Furthermore, the provision of security guarantees is one instrument that the EU cannot wield; only the USA and NATO can do so. EU enlargement cannot provide a similar level of protection.[15] The EU's use of softer measures directly reflects the means available to it and its own 'home-grown' experiences, but realists would question whether it really can wield the full range of conflict prevention instruments, as it persistently claims.

The EU's history and experience have clearly shaped its approach to conflict prevention. But as the next section illustrates, the EU adopted this objective in the wake of events external to it, and concurrently with major international actors (not least the UN and the OSCE).

7.2 Conflict prevention as an EU foreign-policy objective

During the Cold War, 'conflict prevention' meant preventing nuclear war between the USA and the Soviet Union, with a strategy of nuclear deterrence. The Cold War did not, of course, inhibit all violent conflict – intra-state or inter-state – but frequently conflicts became theatres of US–Soviet competition: Afghanistan, Angola, El Salvador, Nicaragua, Vietnam, to name but a few. The UN tried to defuse crises and resolve conflicts, and thus prevent or limit superpower involvement, through the 'quiet diplomacy' of the Secretary-General and peacekeeping, but these efforts were not touted as conflict prevention or preventive diplomacy.[16]

To an extent, the EC member states used the EPC framework to try to reduce Cold War tensions in Europe – as in their collective diplomacy in the CSCE – or to propose solutions to conflicts that could threaten international stability. EPC put forward proposals to end the conflict in Afghanistan and the Middle East, and it supported regional efforts to end the conflicts in Central America. This was not activity aimed at preventing imminent violent conflict, but rather alleviating or resolving it, or creating the conditions for peace in the long term. While EPC was largely unsuccessful in this, it manifested a different and unique approach to violent conflict than that of the superpowers, in that it emphasized the local economic and political causes of conflict, and non-military solutions to it.

With the end of the Cold War, several conflicts ended (Cambodia, Central America, Mozambique), but new ones broke out, often within states. A revitalized UN tried to resolve many conflicts, as did regional organizations. Dealing with these conflicts was expensive. For example, the UN Protection Force (UNPROFOR) in the former Yugoslavia cost over $1 billion a year from 1993 to 1995, and the lives of 120 soldiers; EU member states paid a large part of this cost. The estimated cost in 1996 of the NATO Implementation Force, which enforced the Dayton peace agreement, was $5 billion.[17] And this of course leaves out the costs of the conflict for the people of the former Yugoslavia and neighbouring states, of housing Yugoslav refugees in host countries, of lost trade, and of reconstruction.

The costs of conflicts naturally sparked considerations of how to prevent them from breaking out in the first place. Within Europe, even before the Yugoslav war, some attention was paid to conflict prevention, mainly to ensure that the Cold War ended peacefully. A CSCE summit in November 1990 agreed to create a Conflict Prevention Centre, to try to prevent inter-state conflicts (building on its Cold War confidence-building measures). In 1992, in the wake of the Yugoslav war, the CSCE established a High Commissioner on National Minorities, who could intervene at an early stage to try to prevent tensions over national minority issues from erupting into internal and/or inter-state conflict, and strengthened its capacity to undertake fact-finding and field missions to address security issues between and within states. In June 1992, acting on a request from the UN Security Council, UN Secretary-General Boutros Boutros-Ghali published *An Agenda for Peace*, which contained recommendations for strengthening the UN's capacity to prevent violent conflict. EU member states have been active in supporting OSCE and UN conflict prevention activities, indicating a widespread consensus that conflicts can and should be prevented, and that many international organizations can be useful in this respect.

Given that the EU was increasingly expected to deliver humanitarian aid to, and help reconstruct, conflict-ridden zones (particularly in the former Yugoslavia), there was considerable support within the EU for attempting to prevent conflicts from arising. Conflict prevention is also an area in which the EU could make a distinct contribution, and has an armoury of appropriate tools. In 1994, then Commission President Jacques Delors asserted, 'as many conflicts and tensions are rooted in political, social and economic instabilities, the Union is much better equipped than any other international organization to address related problems'.[18]

In the June 1992 report on CFSP Joint Actions, preventing (and settling) violent conflict was declared an objective for EU foreign policy. Initially, the EU's neighbourhood attracted the most attention. The importance of preventing conflict in Central and Eastern Europe was obvious, as conflict there would seriously affect the EU's security, economic interests and political objectives. Enlargement is considered the primary way to spread security and stability eastwards. But it also became imperative that disputes among the CEECs be resolved *before* enlargement, lest the Union import instability and insecurity, or generate tensions between an enlarged EU and outsiders. Across Central and Eastern Europe, there were inter-state disputes over minority rights and boundaries, and domestic tensions stemming from minorities' grievances, economic hardship and nationalism. Early on, the Union addressed these problems in ways that reflect the underlying assumptions about the sources of conflict. It tried to foster democratization and respect for human and minority rights using conditionality (including, most powerfully, membership conditionality), aid, and diplomatic instruments, and it encouraged regional cooperation. It also engaged directly in mediation, not least in the Pact for Stability.

With the end of the Bosnian war, south-eastern Europe became a significant area for EU foreign policy, and it was concerned to prevent the recurrence of conflict and the outbreak of new conflicts there. In the mid 1990s, it drew up a strategy for reconstruction and peace in the region, based on the offer of association agreements and eventual EU membership, provided countries meet conditions including respect for democratic principles and human rights, good-neighbourliness, and compliance with the peace agreements.

The Union also devoted more attention southwards. As southern member states argued, there were risks to European security from religious fundamentalism and underdevelopment – whose direct impact on the EU would be via increased illegal immigration – as well as the spread of chemical and biological weapons. The Euro-Mediterranean partnership, based on political dialogue, economic and financial cooperation, and cultural exchange, is to 'contribute to the overall aim of preventing conflict and promoting stability'.[19] The Euro-Mediterranean partnership tries to make up for the EU's marginal influence in the Middle East peace process with a long-term, wider-ranging approach to peace and stability in the region.

Beyond the EU's periphery, conflict prevention in Africa became an EU concern, in the wake of conflicts in Liberia (1989–2003), Sierra Leone (1991–2002), Somalia (1992–) and Rwanda (1994). In none of them did the EU intervene, although some member states were active in the UN mission to Somalia, France intervened (eventually and controversially) in response to the Rwandan genocide, and the UK sent soldiers to Sierra Leone. One lesson learned was that outsiders would not readily intervene in conflicts in Africa, so African capacities to prevent and resolve conflicts should be developed. The EU has since declared that it would support African efforts in conflict prevention and peacekeeping.[20] Conflict prevention was a significant chapter at the Africa–Europe summit in April 2000, and was included in the Cotonou agreement.

For all of these activities, at the end of the 1990s, however, the Union still lacked an overall strategy for preventing conflicts. Starting in 1999, though, more effort was devoted to articulating a coherent framework. Several member states (Sweden and Finland, for example) and the Commission were pushing to ensure that the development of the EU's capacity to intervene militarily was balanced by a strengthening of its capacity to use civilian means to try to prevent and resolve conflicts. Civilian and military 'crisis management' capabilities have been under development since the 1999 Helsinki European Council. The June 2001 Göteberg European Council noted, 'the development of the European Security and Defence Policy (ESDP) has, since the outset, also been intended to strengthen the EU's capacity for action in the crucial field of conflict prevention'.[21]

In December 2000, Javier Solana and Chris Patten issued a report to the Nice European Council on 'Improving the Coherence and Effectiveness of European Union Action in the Field of Conflict Prevention'. This led to an open (televized) debate on conflict prevention at the January 2001 meeting of the General Affairs Council, under the Swedish presidency. In May 2001, the Commission issued a communication on conflict prevention. And in June 2001, the Göteberg European Council agreed an 'EU Programme for the Prevention of Violent Conflicts'.

The High Representative for CFSP and the Commission asserted that '[p]reserving peace, promoting stability and strengthening international security worldwide is a fundamental objective for the Union, and preventing violent conflict constitutes one of its most important external policy challenges'.[22] They made a number of recommendations for more effective and coherent policies. The Commission's communication also listed a large number of recommendations for improving the Union's capacity to prevent conflicts in the short and long term.

The General Affairs Council's open debate revealed a convergence of views among the member states. They agreed

> on both the principles on which conflict prevention should be based – such as democracy, the rule of law, respect of human rights and human dignity, in particular expressed in the fight against poverty and in favour of economic development – as well as the means to be employed for concrete action, with priority in the civil area – trade, development cooperation, humanitarian assistance, etc – but also in the last resort, the readiness to use military force for conflict solution.[23]

The foreign ministers further agreed that the EU needed to improve its internal tools, as well as the coherence and consistency of its conflict prevention policies. The Göteberg programme was a significant step towards a coherent EU strategy, and declared:

> In line with the fundamental values of the EU, the highest political priority will be given to improving the effectiveness and coherence of its external action in the field of conflict prevention, thereby also enhancing the preventive capabilities of the international community at large.[24]

The EU will set clear political priorities for preventive actions; improve its early warning and policy coherence; enhance its instruments for long- and short-term prevention; and build effective partnerships for prevention.

These commitments have been repeated many times since. The 2003 European Security Strategy could even be read as a declaration of a commitment first and foremost to prevent conflict: addressing security threats requires 'preventive engagement', or acting before problems become serious. The 2008 report on the implementation of the European Security Strategy declared that 'preventing threats from becoming sources of conflicts early on must be at the heart of our approach'.[25] The Lisbon Treaty declares that one of the goals of EU external action is 'to preserve peace, prevent conflicts and strengthen international security' (Article 21), and that the common security and defence policy shall engage in operations which include 'conflict prevention and peace-keeping tasks, tasks of combat forces in crisis management, including peace-making and post-conflict stabilization' (Article 43). A decade after the Göteberg European Council agreed the EU programme on prevention of violent conflicts the Council again declared that 'preventing conflicts and relapses into conflict' is a primary objective of EU external action.[26]

Why has the EU adopted this policy objective? Again, a mix of self-interested and altruistic motives are at play. Firstly, and obviously, violent conflict is costly for the EU. The CFSP High Representative and Commission argued: 'Conflict bears a human cost in suffering and undermines economic development. It also affects EU interests by creating instability, by reducing trade and putting investments at risk, by imposing a heavy financial burden in reconstruction and ultimately by threatening the security of its citizens. The financial costs of preventing conflict are small compared to the cost of addressing its consequences.'[27] And the consequences of regional conflict could be quite serious, as the European Security Strategy notes: it 'can lead to extremism, terrorism and state failure; it provides opportunities for organized crime. Regional insecurity can fuel the demand for WMD.'[28] There are also less tangible costs, as Reinhardt Rummel points out. Ignoring the human suffering would exact a moral cost, undermining the legitimacy of policies designed to further the EU's shared values, such as respect for human rights. The EU's failure to resolve conflicts can discredit the CFSP (as in the case of Bosnia), and cause tensions with other states.[29]

Secondly, violent conflict makes it virtually impossible to pursue the EU's other foreign-policy objectives, such as the promotion of human rights and democracy or encouragement of regional cooperation. Thirdly, the post-Cold War *zeitgeist* regarding conflict prevention has provided particular actors within the EU with the motive and arguments to push for the continued development of the EU's security dimension: a comprehensive approach to security (beyond territorial defence) resonates with the EU's own history and provides a rationale for the expansion of EU competences in security. Finally, and related to that point, there is an ideational dimension here:

the goal of preventing conflict has become a valued facet of the EU's international identity. As a successful 'peace project' itself, it enjoys considerable legitimacy when trying to impart its experiences to others. This means, however, that failure to prevent conflicts could have negative effects on the EU's credibility and image. And claiming success is well-nigh impossible, as it is hard to determine that the EU was responsible for helping to prevent conflicts, or whether conflicts would not have erupted regardless of outside intervention.

The politics of scale clearly favour collective action to prevent conflicts. The EU can wield appropriate and quite powerful policy instruments, such as development assistance, or the conditional offer of EU membership. The member states can have more influence acting together than separately. Conflict prevention is also one area which plays to the EU's strengths, given the range of instruments that it can wield and its history as an exercise in conflict prevention. This is a key reason why the member states chose to develop the conflict prevention capacity of the EU: the EU could add value.

Several actors have actively pushed to strengthen the EU's capacity to prevent conflicts. The neutrals, Denmark and the Netherlands have been keen to develop civilian instruments alongside new military ones, and consider how these should best be used to prevent conflicts. Strengthening the EU's civilian instruments for conflict prevention could, after all, potentially reduce the need for military force. The Netherlands pushed for an EU conflict prevention role during its 1997 presidency, which then resulted in the 1997 Common Position on conflict prevention in Africa.[30] During its 1999 presidency, Finland actively promoted consideration of the non-military management of crises. Sweden used its 2001 presidency to develop the EU's civilian instruments, reflecting the strong emphasis on conflict prevention in Swedish foreign policy, as well as its preference for civilian over military means.[31] Sweden used its 2009 presidency to push for agreement on an EU concept for EU mediation and dialogue, and since 2010, Finland and Sweden have been advocating the creation of a European Institute for Peace, to boost the EU's mediation capabilities.[32] The larger member states have also pushed for EU conflict prevention activities: France proposed the Pact for Stability in Central and Eastern Europe; Germany pushed for a similar Stability Pact in south-eastern Europe; France and the UK advocate EU support for African conflict prevention capabilities; and Spain and Italy promoted the Euro-Med Partnership. The Commission has also long seen conflict prevention as an area where the Community's civilian instruments are of particular use, which requires a strong Commission voice in the foreign-policy-making process. The European Parliament has repeatedly called on the EU to strengthen its capabilities to prevent conflicts.[33] NGOs (such as International Alert, Saferworld, and International Crisis Group) and think tanks (such as the EU Institute for Security Studies) have made numerous recommendations for improving and strengthening the EU's conflict prevention capacities.[34]

There is clearly much support within the EU for pursuing the objective. Unlike in the cases of the human rights and democracy objectives, the challenges the EU faces in implementing the objective are somewhat less the persistence of divisions between member states (though they do exist, over the details of action in pursuit of the objective in any particular case), and rather more the problems of coordination amongst the various actors involved, within the EU and internationally. Conflict prevention policy exposes the weaknesses of the EU's foreign-policy system, such as the turf wars engendered by the pillar division or continued bureaucratic obstacles. A strengthened capacity to prevent conflicts will have to go hand in hand with a strengthened capacity to formulate and implement foreign policy at the EU level – obviously a slow process, where the crucial ingredient is the member states' willingness to do it.

Although the EU was active in conflict prevention quite early, it was following in the footsteps of other international actors, not least the UN and the OSCE. The development of its strategy was also at the behest of several member states who were already quite involved in conflict prevention (such as Sweden). The adoption of this foreign-policy objective thus followed international trends. But it clearly fits well with the EU's own origins and experiences, which contribute to the uniqueness of EU activity in this field.

7.3 What does the EU mean by conflict prevention?

Since the early 1990s, there has been a proliferation of terms regarding the prevention and settlement of violent conflicts: preventive diplomacy, preventive action, crisis prevention, conflict prevention, conflict resolution, peacemaking, peacekeeping, peacebuilding, conflict management, and crisis management. Some definitions of these terms overlap with each other; the same term can mean different activities. In 2001, the Commission grouped both long-term (which it called the projection of stability) and short-term (quick reaction to nascent conflicts) efforts under the general rubric of conflict prevention.[35] This chimed with the Council's definitions:

- conflict prevention targets the direct causes (trigger factors) *and* more structural root causes of violent conflict;
- crisis management addresses acute phases of conflicts, supporting efforts to end violence; and
- peacebuilding supports initiatives to contain violent conflict and prepare for and sustain peaceful solutions.[36]

Crisis management has been divided into 'civilian' and 'military', indicating either rapid deployment of civilian experts or rapid deployment of military forces. But in practice, the term crisis management (both civilian and military) has been used for activities which should – according to the definitions above – be more properly termed conflict prevention or peacebuilding, as in its ubiquitous use to describe all CSDP missions (and the relevant institutional machinery). Yet the EU has rarely intervened to prevent or put a stop to violence: CSDP missions have instead usually been sent *after* conflicts to train security personnel or sustain peaceful solutions.

7.4 How does the EU pursue the objective?

One of the EU's strengths in the field of conflict prevention is the wide range of instruments that it could wield in an effort to prevent violent conflicts, from aid to CDSP missions. However, for effective conflict prevention, instruments should be used in a coordinated and integrated way. Yet the CFSP High Representative and Commission admitted several years ago that:

> The challenges which face the Union as it sets about improving its coherence and effectiveness for conflict prevention are similar to those which it faces throughout its external action: to establish and sustain priorities for action; to ensure the coherent use of what is now a very broad range of resources in pursuit of those priorities; to deploy those resources in a pro-active, flexible and integrated way; and to build and sustain partnerships with those who share our values and priorities at global, regional, national and local level.[37]

In 2011, this was still a problem, and the Council acknowledged that 'there is scope for reinvigoration of EU efforts to prevent violent conflicts and their recurrence'. In particular, early warning needs to be better strengthened, more emphasis should be put on taking early action (especially mediation), and partnerships with other international actors need to be strengthened.[38] Yet the report that was supposed to be presented at the end of 2011 on the implementation of these commitments has not been published.[39]

Meeting the challenges of effective conflict prevention requires considerable coordination within the EU – and the proliferation of institutions, rules, committees, instruments (many the result of the development of the CSDP) which all relate in some fashion to the conflict prevention agenda has complicated the endeavour considerably (see Table 7.1). Initially, the pillar division created problems: development policy was entirely separate from political and security policy, and there was rivalry between the Commission and Council secretariat. It erupted in a case before the European Court of Justice over which pillar could run a programme to combat the spread of small arms and light weapons in West Africa; the ECJ eventually agreed that this could be included in EU development policy.

The creation of the EEAS was supposed to help alleviate such issues, but has led to new complications. Notably, the number of bodies dealing with various aspects of conflict prevention policy remains very large. But the numbers of personnel engaged in key bodies, such as the Division for Peacebuilding, Conflict Prevention and Mediation, are small – and morale is generally low.[40] For months, some of the key directorate level positions were

Table 7.1 Principal institutions involved in EU conflict prevention policy

European Commission	EEAS	Council of the EU
Service for Foreign Policy Instruments (FPI): plans and administers the Instrument for Stability (reports to Vice President Ashton directly)	Crisis management board: usually chaired by HR/VP, and brings together heads of crisis management bodies (CMPD, CPCC and EUMS), directors of regional and thematic directorates and PSC chair	Key committees:
	Crisis management platform: brings together same individuals as above, minus the PSC chair and HR/VP; is coordinated by the managing director for crisis response and operational coordination	Political and Security Committee (PSC) (provides strategic direction and coordination)
Directorate-General for Development and Cooperation (DG DEVCO): has a Unit for Fragility and Crisis Management	Conflict prevention group: convened by Division for Conflict Prevention, Peacebuilding and Mediation; brings together heads of relevant thematic and geographical directorates and crisis management bodies, chairs of CIVCOM and PMG, and representatives of FPI and DEVCO's fragility unit; reviews early warning, provides analysis, identified policy options, and mainstreams conflict prevention in EU external relations	Political–Military working party (PMG) does preparatory work for the PSC on CSDP
Directorate-General for Enlargement: handles relations with Western Balkans	Crisis Response and Operational Coordination: includes EU situation room and crisis response planning and operations	Committee for Civilian Aspects of Crisis Management (CIVCOM)
	EU Intelligence Analysis Centre (INTCEN): strategic analysis based on intelligence from member states, EU and open sources	There are also working groups on conventional arms exports; global disarmament and arms control; human rights; development cooperation
	Directorate for Security Policy and Conflict Prevention: includes Division for Conflict Prevention, Peacebuilding, and Mediation, which is responsible for conflict analysis and integration of conflict prevention into EEAS' work	EU Military Committee (provides military advice to PSC)
	Crisis Management Planning Directorate (CMPD): responsible for strategic planning of civilian and military CSDP missions	
	Civilian Planning Conduct Capability (CPCC): responsible for planning, deployment and conduct of civilian crisis management	
	EU Military Staff (EUMS): provides early warning, situation assessment, strategic planning; includes an intelligence division	
	EU delegations	
	EU special representatives	

Source: European Peacebuilding Liaison Office, 'Power Analysis: The EU and Peacebuilding After Lisbon', March 2013, available at http://www.eplo.org/assets/files/2.%20Activities/Working%20Groups/EEAS/EPLO_Peacebuilding%20after%20Lisbon_March2013.pdf (last accessed 9 August 2013).

left vacant. Furthermore, there is still duplication – for example, with intelligence being collected and analysed in several locations. There is also still a divide between the Commission and EEAS, with the Instrument for Stability – a key instrument for conflict prevention (see below) – being programmed and managed in the Commission's Service for Foreign-policy Instruments.

The problems of coordination and priority setting are not, by any means, unique to the EU – this infamously bedevils organizations such as the UN, and even in countries which do pay quite a lot of attention to conflict prevention and management, there is striking lack of 'joined-up' policy planning, coordination and implementation. Paddy Ashdown concludes, with respect to the UK, that 'if cohesion and a cross-disciplinary approach is one of the golden rules of conflict prevention and post-conflict reconstruction, then it is impossible to avoid the conclusion that we still have a long way to go to achieve it'.[41]

The rest of this section analyses several measures the EU can use for conflict prevention: early warning; financial assistance; conditionality; sanctions; limits on arms exports; political dialogue and mediation; support for regional cooperation; civilian missions; and military instruments.

Early warning

One lesson that the Union learned from the wars in the former Yugoslavia is that it needed a better capacity for early warning. An effective preventive policy relies on spotting crises before they erupt, and formulating possible responses. After the Amsterdam Treaty, the policy unit was set up for this specific purpose, but it was small. The 2001 Göteberg programme stressed the importance of effective early warning. Since then, the number of bodies within the EU that have a remit to gather information and provide early warning has increased greatly, including INTCEN and the Military Staff. But ten years later, the Council acknowledged that 'early warning needs to be further strengthened within the EU'. In particular, the EU needs to draw on more sources (including member states – which have been reluctant to share intelligence, EU delegations and civil society actors).[42]

Information and analysis must be integrated into the policy-making process if it is to be translated into action. Since 2001, the Commission (now EEAS) has a checklist on the root causes of conflict, which was supposed to be used in drawing up country and regional strategy papers. But an evaluation of Commission support for conflict prevention and peacebuilding (2001–10) found that the checklist was not widely known within the Commission and that very few officials had ever read it. Furthermore, formal conflict analyses were conducted only in a few cases, limiting the extent to which conflict prevention could be incorporated into country and regional strategies, many of which were found to contain no references to relevant conflicts.[43] This did not improve immediately after the EEAS was created: the initial responses to the Arab Spring did not contain references to peace and security matters, and strategies on the Sahel and Sudan/South Sudan have also been criticized for not being strong enough regarding peacebuilding.[44] Every six months, a confidential 'watch list' of countries most at risk is supposed to be agreed by the Political and Security Committee, but this reflects the lowest common denominator of the member states' interests and is too broad to guide policy-making.[45] The watch list also does not analyse the causes of conflicts or how to address them.[46] There is reluctance to introduce sensitive issues, such as risks of conflict (or, as previously seen, human rights and democracy considerations), into relations with third countries.

But once warnings are integrated into discussions, the member states have to agree that action *should* be taken and then what sort of action should be taken, and here countervailing economic, political and security interests, or inertia, or disinterest, may prevent action or water down any agreements that can be reached. Ever since the outbreak of the Yugoslav war in 1991, for example, analysts and diplomats had warned that conflict in Kosovo was likely; yet this did not lead to action that could prevent it. The exigencies of ending the Bosnian conflict even led to an avoidance of discussing the Kosovo issue at the Dayton peace talks, and Milosevic's hold on power in Serbia was tolerated because of his key role in implementing the Dayton agreement. A major diplomatic effort and the imposition of sanctions on Serbia did not take place until 1998, when violence was already erupting in Kosovo.

A more recent case of weaknesses in the warning and analysis system, and of crisis management overtaking conflict prevention, was Mali. The Political and Security Committee discussed the Sahel region in 2010, but it was not prioritized for preventive action at the time.[47] In March 2011, the Foreign Affairs Council agreed an integrated 'Strategy for Security and Development in the Sahel', but it was focused on long-term perspectives (three to ten years), and underestimated the prospects for imminent conflict in Mali (though it makes it quite clear that the region faces challenges including the risk of violent extremism and radicalization, and terrorist-linked security threats).[48] A year later, however, the Malian government was deposed in a coup d'état (by soldiers unhappy with the conduct of the government's fight against Turareg rebels in the north). Mali was then overwhelmed as Islamic fundamentalist and terrorist forces overran the north of the country. In mid 2012, the EU began discussing sending a CSDP mission to train Malian defence forces – a process which one observer described as 'interminable'.[49] When Islamist forces headed south, in January 2013 France intervened with a military mission to help re-take the north of the country, and was eventually aided by ECOWAS forces. The situation is calmer now, and French forces have begun to withdraw, the EU deployed its mission, a UN peacekeeping mission is being deployed to establish stability, and a presidential election was even successfully held in July 2013. One lesson from Mali is the speed with which security threats can develop – and therefore the need for better warning and analysis capabilities to try to anticipate such developments.

Julia Schünemann has noted that if member states can agree, then the EU can act effectively. For example, when violence broke out between Russia and Georgia in the summer of 2008, the EU did react quickly to try to achieve a ceasefire and deploy a monitoring mission. But she also points out that once again, a crisis prompted action; the opportunity to take preventive action earlier had been missed, when the EU failed to support dialogue between Russia and Georgia.[50]

In sum, improving early warning and analysis capabilities is one step towards a more effective conflict prevention policy, but only one step. The EU still tends to react to crises and conflicts, rather than act early to try to prevent them.

Financial assistance

From the mid 1990s, there was a growing recognition (internationally and within the Union) that assistance alone will not prevent conflict; it must be specifically directed towards alleviating the root causes of conflicts. At the UN level, the Secretary-General emphasized the role of development aid in conflict prevention in his 1994 report, *An Agenda for Development*.[51] By summer 1994, donor countries, international organizations and NGOs were evaluating the negative impact of humanitarian and emergency aid on prospects for peacebuilding, primarily because of the experience of the refugee camps just outside Rwanda but also of the earlier experience of relief provision in Somalia.[52]

The EU absorbed and even contributed to these discussions. Programmes must address the root causes of violent conflicts. The ultimate policy goal is 'structural stability', which is 'a situation involving sustainable economic development, democracy and respect for human rights, viable political structures, and healthy social and environmental conditions, with the capacity to manage change without resort to violent conflict'.[53] Importantly, this approach became the basis for the OECD Development Assistance Committee's guidelines on conflict, peace and development cooperation.[54]

The Council agreed that development aid can contribute to the prevention of violent conflicts, if it addresses the causes of conflicts, ensures balanced opportunities among different identity groups, strengthens democratic legitimacy and effectiveness of governance, and builds effective mechanisms for the peaceful conciliation of group interests.[55] In November 2000, the Community's development policy was revised to emphasize poverty reduction as the primary objective, and 'poverty, and the exclusion which it creates, is one of the root causes of conflict'.[56] Conflict prevention is explicitly mentioned in the European Consensus on Development, particularly in terms of the need to address problems of state fragility. Conflict prevention is supposed, therefore, to be 'mainstreamed' in the EU's development and cooperation policies. But, as has been seen previously in this book with respect to the promotion of human rights and democracy, this is difficult to do.

Between 2001 and 2010, the Commission spent approximately €7.7 billion on conflict prevention and peacebuilding; some of this came from the Instrument for Stability (see below), but most from the regular aid budgets. However, over half of the money was spent on only four *post*-conflict situations: the West Bank and Gaza, Afghanistan, Iraq, and Sudan. The rest was scattered on 103 countries or regions.[57] This sum also includes activities to promote democracy (including election observation), civil society and anti-drug activities – thus covering a very wide spectrum of activities.

The Commission's regional and country strategy papers are supposed to assess potential conflict situations, and where there is possible conflict, 'conflict prevention measures will be made an integral part of the overall programmes of the Community'.[58] But this is not done systematically or widely. Where the strategy papers are drawn up in partnership with recipients (as is the case with the ACP countries), they tend to avoid discussing sensitive issues (such as the potential for conflict).[59] Furthermore, the Commission has not been able to make conflict prevention an issue in all the EU's sectoral policies (particularly trade or agricultural policy) or traditional development programmes.[60]

Development and cooperation aid has been used for measures such as demining, demobilization of combatants, security sector reform, and funding peacekeepers (under the African Peace Facility), but this is controversial: development NGOs and other experts have expressed fears that traditional development objectives such as reducing poverty will be negatively affected. Aid for reconstruction and rehabilitation after a conflict is also a major expenditure – such aid comes from the regular development aid programmes and the Instrument for Stability.

The real focus for dedicated conflict prevention funding was first the 2001 Rapid Reaction Mechanism (RRM), which has now been replaced by the Instrument for Stability (IfS). The RRM allowed for rapid assistance in areas such as mediation, re-establishment of civilian administrations, and demobilization. It was set up as the EU began to move seriously in field of conflict prevention and civilian crisis management (after the 1999 Helsinki European Council), but financial resources were limited to around €25 million a year between 2002 and 2006. It funded activities such as clearing landmines in FYROM, reintegrating child soldiers in the DRC, supporting the interim administration in Afghanistan, strengthening the Palestinian Authority's administrative capacities, and monitoring a ceasefire agreement in Sri Lanka.[61]

The new IfS has two aims: in a situation of current or emerging crisis, to contribute to stability; in the context of stable conditions, to help build capacity to address threats. Technical and financial assistance has been given, inter alia, to establish and operate interim administrations (as in Bosnia or Kosovo since the 1990s), for reconstruction, for demobilization and reintegration of former combatants into society, to address the impact of landmines and access to firearms (as in Chad and Libya in 2012), to strengthen the capacity of law enforcement and judicial authorities in fighting terrorism and organized crime (including illicit trafficking in weapons of mass destruction and components), to assist constitutional reform processes (as in Kyrgyz Republic in 2010), to help refugees (as from the Syrian conflict, in 2012) and to promote early warning and confidence-building systems (as in the African Union). The IfS budget is considerably larger than the RRM's was; it is about the same as the CFSP budget, which is used to fund civilian crisis management missions. But the 2014 budget for the IfS is smaller than it was in 2013, and the total budget for 2014–20 increases only very slightly compared to 2007–13 (see Table 3.2).

The IfS, however, is used mostly for short-term crisis response. In 2012, €195.8 million out of a total budget of €286.1 million went for crisis or emerging crisis situations, while €22 million was dedicated to pre- and post-crisis capacity building.[62] The European Parliament has demanded that ten per cent of the IfS funds be devoted to preventive action, but member states have refused to do this – another indication of how crisis response crowds out conflict prevention in the EU foreign-policy-making system.

Conditionality

The EU's most active use of conditionality to try to prevent conflicts has been vis-à-vis other European countries – and as the apparent threat of violent conflict has receded, so has the use of conditionality. Two EU membership conditions are relevant here: respect for minority rights (see section 5.3) and 'good-neighbourliness'. Good-neighbourliness implies a willingness to cooperate with neighbours, but also – more concretely – to resolve disputes peacefully, if necessary by referring them to the International Court of Justice (ICJ).

Good-neighbourliness has been stressed on a number of occasions. In 1992, the Czech Republic and Slovakia were carefully watched to ensure that their break-up was peaceful. In 1993, Hungary and Slovakia were successfully pressed to refer the Gabcikovo dam dispute to the ICJ. A key objective of the 1994–95 Pact for Stability was to encourage the applicant countries to reach bilateral agreements among themselves on borders and the treatment of minorities. In Agenda 2000, the Commission stated that 'before accession, applicants should make every effort to resolve any outstanding border dispute among themselves or involving third countries. Failing this they should agree that the dispute be referred to the International Court of Justice.'[63] The Helsinki European Council reiterated this condition: applicants had to resolve outstanding border disputes before accession, or refer them to the ICJ.[64]

But while the EU's membership conditionality may have helped to avert conflicts over Hungarian minorities or the Gabcikovo dam, it was not even used to try to force a resolution of the decades-old Cyprus conflict (which has been mostly non-violent for the last thirty years but at times quite tense). Conditionality on the Greek Cypriot (Republic of Cyprus) side was dropped so that a settlement was not deemed to be necessary for its accession to the EU. This, however, deprived the EU of one of its most powerful policy instruments to try to force a settlement. And in the end, the Republic of Cyprus joined the EU, leaving the so-called 'Turkish Republic of Northern Cyprus' in a limbo – even though Greek Cypriots had voted overwhelmingly to reject a UN peace plan and Turkish Cypriots had voted overwhelmingly to accept it. This is another instance of one or more member states (in this case Greece, but aided by the indifference of the others) blocking the consistent application of conditionality.[65]

The south-east European countries have been subject to even more stringent conditions tied to the offer of trade relations, assistance, and Stabilization and Association Agreements: countries must protect minority rights, be ready to engage in cross-border cooperation, provide opportunities for displaced persons and refugees to return to their places of origin, and comply with obligations under the peace agreements (including cooperation with the International Criminal Tribunal on the Former Yugoslavia, or ICTY).

In the specific case of Serbia and Montenegro between 2000 and 2006, the EU made it clear that the two entities should remain in a federal state, and that only the single state would conclude a SAA and later accede to the EU. In fact, Solana actively mediated an agreement in 2002 that created the State Union of Serbia and Montenegro (replacing the Federal Republic of Yugoslavia). There were several reasons for this, and preventing further conflict in the region figured highly among them – the EU particularly wanted to avoid any spillover effects from a break-up of Serbia and Montenegro fostering secessionism in Republika Srpksa (within Bosnia) or a hasty decision on Kosovo's status.[66] Yet the federation was untenable from the start, given the differences in political and economic developments and policies in both entities, which stymied the development of their relations with the EU. EU policy occasionally even magnified such differences and fostered moves towards a break-up, as when it broke off negotiations on an SAA with the State Union because *Serbia* was not cooperating with ICTY. When a dissolution became inevitable, the EU stepped in to ensure that a referendum on statehood in Montenegro would not be destabilizing (by mediating an agreement between pro-independence and anti-independence camps on the modalities of the referendum). The resulting vote for independence was recognized by the EU.

The successful use of conditionality depends on the credibility and clarity of the conditions and the benefits on offer – but also on whether the targets can and want to respond to it. Where there are relatively low levels of tension, it has worked well, as in the peaceful break-up of Czechoslovakia and the

State Union, or the Gabcikovo dam dispute. In situations of considerable instability, or where there are countervailing interests (within the EU or in the targets), it has worked less well.

Sanctions

The EU has imposed diplomatic and economic sanctions after a violent conflict has already erupted, to try to prevent further violence. Aid to several countries has been suspended because they were involved in violent conflicts, so as to avoid the misuse of funds for military purposes and to underscore the EU's appeal for a settlement of conflicts (see Table 7.2 for a list of recent sanctions). The EU has imposed arms embargoes and diplomatic and financial sanctions (mainly barring the entry to the EU of persons considered to be a

Table 7.2 EU sanctions in place in conflict or post-conflict situations. July 2013

Country	Measures	Reasons
Afghanistan (Taliban)	Arms embargo; freezing of funds; restrictions on admissions	Involvement in terrorism/war
Bosnia and Herzegovina	Restrictions on admissions and freezing of funds of persons threatening security situation, undermining Dayton peace agreement	Prevention of further violence
Democratic Republic of Congo	Since 2005: arms embargo; freezing of funds of persons violating arms embargo or impeding disarmament; restrictions on admission to EU of persons violating arms embargo, impeding DDR, using children in armed conflict	To prevent resumption of civil war
Eritrea	Since 2010: arms embargo; freezing of funds and restrictions on admissions of persons violating arms embargo or supporting the destabilization of region	To prevent violence
Iraq	Since 2003: arms embargo, freezing of funds of certain persons	To try to stop civil war, insurgency
Ivory Coast	Since 2004: asset freeze for certain individuals threatening peace and ban on exports of equipment for internal repression. Since 2006: CFSP restrictions on admission of certain individuals, arms embargo	To prevent resumption of civil war
Lebanon	Since 2006: arms embargo; ban on certain services; restrictions on admission and freezing of funds for persons suspected of murdering former Prime Minister (such restrictions also imposed on Syria)	To prevent war (civil and regional)

Continued

Table 7.2 *Continued*

Country	Measures	Reasons
Liberia	2001: arms embargo. Since 2002: CFSP restrictive measures. 2003: aid directed to peacekeeping; new aid linked to peace agreement. Since 2006: CFSP measures of arms embargo, diamond embargo, asset freeze and travel restrictions on certain persons reaffirmed. 2007: diamond embargo lifted. 2008: arms embargo for non-governmental entities	To stop civil war and prevent its resumption
Libya	Since 2011: arms embargo; restrictions on admission and freezing of funds on certain persons	To try to prevent further violence, internal repression
Moldova	Since 2003: restrictions on admission of leadership of Transnistrian region considered to be blocking resolution of conflict	To prevent violence
Myanmar	Since 2013: arms embargo	To prevent violence, internal repression
Palestinian Authority/ Hamas	2006: suspension of aid to Hamas government	To prevent violence in region
Sierra Leone	Since 1998: arms embargo; restrictions on admission of members of former military junta. Since 2002: ban on diamond imports	To prevent resumption of civil war
Somalia	Since 2002: arms embargo confirmed, ban on certain services	To prevent resumption of civil war
South Sudan	Since 2011: arms embargo	To prevent violence, war with Sudan
Sudan	Since 1994: arms embargo; since 2005: restrictions on admissions of persons infringing arms embargo or human rights; freezing of funds; ban on certain services	To stop war
Syria	2012–13: arms embargo; since 2012: a long list of sanctions including bans on investment, trade, and aid	To prevent violence, repression

Note: The list does not include EU sanctions on Iran and North Korea (in conformity with UN Security Council resolutions aiming to prevent Iran from developing nuclear weapons and to force North Korea to desist from developing nuclear weapons). Source: European Commission, 'Restrictive measures in force', latest update 31 July 2013.

threat to peace, and freezing their assets) to try to prevent the resumption of civil wars or the outbreak of violent conflict. It has also been active in trying to build an international control regime to prevent the sale of diamonds from conflict zones (the Kimberley process).

Most of the sanctions imposed have been in response to internal conflicts – though there may be significant spillover effects for other countries (as between Liberia, Ivory Coast and Sierra Leone). But the EU has also imposed sanctions to try to prevent wider conflicts. The sanctions on Hamas (see section 6.4) were imposed to try to stop violence between Hamas and Israel. In the case of Lebanon, negative measures have been imposed to try to prevent both civil war within Lebanon and between Hizbollah and Israel.

Sanctions now tend to be 'smart', targeting only certain individuals (or products, as in diamonds or timber). Within the EU, the debate on the utility of sanctions was fuelled by the experiences of sanctions in the former Yugoslavia in the 1990s. Sanctions fostered illegal transactions, smuggling, civilian suffering and trade losses for neighbouring countries.[67]

The most notable exception to this is the extensive sanctions regime in place on Syria since the violent repression of anti-government protests in 2011 and the ensuing civil war. As Clara Portela notes, these are unprecedented sanctions: 'the EU deployed the virtual entirety of measures in the sanctions toolbox within less than a year'.[68] These entail a ban on the import of oil from Syria, a ban on aid, restrictions on individuals considered responsible for repression, an arms embargo and trade restrictions. Controversially, however, in May 2013, France and the UK successfully pushed other more reluctant member states into agreeing to suspend the arms embargo on Syria. This could allow European states to send arms to rebel groups in Syria.[69] The decision is so controversial because not only are some of the rebels fighting the Assad regime known to be Islamic extremists if not terrorist groups (so therefore any arms supplies could fall into their hands), but because it contradicts the EU's third and fourth criteria for arms exports (see Box 7.1 below).

The record of sanctions in actually preventing conflict from breaking out in the first place is far from established. Sanctions threatened and imposed against Serbia in 1998 could not prevent the war in Kosovo, for example. Sanctions imposed after a conflict has broken out inevitably take time to work (if they work at all): they do not seem to be having an effect on the war in Syria (yet), for example – not least because the actions of other international actors (Russia, China, Iran) are directly countering the EU's sanctions. But they are still clearly an important tool in the EU's toolbox.

Limits on arms exports

Any serious attempt to prevent conflicts must address the supply of arms to areas at risk of conflict. But arms industries are powerful lobbies, and states find it difficult to limit the exports on which many jobs can depend. They are also unwilling to limit exports if competitors will simply supply substitutes, so the need for cooperation is evident.

Control of arms exports does not fall within the Common Commercial Policy, so was initially handled under CFSP. In 1991, the member states moved towards harmonization of their arms export policies. The June 1991 Luxembourg European Council noted that member state policies on arms exports were based on common criteria, which could form the basis for a common approach. Seven criteria were listed; an eighth was added a year later by the Lisbon European Council.[70] The eight criteria were later incorporated into the Code of Conduct on Arms Exports, which was signed on 8 June 1998, following a UK presidency initiative. The Code is a list of eight criteria stipulating the conditions under which export licenses should be denied. Member states are to tell each other about licenses they have denied; a member state that approves a license that has been denied by another member state must explain the reasons for so doing. In 2008, the Council agreed a CFSP common position reinforcing the Code (see Box 7.1).[71] It also strengthened the procedures aimed at harmonizing member state export policies. Each year, the member states are to send data on licences refused and granted, and the information is published in an annual report.

Box 7.1 Criteria for arms exports

Member states to consider:

1. Respect for the international obligations and commitments of member states, in particular the sanctions adopted by the UN Security Council or the EU, agreements on non-proliferation and other subjects, as well as other international obligations.
2. Respect for human rights in the country of final destination as well as respect by that country of international humanitarian law.
3. Internal situation in the country of final destination, as a function of the existence of tensions or armed conflicts.
4. Preservation of regional peace, security and stability.
5. Behaviour of the buyer country with regard to the international community, as regards in particular its attitude to terrorism, the nature of its alliances and respect for international law.
6. National security of the member states and of territories whose external relations are the responsibility of a member state, as well as that of friendly and allied countries.
7. Existence of a risk that the military technology or equipment will be diverted within the buyer country or re-exported under undesirable conditions.
8. Compatibility of the exports of the military technology or equipment with the technical and economic capacity of the recipient country, taking into account the desirability that states should meet their legitimate security and defence needs with the least diversion of human and economic resources for armaments.

Source: Council of the EU, Common Position 2008/944/CFSP

The EU has taken a strong stance on anti-personnel land mines. In a series of Joint Actions in 1996 and 1997, the Union supported the Ottawa convention on the prohibition of the use, stockpiling, production and transfer of anti-personnel mines and on their destruction. It also established a moratorium on their production and transfer. This stand clearly distinguishes the Union from the USA, which refused to sign the Ottawa convention.

Combating the spread of small arms and light weapons (SALW) has been another area where the EU has taken the initiative. A CFSP Joint Action on SALW dates from 2002; Commission aid dates back further – and combating the spread of SALW was included in the Cotonou convention. The EU includes small arms issues in political dialogue with developing countries, provides aid to eliminate surplus small arms, promotes regional cooperation to combat illicit trafficking, and funds public awareness programmes.[72]

On a wider scale, the EU has tried to build international consensus on several principles, including: states should import and hold small arms only for legitimate security needs; they should supply small arms only to governments; and they should combat illicit trafficking by implementing border and customs controls.[73] The EU supported the July 2001 UN conference on controlling small arms and light weapons, which, however, reached only an anodyne final agreement, due in large part to US opposition to stronger measures – another area where EU and US positions have diverged. The EU has also strongly supported attempts since 2005 to agree a binding international arms trade treaty (which is also strongly opposed by the USA).

Political dialogue and mediation

Political dialogue is a long-term conflict prevention measure, while mediation is a more short-term one. In April 2001, the Commission argued that dialogue on political issues can have an early warning role, and help bring disputes to an early resolution. But if this is to occur, 'the political dialogue clearly needs to be more focused, time-flexible and robust than is often the case at present'.[74] The Göteberg programme stated that the 'EU's political dialogue will be used in a systematic and targeted way to address potential conflicts and promote conflict prevention'. Given that dialogues are also supposed to cover human rights and democracy, trade, migration issues, and so on, their agendas could become quite overloaded. Furthermore, if political dialogue is to help resolve disputes, the EU needs to have not only an in-depth understanding of the disputes at issue, but also some conception of how it thinks such disputes should be resolved, in the short term. This requires appropriate diplomatic capabilities.

Mediation is an area in which the EU has recognized it needs better resources. In 2009, the Council recommended strengthening the EU's capacities in mediation and dialogue by boosting training programmes for officials, creating more flexible means of using mediation capabilities and cooperating more effectively with other actors (local and international).[75] A Mediation Support Team was then set up within the EEAS Conflict Prevention, Peace-building and Mediation Instruments Division, providing operational support, training and lessons learned to EU officials. The 2011 Council conclusions on conflict prevention state that the EU will further 'strengthen mediation capacities by providing support and training to mediators and their staff and increase their readiness'.[76] Some member states (led by Finland and Sweden), NGOs and MEPs argue still more needs to be done, and have pushed for the creation of a European Institute for Peace, which would train and deploy mediators. This proposal has still not been agreed to at EU level.

The EU has engaged in diplomacy to try to prevent conflicts, resolve conflicts that have already broken out, and prevent their recurrence. The EU has sponsored major multilateral diplomatic initiatives to try to prevent conflicts, such as the Pact for Stability in Central and Eastern Europe, and the Stability Pact for south-eastern Europe. It supports African efforts to develop preventive diplomacy, prompted particularly by British and French pressure. Special representatives have been sent to the former Yugoslavia, Middle East, African Great Lakes region, the Caucasus, Central Asia and the Southern Mediterranean region (though several of these mandates have been controversially discontinued; see Chapter 3).

The presidency and troika visited countries and regions at risk of violent conflict, or where violent conflict has already broken out, in an attempt to prevent the outbreak or escalation of conflict. The French presidency was very active in trying to achieve a ceasefire between Russia and Georgia in August 2008 (ultimately successfully) – though there has since been a stalemate in the region and Russian troops have not withdrawn from Abkhazia and South Ossetia. EU action to try to stop conflict between Hamas (in control of the Gaza Strip) and Israel in late 2008 and early 2009 was less successful – and even marked by a cacophony of voices as not only the Czech presidency and but also, separately, the then French President, Nicholas Sarkozy, toured the region. This sort of activism, though, is probably a thing of the past, as the presidency now plays almost no role in EU foreign policy.

Before Lisbon, the High Representative and Commission were also active: for example, in February 2001, Solana and Patten (joined often by the NATO Secretary-General) spent a considerable amount of time (successfully) working for a peaceful solution to the escalating conflict in the Former Yugoslav Republic of Macadeonia. The Commission on its own has even been involved in mediation. From October 1992, it mediated a dispute between Hungary and Slovakia over a hydroelectric project on the Danube (the Gabcikovo dam). In April 1993, Commission officials successfully secured agreement from both sides to submit the dispute to the ICJ. Undoubtedly, the prospect of being excluded from eventual EU enlargement helped to convince the two sides to compromise.[77] Since the Lisbon Treaty, High Representative

Ashton has engaged in diplomacy to try to resolve conflicts and prevent their recurrence: in April 2013, she successfully brokered a final deal between Serbia and Kosovo that could enable normalization of relations between them.

Support for regional cooperation

In accordance with the EU's own experience, regional cooperation is seen as a way to spread peace. EU enlargement reflects this, but it is also obvious in the emphasis on good-neighbourliness in Europe, and support for building conflict prevention capacities of African organizations. The EU's encouragement of regional groupings in Africa, Central America, Latin America and Asia feeds into this long-term approach to building peace. But there are snags, as discussed in Chapter 4, notably the willingness of states to cooperate with each other. The Euro-Mediterranean partnership was based on the assumption that peace and stability will flow from regional cooperation, yet there has been a lack of progress in the Middle East peace process.

The EU has been very active in trying to boost the conflict prevention and management capacities of African organizations. It helps to strengthen the early warning and analysis capabilities of African organizations, by exchanging information on areas at risk, training analysts, organizing seminars, and providing material assistance.[78] An action plan for support to peace and security in Africa was agreed in November 2004, and there has been active support for African peace support missions: much of the AU mission in Sudan, for example, has been paid for by the EU. In April 2012, the EU offered to assist ASEAN in developing its conflict management and crisis response capacities. Elsewhere cooperation is less developed, partly because other regional organizations are not much engaged in conflict management.

Civilian missions

Ever since the 1999 Helsinki European Council, the EU has been developing a non-military rapid response capability to crises and situations of instability, as discussed in section 3.2. Many of the CSDP missions launched since 2003 have been civilian missions (see Table 3.5). The use of the term 'crisis management' to describe these missions is a misnomer: most often, they are deployed as measures that in some way (directly or indirectly) try to prevent the recurrence of conflict, stabilize post-conflict situations or fight international crime (see Chapter 8). Their relation to a broader strategy is not entirely clear: with the exception of the missions in south-eastern Europe, many seem to be quite ad hoc and reactive, rather than preventive. Furthermore, there is a growing 'capabilities-expectations gap' in this area, and the EU has struggled to meet its 2010 civilian headline goal – both in terms of finding appropriate personnel and deploying them rapidly.

However, the EU's growing expertise in policing, justice and the rule of law is widely appreciated as crucial for state-building. There may be a division of labour emerging with NATO: NATO takes care of the military side, and the EU the civilian side – but the current state of EU–NATO relations means this will be especially difficult to develop, if there is indeed agreement that this is the right route to take.[79]

Military instruments

The 1999 Helsinki European Council made it clear that EU missions would carry out the 'full range of conflict prevention and crisis management tasks defined in EU treaty, the Petersberg tasks'.[80] Since then, some military missions have been launched – but as already noted, these have not generally not been deployed in actual crises. An exception was the brief 2003 Operation Artemis to the DRC, which tried to stabilize a volatile situation in the Bunia region before extra UN troops arrived. EUFOR DRC in 2006 likewise helped to stabilize a dangerous situation so that UN-supervised elections could proceed.

Mostly the military missions pursue objectives related to peacekeeping and peacemaking (in the sense of fostering conflict resolution): 'stabilization' and state-building tasks. One development that initially surprised some observers is the geographical extent of the missions: rather than deploy mainly in Europe (where there could be intense cooperation with NATO), the EU has ventured into Africa. But there is little sense that decisions on deploying troops result from an overall strategy (in spite of the existence of the 2003 European Security Strategy); some of the decisions have been reactive (a request from the UN to act in the Democratic Republic of Congo in 2003, for example) and perhaps taken more to show that the EU could indeed carry out a military operation outside Europe than to implement a strategic vision of the EU's need to stabilize the DRC.

However, there are clearly limits to the EU's willingness to develop the CSDP and its capacity to deploy missions. Two examples illustrate these challenges. First, rather than intervene in Darfur, Sudan, the EU in 2007 agreed, somewhat reluctantly, that it would instead send a mission to try to protect Sudanese refugees in Chad (and to a lesser extent in the Central African Republic). This was a French initiative, and some EU member states were suspicious of French motives, seeing the mission as boosting support for its ally, the Chadian government. Officially it was a one-year 'bridging mission'; in 2009, the UN took over and the EU withdrew. About half of the 3300 troops were French and the EU had to borrow helicopters from Russia because there were no appropriate helicopters available from EU member states.[81]

In autumn 2008, intense fighting broke out in the eastern Democratic Republic of Congo (DRC) between the government and rebel forces supported by Rwanda. Although both the then UK Foreign Secretary David Miliband and

French Foreign Minister Bernard Kouchner spoke strongly about the need for more UN peacekeepers to be sent, when UN Secretary-General Ban-Ki Moon asked the EU to send troops to help the UN's peacekeeping mission there, EU foreign ministers were divided. Belgium and France were supportive, but the UK and Germany were opposed, arguing they were overstretched by deployments elsewhere (Afghanistan). Miliband said that European countries could send troops to the UN mission.[82] None did. This despite the fact that the EU has sent troops to the DRC before and currently has two CSDP missions to the country (EUSEC and EUFOR RD Congo) to help reform the security, police and justice sectors. As Richard Gowan argued, 'The Congo crisis tested three widely proclaimed EU priorities: its partnership with Africa, its strategic support to the UN, and its belief in the need to protect the vulnerable. Yet even combined, these priorities did not create enough momentum for military action.'[83]

The EU and UN had been keen to develop their cooperation – from the UN's point of view, the EU could potentially supply UN missions with experienced and well-equipped troops. In June 2001, pushed by the Swedish Presidency, the European Council approved conclusions on EU–UN cooperation in conflict prevention and crisis management, involving regular meetings at several levels; in September 2003, the EU and UN signed a joint declaration on cooperation in crisis management. EU member states contribute about 40 per cent of the UN's peacekeeping budget, though less than seven per cent of the personnel for UN operations (under UN command; EU member states contribute substantially more to UN-mandated operations such as Operation Althea in Bosnia or ISAF in Afghanistan).[84] But the idea that battle groups could be deployed for UN operations (for example as a 'bridging' mechanism before a larger UN peacekeeping force arrives, as happened in the DRC in 2003) now appears to be a step too far in terms of both the willingness and capabilities of the EU and its member states to do so.

7.5 Evaluation

The extent to which the EU has been developing a strategy on conflict prevention and crisis management, and creating new instruments, is impressive. The EU has recognized that it is well positioned to foster the long-term conditions for peace, by targeting the underlying causes of conflict and contributing to stability. It has also developed capabilities that could help prevent violent conflict in the short term.

But conflict prevention also exposes the weaknesses inherent in the EU's foreign relations system. Long-term conflict prevention is problematic – the resources for it are relatively small, early warning and analysis capabilities need strengthening, and there is a tendency for conflict prevention to lose out to crisis management. Where conflict appears imminent, speed and decisiveness are often of the essence. Yet it can take time to build an EU consensus to act at all, much less with effective instruments. If disputes appear danger-ous, the EU and the member states must agree that a crisis exists, and the EU has to unite behind a strong and decisive message. As the CFSP High Representative and the Commission noted, in situations with a high conflict potential in the short term, conflict prevention efforts 'must be underpinned by vigorous and continuous diplomatic engagement, involving the transmis-sion of clear messages to countries and regions in a situation of political deterioration'.[85] The EU does not always have the capacity and the will to engage so clearly and forcefully.

Then, of course, there are the problems of coordinating the various institu-tions and instruments involved. In addition to the well-known problems of consensus-building and coordination, the EU faces other challenges such as reconciling competing objectives and setting priorities. Conflict prevention is not the EU's only foreign-policy goal, but even the goals central to its long-term conflict prevention strategy – integration, democracy and economic interdependence – are not necessarily compatible with conflict prevention. Conflict prevention is still not fully integrated into policy-making. Priorities must be set, but the EU does not do this well. Short-term considerations can thus easily take precedence over the EU's longer-term strategy; crisis response tends to crowd out conflict prevention.

Conclusion

Conflict prevention is a significant objective for EU foreign policy, and con-siderable effort has been devoted to trying to develop a coherent strategy and strengthening the EU's instruments for conflict prevention. Yet reaction rather than prevention still characterizes the EU's approach to international conflict situations.

Even though the EU adopted the conflict prevention objective after other international actors did so, in many ways, the EU's conflict prevention efforts are unique because they build on the EU's own history and experience. As the International Crisis Group noted, 'The EU has shown considerable commit-ment to the principles and purposes of conflict prevention – arguably more than many traditional great powers – due in no small part to its origins as an economic community that disposed of exclusively "civilian" power.'[86] But the analysis of the causes of violent conflicts and how best to address them is also shared by other actors. Where the EU is unique is that it can muster a large conflict prevention 'toolbox', much more so than any other interna-tional organization, and arguably, more so than the individual member states (consider, for example, the influence of the conditional offer of EU membership).

The extent of the EU's toolbox distinguishes it from other international organizations, which have a clearer mandate to prevent conflicts: the UN, and, within Europe, OSCE and NATO. The OSCE cannot coerce parties to a dispute or conflict but must depend on their goodwill, and its large member-ship (56 states) and consensual decision-making process lead inevitably to watered-down decisions (a problem also for the UN). For all the military power that NATO can bring to bear in favour of conflict prevention or resolution, the range of instruments that the EU can employ is still much larger.

Several of the specific contents of the EU's toolbox are also unique, particu-larly the emphasis on multilateralism and regional cooperation, precisely because it is the export of the EU's own model of conflict prevention. Other aspects of the EU's toolbox are not so unusual, such as the mainstreaming of conflict prevention in development aid, and its new capabilities (civilian and military) for intervening in crisis situations.

Questions for discussion

1. Did the European Union deserve to win the 2012 Nobel Peace Prize?

2. What are the strengths and weaknesses of the EU's policies to prevent violent conflict in third countries?

3. Consider the policy instruments the EU uses to try to prevent conflict: which do you think are the most effective?

Suggestions for further reading

Gross, Eva and Ana E. Juncos, eds. *EU Conflict Prevention and Crisis Management: Roles, Institutions, and Policies*. London: Routledge, 2010.
Schünemann, Julia. 'EU Conflict Prevention 10 Years after Göteberg', Policy Paper no. 1, June 2011, Institut Català Internacional per la Pau.
Tocci, Nathalie. *The EU and Conflict Resolution: Promoting Peace in the Backyard*. London: Routledge, 2007.

CHAPTER EIGHT

The Fight Against International Crime

The objective of fighting international crime was proclaimed as early as 1975, as the motivation for setting up the Trevi group, though little of substance resulted from Trevi discussions. The ramifications of the completion of the single European market and the end of the Cold War then prompted the member states to do more together to tackle international crime, but the issue has really only risen up the EU's agenda since the October 1999 Tampere European Council, which was devoted to discussing Justice and Home Affairs (JHA). In 2000, the Council set priorities for external relations in the JHA field, launching the so-called 'external dimension of JHA'.[1] Since then, this dimension has bloomed, and JHA issues figure highly in the EU's relations with third countries.

There are several unusual characteristics of the objective of fighting international crime, when compared to the other objectives discussed in this book. Firstly, the fight against international crime stands out because of the extent of its internal–external nexus: criminal activity takes place, and criminals cooperate, across national frontiers within the EU and across the EU's external borders. Steps taken to try to increase 'internal' security are interconnected with steps taken to address 'external' criminal threats.[2] Foreign policy and internal EU policy are intertwined. This can be seen vividly in the EU's response to the 11 September 2001 terrorist attacks on the USA: it consisted of agreements on an EU-wide arrest warrant and common penalties for terrorist crimes, as well as the use of more traditional diplomatic and economic foreign-policy instruments.

Secondly, as just indicated, this policy objective has to a large extent developed in reaction to developments outside the EU. From the inclusion of the JHA pillar in the Maastricht Treaty to the successive counter-terrorism action plans and approaches to global migration, outside events seem to be a – if not the – key dynamic prompting EU responses. Conversely, a decline in perceived external threats can lead to less dynamism at the EU level.

Thirdly, the 'fight against international crime' covers a wide range of activities – and crucially, since the mid 1990s there has never been a single policy-making framework encompassing them all.[3] Initially this objective was pursued in different pillars; even after the Lisbon Treaty, competence is still dispersed among many different agencies and institutions, though in general the JHA Council takes decisions, and DG Home Affairs in the Commission is responsible for initiating and implementing decisions. This raises obvious challenges for ensuring overall coherence in foreign policies vis-à-vis third countries.

'Crime' is also quite difficult to define anyway: what is a crime in one national jurisdiction may not be a crime in another, or may be penalized quite differently. In the EU lexicon, the term 'international crime' covers a wide scope of activity, including: illegal trafficking in drugs and human beings; terrorism; euro forgery; cyber crime; intellectual property crime; and VAT fraud.[4] All of these criminal activities can be – and often are – pursued by criminals organized transnationally, so that efforts to fight crime include the fight against international organized crime. This chapter focuses only on the fight against those crimes where the EU has engaged substantially with third countries, namely international terrorism, illegal trafficking in drugs and illegal immigration.

Finally, the fight against international crime is also the one foreign-policy objective considered in this book that is most clearly motivated by self-interest. While pursuit of the other objectives does benefit the Union itself (so that conflict prevention or human rights protection could reduce the number of EU-bound refugees fleeing persecution or war), their fulfilment primarily has beneficial effects for people outside the Union. The rationale for EU external action to fight international crime is to prevent or mitigate the nefarious influence of international criminal activity within the Union's territory, to ensure an 'area of freedom, security and justice' (AFSJ) for EU citizens. The 2005 Strategy for the External Dimension of JHA states this quite clearly: the 'EU's objective in engaging with third countries on JHA issues is to respond to the needs of its citizens'.[5] The EU's attempts to eradicate international crime where it is not so directly affected are few and far between (EU assistance for the fight against Palestinian terrorism is an exception). Fighting international crime is primarily about protecting the EU's fundamental interests and security. The EU has tried to shape its milieu, notably by pressing third countries to adopt its standards and practices in this field, but this milieu goal is a way of achieving what is really a possession goal.

Because of the intricate overlap between fighting international crime within the EU and fighting crime as a foreign policy, section 8.1 traces the evolution of this objective for both internal and external policy. Section 8.2 analyses how the EU defines the three international crimes covered here, and section 8.3 how it pursues the objective vis-à-vis third countries. Section 8.4 evaluates the EU's pursuit of this objective.

8.1 The fight against international crime

International crime clearly needs to be addressed through international cooperation. Numerous UN conventions have been agreed on terrorism and drug trafficking since the 1960s, and the Council of Europe has drafted conventions such as the 1957 European Convention on Extradition and the 1977 European Convention on the Suppression of Terrorism. The fight against illegal immigration is a more recent concern, and less codified at the international level, but individual states have long had their own policies against illegal immigration. The EU was therefore most definitely a latecomer in terms of the fight against international crime. Only with increasing integration – free movement of goods, people, services and capital within the EU – did the member states view cooperation at the EU level as an imperative.[6]

The end of the Cold War in Europe presented EU member states with particular challenges. The post-communist transition in Eastern Europe and the former Soviet Union was accompanied by a rise in domestic and cross-border crime, especially organized crime, although the extent of the rise was frequently exaggerated.[7] Greater cooperation within the EU was justified to counter the perceived threat of Russian and East European criminality spilling into Western Europe over the more open post-Cold War borders.[8] The threat from the former Yugoslavia was seen as even greater. Crime in the former Yugoslavia flourished as a result of the wars, with deleterious effects on political and economic life in the region and on the EU. The region is still considered to be a significant transit route for illegal drugs (mainly heroin from Afghanistan) and for illegal immigrants, including 'trafficked women'.[9]

These developments prompted the strengthening of cooperation within the EU on JHA issues, including incorporating an explicit 'external dimension' into that framework. The 1999–2003 Tampere multiannual programme noted that it is essential that 'the Union should also develop a capacity to act and be regarded as a significant partner on the international scene'.[10] In 2000, the Council responded with a document which is the first development of the 'external dimension of the JHA'.[11] Justice and home affairs issues were to be incorporated into EU external policy on the basis of a cross-pillar approach and cross-pillar measures (relying mostly on first and second pillar instruments). Cooperation with third countries would be developed on migration, organized crime, terrorism, drug-trafficking and other crimes. Europol was instructed to conclude cooperation agreements with third states and international organizations.

Initially, there was only mixed progress in these various areas. However, in response to the terrorist attacks of 11 September 2001 on the USA, there were breakthroughs in fulfilling the Tampere agenda, including agreement on a common definition of 'terrorism', on a European arrest warrant, and on the establishment of Eurojust, a unit to foster coordination among national investigating and prosecuting authorities in relation to serious crime (including terrorism, drug trafficking and human trafficking). The 2003 European Security Strategy named terrorism and organized crime (involved in cross-border trafficking in drugs, weapons, illegal migrants and weapons) as two of the five key threats to European security.

The terrorist attacks in Madrid on 11 March 2004 sparked further agreements, including the establishment of an EU counter-terrorism coordinator. An EU border agency, Frontex, become operational in 2005; it has led patrols to combat illegal immigration off the Canary Islands and in the Mediterranean. The 2004–9 Hague Programme contains does not contain much on the external dimension, but instead requests that a separate strategy be developed.[12] In December 2005, the Council agreed a 'strategy for the external dimension of JHA', which named the key priorities for the EU as addressing the threats of terrorism, organized crime, corruption and drugs and the challenge of managing migration flows.[13] The same month, the European Council approved a counter-terrorism strategy and a global approach to migration. The 2009–13 Stockholm Programme contains a much longer section on the external dimension than the Tampere and Hague programmes did – reflecting the growing importance of cooperation with third countries on JHA issues. External cooperation is to focus on migration and asylum, security (including combating organized crime, terrorism and drugs), information exchange, justice (promoting human rights and good governance, fighting corruption) and civil protection (developing capacities to prevent and respond to catastrophes and terrorist attacks).[14] In 2010, the Council approved an Internal Security Strategy, which aims to protect EU citizens through better crime prevention and response to man-made and natural disasters. The Strategy explicitly recognizes the interdependence between internal and external security, and calls for more international cooperation to combat threats – including by involving 'internal' security bodies in EU crisis management missions in third countries.[15]

But despite the perceived threats and the acknowledged need to cooperate to counter them, cooperation requires the member states to agree on highly sensitive matters, and they are often reluctant to do so.[16] Documents from the Counter-Terrorism Coordinator, for example, repeatedly contain exhortations for the member states to share information with relevant EU agencies (such as Europol).[17] The EU has churned out a bewildering number of ambitious 'strategies', 'comprehensive plans', 'global approaches', 'action plans', and 'action-oriented plans', all listing measures to be taken in the short and medium term within the EU and outside it, but implementing them all is much more of a problem (and a few initiatives are launched and then never referred to again).[18] The European economic crisis has affected the pursuit of this objective as well; for example, Europol's budget went from €84.15 million in 2012 to €75.18 million in 2013.[19] Implementing all the various initiatives is obviously more of a challenge in conditions of austerity.

Coordination and cooperation among all the various institutions involved in the internal and external dimension of JHA are serious challenges, which the Lisbon Treaty has not eased. The necessity for coherence is repeatedly acknowledged. The Council's 2000 report on the external dimension suggested various ways in which JHA matters could be incorporated in foreign policy. Member states' diplomatic missions and Commission delegations in third countries are supposed to be aware of JHA issues. All Council working groups, especially those on relations with particular regions, should cover JHA issues. The member states should cooperate on JHA matters within other international organizations.[20] But there were turf battles between foreign ministries and interior and justice ministries, replicated in the EU: there were separate Council working groups on terrorism in the second and third pillars, and within the Commission, the Directorate-Generals for External Relations and for Justice, Freedom and Security did not always coordinate their activities well.

The Lisbon Treaty simplified the EU, but foreign policy and JHA/internal security matters are still dealt with under two different policy-making frameworks, the former more intergovernmental and the latter more supranational. Although the creation of the EEAS was supposed to help foster more coherent foreign-policy-making, JHA issues (with the exception of counter-terrorism) are notably absent from its organizational structure. The two counter-terrorism working groups are chaired by the presidency (not the EEAS, as is the case for most other working groups under the Foreign Affairs Council) and the lead DG is Home Affairs (it used to be DG External Relations in the old pre-Lisbon Commission).[21] DG Home Affairs deals with matters such as immigration, organized crime and terrorism, and DG Justice with some aspects of the fight against drug trafficking.[22] In addition, there are the various agencies and bodies, including Europol, Eurojust, Frontex, IntCen and the European Monitoring Centre for Drugs and Drug Addiction, as well as the Counter-Terrorism Coordinator, who should cooperate with each other (and the EEAS and the relevant Commission DGs) if foreign-policy-making regarding the fight against international crime is to be coherent. There has also been a struggle for control over the policy agenda between the member states (and the Council) and EU institutions, even though formally there has been a transfer of agenda setting power in the JHA areas from the Council/ European Council to the Commission.[23]

The plea for coherence remains. In a 2010 communication on the Internal Security Strategy, the Commission noted that 'Internal security cannot be achieved in isolation from the rest of the world, and it is therefore important to ensure coherence and complementarity between the internal and external aspects of EU security.' Therefore security (the fight against international crime) should be integrated into strategic partnerships, into dialogue with third countries and regional groupings, and into EU funding.[24] As we have already seen in the cases of the promotion of human rights, democracy, good governance and the prevention of conflict, such coherence is difficult to achieve.

The rest of this section traces the rise of three crimes – terrorism, illegal immigration and illegal drug trafficking – on the EU's crime-fighting agenda. They were all dealt with, to some degree, in the Trevi group and all are listed explicitly in the Maastricht and Amsterdam Treaty JHA provisions, the 1999 Tampere European Council conclusions, the 2003 European Security Strategy, and the 2005 Strategy for the External Dimension of JHA.

Terrorism

Fighting terrorism was the rationale for setting up the Trevi group in 1975, and its first objectives were: cooperation in the fight against terrorism, exchange of information about terrorist groups, and equipment and training of police organizations in anti-terrorist tactics. Trevi's focus was primarily internal, in the sense of fighting terrorism (whatever its provenance) within the territory of the Community, not outside it.

But countering terrorism became a consideration for relations with third countries in the 1980s. The UK, Italy and Germany in particular were hit by terrorists from the Middle East and Mediterranean, and pushed for a collective response from EPC.[25] In 1984, the member states agreed a set of principles on cooperation against international terrorism, including a joint response in the event of a terrorist attack involving the abuse of diplomatic immunity.[26] In January 1986, they agreed to cooperate on the control of persons entering or circulating within the Community (indicating that policy-makers already saw a link between migration policy and international crime), and not to export arms to countries clearly implicated in supporting terrorism.[27] More coercive measures were taken later in 1986, including diplomatic sanctions against Libya and Syria.[28] But the EPC response to Libya was not robust enough for the USA, which launched a punitive air raid on Libya in 1986. The EU's less confrontational approach to Libya and Iran – both accused of sponsoring terrorism – led to disagreements with the USA in the 1980s and 1990s in particular.

The Maastricht Treaty JHA provisions list terrorism as a priority for police cooperation. But sensitivities about national sovereignty still prevented substantial agreements among the member states, much less binding ones. For example, they could not reach an agreement on extraditing alleged terrorists to another member state because there was no agreement on a common definition of terrorism: one state's terrorist was another state's freedom fighter deserving of political asylum. The Amsterdam Treaty, which left cooperation in the fight against international crime largely within the third pillar, did not vastly improve the possibilities for agreement.

In 1998, the Council and Commission declared that there should be intensified police and judicial cooperation against terrorism. The member states should agree a definition of terrorism and minimum penalties, to ensure that the crime received an equivalent response throughout the EU. Europol and the member states were to exchange information on terrorism. Member states should reduce delays in extradition procedures.[29] The 1999 Tampere European Council also called for stepping up cooperation against crime, including terrorism. Joint investigative teams should be set up to combat terrorism, and drug and human trafficking, and information from the member states shared with Europol.[30]

But tackling terrorism only became a higher priority after the 11 September 2001 terrorist attacks on the USA. The European Council held an extraordinary meeting in Brussels on 21 September and agreed an action plan. Many of the measures had already been under discussion within the EU for some time, but proponents could now successfully argue that their adoption was more urgent.[31] Most of the measures are 'internal', in the sense that they deal with the terrorist threat as it manifests itself on EU territory. They are also strikingly cross-pillar:

- agreement on a European arrest warrant and a common definition of terrorism;
- implementation of the entire Tampere action plan as quickly as possible;
- identification of presumed terrorist and terrorist organizations in Europe;
- member states to share with Europol, 'systematically and without delay', information on terrorism;
- Europol to set up a special anti-terrorist team as soon as possible;
- Europol and the relevant US authorities to reach a cooperation agreement;
- implementation of existing international conventions on the fight against terrorism;
- the Council to take urgent measures to end the funding of terrorism and member states to ratify the UN Convention for the Suppression of the Financing of Terrorism;
- the Transport Council to take necessary measures to strengthen air transport security;
- and the General Affairs Council to evaluate the EU's relations with third countries in light of the extent to which those countries support terrorism.[32]

Absent from the plan is the use of military instruments. While some member states participated in the US-led military action in Afghanistan to oust the Taliban and capture al-Qaeda members, the EU's approach was civilian. (Indeed, there is still disagreement over the extent to which CSDP resources should be used to fight terrorists[33] – though more recently, there has been agreement to use civilian and military missions to help third countries combat terrorism, and the first CSDP mission to do so was recently deployed in Niger; see section 8.3.)

There has been some progress in implementing the 2001 action plan. The EU drew up a list of terrorists and terrorist organizations whose financial assets were then frozen, a measure insisted upon by the USA. Many of the terrorists on the list are members of the Basque terrorist group, ETA, and the organizations banned include several based in EU member states (such as the Real IRA, Ulster Freedom Fighters and the Greek Revolutionary Organization

17 November).[34] EU member states were clearly able to take advantage of the 11 September response to promote their particular security interests.

In November 2001, the Council upgraded the money laundering directive to encompass the proceeds of all serious crime including terrorism. On 6 December, Europol set up a specialist anti-terrorist team and signed a cooperation agreement with the USA. The Laeken European Council, 14–15 December 2001, reached political agreement on the arrest warrant and on a common definition of and minimum penalties for terrorism. In July 2002, both measures were formally agreed.[35] The arrest warrant supplants the existing system of extradition between the member states, and means suspects can be handed over to another EU member state on the basis of a single document. The warrant covers terrorism and 31 other serious crimes such as drug trafficking, fraud and trafficking in human beings.[36]

The 2003 European Security Strategy labelled terrorism as a 'growing strategic threat to the whole of Europe', and asserted that 'concerted European action is indispensable'. It called for more coherent and capable EU policy to address the threat. Following the March 2004 Madrid terrorist bombings, the EU issued a declaration on combating terrorism, which implemented the constitutional treaty's solidarity clause, established a counter-terrorism coordinator, and called for a long-term strategy to address all the factors contributing to terrorism.[37]

In December 2005 (following terrorist attacks in London in July 2005), the European Council agreed a Counter-Terrorism Strategy, which is based on four strands: preventing terrorism (addressing the causes of 'radicalization'), protecting citizens and infrastructure (for example, through better border security), pursuing terrorists (disrupting networks, cutting of funding and access to materials, bringing them to justice) and responding to consequences of attacks (improving disaster response capabilities).[38] Periodic reports on implementing the Counter-Terrorism Strategy are prepared by the Counter-Terrorism Coordinator, and group measures according to the four strands. There are clear overlaps also with the Internal Security Strategy (see above).

The member states are still reluctant to cede too much power to the EU level and are unwilling to share intelligence (perhaps out of mistrust of other member states). For example, the Counter-Terrorism Coordinator can do little more than encourage and cajole the member states to act together to fight terrorism. In an interview with the *Financial Times* in March 2005, the then counter-terrorism coordinator, Gijs de Vries, admitted that member states had been slow to implement EU legislation and measures, and were reluctant to swap intelligence and foster police and judicial cooperation.[39] In March 2007, de Vries stepped down after his three-year mandate, and his replacement, Gilles de Kerchove, was nominated only seven months later.[40] Member states prefer to exchange information with each other, or to meet in smaller, more informal groups such as the G6 (France, Germany, Italy, Poland, Spain and the UK).

Terrorism loomed very large in public fears and policy-making in the early 2000s, for obvious reasons. Since then, however, it has become somewhat less of a menace. Europol issues an annual 'Terrorism Situation and Trend Report', which has illustrated a decreasing number of terrorist attacks in EU member states since 2007 (581 in 2007; 174 in 2011).[41] There are still serious concerns about the threat of terrorism emanating from the Arabian peninsula (Yemen) and the Sahel (especially Mali, Niger and Nigeria). But there is now much more focus on the threat of 'home-grown' terrorism (such as resulted in the 2005 London bombings), which has led to more attention to addressing the 'root causes' of such terrorism by countering radicalization (the 'prevent' strand of the counter-terrorism strategy). The internal rather than external dimension of counter-terrorism has become more predominant. There has also been what the counter-terrorism coordinator called 'CT fatigue' – there is much less sense of urgency in counter-terrorism policy.[42]

The EU, like other international actors, links terrorism and other international crimes, notably drug trafficking, money laundering, and illegal immigration. The UN Security Council, in Resolution 1373 (2001) on fighting terrorism, noted 'the close connection between international terrorism and transnational organized crime, illicit drugs, money-laundering illegal arms-trafficking, and illegal movement of nuclear, chemical, biological and other potentially deadly materials' (paragraph 4). Implementing Resolution 1373 requires action in many areas: financial law and practice; customs law and practice; immigration law and practice; extradition law and practice; police and law enforcement work; capacity-building for the judiciary; and the fight against networks related to terrorism (namely illicit drug trafficking).[43]

The EU also links the fight against international terrorism to an even wider agenda. The June 2002 Seville European Council declared that the EU's actions against terrorism would include devoting greater efforts to conflict prevention and to promoting human rights, democracy and arms control.[44] One of the measures that appears on the regular 'action plans' and progress reports is, 'promote good governance, democracy, education and economic prosperity outside the EU'. Eradicating the roots of terrorism by eradicating poverty is also a regular theme in EU declarations.[45] The proclaimed links between all of these objectives are not only not entirely clear, but as we have seen in previous chapters, make it difficult for the EU to set priorities. Furthermore, if for the EU, fighting terrorism really does depend on spreading good governance, democracy, human rights protection and prosperity, then the various weaknesses in EU policies to promote them noted in previous chapters could be a serious impediment to that goal.

Illegal immigration

Although illegal immigration was discussed in the Trevi framework, the member states really only recognized the need for collective action in this area in the early 1990s, when the combined effects of the collapse of communism in Eastern Europe and the Yugoslav wars increased the number of refugees and immigrants arriving in the EU – at a time when border controls between EU member states were disappearing. It is a prominent priority in the Maastricht Treaty, and since the Amsterdam Treaty transition period, Community decision-making rules (including a key role for the European Commission) have applied to the policy area. While terrorism appears to have diminished in terms of its prominence as an EU foreign-policy objective in recent years, the same cannot be said of countering illegal immigration. Certainly this objective has received considerable attention in the wake of the Arab Spring (and the related concerns that turmoil in the southern Mediterranean would result in mass influxes of migrants into Europe) and the eurozone crisis (which resulted in higher unemployment – and therefore pressure to prevent migration to Europe).

Since the 1980s, migration into the EU has been 'securitized': it has been socially constructed as a security question, as a danger to public order, cultural identity and domestic and labour market stability.[46] This has justified implementing more restrictive migration policies. Fighting illegal immigration is often portrayed as the fight against human smuggling and trafficking networks, even though most illegal immigration is due to people staying on after their visas have expired.[47]

Paradoxically, the EU member states have not entirely agreed what *legal* immigration is, although there is a growing body of EU law on admission (including visa policies), residence and integration of immigrants, as well as on minimum standards for determining asylum status and for treating asylum seekers. Essentially, though, 'illegal immigration' is a contravention of *national* immigration law, but the fight against it increasingly takes place at the EU level. As Andrew Geddes argues, the member states are using the EU 'as a mechanism for restricting those forms of migration that their policies define as unwanted'.[48] Because movement within the Schengen area is so free (with no border controls on people), EU member states are particularly concerned to 'harden' the Schengen border. This has led to increasing attention to strengthening border controls, and ensuring that third countries 'manage' (that is, really, 'prevent') migration to the EU.

Since the mid 1990s, the EU has increasingly agreed measures directed at third countries to try to prevent illegal immigration and to force them to take back illegal immigrants found on EU territory. Some measures are quite soft (information campaigns against illegal immigration in transit countries and countries of origin), others are 'harder' (such as the conclusion of re-admission agreements, see section 8.3).

In February 2002, the Council approved a comprehensive plan to combat illegal immigration and trafficking of human beings.[49] The plan includes numerous measures for the short and medium term, including uniform visa standards, consideration of an EU border service, conclusion of re-admission agreements with third countries, and harmonization of laws on illegal employment. The JHA Council in June 2002 asserted that combating illegal immigration and human smuggling and trafficking is a 'priority objective' and must be integrated to a greater extent into the EU's external relations.[50]

At the Seville European Council, 21–2 June 2002, several member states, led by Spain and the UK, called for the EU to make aid to third countries conditional on their efforts to stop migration movements towards the EU and on their willingness to take back illegal immigrants.[51] They appeared to be responding to the popularity of anti-immigrant parties in several recent elections (in Denmark, France and the Netherlands). France and Sweden blocked the use of economic sanctions as too draconian, but re-admission agreements under negotiation were to be concluded as soon as possible, and mandates approved for negotiating agreements with countries already identified by the Council. In 2004, the Council created Frontex, the European border agency, which is to help member states by sharing information on risks, providing training for border personnel, assisting in returning illegal immigrants to their country of origin, and boosting border controls if there is a 'crisis' at an external border (as there was in November 2010 on Greece's border with Turkey). Human rights campaigners argue that Frontex patrols are about turning people away, and that not enough is done to ensure that asylum seekers are not among those seeking entry and that they are not returned to a country where serious human rights violations occur. [52]

In December 2005, the European Council agreed a 'global approach to migration', which in the first instance was focused on Africa and the Mediterranean region, and in 2007, extended to Eastern and South-Eastern Europe.[53] The EU pledged to increase joint patrols and border surveillance to prevent illegal immigration (and loss of life by people trying to get into the EU), enhance its dialogue and cooperation with African and neighbouring countries, expand information campaigns on legal migration opportunities and the risks of illegal immigration, conclude re-admission agreements, and organize joint return flights (with the help of an EU 'Return Fund'). Both global approaches call for 'cheaper and more easily available remittances services' (so that migrants can send money home), but these will have to conform to tighter EU provisions on money-laundering (to combat 'terrorism financing').[54] In 2007, the Commission added the idea to facilitate circular migration by concluding 'mobility partnerships' with certain (cooperative) countries.

In 2011, the Arab Spring prompted what the Commission called a 'migration crisis' and the then Italian Interior Minister described as a looming 'invasion' of refugees from Tunisia, Libya and Egypt. But the Italian minister's prediction of 1.5 million refugees did not come to pass: about 45,000 persons sought refuge in Italy and Malta in the first six months of 2011 (the vast majority of people fleeing conflict and unrest in the southern Mediterranean went to countries of the southern Mediterranean).[55] But the fear of a mass influx of refugees was enough to prompt the French government to impose checks on Schengen visa holders, leading to tensions between Italy and France. The Schengen crisis subsided, but led to reforms of the system (to allow for the temporary reintroduction of internal border controls in crises). For the purposes of this chapter, however, what is significant is that the Arab Spring led to a renewed Global Approach to Migration and Mobility, in which the EU declared it would establish new partnerships (called Dialogues for Migration, Mobility and Security) with southern Mediterranean countries. Significantly, the emphasis continues to be on enforcing border controls (such as developing a European Border Surveillance System termed EUROSUR) and pressing third countries to 'manage' migration vis-à-vis the EU.[56] The EU institution driving this agenda is DG Home, not the EEAS, which is more inclined to place migration within the wider context of overall relations and less concerned only with limiting migration.[57]

The fight against illegal immigration is still tied to a whole host of other objectives, including promoting human rights and democracy, combating poverty and preventing conflict. This again raises the issue of how compatible the EU's objectives are. It also raises the question of whether the underlying motivation for conflict prevention or poverty reduction or the promotion of human rights and democracy is actually control of migration flows. As the 2002 Seville European Council declared, 'closer economic cooperation, trade expansion, development assistance and conflict prevention are all the means of promoting economic prosperity in the countries concerned and thereby reducing the underlying causes of migration flows' (paragraph 33). The emphasis on addressing 'root causes' is typical of the EU's approach to other issues (such as terrorism and violent conflict); whether the EU is capable of addressing *all* of the proposed measures, and ensuring they fit together, is the basic problem. But, as seen in the case of the response to the Arab Spring 'migration crisis', there are institutions (and member states) that have a different perspective, in which controlling/preventing migration is the overriding concern.

Drugs

Like terrorism and illegal immigration, the fight against illegal drug trafficking was discussed within Trevi and listed as a priority for police cooperation in the Maastricht Treaty. Since the early 1990s, it has been increasingly incorporated into the EU's foreign relations, as part of the EU's overall drugs strategy. These are multiannual strategies, endorsed by the European Council; the first covered 1990–94, the most recent covers the 2013–20 period.[58] They are accompanied by 'action plans'. The drugs strategies take a comprehensive approach to reducing the demand for and supply of illicit drugs. They propose action within the EU, against illicit drug cultivation or manufacture, for example. They also propose external action. Drugs concerns are supposed to be taken on board when determining policy priorities vis-à-vis major producing or transit countries.

The current drugs strategy proposes to fight international drug trafficking networks by stepping up police, customs and judicial cooperation within the EU, integrating drug control into development cooperation, and cooperating with third countries and international organizations. With respect to the latter, the EU member states are to adopt common EU positions in various international fora that deal with drugs policy, above all at the UN. The need for a coherent foreign-policy approach is highlighted:

> The EU and its Member States should guarantee the integration of the EU Drugs Strategy and its objectives within the EU's overall foreign-policy framework as part of a comprehensive approach that makes full use of the variety of policies and diplomatic, political and financial instruments at the EU's disposal in a coherent and coordinated manner. The High Representative supported by the EEAS should facilitate this process.[59]

In June 2010, the Council agreed a European Pact to Combat International Drug Trafficking – Disrupting Cocaine and Heroin Routes. This calls for improved internal coordination and cooperation, but also the need to create partnerships with third countries, and to design foreign policies that take into account the 'situation and needs of the source and transit countries'.[60] Action plans have been agreed with third countries to provide a framework for cooperation on fighting drug trafficking with Latin America and the Caribbean, Afghanistan, Central Asian states, Western Balkan states and West African states.

The EU's comprehensive approach to the fight against illegal drug trafficking, based on civilian instruments, puts it at odds with the USA's 'war on drugs', which has involved the use of military force. In Colombia, for example, the USA provides military aid to help end the internal conflict there and to counter drug trafficking.[61]

8.2 How does the EU define international crime?

Under the Amsterdam Treaty, the member states are to agree definitions of particular crimes and how they should be punished. By 2004, the EU had agreed definitions and penalties with respect to terrorism, human trafficking and drug trafficking. The European Commission has been active in proposing common definitions of crimes and the relevant penalties. In doing so, it relies to a large extent on definitions in international conventions.

Reaching agreement on a definition of terrorism did not happen until after 11 September 2001. At the time, only six member states had specific laws or legal instruments concerning terrorism: France, Germany, Italy, Portugal, Spain and the UK (all of whom had direct and tragic experience of terrorism). But numerous international conventions on aspects of terrorism have been agreed, and the European Commission used these to arrive at a common definition.[62] In December 2001, the JHA Council reached agreement on a definition, then formalized in a June 2002 Framework Decision. Over ten years later, this remains the EU's definition of terrorism.

The Council agreed that a 'terrorist act' aims to intimidate a population; unduly compel a government or an international organization to perform or abstain from performing any particular act; or destabilize or destroy the fundamental political, constitutional, economic or social structures of a country or an international organization. It includes:

- attacks upon a person's life which may cause death;
- kidnapping or hostage taking;
- causing extensive destruction to a government or public facility, a transport system, an infrastructure system, a public place or private property;
- seizure of aircraft, ships or other means of public or goods transport;
- manufacture, possession, or use of weapons, explosives, or of nuclear, biological or chemical weapons;
- release of dangerous substances, or interfering with or disrupting the supply of water, power or any other fundamental natural resource;
- threatening to do the above; or
- participating in or directing the activities of a terrorist group.[63]

In the February 2002 comprehensive plan to combat illegal immigration, 'illegal immigration' refers to the general illegal entry and residence of persons in the EU, encompassing those who enter illegally (without the proper documents), and those who enter legally but remain after their visa or work permit expires. Those who enter illegally may do so on their own accord, or be smuggled in by others, or be the victims of traffickers. 'Smuggling' and 'trafficking' of human beings are different criminal activities, as distinguished in the 2001 UN Convention against Transnational Organized Crime and related protocols. Smugglers are paid by would-be immigrants to facilitate their entry into the EU. In late 2001, the JHA Council reached political agreement on a directive defining the facilitation of unauthorized entry, movement and stay, and a Framework Decision on strengthening the penal framework to prevent the facilitation of unauthorized entry and residence. Trafficking involves the intent to exploit a person, independent from the question as to how the victim came to the location where the exploitation takes place.[64] The most appalling cases of trafficking involve women or children brought into the EU for the purposes of prostitution and sexual exploitation. In July 2002, the Council approved a Framework Decision on combating trafficking in human beings, which was replaced by an EU Directive in 2011.[65]

EU agreement was more difficult to reach regarding drug trafficking, because there are quite significant differences in national drug policies, particularly on the personal use of 'soft drugs' (such as cannabis). In May 2001, the Commission proposed a definition of and penalties for illicit drug trafficking. Illicit drug trafficking is 'the act, without authorization, of selling and marketing as well as, for profit, of cultivating, producing, manufacturing, importing, exporting, distributing, offering, transporting or sending or, for the purpose of transferring for profit, of receiving, acquiring and possessing drugs'.[66] 'Drugs' are the substances covered by three UN conventions[67] and a 1997 EU Joint Action on new synthetic drugs. But the JHA Council could not initially agree on penalties for offences involving small quantities of drugs; eventually, in November 2004, it did agree on a Framework Decision laying down minimum penalties.[68]

8.3 How does the EU pursue the objective?

The foreign-policy instruments that the EU uses to fight international crime are primarily financial and technical assistance, international agreements, dialogue, conditionality, and civilian missions.

Aid to fight international crime

Assistance to third countries to fight crime began in the mid 1990s. The money comes mainly from existing aid programmes. In line with the 'root causes' approach, aid to reduce poverty and for sustainable development is considered to contribute to the fight against international crime, and democracy aid bolsters the fight against international crime: consolidated democracies will mean less crime. But the fight against international crime – like the promotion of human rights, democracy and conflict prevention – is also supposed to be mainstreamed into the EU's aid programmes.[69] This, as discussed in previous chapters, is not easy, not least because there are now numerous objectives that are supposed to be mainstreamed into the EU's relations with third countries.

The most significant funding is allocated to the fight against illegal immigration. In 2001, on the recommendation of the Tampere European Council, a special budget line was created, 'cooperation with third countries in the area of migration', to help them 'manage' migration flows (mainly through better border management). The 2001 budget was €10 million; in 2003, this doubled to €20 million.[70] In 2004, this was replaced by a special programme for aid to third countries in the area of migration and asylum: AENEAS. For 2004–6, the total budget was €120 million, quite an increase in funding. In 2007, AENEAS was replaced by a thematic programme on cooperation with countries in areas of migration and asylum. The funding for 2011–13 was €179 million. This aid is to support third countries to better 'manage' migratory flows, which will thus lower migratory pressures on the EU. It goes primarily to countries in the southern Mediterranean, Africa, Eastern Europe and Central Asia (the major areas of origin and transit of migrants to the EU). The money supports activities such as information on legal migration and employment opportunities in the EU, border management to prevent illegal migration, building capacity in security of travel documents, support for reintegration of returnees, and protecting migrants from racism and xenophobia.[71]

But most aid to third countries related to migration issues comes from aid programmes. In December 2005 European Council agreed that up to three per cent of the EU's relevant financial instruments for external action should be allocated to areas related to migration. From 2005 to 2010, €800 million from thematic and geographic funding programmes was spent on various migration-related projects in third countries.[72]

The Global Approach to Migration and Mobility indicates that there are four core priorities for EU assistance (and dialogue) with third countries: facilitating legal migration and mobility; preventing and reducing illegal immigration; promoting international protection (of asylum seekers); maximizing the development impact of migration and mobility.[73] But considering that reducing migratory pressures on the EU remains such a public concern, it is the second priority that is given most attention. The EU wants third countries not only to prevent illegal immigrants from leaving for the EU, but to stop people who are passing through their countries on their way to the EU.

There is no dedicated budget line or programme to help third countries fight terrorism. The Instrument for Stability can fund, in a crisis situation, 'measures to strengthen the capacity of law enforcement and judicial authorities involved in the fight against the illicit trafficking of people, drugs, firearms and explosive materials', and in a stable situation, measures to strengthen the capacity of such authorities to handle also the fight against terrorism and organized crime. And as of 2006, Community aid to the tune of €400 million was provided to 80 countries to help them implement UN Security Council Resolution 1373 on fighting terrorism.[74] The CFSP budget has also been used for the fight against terrorism. In 1997, the EU set up a programme to help the Palestinian Authority counter terrorist activities emanating from the territories under its control. Between 1997 and 2003, €13.6 million was provided for training and assistance to strengthen the Palestinian Authority's organizational and operational capacity for anti-terrorism.[75]

With respect to both the fight against illegal immigration and the fight against terrorism, the Commission proposed for the 2014–20 period that the Home Affairs budget will support two home affairs policies, through an asylum and migration fund and an internal security fund (which will be funded with €6.1 billion, considerably less than the €10.9 billion the Commission suggested)[76]. Significantly, both of these funds will have an 'external dimension' – supporting actions in third countries, 'for example in relation to the resettlement of refugees, implementation of re-admission agreements, regional protection programmes, as well as cooperation with third countries to fight against trafficking of human beings, prevent terrorism and reinforce their external borders'.[77] All of these actions are to be implemented by the Commission in partnership with third countries, and this is all supposed to be fully coherent and complementary to the Union's foreign policy. As already indicated above, this seems to show the intention of DG Home Affairs to be involved more directly in external relations with respect to the fight against terrorism and illegal migration – and therefore the challenge of ensuring that the EU's actions in third countries are coherent will undoubtedly increase.

As for the fight against drug trafficking, by 2000, the Commission was already running programmes in over 100 third countries, with projects ranging from drug abuse treatment, to alternative crop development, customs and police cooperation, and measures to combat money laundering. Priority is given to the 'cocaine trafficking route' in Latin America and the Caribbean, and the 'heroin trafficking route' from Afghanistan.[78] As with terrorism, it is not entirely clear how much the EU spends on fighting drug trafficking, as there is no dedicated fund for this objective.

Agreements

In line with the EU's preference for basing its relations with third countries on legal agreements, the role that such agreements play in its fight against international crime is growing. Increasingly, EU agreements with third countries contain commitments to fight international crime. The association agreements concluded with southern Mediterranean countries and southeast European countries include provisions for cooperation in the fight against money laundering, organized crime (including human trafficking), illicit drugs and terrorism. The Cotonou agreement contains a clause pledging both sides to cooperate in the fight against terrorism, and anti-terrorism clauses have also been included in the association agreement with Chile, and cooperation agreements with Tajikistan, Andean Community and Central America.[79]

The EU and the USA have concluded several agreements on JHA matters. In June 2003, they concluded agreements on mutual assistance in criminal matters (terrorism and other crimes) and extradition (the first ever on third pillar matters). The negotiations sparked considerable criticism from civil liberties groups, fearful that fundamental human rights will be violated, particularly in the practice of extradition.[80] Other agreements include one on ship container security (2004), on terrorist financing (2010), and on passenger name records (2007), this last one generating considerable criticism from MEPs and civil liberties groups over concerns that the data would not be adequately protected by the USA.

Also controversial are re-admission clauses and agreements. At the end of 1995, the Council agreed that re-admission clauses should be included in Community and mixed agreements with third countries, on a case by case basis. The June 2002 Seville European Council then decided that *every* agreement concluded with third countries should include a clause on joint management of migration flows and on compulsory re-admission in the event of illegal immigration. The Commission has argued this will help to strengthen the obligation under international law for countries to re-admit their own nationals.[81] The re-admission clauses generally state that the two parties will cooperate on re-admitting nationals illegally present on the territory of the other party, and (sometimes) that they will conclude a re-admission agreement. As of July 2011, re-admission clauses were in agreements with twenty-seven countries (in Latin America, Asia, the southern Mediterranean, Central Asia, Eastern Europe and south-eastern Europe), the Cotonou agreement, and agreements with the Andean Community and Central America.[82]

The re-admission clause is similar to the human rights clause in that it is supposed to appear in all external agreements; third countries, though, do object to its inclusion and thus far it has not has not been included in every recent agreement. Unlike the human rights clause, the re-admission clause is not an essential element of the agreement, so that contravention of it cannot lead to the suspension or termination of the agreement.

Re-admission agreements go further. In the last decade, many member states have concluded re-admission agreements with third countries. In these, a third country must agree to re-admit not only its own nationals but the nationals of other countries who have transited through its territory on their way to the EU member state. Thus, instead of examining the asylum request themselves, EU member states can expel an asylum-seeker to a 'safe' country of transit. Re-admission agreements place the onus on third countries to control movements of their own and other countries' nationals to the EU. This is an export of EU border controls: third countries have to adapt to an EU member state's standards on controlling the movement of people (as in imposing visa requirements, checking that travel documents have not been forged, controlling ports and other possible points of entry and exit, and so on). Such agreements were concluded between EU member states (particularly Germany and the Scandinavian states) and the CEECs; as a result, the CEECs concluded re-admission agreements with *their* neighbours, thus passing the restrictive policies further along.[83] EU member states now conclude such agreements with a wide variety of countries.

The practice is also replicated at the EU level – and has become a very important priority for the EU. The agreements are so valuable because under them, the EU could deport a larger number of 'illegals' back to third countries, thus contributing to its 'return policy' which ensures 'public support for elements such as legal migration and asylum'.[84]

Since 2004, EU re-admission agreements have been concluded with Hong Kong, Macao, Sri Lanka, Albania, Russia, Ukraine, FYROM, Serbia, Bosnia and Herzegovina, Montenegro, Moldova, Pakistan and Georgia. Several of the ENP action plans (most notably Morocco's) insist that the neighbours must conclude re-admission agreements with the EU as a 'benchmark' which has to be met if relations are to develop.

Re-admission agreements have not been widely welcomed by third countries, as they consider the agreements to be solely in the EU's interest (with considerable justification). The Commission has admitted that it may need to offer incentives to third countries, and the AENEAS programme was designed to do just that.[85] Since December 2005, the EU has also agreed that visa facilitation should go hand-in-hand with re-admission agreement negotiations – thus offering third countries an incentive to negotiate the latter (and disappointment if they do not). Visa facilitation agreements are now routinely concluded with those countries that are also negotiating a re-admission agreement. But there is a hard edge to this policy: countries cannot conclude a visa facilitation agreement without also concluding a re-admission agreement.[86] In a 2011 evaluation of the re-admission agreements, the Commission argued that the incentives offered thus far were still not enough to convince countries such as Morocco, China or Algeria to conclude an agreement. In the case of China and Algeria, member states were refusing to consider a visa facilitation agreement; in the case of Morocco, the financial incentives are also considered insufficient. The Commission thus proposed that third countries be offered a coherent 'mobility package', which would include incentives and the re-admission agreement.[87]

Since 2008, the EU has concluded 'Mobility Partnerships' with five countries: Cape Verde, Moldova, Georgia, Armenia and Morocco. The negotiating partner on the EU side is DG Home Affairs – not the EEAS – and the Commission claims these are political declarations in which the parties agree to cooperate on a variety of issues related to mobility and migration management. Critics, however, detect a harsher approach: essentially, the Mobility Partnerships 'require third countries to adopt European security policy instruments: re-admission agreements with the EU; working arrangements with Frontex; cooperation in joint surveillance operations in the Mediterranean sea; and capacity building in other aspects of integrated border management as the *sine qua non* to access highly provisional "benefits" such as visa facilitation agreements and labour and circular migration schemes, flanked by capacity-building financial measures'.[88]

Dialogue

The fight against international crime, like the other objectives covered in this book, has been increasingly incorporated into the EU's dialogues with third countries. In June 2000, the Council agreed that existing institutional frameworks (provided by association or cooperation agreements) should be used for dialogue with third countries on JHA issues.[89] Multilateral fora such as the Stability Pact for South-eastern Europe, the Euro-Mediterranean process and ASEM discuss JHA issues, as do EU–Africa, EU–Latin America and EU–Western Balkans meetings. The EU also formulates 'action plans' with third countries, which set up a framework for cooperation. For example, the ENP action plans contain extensive provisions and benchmarks on JHA issues. The Belgian presidency complained in late 2001 that the external aspect of JHA was pursued in too many different frameworks, and therefore lacked an integrated, overall approach, but since then it would not appear that the number of frameworks has diminished.[90] As part of the new Global Approach to Migration and Mobility, the Commission (not EEAS) also conducts 'migration missions' to facilitate dialogue and cooperation with third countries – primarily in sub-Saharan Africa and Eastern Europe.[91]

Since the 11 September terrorist attacks, cooperation and dialogue with the USA has intensified. Before, while the fight against international crime was a common objective of transatlantic cooperation (see the 1995 Transatlantic Agenda), the EU had not been willing to open up Council JHA structures to US representatives. Afterwards, the EU member states agreed to associate the USA with Council working groups, Europol, Eurojust and the Police Chiefs Operational Task Force. Several agreements on JHA matters have since been concluded, fostering even deeper dialogue. An agreement between Eurojust and the USA was finalized in 2006.[92]

Russia is also clearly an important partner for the EU in the fight against international crime, because it is seen as a source of criminal activity. The June 1999 Common Strategy on Russia contained two JHA-relevant aspects: (1) cooperation in the fight against organized crime, money laundering, trafficking in human beings, drugs and stolen vehicles, and illegal immigration; and (2) support for judicial and administrative reform, to strengthen the rule of law.[93] In March 2000, the EU and Russia agreed a Plan on Common Action on combating organized crime, to give effect to the Common Strategy provisions. It consists mostly of measures that the EU wants Russia to take: for example, Russian judicial authorities should devote attention to financial crime, human trafficking, arms and drug trafficking, and illegal immigration. The EU member states and Russia will exchange information and intelligence on field of organized crime, and Europol will cooperate with competent Russian federation agencies.

One of the four 'common spaces' which the EU is establishing with Russia covers 'freedom, security and justice'. In addition to the visa facilitation and re-admission agreement discussed above, this 'common space' also includes a 2003 agreement between Europol and Russia on cooperation, a 2006 agreement between Frontex and Russia, and ongoing negotiations between Eurojust and Russia on cooperation.[94]

Conditionality

The EU's most extensive use of conditionality is in relation to candidate countries: they must implement the JHA *acquis* (including the Schengen agreement) before they join the EU. For the CEECs, this was costly, in terms of the additional resources that they have to devote to policing borders and the loss of trade across the borders. The conditions have since become tighter due to concerns that Bulgaria and Romania were admitted into the EU before they had adequately dealt with domestic problems of organized crime. The pressure on candidates does not end with accession: current member states will lift internal border controls with new member states only after the Council decides that they are implementing properly the Schengen *acquis*. Turkey is expected to sign a re-admission agreement before it completes accession negotiations.

Conditionality has also crept into the EU's relations with other countries, although the extent to which it is actually applied varies. The CFSP Common Position on Arms Exports (see Table 7.3) includes the buyer country's 'attitude towards terrorism' as a consideration for export licences. Under the GSP regime, developing countries could be withdrawn from the list of beneficiaries if there are serious shortcomings in customs controls on the export or transit of drugs, or a failure to comply with international conventions on money laundering. But preferences have not yet been withdrawn for these reasons. From 1990 to 2006, a special incentive scheme under the GSP applied to eleven Latin American countries, to support their fight against illicit drug production and trafficking.[95] But it was found to be incompatible with WTO trading rules; instead the new scheme grants preferences to developing countries if they ratify and implement a series of international conventions – including the UN Conventions on Narcotic Drugs, on Psychotropic Substances, and against Illicit Traffic in Narcotic Drugs and Psychotropic Substances.[96]

Third countries' records in the fight against international crime are now coming under scrutiny. The 2001 action plan against terrorism indicates that the Council will systematically evaluate third countries' contribution to combat terrorism, but what action the EU would take if third countries are not cooperative is not made explicit.

Cooperative countries have been rewarded: Tajikistan and Pakistan were rewarded for helping to oust the Taliban regime in Afghanistan, even though neither adequately respects human rights and democratic principles. In late 2001, TACIS aid to Tajikistan was resumed, having been suspended because of violations of human rights and democracy in the country.[97] In October 2001, the EU switched its previous position on Pakistan and agreed to increase EU aid and grant it additional trade preferences (for textiles) under the GSP regime. In November 2001, the EU signed a cooperation agreement with Pakistan – an agreement that had previously been put on hold because of

General Musharraf's coup d'état (see section 6.5). For 2007–13, EU aid to Pakistan was increased substantially.

A preference for engagement over isolation was also evident in relations with Libya before 2011, a state found to have sponsored terrorism. In 1992, the EU implemented UN Security Council sanctions on Libya, imposed because of Libya's involvement in the 1988 bombing of a civilian airliner over Lockerbie, Scotland. Libya was also ostracized, excluded from the Euro-Mediterranean process begun in 1995, but the EU did not follow the USA in banning investment in Libya and vigorously protested the extraterritorial reach of its 1996 Iran–Libya Sanctions Act. Once Libya handed over the suspects in the Lockerbie bombing, the EU was willing to consider opening to it, inviting Libya to be an observer in the Euro-Mediterranean process in 2000. An ad hoc dialogue on migration dialogue was ongoing from 2005, in spite of concerns about human rights and democracy in that country. The 2011 uprising and subsequent war in Libya did not bring a halt to the concerns over migration – indeed not even a year after the Ghaddafi regime had fallen, the EU was evaluating Libya's need for assistance with border management.[98]

In the fight against illegal immigration, the EU seems to increasingly favour more coercive political measures. As seen above, visa facilitation is now conditional on the third country concluding a re-admission agreement with the EU. In June 2002, the JHA Council warned that third countries must prevent the departure or transit of vessels carrying illegal immigrants heading for the EU. Failure to do so without good cause could lead to an 'appropriate early political response'.[99] Later the same month, the Seville European Council warned that '[i]nadequate cooperation by a country could hamper the establishment of closer relations between that country and the Union'. If the Council found that a third country had not cooperated in the joint management of migration flows, it could 'adopt measures or positions under the Common Foreign and Security Policy and other European Union policies, while honouring the Union's contractual commitments and not jeopardizing development cooperation objectives'. ENP benchmarks in the action plans include a willingness to cooperate on JHA issues (including by agreeing to a re-admission agreement), and the development of relations with the EU is supposed to depend on meeting the benchmarks. So far, however, no third country has been singled out for such treatment on the basis of failure to cooperate over migration issues.

Civilian and military missions

The most recent additions to the EU's 'toolbox' in the fight against international crime are principally CSDP civilian and military missions (see Table 3.5). Many of the missions agreed thus far have mandates and objectives that are directly related to international crime. The EU Police Mission (EUPM) in Bosnia and Herzegovina, which operated from 2003 to 2012, was to assist the establishment of a professional police force, which will help fight international crime. It trained local police, and updates operational rules and standards. The mandate for EUFOR Bosnia touches on the fight against organized crime (in so far as this is part of the Stabilization and Association Process). The two police missions in FYROM (EUPOL Proxima and EUPAT) were to help Macedonian authorities consolidate law and order including fighting against organized crime. EUBAM Moldova/Ukraine is explicitly directed against trafficking in arms, people and drugs (which have been fostered by authorities in the renegade Transnistria region). EUJUST Themis supported the reform of Georgia's criminal justice sector. The EU mission in Kosovo is a rule of law mission, with the fight against organized crime as a priority. EUPOL COPPS in the Palestinian Territories is to help the Palestinian police fight against terrorists. EUPOL Afghanistan is to help police reform, which should help combat, among other things, drug trafficking. EUJUST LEX in Iraq is to train officials in criminal investigation.

Most recently, the EU has responded to the crisis in the Sahel with three CSDP missions. In 2012, a civilian mission to Niger was launched to support and train forces there to help combat terrorism and organized crime. In 2013, a military mission was sent to Mali to train and advise armed forces to help 'neutralize' organized crime and terrorist threats (that is, Al-Qaeda, involved in fighting in northern Mali in 2012).[100] In May 2013, the Council approved a border assistance mission to Libya (EUBAM Libya), to help the country strengthen its borders and fight organized crime and terrorism, primarily through training and advice. This is not only related to migration from Libya to the EU, but more significantly, the extent to which armed groups and arms have crossed Libya's land borders (arms from a chaotic Libya were used in the rebellion in Mali).[101]

Most of these missions are quite small (a drop in the ocean in a place like Afghanistan), and of short duration. They depend on the agreement of the host state – usually not an issue, though FYROM objected to the extension of the EU police mission because it felt it would jeopardize its chances of opening membership negotiations with the EU.[102] In the case of Bosnia and Herzegovina, the mission was criticized for being weak and premature: it was to monitor and mentor the Bosnian police, but when EUPM was deployed, there were three very divided police forces (Bosniak, Croat and Serb) so much more fundamental reform was needed.[103]

Nonetheless, the deployment of such civilian and military missions could potentially increase the EU's ability to fight international crime, if only because of the material help they can give third countries. However, they are being deployed to fight what *the EU* sees as the biggest problems in terms of the fight against international crime, and not necessarily what people in the targeted countries may view as their biggest problems. For example, the European Security Strategy (p. 6) states: 'Restoring good government to the Balkans, fostering democracy and enabling the authorities there to tackle organized crime is one of the most effective ways of dealing with organized crime within the EU.' But as Felix Berenskoetter points out, in the case of Bosnia and Herzegovina, it is not clear that Bosnians agree that their greatest problem is organized crime; in fact, there is still a lack of public trust in the police there, given that they were often involved in ethnic cleansing.[104]

8.4 Evaluation

The external dimension of JHA is still evolving, and effective and coherent policy-making mechanisms in this area are still being developed. But a few broad trends seem apparent. Firstly, the EU is increasingly willing to use both carrots and sticks to pursue the objective of fighting international crime. While there is still a preference for using positive incentives and engagement, the 'power bloc' image seems to fit best. The EU's approach is still civilian, which distinguishes it from the US approach to fighting terrorism and drugs, in which the use of military instruments is prominent.

Secondly, the EU makes links not just between terrorism, illegal immigration and drug trafficking, but also between fighting international crime and the wider agenda of promoting equitable and sustainable development, poverty reduction, the rule of law, democracy and conflict prevention. Again, the underlying assumption is that these objectives are all compatible, and will easily reinforce each other. Yet there are clearly potential, and actual, contradictions in policies that link the objectives but do not explicitly set priorities among them. Which comes first, preventing conflict or preventing illegal immigration or fostering the protection of human rights? Will countries that enforce border controls well (which could conceivably involve heavy police and military action) but do not have a good human rights record still be given additional aid and other benefits from the EU? We have already seen that countries considered to be crucial in the fight against terrorism (namely Pakistan) have been granted benefits even though their poor democratic records previously excluded them from benefits. The prevalence of such security considerations seem to indicate that the fight against international crime is actually one of the EU's highest priorities. Realists would certainly argue that it should be, as states – or conglomerations of states – are concerned above all about their security and the fight against international crime (including illegal immigration) is a security strategy.

Thirdly, the implications of the JHA agenda for the EU's place in the world are large. There is, as Jörg Monar points out, a strong dynamic of inclusion and exclusion in JHA cooperation. The EU has created a dichotomy between a 'safe inside' and an 'unsafe outside'.[105] As Jan Zielonka argues, hardening borders is not the most effective way to combat international crime (in fact, hard borders create a demand for illegal activities, as people try to circumvent them), but the trend is still towards hardening the EU's external border.[106] As discussed in Chapter 4, the EU has tried to lessen the potential for tensions between 'ins' and 'outs' by encouraging cross-border cooperation. This is incompatible with a hard EU border. A hard border also contradicts trends towards greater interdependence, as well as the rationale for the creation of the EU itself.

Conclusion

The foreign-policy objective of the fight against international crime did not arise first from within the EU: other international organizations and the member states themselves had long been involved in this area before the EU was. But the external aspects of the fight against international crime have 'spilled over' from the internal development of the JHA agenda. As borders lose meaning within the EU, protecting the EU's external border has become more important.

The role of external events in pushing the member states to cooperate on the external aspects of JHA is also very significant. The collapse of communism in Eastern Europe, the terrorist attacks of 11 September 2001, the arrival of asylum seekers and would-be immigrants from places far and near, have all contributed to the perceptions that the EU's security – and that of the member states – must be protected through cooperation at the EU level. Crime is a security threat. Public opinion feeds into this: fears of terrorism, of foreign mafias, of immigrants (both illegal and legal) prompt responses from governments and more cooperation at the EU level. But the factors creating a demand for more EU cooperation do not translate smoothly or easily into actual cooperation: national sensitivities about sovereignty and autonomy in this field, and the familiar challenges of cross-pillar coordination, can work to impede the negotiation and implementation of EU-level measures.

In pursuing this objective, the EU has increasingly been drawn to coercive measures, following examples set by the member states and other international actors (notably the USA). Concluding a re-admission agreement with the EU is fast becoming a condition for many countries. Its approach is largely civilian, however, though military forces may be used to help train security forces in third countries. And there is still a lingering preference for legal instruments, for positive incentives, for adopting to standards set at the international level (in UN conventions, for example). External agreements now contain clauses on fighting terrorism, illegal immigration and drug trafficking, but these are not essential elements of the agreements. Dialogue too is important – the fight against international crime is one more item for discussion in institutionalized dialogues. The EU's pursuit of this objective thus retains unique elements.

Questions for discussion

1. Analyse the limits to EU 'integration' in the field of fighting international crime.

2. Does the fight against terrorism and illegal immigration trump the other foreign-policy objectives considered in this book?

3. Consider the instruments that the EU uses to try to prevent or reduce international crime: which do you think are most effective?

Suggestions for further reading

Bossong, Raphael. 'The Action Plan on Countering Terrorism: A Flawed Instrument of EU Security Governance', *Journal of Common Market Studies*, 46, 1 (2008).

Carrera, Sergio, Joanna Parkin and Leonhard den Hertog, 'EU Migration Policy after the Arab Spring: The Pitfalls of Home Affairs Diplomacy', Notre Europe/CEPS Policy Paper 74, 26 February 2013.

Coolsaet, Rik. 'EU Counterterrorism Strategy: Value Added or Chimera', *International Affairs*, 86, 4 (2010).

Monar, Jörg. 'The Dynamics of Justice and Home Affairs: Laboratories, Driving Factors and Costs', *Journal of Common Market Studies*, 39, 4 (2001).

CHAPTER NINE

Conclusion

This book has analysed why and how the EU pursues five particular foreign-policy objectives: the promotion of regional cooperation; the promotion of human rights; the promotion of democracy and good governance; the prevention of violent conflict; and the fight against international crime. Two guiding questions were posed at the outset: is the EU's pursuit of these objectives the result of internal, and therefore unique, dynamics; and how unique are the methods and instruments used by the EU to try to achieve the objectives? The first section of this chapter sums up the answers to those questions. Section 9.2 then considers how committed the EU really is to pursuing these five objectives, while the last section opens up a discussion on the effectiveness of the EU's policies to pursue these objectives.

9.1 How unique an international actor is the EU?

An easy stab at answering the first question posed would be to consider whether the member states would pursue these objectives if the EU did not exist. Certainly most, if perhaps not all, of the member states do pursue at least four of the five objectives outside the EU context, though with considerably varying degrees of enthusiasm. The promotion of human rights, the promotion of democracy and good governance, the prevention of violent conflict, and the fight against international crime all generally appear on the national foreign-policy agendas of the member states. Such goals are shared by the member states, as well as numerous other actors, and have been promoted especially since the end of the Cold War. The encouragement of regional cooperation is the exception, where the EU has the comparative advantage, though other international actors also promote regional cooperation, albeit to a lesser extent. But strictly in terms of its choices of foreign-policy objectives, the EU does not appear to be such a unique international actor: its objectives are less the product of unique internal dynamics or its 'constitutive values', and more a reflection of the global zeitgeist.

The adoption by the EU of most of the foreign-policy objectives considered here followed international developments and/or came as the result of a push from particular member states (and sometimes other actors such as the EP or European Commission) already committed to the objectives. The EU has, for the most part, been responding to 'normative globalization' or reacting to the problems thrown up by interdependence, not to specific demands from external actors. However, although the decisions to adopt these particular foreign-policy objectives do not by and large derive from any constitutive values of the EU, the objectives do seem to be considered important elements of the kind of collective identity the EU member states wish to project.

A striking aspect of the selection and articulation of the objectives is that the smaller member states have often been at the forefront, pushing for them, and that the EU institutions often add input. At this stage of the policy process, then, a directoire of the large states is not dictating the EU's foreign policy.

For example, the European Parliament and member states such as the Netherlands pushed for an external human rights policy, and the events in Central and Eastern Europe helped to convince other member states and the European Commission of the merits of pursuing a policy based on conditionality (especially as protection of human rights in the former communist world was seen to enhance the European security environment). The EU's adoption of the democracy and good governance objective followed on from the spread of democracy throughout the world, and from the consensus – developed in the international donor community – that democracy and good governance were good for development, as well as the acceptance by policy-makers of the democratic peace proposition. In both the case of human rights and that of democracy and good governance, there is an internal/external policy gap; the lack of a strong internal human rights regime and the democratic deficit indicate that the EU is not projecting its 'founding values' to the international arena.

Conflict prevention was becoming a general concern for many actors (EU member states as well as outsiders) when the EU also adopted it, although the EU's history and experiences mean it can make a unique contribution to the field. The member states agreed to pursue the fight against international crime at the EU level only in response to both worrying external developments and increasing European integration. Cooperation at the EU level was seen to be imperative if the EU was to provide an area of security for its citizens, and cooperation had to extend to relations with third countries if the objective of fighting international crime was to be addressed at all adequately. The encouragement of regional cooperation is the exception here: from the 1960s, various national and Community actors have pushed for the Community (then Union) to support promising regional groupings, based on their own experiences of regional integration within the EU. Support for regional cooperation is a policy largely (and rather logically) carried out at the EU level.

As discussed in the chapters, member states have pushed for the EU to adopt these objectives for a number of 'self-interested' and 'altruistic' reasons. Considerations of national (and EU-wide) security and economic interests

– and appreciation of the benefits of the politics of scale – have prompted support for the EU's pursuit of the objectives; this is especially evident with conflict prevention and the fight against international crime, but is apparent with respect to the other objectives as well. As seen repeatedly in this book, a belief in the interconnections between human rights, democracy, good governance, the fight against international crime, regional cooperation, conflict prevention, sustainable development and prosperity pervades the EU's foreign policy.

In a more ideational vein, the pursuit of these objectives also feeds into perceptions of the EU's international identity, that is, the identity the EU (and its member states) would like to project. With respect to the promotion of human rights, and of democracy and good governance, there is a clear view that the EU must pursue such objectives: Europe is a region populated by democracies with strong human rights traditions, therefore collective foreign policies must reflect such values. There is also a clear awareness that the EU has a distinct comparative advantage in its pursuit of two other objectives: it has a unique legacy of conflict prevention and regional cooperation to share with others. By positioning itself as a uniquely legitimate and credible actor in such fields, it stands out in the crowd, boosting its own actorness. It is no surprise then that the EU institutions have been active in the policies to promote regional cooperation and prevent conflict.

With respect to four of the five objectives, there is also a strong strain of 'altruism': a belief that promoting regional cooperation, human rights, democracy and good governance, and preventing conflict is beneficial primarily for the people who are the objects of such policies. That belief is fuelled not just by a liberal internationalist outlook shared widely by numerous international actors (the UN, the OSCE, and so on), but also by the European experience: Europe has been peaceful and prosperous because of integration, the spread of democracy, robust human rights protection; this model can and should be spread elsewhere. The fight against international crime is a different case, because the EU concentrates mostly (though not exclusively) on fighting the effects of international crime on the EU itself.

However, just because the EU is motivated to adopt the objectives, it does not follow automatically that effective, coherent and consistent policies to pursue them will be agreed and implemented (see below). The reasons above just explain why the objectives are EU foreign-policy objectives in the first place.

So if the choice of these foreign-policy objectives does not greatly distinguish the EU from other international actors, is the way in which it pursues them more unique? Here the case for a *sui generis* identity is much stronger, for two reasons. Firstly, many policy instruments that the EU uses are distinctive: legal agreements with other actors, support for international agreements and conventions, institutionalized dialogue, the conditional promise of EU membership. A few of these could only be wielded by the EU, not by member states (the offer of EU membership, bloc-to-bloc agreements and regional dialogue, for example). The EU's preferred policy instruments also distinguish it from other major international actors, notably the USA. Other international organizations cannot employ as wide a range of instruments as the EU can. The EU is also developing an expertise in 'civilian crisis management' which is rapidly becoming one of the crucial foreign-policy skills desired even by the USA and NATO; but the UN in particular was in this business long before the EU, and the EU's approach does not differ greatly from the UN's.

Secondly, the EU tends to rely on persuasion and incentives rather than coercion, although non-violent coercion is used as well – especially in the (inconsistent) application of negative measures (and in this respect, the EU and other international actors behave similarly). However, conditionality, it should be stressed, is usually supposed to be applied in accordance with legal rules, such as the human rights clause. The preference for incentives is present even in the EU's fight against international crime, though the EU has taken a much more assertive stance in its demands on third countries over illegal immigration in particular (where the power bloc image certainly seems to fit). The fundamental problem, of course, is that the EU is not very good at delivering incentives that it has promised, or at least delivering them quickly, and those incentives may not be adequate for the job they are supposed to do.

To a great extent the reluctance to use coercion reflects the difficulties of trying to reach agreement among the member states. The imposition of negative measures generally requires unanimity, so the logic of diversity can block collective agreement. While in some situations, there may be reluctance to use negative measures because of (quite understandable and appropriate) doubts about their utility and effectiveness, in many others, member states block the use of negative measures because they are protecting national interests. The imperatives of compromise thus tend to rule out coercion (and certainly the consistent use of it); persuasion becomes the easier option to pursue.

To sum up then, the EU may not be so unique in its choice of foreign-policy objectives, but the way it pursues them does distinguish it from other international actors who are pursuing similar objectives. What it does is less unique than how it does it. Dialogue and institutionalized cooperation are fundamental, though this can often be the result of disagreements among the member states to do more. For some, this is deplorable as it means the USA has to confront nefarious characters and deal with military threats. For others, the EU's preference for dialogue and cooperation is admirable. In the course of a century Europe went from being war-torn, and half of it smothered by communism for several decades, to being, for the most part, a 'Kantian paradise'; surely that is progress in international politics, as the 2012 Nobel Peace Prize committee affirmed. But no wonder there is a debate about the

EU's international identity, about its role in international relations – is the EU a distinctive civilian power, an occasional (though inconsistent) power bloc, a hybrid of civilian power and power bloc, or a flop, an appeaser, an irrelevance? At times it may look as though the first category fits; at others, the second and third may fit best; while those with a dim view of the effectiveness of all of them, prefer the last category.

9.2 How important are the objectives for the EU?

The pursuit of all five objectives has clearly become a significant facet of the EU's international identity – as the repeated proclamations that the EU is in the business of pursuing them illustrate. The rhetorical commitment to all of them is reiterated again and again, creating expectations that the EU will act – among insiders and outsiders. But how serious is the EU about trying to achieve them, *really*?

How many sacrifices, as Wolfers puts it, does the EU make to achieve these foreign-policy objectives? Certainly the amount of money, as a whole and as a percentage of the EU's budget, that it spends on pursuing the objectives is not that large – and as can be seen in Table 3.2, maintaining funding for external programmes in an austere economic environment is difficult. Furthermore, most of the EU's aid budget usually goes to traditional development activities – and the extent to which achievement of the policy objectives is incorporated into these activities is variable. The diplomatic and institutional resources devoted to pursuing the objectives are more significant, judging from the number of agreements it negotiates or concludes with third countries and regional groupings, the growing number of civilian and military missions launched (though they tend to be small and short-term), and the innumerable action plans and strategies approved.

Yet time and again, we have seen that where national economic and strategic interests came into play, the EU could not implement consistent policies: it says one thing in one case, and another thing in a similar case; it cannot maintain positions over time, even where conditions 'on the ground' have not improved; it implements sanctions here but not there (in similar situations); it grants incentives here but not there (in similar situations). Decisions are often lowest common denominator compromises, and can be later watered down, or reversed, or implemented patchily, or even contravened by individual member states. While flexibility in policy-making can be a virtue, the extent of the inconsistencies are a sign that the EU and its member states are simply not *that* committed to making sacrifices for common policies – particularly to pursue the milieu goals. It is impossible to drop them (especially if they are seen as important elements of a collective identity), but the EU member states do not often sacrifice key interests to pursue the milieu goals through the EU. The logic of diversity blocks EU action, and member states' material interests can prevail over the longer-term agenda of promoting human rights, democracy, and regional cooperation, and preventing conflict. Perhaps surprisingly, even where the EU's objective is more of a possession goal – the fight against international crime – the member states have resisted sharing information or building strong collective institutions (for example, the counter-terrorism coordinator) to pursue it.

Since the second edition of this book was published, a number of trends regarding the foreign-policy objectives can be discerned. Firstly, the promotion of regional cooperation remains important, but it is muted by a parallel, separate process of engaging bilaterally with third countries, in strategic partnerships above all. This reflects the prevalence of material interests (especially in free trade areas with key trading partners) compared to the more idealistic promotion of regional cooperation. Secondly, there have been serious efforts made to try to improve the coherence of the EU's human rights and democracy promotion policies – with results yet to be discerned. Nonetheless, these efforts to overcome the challenges of coherence and coordination are noteworthy. Thirdly, crisis management continues to crowd out conflict prevention, though here again some efforts have been made to try to boost the resources and attention given to conflict prevention. Fourthly, concerns about the threat of terrorism have subsided, draining urgency from the need for coherence in the fight against terrorism, while the perceived threats from illegal migration continue to drive ever more activity at EU level to try to combat it.

These five objectives are not necessarily compatible with each other, not to mention with other policy objectives. Regional cooperation, human rights, democracy and good governance, conflict prevention, international crime – along with environmental policy, economic policy, energy policy, and so on – are all supposed to be 'mainstreamed' throughout the EU's relations, in its aid programmes, in its dialogues, in legal agreements. The fact that the EU also continually notes that mainstreaming is not complete is surely an indication of how difficult it is to do. But there is a deeper issue as well, in that coherent foreign-policy-making requires good internal communication and coordination, and this book has illustrated that the perennial challenge of ensuring coherence in the EU's external policies has not (yet) been resolved, despite the Lisbon Treaty reforms. The EU's foreign-policy-making system remains very complex (with the added issue that it has been undergoing considerable change), and turf wars have not disappeared. Indeed, although the aim of the Lisbon Treaty was in fact to allow for more coherent foreign-policy-making (through the EEAS and the 'double-hatted' High Representative), evidence that this is not happening is abundant. Particularly striking is the fact that trade policy, migration policy, development policy, and 'traditional' foreign policy seem to be on different (perhaps not even parallel) 'tracks'. The EU is pursuing free trade agreements with key economic partners and strategic partnerships with a partially overlapping but different set of 'powers'; migration policy is driven by different dynamics which complicate the inclusion of migration in a comprehensive relationship with third countries; and the making of development policy is complicated by rivalry between the EEAS and DG DEVCO. Commentators and observers have made recommendations on how the foreign-policy-making machinery could be better coordinated, and reforms may be made to enable this in the next few years. But for now, obstacles to better coordination have prevented more coherent policy-making.

The logic of diversity also prevents the prioritizing of objectives, which makes long-term coherent strategies to pursue them virtually impossible: short-term considerations can easily prevail. The EU's capabilities are not infinitely expandable, and hard decisions have to be made about where to devote funding and resources. Yet setting priorities is not a strong point of the complex EU foreign-policy-making system. As Sven Biscop has argued,

> For in the absence of clear priorities, the EU rarely takes to the initiative on the key foreign-policy issues of the moment (contrary to the other great powers) or, when it does, its initiatives tend to be fragmented and stove-piped. Consequently, it is not very successful in prevention, despite its rhetoric, and to which it has not been able to prevent, it tends to react late. Furthermore, the allocation of the means bears no relation to any prioritization of objectives.[1]

This is not to diminish the significant fact that the EU is still pursuing milieu goals – the member states did not have to agree to pursue them in the first place, nor to their continued prominence in the EU's foreign relations. At some level – which is not wholly superficial – they are important for the EU and its member states, or money and time would not be spent at all trying to pursue them. But there is quite a large gap between rhetoric and practice, a gap which is damaging the EU's credibility in international relations. Member state priorities and interests often differ, and reconciling these is decidedly difficult.

9.3 How effective an international actor is the EU?

One large issue that this book does not cover in great depth, due to a lack of space, is how effective the EU has been in actually achieving the objectives. Certainly the EU is not without influence, especially vis-à-vis its European neighbours (and would-be EU member states) and countries highly dependent on it for trade and/or aid. And admittedly attributing 'success' (difficult to measure in any event) to the EU, rather than, say, to domestic actors or other international actors or beneficial international developments or just plain luck, is largely an exercise in supposition in the absence of detailed case studies. If the EU's policy is not effective – as in encouraging democracy and human rights in a host of countries around the world – the 'fault' does not necessarily lie with the EU. It is very difficult to force third countries to do something that they patently do not want to do.

However, a few broad-brush conclusions about the EU's effectiveness – and potential effectiveness – are offered here, to stimulate debate and hopefully further research. The first is that we must surely question the extent to which the EU can be effective at all if the member states and institutions can find it so difficult to agree and then maintain any unity achieved. 'Presence' and the radiating effects of the EU's soft power (the attraction of its model) may make a difference in international relations (perhaps only in the long run), but if the EU wants to achieve certain outcomes (as it repeatedly proclaims it does), then actorness becomes critical. The inconsistencies of EU policies, the lack of agreement to devote more resources to the pursuit of particular policies (and to external relations in general), and the sometimes contradictory messages sent by different EU actors (as well as the internal coordination problem) do not give the impression of a unified international actor that can expect to be effective. This is a perennial problem, though the continuous institutional tinkering undertaken is a sign that there is some agreement to try to tackle it.

Secondly, effectiveness is strongly related to the EU's image in the 'eyes of others'.[2] The EU's influence could arguably be strengthened if its pursuit of foreign-policy objectives was better legitimized: the EU should do as it wishes others to do. The EU model of regional integration and conflict prevention is an asset that grants the EU considerable influence. But the lack of a strong internal human rights regime, the lack of international accountability in the area of human rights, and the democratic deficit cast doubt on the EU's legitimacy in these areas. Although the EU can refer to universal values and global trends to justify its promotion of human rights and democracy, it will always be susceptible to charges of double standards, which eat away at the EU's potential influence. This is in addition to the effects of the euro crisis on the EU's standing in international affairs: the repeated failures to resolve it dented the EU's credibility, in particular because third countries were negatively affected.[3] Furthermore, there are plenty of other actors 'out there' offering different perspectives and enticing resources. Pursuing milieu goals is difficult in this environment. With alternative sources of financial assistance, the relationship between the EU and non-Western countries is less asymmetrical, for a start. But although the EU uses the language of partnership in its relations with many third countries, it still requires them to accept EU rules and norms. This can prompt resistance. The EU's attractiveness, which made it the cornerstone of European order in the post-Cold War world, has declined.[4] Because the EU repeatedly, sometimes loudly, declares that it *is* trying to effect change, to achieve its objectives, its internal and external legitimacy could suffer it it does not adjust its policies to accommodate the changing world, and thus stand a chance of exercising influence.

Pinning a single international identity on the EU is, as we have seen, not easy: sometimes it appears to be a civilian power, using persuasion to pursue milieu goals; other times, it looks like a power bloc, seeking to protect and promote its geopolitical and economic interests; occasionally the hybrid of civilian power and power bloc may also fit. But the EU also flirts dangerously with failure and irrelevance. Fundamentally the problem remains that of reaching and maintaining agreement on objectives and on the means to be used to try to reach them: the underlying tensions between a desire to preserve national prerogatives in foreign relations and a desire to project a collective international identity persist. The EU is in a bind: external effectiveness will make it a more attractive focus for the member states, but to achieve this, the member states must first agree to strengthen the system and the resulting foreign policies. A more multipolar world, in which fulfilling preferences and protecting interests are more challenging, could foster an appreciation of the benefits of strengthening EU actorness in foreign policy, but the general decline in public support for the EU and some of the recent debates in member states (with open discussion of leaving the EU in the UK, for example) do not augur well for this – yet.

Negative Measures Imposed by the EU for Violations of Human Rights and Democratic Principles 1988–2013

Country	Use of human rights clause to suspend development cooperation/ aid?	Action Taken	Reason
ACP Countries			
Burundi	No	1993–4: aid suspended. 1997–8: no new programmes launched, except to support peace process. Cooperation then gradually resumed.	1993 and 1997: coup d'état; security situation.
Central African Republic	1996: no; 2003: yes	1996–97: aid suspended. From 2003: macro-economic aid suspended. 2005: cooperation resumed.	Violations of human rights and democracy; security concerns (1996); coup d'état (2003).
Comoros	1995: no; 1999: yes	1995: cooperation slowed until 1996 elections. 1999: consultations; ongoing programmes continue, new programmes implemented only gradually. 2002: relations normalized.	Coup d'état (1995 and 1999).
Congo	No	1997–2002: full suspension of development cooperation.	Security situation and human rights abuses.
Democratic Republic of Congo (formerly Zaire)	No	From 1992: cooperation suspended (aid in 1994 for Rwandan refugees); aid gradually resumed in 1997.	Setbacks in democratization process.

Continued

Country	Use of human rights clause to suspend development cooperation/ aid?	Action Taken	Reason
Equatorial Guinea	No	Since 1992: no new cooperation operation implemented (*ad hoc* decision). 1997: gradual resumption depending on progress.	Violations of human rights and democracy.
Ethiopia	No	2005–6: budget support frozen.	Violations of democracy, human rights.
Fiji	2000 and 2007: yes	2000: consultations; cooperation suspended. 2003: cooperation resumed. From 2007: development aid redirected to NGOs, cancellation of allocations for sugar imports.	Coup d'état (2000 and 2007).
The Gambia	No	1994: cooperation maintained only if meets basic needs. Since 1997: aid resumed gradually following transition to democratic civilian rule.	Coup d'état.
Guinea	Yes	2004: consultations; 2005: aid redirected to political projects. 2009: more consultations; suspension of ongoing projects; travel bans; assets freeze; arms embargo. December 2012: aid resumed after transition to democracy commences; other measures still in place.	Worsening of democratic climate; coup d'état in 2008; violent crackdown on protesters in 2009.
Guinea-Bissau	Yes	1999: consultations; 2003: consultations. No negative measures adopted either time. 2011: suspension of development cooperation in certain sectors; 2012: assets freeze and travel bans.	Interruption of democratization process (1999); coup d'état (2003); mutiny (2010); coup d'état (2012).
Haiti	1991 and 1997: no; 2000: yes	1991: cooperation suspended (*ad hoc* measure). 1994: cooperation resumed following elections. 1997: cooperation slowdown. 2000: consultations; suspension of budget aid and new aid, aid redirected to democracy projects. 2005: negative measures lifted.	Coup d'état (1991); lack of political agreement (1997); lack of respect for democratic principles (2000).

Country	Use of human rights clause to suspend development cooperation/ aid?	Action Taken	Reason
Ivory Coast	2000 and 2001: yes; 2010: no	2000: consultations; ongoing programmes continue, new aid directed to political reform programmes. 2001: consultations; new aid directed to political projects. 2002: relations normalized. Since 2004: asset freeze for certain individuals threatening peace and ban on exports of equipment for internal repression. Since 2006: restrictions on admission of certain individuals, arms embargo. December 2010: assets freeze and visa bans on individuals and companies; some sanctions lifted from April 2011; some remain in place.	Violations of human rights and democracy (coup d'état, 1999), civil war; 2011: incumbent president initially refused to cede power to election winner.
Kenya	No	1991: aid suspended (*ad hoc* measure). 1996: aid resumed slowly.	Lack of progress in political field.
Liberia	1990: no; 2001 and 2003: yes	1990: only humanitarian aid provided until 1994 (*ad hoc* decision). 2001: consultations; ongoing projects continue but new projects linked to political progress; arms embargo imposed. 2003: current projects continue with some aid directed to peacekeeping; new aid linked to peace agreement. Since 2006: arms embargo, diamond embargo, assets freeze and travel restrictions on certain persons. 2007: diamond embargo lifted.	Violations of human rights and democratic principles, corruption; civil war.
Madagascar	Yes	Since 2010: budget aid suspended; no aid through government.	Coup d'état.
Malawi	No	1992: aid freeze (*ad hoc* measure); aid resumed after 1993 referendum.	No progress in political field.

Continued

Country	Use of human rights clause to suspend development cooperation/ aid?	Action Taken	Reason
Mali	No	2012: no aid to government, only support for local population; 2013: aid resumed.	Coup d'état.
Mauritania	Yes	2005: consultations; redirection of funds to political projects. 2009: ongoing projects suspended; 2010: cooperation gradually resumed.	Coups d'état (2005 and 2008).
Mozambique	No	2009: 'donor strike' – budget support frozen; 2010: support resumed.	Lack of progress re governance, democracy.
Niger	Yes	January 1996: aid suspended for 6 months; 1999: consultations; ongoing programmes continued, new programmes opened gradually. 2010: cooperation suspended; 2011: cooperation resumed after constitutional order restored.	Coup d'état (1996, 1999, 2010).
Nigeria	No	1993: new aid programmes reviewed on case-by-case basis and some diplomatic sanctions. 1995: cooperation suspended and diplomatic sanctions imposed. 1998–99: cooperation resumed and sanctions lifted with return to civilian democratic rule.	Lack of democracy; execution of Ken Saro-Wiwa.
Rwanda	No	1994: aid suspended fully. 1998: aid resumed gradually.	Genocide, human rights abuses, security situation.
Sierra Leone	No	1997: existing aid programmes discontinued. 1998: arms embargo and restrictions of admission for members of former junta. 2000–2: import ban on diamonds. Since 2002: relations gradually normalized.	Coup d'état; civil war.
Somalia	No	Since 1990: *de facto* aid suspension; mid 2000s: aid resumes.	Civil war; violations of human rights.

Country	Use of human rights clause to suspend development cooperation/ aid?	Action Taken	Reason
Sudan	No	Since 1990: new aid projects suspended (*ad hoc* measure). Since 1994, arms embargo. 2002: normalization process launched, 2005: relations normalized. Since 2005: restrictions on admission and assts freeze of certain persons.	Civil war; terrorism; violations of human rights and democratic principles.
Togo	1992: no; 1998 and 2004: yes	1993: new programmes frozen (*ad hoc* measure). 1998: aid suspension confirmed after consultations. 2004: aid still suspended after consultations. 2007: EU resumes cooperation.	Interruption of democratization process (1993 and 1998). Lack of freedom in electoral process, lack of human rights (2004).
Zimbabwe	Yes	Since 2002: arms embargo and diplomatic sanctions; financial and other sanctions imposed on government officials; aid suspended. 2011: EU began lifting some restrictions on some individuals; March 2013: lifted restrictions on most individuals. 2012: suspended measures regarding development cooperation.	Violations of democracy.
European countries:			
Belarus	Yes (re aid)	Since 1997: technical aid programmes halted and signature of agreement postponed. From 2002: ban on high-level contact; from 2004 restrictions on admission and freezing of funds for certain persons who violated democratic and human rights standards. These measures were suspended in 2008, but re-imposed in 2011. Since 2007: GSP suspended.	Violations of human rights and democracy; violations of diplomatic protocol; fraudulent elections (2004, 2010) and human rights violations; GSP – violations of trade union rights.

Continued

Country	Use of human rights clause to suspend development cooperation/ aid?	Action Taken	Reason
Croatia	No	1995: suspended from PHARE; reconstruction aid resumed in 1996; eligible for full aid from 2000.	Violations of human rights and democracy, peace agreements.
Russia	No	1995: cooperation agreement conclusion delayed for 6 months; 2000: TACIS aid directed to human rights projects for 6 months.	War in Chechnya (consequences for civilians).
Serbia	No	1992–6: diplomatic and economic sanctions. From 1998: no technical or reconstruction aid and some economic sanctions. October 2000: aid resumed and most sanctions revoked.	War (1992–5); violations of human rights in Kosovo (1998).
Middle Eastern countries			
Syria	no	2011: aid fully suspended; range of other sanctions imposed.	Human rights abuses; conflict (civil war).
Asian countries:			
Burma/ Myanmar	No	1988: most aid suspended. 1990: arms embargo. 1991: no defence cooperation. 1996, diplomatic sanctions. 1997: suspension from GSP. 2000, no exports allowed that could be used for repression; assets of certain governmental officials frozen; ban on some investment. Aid only for projects on human rights, poverty alleviation, provision of basic needs. 2007: ban on exporting equipment for, importing products from, and investment in these sectors: timber; mining of metals, minerals and precious and semi-precious stones. 2012: most measures suspended; 2013: most measures lifted but arms embargo remains.	Suspension of democracy and violations of fundamental rights.

Country	Use of human rights clause to suspend development cooperation/ aid?	Action Taken	Reason
Cambodia	No	1997–9: new aid suspended.	Suspension of democracy.
China	No	June 1989–October 1990: some aid and cooperation suspended, diplomatic sanctions. Arms embargo still in force.	Violations of human rights (Tiananmen Square massacre).
Indonesia	No	1999: arms embargo and military cooperation suspended, for 4 months.	Human rights violations in East Timor.
Pakistan	No	1999: signature of cooperation agreement suspended, until November 2001.	Coup d'état.
Tajikistan	No	1997: TACIS aid suspended. 2000: some assistance provided. 2001: aid resumed.	Violations of democracy and human rights; civil war.
Uzbekistan	No	2005: arms embargo, restrictions on admission of certain persons. 2007: visa restrictions suspended. 2009: arms embargo and other restrictions lifted.	Violations of human rights (Andijan massacre).
Latin American countries			
Cuba	No	2003: light diplomatic sanctions imposed (no high-level visits; member states' participation in cultural events downgraded; dissidents to be invited to attend embassy national days). 2005: sanctions suspended and formally removed in 2008.	Violations of human rights (arrests of journalists and dissidents).
Guatemala	No	1993: no new aid. In 1997, aid resumed to support peace process.	Suspension of constitutional regime.
Honduras	No	2009: budget support suspended, political contacts restricted; 2010: cooperation resumed.	Coup d'état.

Continued

Country	Use of human rights clause to suspend development cooperation/ aid?	Action Taken	Reason
Nicaragua	No	Since 2009: no budget support.	Fraudulent elections.
Peru	No	1992: new aid suspended for 11 months. 2000: aid frozen; 2001: aid resumed.	Violations of democracy.

Note: The list does not include sanctions imposed in conformity with UN Security Council decisions (as in Afghanistan, Angola, Iraq, Libya or the Federal Republic of Yugoslavia). See Table 7.2 for a list of measures currently imposed for security reasons.

Sources: Council of the EU press releases; Commission press releases; European Commission, 'European Union restrictive measures (sanctions) in force', July 2013; Karin Arts, *Integrating Human Rights into Development Cooperation: The Case of the Lomé Convention* (The Hague: Kluwer Law International, 2000), annex 5; Andrew Bradley, 'An ACP perspective and overview of Article 96 cases', ECDPM (European Centre for Development Policy Management) Discussion Paper no. 64D (Maastricht, August 2005); Gordon Crawford, *Foreign Aid and Political Reform: A Comparative Analysis of Democracy Assistance and Political Conditionality* (Houndmills: Palgrave, 2001); Karen Del Biondo, 'EU aid conditionality in ACP countries: explaining inconsistency in EU sanctions practice', *Journal of Contemporary European Research*, 7, 3 (2011); Hadewych Hazelzet, 'Suspension of development cooperation: an instrument to promote democracy?', ECDPM (European Centre for Development Policy Management) Discussion Paper no. 64B (Maastricht, August 2005); Clara Portela, *European Union Sanctions and Foreign Policy: When and Why Do They Work?* (London: Routledge, 2010).

Notes

Chapter 1   Introduction: Conceptualizing EU foreign policy

1 See Mark Leonard, *Why Europe Will Run the 21ˢᵗ Century*, New York: Fourth Estate, 2005; Ian Manners, 'Normative power Europe: a contradiction in terms?', *Journal of Common Market Studies*, 40, 2 (2002); Hanns W. Maull, 'Europe and the new balance of global order', *International Affairs*, 81, 4 (2005); John McCormick, *The European Superpower*, Houndmills: Palgrave Macmillan, 2007; Andrew Moravcsik, 'The quiet superpower', *Newsweek*, 17 June 2002; Tommaso Padoa-Schioppa, *Europa, forza gentile*, Bologna: Il Mulino, 2001; Rockwell Schnabel, *The Next Superpower? The Rise of Europe and its Challenge to the United States*, London: Rowan and Littlefield, 2005; Helene Sjursen, ed., *Civilian or Military Power? European Foreign Policy in Perspective*, London: Routledge, 2007; Mario Teló, *Europe: A Civilian Power?* Houndmills, Palgrave Macmillan, 2005; and Richard Whitman, *From Civilian Power to Superpower? The International Identity of the European Union*, London: Macmillan, 1998. Of course there have always been those who argue that the EU cannot fill such an exalted position in international relations: see in particular, Robert Kagan, *Of Paradise and Power: America and Europe in the New World Order*, London: Atlantic Books, 2003.

2 Giovanni Grevi, *The Interpolar World: A New Scenario*, Occasional Paper no. 79, Paris: European Union Institute for Security Studies, 2009.

3 This takes Hazel Smith's definition of foreign policy ('the capacity to make and implement policies abroad which promote the domestic values, interests and policies of the actor in question'), but emphasizes the relationships with other international actors. Hazel Smith, *European Union Foreign Policy: What It Is and What It Does*, London: Pluto Press, 2002, p. 7.

4 See the definition in Michael Smith, 'The European Union, foreign economic policy and the changing world arena', *Journal of European Public Policy*, 1, 2 (1994): 287.

5 Gunnar Sjöstedt, *The External Role of the European Community*, Westmead: Saxon House, 1977, pp. 77–86. He set out two additional structural requirements: decision-making and monitoring facilities which prepare and control external actions; networks of agents and channels for implementing external actions (p. 75).

6 Arnold Wolfers, *Discord and Collaboration: Essays on International Politics*, Baltimore: Johns Hopkins University Press, 1962, p. 71.

[7] Only with the 1993 Maastricht Treaty did the European Union come into being (see Chapter 2).

[8] 'Declaration on European Identity by the Nine Foreign Ministers, Copenhagen, 14 December 1973', document no. 2/5, in Christopher Hill and Karen E. Smith, eds, *European Foreign Policy: Key Documents*, London: Routledge, 2000, p. 95.

[9] 'Declaration by the European Council on the international role of the European Community (The Rhodes Declaration), Rhodes, 3 December 1988', document no. 2/17, in Hill and Smith, eds, *European Foreign Policy*, pp. 149–51.

[10] Simon Nuttall, *European Foreign Policy*, Oxford: Oxford University Press, 1992, pp. 123–4.

[11] Council of Foreign Ministers, 'Report to the European Council in Lisbon on the likely development of the Common Foreign and Security Policy (CFSP)', Annex to the Conclusions of the Presidency, Lisbon, European Council, 26–7 June 1992, *EC Bulletin* no. 6, 1992. A CFSP Joint Action is a decision to take operational action on a particular issue (see Chapter 2).

[12] European Council, 'A secure Europe in a better world: European security strategy', Brussels, 12 December 2003.

[13] Wolfers, *Discord and Collaboration*, pp. 73–6.

[14] Carmen Gebhard, 'Coherence', in Christopher Hill and Michael Smith, eds, *International Relations and the European Union*, 2nd edn, Oxford: Oxford University Press, 2011, p 107. Arguably, agreement among three member states is the most crucial: France, Germany and the UK. When they fall out over an issue (such as the 2003 Iraq war or the response to violence in Libya in 2011), there can be no common policy; when they agree (as in the case of the Iranian nuclear issue for the past decade), then other member states tend to follow their lead.

[15] Gebhard, 'Coherence', pp. 107–8.

[16] Stanley Hoffmann, 'Obstinate or obsolete? The fate of the nation state and the case of Western Europe', *Daedalus*, 95 (1966): 881–2.

[17] Ulrich Krotz, 'Momentum and impediments: why Europe won't emerge as a full political actor on the world stage soon', *Journal of Common Market Studies*, 47, 3 (2009): 565–8.

[18] See Christopher Hill, 'The capability–expectations gap, or conceptualizing Europe's international role', *Journal of Common Market Studies*, 31, 3 (1993).

[19] Stanley Hoffmann, 'Towards a common European foreign and security policy?', *Journal of Common Market Studies*, 38, 2 (2000): 189. Emphasis added.

[20] Robert Cooper, *The Breaking of Nations: Order and Chaos in the Twenty-First Century*, London: Atlantic Books, 2003.

[21] Kagan, *Of Paradise and Power*.

[22] See David Baldwin, ed., *Neorealism and Neoliberalism: The Contemporary Debate*, New York: Columbia University Press, 1993; Andrew Moravcsik, *The Choice for Europe: Social Purpose and State Power from Messina to Maastricht*, London: UCL Press, 1998.

[23] Krotz, 'Momentum and impediments', p. 563.

[24] David Allen, 'The European rescue of national foreign policy?', in Christopher Hill, ed., *The Actors in Europe's Foreign Policy*, London: Routledge, 1996, p. 303.

[25] Jean-Marie Guehenno, 'A foreign policy in search of a polity', in Jan Zielonka, ed., *Paradoxes of European Foreign Policy*, The Hague: Kluwer Law International, 1998, p. 30.

[26] Christopher Hill and William Wallace, 'Introduction: actors and actions', in Hill, ed., *The Actors in Europe's Foreign Policy*, p. 8.

[27] Daniel C. Thomas, 'Still punching below its weight? Coherence and effectiveness in European Union foreign policy', *Journal of Common Market Studies*, 50, 3 (2012): 472.

[28] The seminal work is Robert Keohane and Joseph S. Nye, *Power and Interdependence*, 2nd edn, Glenview, IL: Scott, Foresman and Co., 1989.

[29] Roy Ginsberg, 'Conceptualizing the European Union as an international actor: narrowing the theoretical capability–expectations gap', *Journal of Common Market Studies*, 37, 3 (1999): 438.

[30] Ginsberg, 'Conceptualizing the European Union', pp. 437–8; Philippe Schmitter, 'Three neofunctional hypotheses about international integration', *International Organization*, 33, 2 (1969). In neo-functionalist theory, externalization is one way which integration might proceed.

[31] Turkey, Montenegro and Serbia are currently negotiating entry with the EU (though Turkey's progress has been slow because it has not met all of the EU's conditions for negotiating). Iceland began negotiations in June 2011, but in 2013 froze the process after parties hostile to membership won elections. The Former Yugoslav Republic of Macedonia (FYROM) is a candidate countries, awaiting the start of negotiations, though Greece is currently blocking FYROM's progress due to bilateral disputes. Bosnia and Herzegovina, Albania and (perhaps) Kosovo have been promised eventual membership. Hopefuls on the sidelines include Ukraine, Moldova, Georgia, Armenia and Azerbaijan.

[32] Joseph Weiler, 'The evolution of mechanisms and institutions for a European foreign policy: reflections on the interaction of law and politics', European University Institute Working Paper no. 85/202, Florence: European University Institute, 1985, p. 21.

[33] See Peter Haas, 'Introduction: epistemic communities and international policy coordination', *International Organization*, 46, 1 (1992).

[34] The classic neo-functionalist texts are Ernest Haas, *The Uniting of Europe: Political, Economic and Social Forces 1950–1957*, London: Stevens and Sons, 1958, and Leon Lindberg, *The Political Dynamics of European Economic Integration*, Stanford: Stanford University Press, 1963.

[35] Michael Smith, 'Does the flag follow trade? "Politicisation" and the emergence of a European foreign policy', in John Peterson and Helene Sjursen, eds, *A Common Foreign Policy for Europe?* London: Routledge, 1998, quotations on pp. 78, 94.

[36] See Alexander Wendt, 'Anarchy is what states make of it: the social construction of power politics', *International Organization*, 46, 2 (1992), and 'Collective identity formation and the international state', *American Political Science Review*, 88, 2 (1994).

[37] Philippe de Schoutheete, *La coopération politique européenne*, Brussels: Editions Labour, 1980, pp. 118–20.

[38] See, for example, Knud Erik Joergensen, 'PoCo: The diplomatic republic of Europe', in Knud Erik Joergensen, ed., *Reflective Approaches to European Governance*, London: Macmillan, 1997, and Michael E. Smith, *Europe's Foreign and Security Policy: The Institutionalization of Cooperation*, Cambridge: Cambridge University Press, 2004, especially chapter 7.

[39] See Ginsberg, 'Conceptualizing the European Union', p. 439, and Roy Ginsberg, *Foreign Policy Actions of the European Community: The Politics of Scale*, Boulder: Lynne Rienner, 1989, pp. 4, 59.

[40] Ben Tonra, *The Europeanisation of National Foreign Policy: Dutch, Danish and Irish Foreign Policy in the European Union*, Aldershot: Ashgate, 2001, p. 19.

[41] Ronald Jepperson, Alexander Wendt and Peter Katzentstein, 'Norms, identity and culture in national security', in Peter Katzenstein, ed., *The Culture of National Security: Norms and Identity in World Politics*, New York: Columbia University Press, 1996, p. 59.

[42] Henrik Larsen, 'Concepts of security in the European Union after the Cold War', *Australian Journal of International Affairs*, 54, 3 (2000): 352.

[43] The implied 'global' extent of this is admittedly misleading. It may be more accurate to set the limits of normative globalization to Western and Central Europe, North America, and other scattered territories, as certain areas of the world seem robustly immune to the spread of international norms such as the protection of human rights. But international human rights conventions have been ratified (if not implemented) by most states, and domestic actors in societies where human rights are violated often demand fulfilment of those standards. A broad enough consensus on some norms can justify the use of the term 'global' rather than just 'Western' (and there are disagreements within the 'West' on norms).

[44] Whitman, *From Civilian Power to Superpower?*, p. 2.

[45] Karin Arts notes that the EC approach to development cooperation is distinctive in 'its emphasis on creating legally binding frameworks for development cooperation'. Karin Arts, *Integrating Human Rights into Development Cooperation: The Case of the Lomé Convention*, The Hague: Kluwer Law International, 2000, p. 2.

[46] François Duchêne, 'The European Community and the uncertainties of interdependence', in Max Kohnstamm and Wolfgang Hager, eds, *A Nation Writ Large? Foreign-Policy Problems before the European Community*, London: Macmillan, 1973, pp. 19–20.

[47] Lily Gardner Feldman, 'Reconciliation and legitimacy: foreign relations and the enlargement of the European Union', in Thomas Banchoff and Mitchell P. Smith, eds, *Legitimacy and the European Union: The Contested Polity*, London: Routledge, 1999, p. 67.

[48] Hill and Wallace, 'Introduction', pp. 9–10; quote on p. 9.

[49] Stephan Keukeleire, 'The European Union as a diplomatic actor: internal, traditional and structural diplomacy', *Diplomacy and Statecraft*, 14, 3 (2003): 47.

[50] See Johann Galtung, *The European Community: A Superpower in the Making*, London: George Allen and Unwin, 1973, and David Mitrany, 'The prospect of integration: federal or functional?', in Joseph S. Nye, Jr, ed., *International Regionalism*, Boston: Little, Brown and Co., 1968.

[51] Jan Zielonka, 'How new enlarged borders will reshape the European Union', *Journal of Common Market Studies*, 39, 3 (2001): 509.

[52] Gregory Flynn and Henry Farrell, 'Piecing together the democratic peace: the CSCE, norms and the "construction" of security in post-Cold War Europe', *International Organization*, 53, 3 (1999): 528.

[53] K. J. Holsti, *International Politics: A Framework for Analysis*, 7th edn, Englewood Cliffs, NJ: Prentice-Hall, 1995, pp. 125–6.

[54] Joseph S. Nye, Jr, *Soft Power: The Means to Success in World Politics*, New York: Public Affairs, 2004, p. 5.

[55] Nye, *Soft Power*, p. 7.

[56] These are broadly the three categories laid out by Christopher Hill in 'European foreign policy: power bloc, civilian model – or flop?', in Reinhardt Rummel, ed., *The Evolution of an International Actor: Western Europe's New Assertiveness*, Boulder: Westview, 1990.

[57] Karen E. Smith, 'Beyond the civilian power debate', *Politique Européenne*, no. 17, automne 2005, pp. 68–9. The idea of the EU (or EC) as a civilian power has a long history, and has been debated extensively in the literature. Two important early articles are by Duchêne, 'The European community', and Hedley Bull, 'Civilian power Europe: a contradiction in terms?', *Journal of Common Market Studies*, 21, 1–2 (1982).

[58] These are the ends referred to by Duchêne, 'The European Community', and Hanns Maull, 'Germany and Japan: the new civilian powers', *Foreign Affairs*, 69, 5, (1990). Although Ian Manners makes a distinction between 'normative power' and 'civilian power', the values of a 'normative power EU' fit easily here. Manners, 'Normative power Europe'.

[59] Stelios Stavridis, 'Why the "militarising" of the European Union is strengthening the concept of a *"Civilian Power Europe"*', Robert Schuman Centre Working Paper no. 2001/17, Florence: European University Institute, 2001, pp. 17–20.

[60] Göran Therborn, 'Europe in the twenty-first century: the world's Scandinavia?', in Peter Gowan and Perry Anderson, eds, *The Question of Europe*, London: Verso, 1997, p. 380.

Chapter 2   The evolution of the EU as an international actor

[1] David Allen and Michael Smith, 'Western Europe's presence in the contemporary international arena', *Review of International Studies*, 16, 1 (1990); Charlotte Bretherton and John Vogler, *The European Union as a Global Actor*, 2nd edn, London: Routledge, 2006, pp. 27–9.

[2] Sjöstedt, *The External Role*, p. 15.

[3] Some theorists, however, argue that the Communities were above all a means for Europe's states to revive their economies and ensure the survival of the welfare state; others point to the role that domestic economic interests played in pushing for economic integration. On the first view, see Alan Milward, *The European Rescue of the Nation State*, London: Routledge, 1992; on the second, Moravcsik, *The Choice for Europe*.

[4] On US insistence, West Germany received reconstruction funding under the 1947 Marshall Plan. On the US role in encouraging European integration, see Geir Lundestad, *"Empire" by Integration: The United States and European Integration 1945–1997*, Oxford: Oxford University Press, 1998.

[5] 'The Schuman Declaration, 9 May 1950', document no. 1/4 in Hill and Smith, eds, *European Foreign Policy*, p. 13.

[6] For QMV, each member state has a number of votes which is more or less proportional to its population size (though small member states are actually 'over-represented', while large member states are under-represented). So in the EU-27 through 2013, Germany, France, Italy, UK had 29 votes each, while tiny Malta had 3 votes. A proposal must receive 258 votes out of the total of 345, but a qualified majority must also comprise a majority of member states and represent at least 62 per cent of the EU's population. Under the Lisbon Treaty, the system will change provisionally from 2014 and definitively from 2017: a proposal will need the support of 55 per cent of member states representing at least 65 per cent of the EU's population.

[7] The European Commission and the Council are based in Brussels, Belgium. The European Parliament holds most of its plenary sessions in Strasbourg, France and its committee meetings in Brussels. The European Court of Justice is based in Luxembourg.

[8] For a comprehensive history of EPC, see Simon Nuttall, *European Political Co-operation*, Oxford: Clarendon Press, 1992.

[9] The following countries have joined the EU since the end of the Cold War: Austria, Finland and Sweden in 1995; Cyprus, the Czech Republic, Estonia, Hungary, Latvia, Lithuania, Malta, Poland, Slovakia and Slovenia in 2005; Bulgaria and Romania in 2007; and Croatia in 2013.

[10] They were supported by the European Court of Justice (Opinion 1/94), which held that only some aspects of trade in services and intellectual property fell under the CCP.

[11] The budget is unusual compared to other international organizations, because it is based on Community revenue sources: customs duties, agricultural levies, a proportion of Value-Added Tax levied in the member states, and national contributions (weighted by relative GNP). The Commission proposes the budget and the Council and EP approve it. The budget is actually rather small, just under 1 percent of Community GDP in 2013. Most of it is devoted to the Common Agricultural Policy, which supports farming, and structural and cohesion funds, which go to poor regions.

[12] Over the years, there have been several calls to 'budgetize' the EDF (that is, to incorporate aid to the ACP countries into the EC budget), but the member states prefer intergovernmental decision-making for the EDF.

[13] European Parliament, Council and Commission, 'The European consensus on development', in *Official Journal of the European Union* (hereinafter *OJ*), C 46, 24 February 2006.

[14] With one exception: following the 1987 Single European Act, a small EPC secretariat was set up within the Council secretariat in Brussels.

[15] David Allen, '"Who speaks for Europe?" The search for an effective and coherent external policy', in John Peterson and Helene Sjursen, eds, *A Common*

Foreign Policy for Europe? London: Routledge, 1998. M. E. Smith (*Europe's Foreign and Security Policy*) describes the evolution of the CFSP pillar as one in which cooperation has been increasingly 'institutionalized'.

[16] Gisela Müller-Brandeck-Bocquet, 'The New CFSP and ESDP Decision-Making System of the European Union', *European Foreign Affairs Review*, 5, 4 (2000): 261.

[17] See Giesela Müller-Brandeck-Bocquet and Carolin Rüger, eds, *The High Representative for the EU Foreign and Security Policy – Review and Prospects*, Baden-Baden: Nomos, 2011.

[18] The PSC can also meet in the formation of the Political Committee, so this 'national element' of the CFSP is not quite extinguished.

[19] Michael E. Smith, 'The legalization of EU foreign policy', *Journal of Common Market Studies*, 39, 1 (2001).

[20] See Nuttall, *European Foreign Policy*, pp. 256–7.

[21] The euro did not exist in 1994; rather, ECUs (European Currency Units) were the composite currency unit used to denominate the budget. The euro replaced the ECU at the value of 1 ECU to €1. European Commission, 'The community budget in facts and figures 1994 edition', SEC 94 (1100); EU Budget 2011, Financial Report http://ec.europa.eu/budget/financialreport/expenditure/global/index_en.html#CFSP (last accessed 5 April 2013).

[22] Jolyon Howorth, 'European defence and the changing politics of the EU: hanging together or hanging separately?', *Journal of Common Market Studies*, 39, 4 (2001); 'Franco-British declaration on European defence', St Malo, 4 December 1998, document 3/15 in Hill and Smith, eds, *European Foreign Policy*.

[23] 'Charlemagne: Berlin Minus', *The Economist*, 10 February 2007; Simon Taylor, 'EU–NATO – room for improvement', *European Voice*, 7–13 June 2007.

[24] On the 'spillover' of economic integration into the JHA field, see Jörg Monar, 'The dynamics of justice and home affairs: laboratories, driving factors and costs', *Journal of Common Market Studies*, 39, 4 (2001): 754–5.

[25] The Schengen agreement was signed by France, Germany and the Benelux countries in June 1985, but implemented only in 1995. It provides for the elimination of border checks inside the Schengen area, and stronger checks at external borders. Other EU member states have since joined, but the UK and Ireland remain outside Schengen (though may take part in some of the Schengen *acquis*), and Denmark can opt out of certain measures, while Norway and Iceland joined, to maintain the Nordic Passport Union with Denmark, Finland and Sweden.

[26] European Council, 'Laeken declaration on the future of the European Union', Presidency Conclusions SN/300/1/01 REV1,14–15 December 2001, p. 21.

[27] The British opt-out will be extended, and any member state can pull an 'emergency brake', suspending the legislative procedure for measures that affect its criminal justice system.

[28] Tonra, *The Europeanisation of National Foreign Policy*, p. 258.

[29] Sikorski represented the EU before the European Parliament's Foreign Affairs Committee and at a meeting with Uzbekistan. In twelve countries with no EU delegations, Polish embassies represented the EU. Karolina Pomorska and Sophie Vanhoonacker, 'Poland in the driving seat: a mature presidency in turbulent times', *The JCMS Annual Review of the European Union in 2011*, p. 79.

[30] See Katie Verlin Laatikainen, 'Multilateral leadership at the UN after the Lisbon Treaty', *European Foreign Affairs Review*, 15, 4 (2010).

[31] Niklas Helwig, Paul Ivan and Hrant Kostanyan, *The New EU Foreign Policy Architecture: Reviewing the First Two Years of the EEAS*, Brussels: Centre for European Policy Studies, 2013, pp. 13–14.

[32] See Miranda Green, 'Lunch with the FT', interview with Baroness Ashton, *Financial Times*, 10/11 July 2011; Ian Traynor, 'On the lady's service', *e-sharp!*, January-February 2011; Thomas Raines, 'Europe eats its young', *The World Today*, July 2011. For overviews of Ashton's troubles, see David Allen and Michael Smith, 'Relations with the rest of the world', in *The JCMS Annual Review of the European Union in 2010* and *The JCMS Annual Review of the European Union in 2011*.

[33] Joint letter from the Foreign Ministers of Belgium, Estonia, Finland, France, Germany, Italy, Latvia, Lithuania, Luxembourg, the Netherlands, Poland and Sweden, to the High Representative of the Union for Foreign Affairs and Security Policy and Vice President of the European Commission, Catherine Ashton, 8 December 2011, available at: http://www.eerstekamer.nl/eu/documenteu/_joint_letter_from_the_foreign/f=/vixkc59lj4ja.pdf (last accessed 13 May 2013).

[34] See Steven Erlanger, 'Catherine Ashton', *New York Times*, 13 February 2011; Julian Borger, 'EU anger over British stance on UN statements', *Guardian*, 20 October 2011. In October 2011, the Council agreed arrangements on EU statements in multilateral organizations, to try to deal with the UK's objections. See Steven Blockmans, 'The European external action service one year on: first signs of strengths and weaknesses', CLEER Working Paper 2012/2, The Hague: TMC Asser Institute, 2012, p. 33.

[35] Hylke Dijkstra, 'European external action service: towards the 2013 review', *Studia Diplomatica*, 45, 4 (2012): 7–8.

[36] See Desmond Dinan, 'Governance and institutions: implementing the Lisbon Treaty in the shadow of the Euro crisis', in *The JCMS Annual Review of the European Union in 2010*, pp. 113–15.

[37] 'European Union external action', *EEAS Review* (July 2013), Foreword by Catherine Ashton.

[38] Figures from European Union External Action, *EEAS Review* (July 2013). On morale in the EEAS, see European Peacebuilding Liaison Office, 'Power Analysis: The EU and Peacebuilding After Lisbon', March 2013, pp. 12 and 14; David Allen and Michael Smith, 'Relations with the rest of the world', *The JCMS Annual Review of the European Union in 2011*, p. 163. In comparison approximately 4,300 UK-based staff work for the British Foreign Office, alongside 9,000 local staff employed overseas. House of Commons, Foreign Affairs Committee – Seventh Report: The Role of the FCO in UK Government, 27 April 2011, paragraph 168.

[39] See the special issue edited by Sophie Vanhoonacker, Petar Petrov and Karolina Pomorska, 'The emerging EU diplomatic system', *The Hague Journal of Diplomacy*, 7, 1 (2012).

[40] Ana E. Juncos and Karolina Pomorska, 'Invisible and unaccountable? National representatives and council officials in EU foreign policy', *Journal of European Public Policy*, 18, 8 (2011).

Chapter 3   The EU's foreign-policy instruments

1   David Baldwin, *Economic Statecraft*, Princeton: Princeton University Press, 1985, pp. 8–9.

2   The scheme is based on one formulated by Harold Lasswell. Baldwin, *Economic Statecraft*, pp. 13–14. It is similar to the one used by C. Hill, though he prefers cultural instruments to propaganda. Cultural instruments seek to influence peoples in other states, but is 'softer' than propaganda. Christopher Hill, *The Changing Politics of Foreign Policy*, Houndmills: Palgrave, 2003, pp. 138, 152–4. The EU sponsors cultural events in third countries, but this is not a well-developed EU instrument.

3   As of March 2013, there were nine free-trade agreement negotiations under way, nine agreements had been negotiated but had yet to enter into force, and 28 agreements were already in force. European Commission, 'Memo: the EU's free trade agreements – where are we?', Reference MEMO/13/282, 25 March 2013.

4   European Commission, 'Global Europe: competing in the world. a contribution to the EU's growth and jobs strategy', COM (2006) 567 final, 4 October 2006, p. 9.

5   European Commission, 'Trade, growth and world affairs: trade policy as a core component of the EU's 2020 strategy', COM (2010) 612 final, 9 November 2010, p. 4.

6   Respect for democratic principles and human rights is a formal condition for receiving assistance from the European Bank for Reconstruction and Development, but no other international actor includes in its external agreements a human rights clause. Since 2007, US trade agreements with third countries include 'enforceable' labour standards (based on the International Labour Organization's core labour standards), which allow the USA to impose sanctions if the standards are violated ('A dubious deal', *Economist*, 19 May 2007).

7   Fabienne Bossuyt, 'The social dimension of the new generation of EU FTAs with Asia and Latin America: ambitious continuation for the sake of policy coherence', *European Foreign Affairs Review*, 14, 5 (2009): 719–20.

8   Arts, *Integrating Human Rights*, p. 2.

9   See Enzo Grilli, *The European Community and the Developing Countries*, Cambridge: Cambridge University Press, 1993, pp. 150–1.

10   European Commission, 'The EU's new generalised scheme of preferences (GSP)', December 2012; available at: http://trade.ec.europa.eu/doclib/docs/2013/february/tradoc_150582.pdf (last accessed 10 June 2013).

11   See Stefan Lehne, 'The role of sanctions in EU foreign policy', Carnegie Endowment for International Peace, 14 December 2012; Constanty Gebert, 'Shooting in the Dark? EU Sanctions Policies', European Council on Foreign Relations, Policy Brief, 15 January 2013.

12   European Commission, 'Budget 2012 in figures', http://ec.europa.eu/budget/figures/2012/2012_en.cfm (last accessed 3 May 2013).

13   OECD, Development Assistance Committee, 'Peer Review: European Union 2012', p. 56. In 2011, the Union was the second largest donor, after the USA.

In 1994–95, the Community distributed aid to 160 recipient countries, so it has been prioritizing its aid distribution to some extent.

14 European Commission, 'Increasing the Impact of EU Development Policy: An Agenda for Change', COM (2011) 637 final, 13 October 2011, p. 9–10; Council of the European Union, 'Council Conclusions on Increasing the Impact of EU Development Policy: An Agenda for Change', Foreign Affairs Council meeting of 14 May 2012.

15 The European Consensus on Development, in *OJ* C 46, 24 February 2006.

16 Sarah Delputte and Fredrik Söderbaum, 'European Aid Coordination in Africa: Is the Commission Calling the Tune?', in Stefan Gänzle, Sven Grimm and Davina Makhan, eds, *The European Union and Global Development*, Houndmills: Palgrave Macmillan, 2012, p. 54.

17 OECD, 'Peer Review: European Union 2012', p. 54.

18 CONCORD (a European NGO confederation), 'Spotlight on EU Policy Coherence for Development', 2011 Report. On the specific case of the incoherence between the common fisheries policy and development policy, see Charlotte Bretherton and John Vogler, 'Towards an EU policy for sustainable development?', in Gänzle, Grimm and Makhan, eds, *The European Union and Global Development*.

19 Helwig, Ivan and Kostanyan, *The New EU Foreign Policy Architecture*, pp. 39–40.

20 Though CFSP decisions do also include promises of aid or trade agreements.

21. Aidan Cox and Jenny Chapman, *The European Community External Cooperation Programmes: Policies, Management and Distribution*, London and Brussels: Overseas Development Institute and European Commission, 1999, p. 3.

22 OECD, 'Peer Review: European Community 2012', p. 4.

23 BOND (a network of UK NGOs), 'Renewing Europe's role as a global development actor: BOND submission to the future of Europe convention', London, 2002; Concord (a network of European NGOs), 'Hold the applause! EU Governments risk breaking aid promises', April 2007; available at www.concordeurope.org (last accessed 13 January 2014), p. 45.

24 European Commission, 'Report on the implementation of macro-financial assistance to third countries in 2011'. COM (2012) 339 final, 28 June 2012, p. 15.

25 European Investment Bank, *Activity Report 2012*, pp. 28–9; available at: http://www.eib.org/attachments/general/reports/ar2012en.pdf (last accessed 3 May 2013).

26 The member states are supposed to harmonize their export credit systems, and the ECJ ruled in 1975 that export credits fall under EC competence, but the member states have resisted 'handing over' this instrument.

27 Elfriede Regelsberger, 'The EU as an actor in foreign and security policy: some key features of CFSP in an historical perspective', *CFSP Forum*, 5, 4 (2007), available at: http://www.lse.ac.uk/internationalRelations/centresandunits/EFPU/FORNETarchive.aspx (last accessed 20 August 2013).

28 See the Council website, 'CFSP statements', for each year (avoiding incorrectly placed statements): http://www.consilium.europa.eu/policies/foreign-policy/cfsp-statements?lang=en&BID=73 (last accessed 3 May 2013).

29 See http://eeas.europa.eu/statements/hr/index_en.htm#top for a list of statements by the High Representative (last accessed 11 June 2013).

[30] Helwig, Ivan and Kostanyan, *The New EU Foreign Policy Architecture*, pp. 21–2.

[31] These included respect for democracy and human rights, guarantees for the rights of minorities, acceptance of the principle of the inviolability of frontiers, and honouring security commitments.

[32] On Angola, see Nicholas van Praag, 'European political cooperation and Southern Africa', in David Allen, Reinhardt Rummel, and Wolfgang Wessels, eds, *European Political Cooperation: Towards a Foreign Policy for Western Europe*, London: Butterworth Scientific, 1982, p. 137. On North Korea, see General Affairs Council, 'Conclusions on European Union lines of action towards North Korea', press release no. 1343/00 (presse 435), 20 November 2000.

[33] Daniel Korski and Richard Gowan, 'Can the EU rebuild failing states? A review of Europe's civilian capacities', European Council on Foreign Relations, October 2009, p. 23.

[34] NATO, 'Active engagement, modern defence: strategic concept for the defence and security of the members of the North Atlantic Treaty Organization', adopted by heads of state and government at the NATO Summit in Lisbon, 19–20 November 2010.

[35] See Annegret Bendiek and Hannah Whitney-Steele, 'The financing of the EU's common foreign and security policy', SWP Comments 16, Berlin: Stiftung Wissenschaft und Politik, 2006; Esther Barbé and Benjamin Kienzle, 'Security provider or security consumer? The European Union and conflict management', *European Foreign Affairs Review*, 12, 4 (2007).

[36] The first three conditions were set by the June 1993 Copenhagen European Council; the last by the December 1999 Helsinki European Council.

[37] See Myrto Hatzigeorgopoulos, 'The role of EU battlegroups in European defence', ESR 56, European Security Review, ISIS Europe, June 2012. http://www.isis-europe.eu/sites/default/files/publications-downloads/esr56_EUBattlegroups-June2012%20MH_2.pdf (last accessed 13 January 2014).

[38] See CSDP Mission Analysis Partnership (MAP), hosted by ISIS Europe, 'Mission Personnel 2012'. Available at: http://www.csdpmap.eu/mission-personnel (last accessed 8 May 2013).

[39] Gebhard, 'Coherence', pp. 107–8.

Chapter 4   Regional cooperation

[1] 'Regionalism' is the 'conscious policy of states, a top-down process, seeking greater regional co-operation on a range of issues from security to the economy'. Marukh Doctor, 'Why bother with inter-regionalism? Negotiations for a European Union-Mercosur agreement', *Journal of Common Market Studies*, 45, 2 (2007): 286–7.

[2] European Commission, 'Communication on European Community support for regional economic integration efforts among developing countries', COM (95) 219 final, 16 June 1995, p. 3.

[3] Annegret Bendiek and Heinz Kramer, 'The EU as a "strategic" international actor: substantial and analytical ambiguities', *European Foreign Affairs Review*, 15, 4 (2010): 461.

4 See the excerpts of two documents in Peter M. R. Stirk and David Weigall, *The Origins and Development of European Integration*, London: Pinter, 1999: 'Summary of discussion on problems of relief, rehabilitation, and reconstruction of Europe, US Department of State, 19 May 1947' (pp. 45–6) and 'Committee of European Economic Cooperation: General Report, July–September 1947' (pp. 51–2).

5 Kenneth Waltz, 'Reductionist and systemic theories', in Robert Keohane, ed., *Neorealism and its Critics*, New York: Columbia University Press, 1986, pp. 58–9.

6 European Commission, COM (95) 219, p. 8. See also the similar views of several experts interviewed in Renata Goldirova, 'The EU: A model impossible to export?', *EUObserver.com*, 22 March 2007.

7 Philomena Murray and Edward Moxon-Browne examine the 'template' issue in 'The EU as a template for regional integration? The case of ASEAN and its committee of permanent representatives', *Journal of Common Market Studies*, 51, 3 (2013); Reuben Wong argues that the EU is a 'reference point' but not a model for ASEAN, in 'Model power or reference point? The EU and the ASEAN Charter', *Cambridge Review of International Affairs*, 25, 4 (2012).

8 Jörg Monar, 'Political dialogue with third countries and regional political groupings', in Elfriede Regelsberger, Phillipe de Schoutheete de Terverant, and Wolfgang Wessels, eds, *Foreign Policy of the European Union: From EPC to CFSP and Beyond*, Boulder: Lynne Rienner, 1997, p. 266; Catherine Flaesch-Mougin, 'Competing frameworks: the dialogue and its legal bases', in Geoffrey Edwards and Elfriede Regelsberger, eds, *Europe's Global Links: The European Community and Inter-Regional Cooperation*, London: Pinter, 1990, p. 30.

9 Fredrik Söderbaum, Patirk Stålgren and Luk Van Langenhove, 'The EU as a global actor and the dynamics of interregionalism: a comparative analysis', *Journal of European Integration*, 27, 3 (2005).

10 Elfriede Regelsberger, 'The dialogue of the EC/Twelve with other regional groups', in Edwards and Regeslberger, *Europe's Global Links*, pp. 12–13.

11 See European Commission, COM (2006) 567, and COM (2010) 612.

12 Söderbaum, et al., 'The EU as a global actor', p. 371.

13 European Council, 'A secure Europe in a better world', p. 9.

14 European Commission, 'Euro-Med Partnership Regional Strategy Paper 2002–2006 and Regional Indicative Programme 2002–2004 ' (2001), p. 6.

15 As the press releases announcing the launch of negotiations for association agreements with the Andean Community (IP/07/834, 14 June 2007) and the Central America Community (IP/07/981, 29 June 2007) both assert.

16 Mary Farrell, 'A triumph of realism over idealism? Cooperation between the European Union and Africa', *Journal of European Integration*, 27, 3 (2005): 266.

17 Grilli, *The European Community*, pp. 335–6.

18 Carolyn Jenkins and Lynne Thomas, 'African regionalism and the SADC', in Mario Teló, ed., *European Union and New Regionalism*, Aldershot: Ashgate, 2001, p. 153.

19 Nuttall, *European Political Co-operation*, p. 234.

20 'Cairo Declaration', Africa-Europe summit under the aegis of the OAU and the EU, Cairo, 3–4 April 2000, paragraph 2.

21 Council of the EU, 'The EU and Africa: towards a strategic partnership', document no. 15961/05 (Presse 367), 18 December 2005.

22 Council of the EU, 'The Africa-EU strategic partnership: a joint Africa-EU strategy', document 16344/07, 9 December 2007, paragraph 111.

23 In addition, two EPAs will be concluded with Caribbean and Pacific groups. The EU's strategy is also incoherent in that under the 2001 'Everything But Arms' (EBA) initiative, the world's 48 poorest countries (all but 9 in the ACP group) have almost entirely duty-free access to the EU market. The ACP beneficiaries of EBA thus have little incentive to join (reciprocal) EPAs. But if they do not join an EPA, and still remain in a regional economic community, the only way they could prevent *de facto* liberalization of their own markets would be to erect barriers between their economies and their regional partners, thus blocking regional trade. Mayur Patel, 'Economic partnership agreements between the EU and African countries: potential development implications for Ghana', report for Realizing Rights, June 2007, p. 24. http://www.realizingrights.org/pdf/EPAs_between_the_EU_and_African_Countries_-_Development_Implications_for_Ghana.pdf (last accessed 20 August 2013).

24 Council of the EU, 'The Africa-EU strategic partnership' (2007), paragraph 99.

25 The member states of SADC are: Angola, Botswana, Democratic Republic of Congo, Lesotho, Malawi, Mauritius, Mozambique, Namibia, South Africa, Swaziland, Tanzania, Zambia and Zimbabwe.

26 Secretariat of the African, Caribbean and Pacific Group of States, 'press release: consensus on economic partnership agreements between EU and ACP countries', Berlin, 14 March 2007. There are internal disagreements within the Commission, with trade officials keen on liberalization, and development officials less so. I am grateful to Mary Farrell for pointing this out to me.

27 Nuttall, *European Political Co-operation*, p. 291.

28 For the quote: Christian Koch, 'GCC–EU relations: the news again is "no news"', *Gulf Research Center: GCC–EU Research Bulletin*, no. 5, July 2006, p. 3.

29 Abdulla Baabood, 'Dynamics and determinants of the GCC states' foreign policy, with special reference to the EU', in Gerd Nonneman, ed., *Analyzing Middle East Foreign Policies*, London: Routledge, 2005, pp. 162, 164–8. See also Abdulla Baabood and Geoffrey Edwards, 'Reinforcing ambivalence: the interaction of Gulf states and the European Union', *European Foreign Affairs Review*, 12, 4 (2007): 547–53.

30 Christian Koch, 'A union in danger: where the GCC is headed is increasingly questionable', Gulf Research Center Foundation, 10 December 2012.

31 Association agreements were concluded with Greece (1961) and Turkey (1963); more limited agreements were concluded with Cyprus (1972), Egypt (1972), Israel (1964, 1970), Lebanon (1965, 1972), Malta (1970), Morocco (1969), Tunisia (1969), Spain (1970) and Portugal (1972). More substantial agreements were later concluded with Israel (1975), Algeria (1976), Morocco (1976), Tunisia (1976), Egypt (1976), Lebanon (1977), Jordan (1977), and Syria (1977).

32 Grilli, *The European Community*, pp. 188–9.

33 Esther Barbé, 'Balancing Europe's eastern and southern dimension', in Jan Zielonka, ed., *Paradoxes of European Foreign Policy*, The Hague: Kluwer Law International, 1998.

[34] Geoffrey Edwards and Eric Philippart, 'The Europe–Mediterranean partnership: fragmentation and reconstruction', *European Foreign Affairs Review*, 2, 4 (1997): 470–4.

[35] 'Conclusions of the European Council on relations with the Mediterranean countries, Corfu, 24–25 June 1994', document no. 4b/52, in Hill and Smith, eds, *European Foreign Policy*, pp. 348–9.

[36] Bretherton and Vogler, *The European Union*, p. 161.

[37] Claire Spencer, 'The EU and common strategies: the revealing case of the Mediterranean', *European Foreign Affairs Review*, 6, 1 (2001): 49.

[38] European Council, 'Common strategy of 19 June 2000 on the Mediterranean Region(2000/458/CFSP', in *OJ* L 183, 22 July 2000.

[39] European Commission, 'Wider Europe – neighbourhood: a new framework for relations with our southern and eastern neighbours', COM (2003) 104 final, 11 March 2003, p. 4.

[40] At the time of writing, Action Plans had been agreed with all of the Mediterranean partners except for Algeria, Libya and Syria.

[41] See, for example: Richard Gillespie, 'The Union for the Mediterranean: An Intergovernmentalist Challenge for the European Union?', *Journal of Common Market Studies*, 49, 6 (2011).

[42] Raffaella del Sarto and Tobias Schumacher, 'From EMP to ENP: what's at stake with the European neighbourhood policy towards the southern Mediterranean?', *European Foreign Affairs Review*, 10, 1 (2005): 28–9.

[43] European Commission, 'A partnership for democracy and shared prosperity with the southern Mediterranean', COM (2011) 200 final, 8 March 2011, p. 5.

[44] Ibid., p. 11.

[45] 'Joint declaration of the Community–ASEAN Foreign Ministers' Conference, Brussels, 20–21 November 1978', document no. 4c/31 in Hill and Smith, eds, *European Foreign Policy*, p. 435.

[46] Nuttall, *European Political Co-operation*, p. 289.

[47] Bandar Seri Begawan plan of action to strengthen the ASEAN–EU enhanced partnership (2013–17), agreed at the 19th EU–ASEAN ministerial meeting, 27 April 2012.

[48] Anja Jetschke and Clara Portela, 'ASEAN–EU relations: from regional integration assistance to security significance?', GIGA Focus no. 3, 2013, Hamburg: German Institute of Global and Area Studies, p. 3.

[49] Sangeeta Khorana and Maria Garcia, 'European Union–India trade negotiations: one step forward, one back?, *Journal of Common Market Studies*, 51, 4 (2013).

[50] Council of the EU, 'The EU and Central Asia: strategy for a new partnership', document no. 10113.07, 31 May 2007, p. 6.

[51] European External Action Service and European Commission, 'Progress Report on the implementation of the EU strategy for Central Asia: implementation review and outline for future orientations', doc 11455/12, 28 June 2012, p. 9; Council of the European Union, 'Joint Progress Report by the Council and the European Commission to the European Council on the implementation of the EU Central Asia strategy', document no. 11402.10, Brussels, 28 June 2010, p. 3.

[52] Christopher Piening, *Global Europe: The European Union in World Affairs*, London: Lynne Rienner, 1997, pp. 120–1.

[53] 'Joint communique of the conference of Foreign Ministers of the European Community and its member states, Portugal and Spain, the states of Central America and the Contadora states, San Jose, Costa Rica, 28–29 September 1984', document no. 4c/30 in Hill and Smith, eds, *European Foreign Policy*, p. 431.

[54] The six states are Costa Rica, El Salvador, Guatemala, Honduras, Nicaragua and Panama; those six states plus Belize form the Central American Integration System. The San José dialogue and the various cooperation agreements, however, do not include Belize.

[55] Nuttall, *European Political Co-operation*, p. 90. The members are: Argentina, Bolivia, Brazil, Chile, Columbia, Costa Rica, Dominican Republic, Ecuador, El Salvador, Guatemala, Honduras, Mexico, Nicaragua, Panama, Paraguay, Peru, Uruguay, Venezuela and a CARICOM (Caribbean Community) representative.

[56] Piening, *Global Europe*, pp. 129–30.

[57] European Commission, 'An EU–Caribbean partnership for growth, stability and development' COM (2006) 86 final, 2 March 2007. Formed in 1990, CARIFORUM members are: Antigua and Barbuda, Barbados, Bahamas, Belize, Dominica, Dominican Republic, Grenada, Guyana, Haiti, Jamaica, St Kitts and Nevis, St Lucia, St Vincent and the Grenadines, Suriname, and Trinidad and Tobago. Cuba is also a member, since it is in the ACP group but is not a Cotonou signatory (and will not participate in the EPA).

[58] Venezuela withdrew from the Andean community in 2006, after the other members began negotiating free trade agreements with the USA.

[59] On the problems in the EU–Mercosur negotiations, but also on the remarkable continuation of negotiations despite the problems, see Doctor, 'Why bother with inter-regionalism'.

[60] Doctor, 'Why bother with inter-regionalism', p. 290.

[61] European Commission, 'Report to the general affairs council on the promotion of intra-regional cooperation and "bon voisinage"', 6 March 1995, p. 1.

[62] 'Political Declaration adopted at the conclusion of the final conference on the pact on stability in Europe and list of good-neighbourliness and cooperation agreements and arrangements', *EU Bulletin*, no. 3, 1995, p. 113.

[63] Alyson J. K. Bailes, 'The role of subregional cooperation in post-Cold War Europe', in Andrew Cottey, ed., *Subregional Cooperation in the New Europe*, London: Macmillan, 1999, pp. 158–9.

[64] Richard G. Whitman and Ana E. Juncos, 'Relations with the Wider Europe', in Nathaniel Copsey and Tim Haughton, eds, *The JCMS Annual Review of the European Union in 2010*, pp. 199–200.

[65] Council of the EU, 'Conclusions on the principle of conditionality governing the development of the European Union's relations with certain countries of south-east Europe', 29 April 1997, in *EU Bulletin*, no. 4, 1997, pp. 132–4.

[66] See Finnish Presidency and the European Commission, 'Report to the European Council on EU Action in support of the Stability Pact and South-East Europe', Press release no. 13814/99, 6 December 1999; Council of the EU, 'Common Position1999/345/PESC of 17 May 1999 Concerning the Launching of the Stability Pact of the EU in South-Eastern Europe', *OJ* L133, 28 May 1999.

[67] Milica Delevic, *Regional Cooperation in the Western Balkans*, Chaillot Paper no. 104, Paris: EU Institute for Security Studies, 2007.

[68] European Commission, COM (95) 219, p. 3.

[69] Such funding formed a prominent part of the previous schemes for aiding the Central and East European countries (PHARE), the former Soviet republics (TACIS), South-East European countries (CARDS), and Mediterranean non-member countries (MEDA). European Commission, COM (95) 219, p. 20.

[70] European Commission, 'Regional Strategy Paper (2007–2013) for the Euro-Mediterranean Partnership', p. 54.

[71] Council of the EU, 'The EU and Africa: Towards a Strategic Partnership', (2005) p. 2.

[72] European Commission, 'Annual Report 2011: The African Peace Facility', available at http://ec.europa.eu/europeaid/where/acp/regional-cooperation/peace/documents/2011_annual_report_on_the_african_peace_facility_en.pdf (last accessed 2 July 2013).

[73] Council of the EU, 'Action plan for ESDP support to peace and security in Africa', document no. 10538/4/04, 16 November 2004.

[74] In 1992, the EU formalized its ties with the European Free Trade Association (EFTA), in the European Economic Area agreement. This was not, however, aimed at strengthening EFTA as a regional grouping, but at extending the single European market to EFTA members in response to their concerns about marginalization. In the event, several EFTAns applied and then acceded to the EU, while Switzerland opted out of the EEA. The EEA thus embraces the EU, Iceland, Liechtenstein and Norway.

[75] European Commission, COM (95) 219, p. 18.

[76] See Flaesch-Mougin, 'Competing frameworks'. The Euro-Arab dialogue centred on economic issues, while that with the Front Line States covered political issues. The EP is often involved in dialogues with parliamentarians from regional groupings (such as the Latin American and Central American Parliaments, and the ASEAN Interparliamentary Organization), as well as the EC-ACP joint assembly.

[77] Julie Gilson, 'New interregionalism? The EU and East Asia', *Journal of European Integration*, 27, 3 (2005): 309.

[78] Monar, 'Political dialogue with third countries', pp. 269–70.

[79] See, for example, Arvind Panagariya, 'The regionalism debate: an overview', *The World Economy*, 22, 4 (1999); special report on 'The Gated Globe', *The Economist*, 12 October 2013.

[80] For a brief account of this debate, see Richards and Kirkpatrick, 'Reorienting interregional co-operation', pp. 685–8.

[81] Andrew Hurrell and Louise Fawcett, 'Conclusion: regionalism and international order?', in Fawcett and Hurrell, eds, *Regionalism in World Politics*, Oxford: Oxford University Press, 1995.

[82] See Boutros Boutros-Ghali, *An Agenda For Peace*, New York: United Nations, 1992, paragraph 64.

[83] Müller-Brandeck-Bocquet, 'Perspectives for a new regionalism', p. 579.

[84] See Karen E. Smith, 'Speaking with one voice? European Union coordination on human rights issues at the United Nations', *Journal of Common Market Studies*,

44, 1 (2006), and 'The European Union and the politics of legitimization at the United Nations', *European Foreign Affairs Review*, 18, 1 (2013).

[85] Karen E. Smith, 'The limits of "proactive cosmopolitanism": EU policy towards Burma, Cuba and Zimbabwe', in Ole Elgström and Michael Smith, eds, *The European Union's Roles in International Politics*, London: Routledge, 2006.

[86] Keukeleire, 'The European Union as a diplomatic actor', p. 47.

[87] Mario Teló, 'Reconsiderations: three scenarios', in Teló, ed., *European Union and New Regionalism* (2001), p. 265.

Chapter 5 Human rights

[1] On this distinction, see Kathryn Sikkink, 'The power of principled ideas: human rights policies in the United States and Western Europe', in Judith Goldstein and Robert Keohane, eds, *Ideas and Foreign Policy*, Ithaca: Cornell University Press, 1993, pp. 141–2. Principled beliefs are 'normative ideas that specify criteria for distinguishing right from wrong and just from unjust'. Causal beliefs 'provide guides for individuals on how to achieve their objectives.' Judith Goldstein and Robert Keohane, 'Ideas and foreign policy: an analytical framework', in Goldstein and Keohane, eds, *Ideas and Foreign Policy*, pp. 9–10.

[2] George Kennan, 'Morality and foreign policy', *Foreign Affairs*, 64, 2 (1985).

[3] See Dilys Hill, 'Human rights and foreign policy: theoretical foundations', in Dilys Hill, ed., *Human Rights and Foreign Policy*, Houndmills, Macmillan, 1989.

[4] See Thomas Franck, 'Are human rights universal?', *Foreign Affairs*, 80, 1 (2001); Mahmood Monshipouri, *Democratization, Liberalization and Human Rights in the Third World*, Boulder: Lynne Rienner, 1995, pp. 17–19.

[5] For a robust denunciation of Western motivations, see John-Jean Barya, 'The New Political Conditionalities of Aid: An Independent View from Africa', *IDS Bulletin*, 24, 3 (1993).

[6] See R.J. Vincent, 'Human rights in foreign policy' in D. Hill, ed., *Human Rights and Foreign Policy* (1989).

[7] See Comité des Sages, 'Leading by example: a human rights agenda for the European Union for the Year 2000', reprinted in Philip Alston, ed., *The EU and Human Rights*, Oxford: Oxford University Press, 2000; Dick Oosting (director, Amnesty International), '"Fortress Europe" asylum system is no respecter of human rights', *European Voice*, 27 September–3 October 2001; Gráinne de Búrca, 'The road not taken: The European Union as a global human rights actor', *American Journal of International Law*, 105, 4 (2011).

[8] Leaders of countries that have been targeted by EU negative sanctions, such as Castro in Cuba or Mugabe in Zimbabwe, frequently point to the EU's own failings ('neo-colonialism', racism, etc). The Council wants 'core scripts' on key human rights issues in EU member states to be used in political dialogue meetings, to 'address accusations of double standards' – indicating that such accusations are made often by the EU's partners. Council of the EU, 'Mainstreaming human rights across CFSP and other EU policies', document no. 10076/06, 7 June 2006, p. 2.

9 Andrew Williams, *EU Human Rights Policies: A Study in Irony*, Oxford: Oxford University Press, 2004, chapter 6. He further argues that the myth ignores negative aspects of European history such as the legacy of colonial rule. See also de Búrca, 'The road not taken' on the omission of human rights from the EEC Treaty. In comparison, the 1953 draft European Political Community treaty stated that the Political Community was 'to contribute towards the protection of human rights and fundamental freedoms in Member States' (Article 2), and part I of the ECHR was to have been an integral part of the treaty (Article 3).

10 Andrew Clapham, *Human Rights and the European Community*, Baden-Baden: Nomos Verlagsgesellschaft, 1991, p. 29.

11 European Parliament, Council and Commission, 'Joint declaration by the European Parliament, the Council and the Commission concerning the protection of fundamental rights', *OJ* C 103, 27 April 1977.

12 The social chapter started life as the charter of fundamental social rights, a declaration of 11 member states (bar the UK) in December 1989; it was appended to the Maastricht Treaty as a protocol, because the UK blocked its incorporation into the treaty. A new UK government dropped the objections during the Amsterdam Treaty negotiations.

13 Williams, *EU Human Rights Policies*, pp. 102–5.

14 Williams, *EU Human Rights Policies*, p. 109.

15 Unusually, the Charter was drafted by a convention composed of member state representatives, MEPs, Commission representatives, and national MPs. This set a precedent for the convention that later drafted the constitutional treaty.

16 Under a special protocol, the ECJ will not have the ability to find the UK or Poland in breach of the Charter.

17 European Commission, '2012 report on the application of the EU Charter of Fundamental Rights', Luxembourg: Office of the Official Publications of the EU, 2013; Council of the European Union, 'EU Annual Report on Human Rights and Democracy in the World in 2012', document 9431/13, 13 May 2013.

18 See, for example, European Parliament resolution of 16 February 2012 on the recent political developments in Hungary (2012/2511(RSP)), P7_TA(2012)0053. In April 2013, European Commissioner Viviane Reding indicated the Commission could launch infringement proceedings against Hungary because constitutional changes made were considered to potentially violate EU laws and principles.

19 Amnesty International, 'Annual Report 2006–7: Human Rights and the EU', 23 May 2007, p. 1. It should be stressed that the EU member states also disagree over particular human rights (from conditions of detention to the right to abortion).

20 Benjamin Ward, 'Europe's own human rights crisis', in Human Rights Watch, *World Report 2012*.

21 European Council, Copenhagen, 'Declaration on democracy', *EC Bulletin*, no. 3, 1978, pp. 5–6. This signalled to the democratizing states of southern Europe – Greece, Portugal and Spain – that the EC would use the 'carrot' of membership to boost democratic forces. Yet the Community had continued with

'business as usual' under the 1961 association agreement with Greece, and had concluded trade agreements with Spain in 1970 and Portugal in 1972.

22 The Lisbon Treaty states that the Union is founded on values which include the rights of persons belonging to minorities.

23 Williams, *EU Human Rights Policies*, p. 81.

24 The basic international framework for the protection of human rights is the 'International Bill of Human Rights': the 1948 Universal Declaration of Human Rights, and the two International Covenants on Civil and Political Rights, and on Economic, Social and Cultural Rights, which entered into force in 1976. Over two-thirds of all the world's states have ratified the covenants, including all of the EU member states (although some have made significant reservations to certain provisions). There are also other important treaties, such as the Genocide Convention and the Convention against Torture. The USA has ratified only the Genocide Convention (in 1989), the International Covenant on Civil and Political Rights (in 1992, though hedged with serious reservations), the Convention on the Elimination of Racial Discrimination and the Convention against Torture (both in 1994). It is not even a party to the Inter-American Convention on Human Rights.

25 Kenneth Dyson, 'The Conference on Security and Cooperation in Europe: Europe before and after the Helsinki final act', in Kenneth Dyson, ed., *European Détente: Case Studies in the Politics of East-West Relations*, London: Frances Pinter, 1986, p. 99.

26 Alfred Pijpers, 'European political co-operation and the CSCE process', *Legal Issues of European Integration*, 10, 1 (1984): 147–8.

27 See Margaret Thatcher, *Downing Street Years*, London: Harper Collins, 1993, p. 457, and Dominique Moïsi, 'French policy toward Central and Eastern Europe' in William Griffth ed., *Central and Eastern Europe: The Opening Curtain?* Boulder: Westview, 1989, pp. 359–62.

28 Karl Birnbaum and Ingo Peters, 'The CSCE: a reassessment of its role in the 1980s', *Review of International Studies*, 16, 4 (1990): 309. Emphasis in the original.

29 Peter Baehr, *The Role of Human Rights in Foreign Policy*, Houndmills: Macmillan, 1994, chapter 11.

30 Sikkink, 'The power of principled ideas', p. 154.

31 Grilli, *The European Community*, p. 102.

32 See *EC Bulletin* no. 6, 1977, point 2.2.59; *Agence Europe* no. 2793, 21 November 1979.

33 Michael Addo, 'Some issues in European Community aid policy and human rights', *Legal Issues in European Integration*, 1 (1998), pp. 79–80.

34 European Parliament, *The European Parliament and Human Rights*, Luxembourg: OOPEC, 1994, p. 7.

35 Ann Florini, 'The evolution of international norms', *International Studies Quarterly*, 40, 3 (1996): 375.

36 As in European Parliament, 'Resolution for the year 1983/1984 on human rights in the world and community policy on human rights', *OJ* C 172, 2 July 1984, p. 38.

37 'Letter to the President of the European Parliament: Memorandum on EPC and Human Rights', Document no. 86/137, in *European Political Cooperation*

Documentation Bulletin, 2, 1 (1986). An EPC working group on human rights was created in 1987.

38 European Political Cooperation, 'Statement by the Twelve on human rights', Brussels, 21 July 1986, reprinted in Press and Information Office of the Federal Republic of Germany, *European Political Co-operation (EPC)*, 5th edn (1988), p. 264.

39 The Commission in particular was reticent to abandon the neutral approach. Michael Zwamborn, 'Human rights promotion and protection through the external relations of the European Community and the Twelve', *Netherlands Quarterly of Human Rights*, 7, 1 (1989): 19–20.

40 Conditionality was only implicit in 1988: the EC concluded a cooperation agreement with the fastest reforming country, Hungary, and would not consider talks with others until they launched reforms. By mid 1989, the conditionality of EC aid and agreements was explicit. See Karen E. Smith, *The Making of EU Foreign Policy: The Case of Eastern Europe*, London: Macmillan, 2004, chapters 3 and 4.

41 Gordon Crawford, *Promoting Democracy, Human Rights and Good Governance through Development Aid*, Working Paper on Democratization no. 1, Leeds: University of Leeds Centre for Democratization Studies, 1996, pp. 32–3.

42 Ole Elgström, 'Lomé and post-Lomé: asymmetric negotiations and the impact of norms', *European Foreign Affairs Review*, 5, 2 (2000): 184. Economic conditionality was widely used in the 1980s by the international financial institutions and major donors; political conditionality was new.

43 European Council, Luxembourg, 'Declaration on human rights', *EC Bulletin*, no. 6, 1991, pp. 17–18. The Lomé IV convention, signed in 1989, contained an article (5) which states that development entailed respect for and promotion of all human rights. But there was no mechanism for enforcing article 5 in the convention.

44 Development Council and member states, 'Resolution on human rights, democracy and development', *EC Bulletin*, no. 11, 1991, pt 2.3.1.

45 European Union statement on human rights, *EU Bulletin*, no. 12, 1998, p. 112.

46 Council of the European Union, 'EU strategic framework and action plan on human rights and democracy', document no. 11855/12, 25 June 2012, p. 2.

47 European Union statement on human rights, *EU Bulletin*, no. 12, 1998, p. 112.

48 European Council, 'A secure Europe in a better world', p. 10.

49 Council of the EU, 'EU strategic framework', p. 1.

50 Jack Donnelly, 'An overview', in David Forsythe, ed., *Human Rights and Comparative Foreign Policy*, Tokyo: United Nations University Press, 2000, p. 311.

51 Williams, *EU Human Rights Policies*, p. 171.

52 David Chandler, *From Kosovo to Kabul: Human Rights and International Intervention*, London: Pluto Press, 2002, pp. 53–88.

53 For more on the cases of inconsistency, see Klaus Brummer, 'Imposing sanctions: The not so "normative power Europe"', *European Foreign Affairs Review*, 14, 2 (2009).

54 Uwe Puetter and Antje Wiener, 'Accommodating normative divergence in European foreign policy co-ordination: the example of the Iraq crisis', *Journal of Common Market Studies*, 45, 5 (2007): 1085.

[55] See above all, Richard Youngs, ed., *Survey of European Democracy Promotion Policies 2000–2006*, Madrid: FRIDE, 2006; see also Brummer, 'Imposing sanctions', pp. 204–5.

[56] Youngs, ed., *Survey of European Democracy Promotion Policies*, pp. 53–4, 59.

[57] Franziska Brantner, 'Europe's new diplomats', *EurActiv* (www.euractiv.com, last accessed 13 January 2014), 23 November 2010.

[58] European Commission and High Representative of the EU for Foreign Affairs and Security Policy, 'Human rights and democracy at the heart of EU external action – towards a more effective approach', COM (2011) 886 final, 12 December 2011; Council Decision 2012/440/CFSP of 25 July 2012 appointing the European Union Special Representative for Human Rights, OJ L 200/21, 27 July 2012.

[59] Judy Dempsey, 'Selling Europe's human rights: loud and clear or softly-softly?', *Judy Dempsey's Strategic Europe* blog, 27 June 2013, Carnegie Europe, http://www. carnegieeurope.eu/strategiceurope/?fa=52223 (last accessed 5 July 2013).

[60] Vincent, 'Human rights in foreign policy', p. 58.

[61] European Commission, 'Democratisation, the rule of law, respect for human rights and good governance: the challenges of the partnership between the European Union and the ACP States', COM (1998) 146 final, 12 March 1998, p. 4.

[62] Council of the EU, 'Common position of 11 June 2001 on the International Criminal Court (2001/931/CFSP)', OJ L 155, 12 June 2001.

[63] In 1989, an optional protocol abolishing the death penalty was added to the International Covenant on Civil and Political Rights. In 1983, a protocol abolishing the death penalty was added to the ECHR (which all EU member states have ratified); in 1990, a similar protocol was added to the American Convention on Human Rights.

[64] Regulation no. 978 (2012), OJ L 1303, 31 October 2012. To qualify for extra preferences, countries must ratify and implement 15 core human rights and ILO conventions, and 12 other conventions related to environment and governance principles. Yet EU member states have not (yet) ratified all of the listed conventions as of August 2013: Malta has not ratified the Genocide Convention, Italy and Malta have not ratified the Stockholm Convention on Persistent Organic Pollutants, and the Czech Republic and Germany have not ratified the UN Convention against Corruption.

[65] European Council, Luxembourg, 'Declaration on human rights', p. 17.

[66] Marika Lerch and Guido Schwellnus, 'Normative by nature? The role of coherence in justifying the EU's external human rights policy', in Helene Sjursen, ed., *Civilian or Military Power? European Foreign Policy in Perspective*, London: Routledge, 2007, p. 149.

[67] European Commission, 'Report on the implementation in 1993 of the Resolution on human rights, democracy and development', COM (94) 42 final, 23 February 1994, p. 11. The Council also prefers positive measures. See Council of the EU, 'Conclusions on the EU's role in promoting human rights and democratisation in third countries', Luxembourg, 25 June 2001, paragraph 14. The foreword to the 2012 Annual Report on Human Rights (p. 8) puts it like this: 'We do this not only by "pointing fingers"—as we must, when grave human rights violations occur—but also by "joining hands" in order to provide

concrete support and guidance in the implementation of human rights obligations.'

68 Demetrios James Marantis, 'Human rights, democracy, and development: the European Community model', *Harvard Human Rights Journal*, 7 (1994): 12–16.

69 Margo Picken, 'Ethical foreign policies and human rights: dilemmas for non-governmental organisations', in Karen E. Smith and Margot Light, eds, *Ethics and Foreign Policy*, Cambridge: Cambridge University Press, 2001, p. 100.

70 See Berlin European Council conclusions, 24–25 March 1999.

71 The EU did cobble together a CSDP mission to help deliver aid, if the UN requested it – but the UN made no such request and the mission was never launched (see Table 3.5).

72 Afghanistan and Iraq also did not have agreements with the EU until recently; in the recent past their human rights records (under the Taliban or Saddam Hussein) were extremely poor. But a cooperation agreement with Iraq should enter into force soon, and an agreement with Afghanistan could be finalized shortly. Since Venezuela left the Andean Community in 2006, it is no longer linked by an agreement with the EU; whether the current government of Venezuela would be inclined to negotiate one is not clear.

73 The EU began negotiations on a trade and cooperation agreement with Iran in 2002, and used them to press Iran to discuss human rights issues. But the exigency of shutting down Iran's uranium enrichment programme has largely superseded the human rights conditionality. Richard Youngs, *Europe and the Middle East: In the Shadow of September 11*, London: Lynne Rienner, 2006, pp. 67–92.

74 'European Parliament, 'Resolution on the human rights and democracy clause in European Union agreements (2005/205(INI)' P6_TA(2006)0056, 14 February 2006, paragraph 3.

75 Council decision reported in *EU Bulletin*, no. 5, 1995, pt. 1.2.3., p. 9. From 1992, it was incorporated into agreements with other European states. Free trade agreements do not normally contain the human rights clause because they are linked with a 'passarelle' clause to a framework agreement which does contain it; if there is no framework agreement with the third country (as was the case with Colombia and Peru), then a human rights clause is included in the free trade agreement. Council of the EU, Annual Report on Human Rights 2012, p. 59.

76 Otherwise suspension or termination would have to be based on the impossibility of treaty performance, or a fundamental change of circumstances. See Eibe Riedel and Martin Will, 'Human rights clauses in external agreements of the EC' in Philip Alston, ed., *The EU and Human Rights*, Oxford: Oxford University Press, 1999, pp. 724–5; European Commission, 'Communication on the inclusion of respect for democratic principles and human rights in agreements between the community and third countries' COM (95) 216 final, 23 May 1995, p. 8. The clause in agreements with other European countries includes respect for market economic principles.

77 European Commission, DG RELEX/B2 – Treaties Office, 'Inventory of agreements containing a suspension-human rights clause'. 7 July 2011.

78 New Zealand, for example, argued that political and economic issues should be kept separate. *European Voice*, 4–10 February 1999.

79 Marcela Szymanski and Michael E. Smith, 'Coherence and conditionality in European foreign policy: negotiating the EU–Mexico global agreement', *Journal of Common Market Studies*, 43, 1 (2005); Fabienne Zwagemakers, 'The EU's conditionality policy: a new strategy to achieve compliance', IAI Working Papers 12/03, Rome: Istituto Affari Internazionali, January 2012, p. 10.

80 Several blogs have reported Canada's resistance; see Stuart Trew, ' First nations and other "funny issues" not covered by human rights clause in Canada–EU deal: diplomat', The Council of Canadians Acting for Social Justice, 13 June 2013 (http://www.canadians.org/content/first-nations-and-other-%E2%80%9C funny-issues%E2%80%9D-not-covered-human-rights-clause-canada-eu-deal; last accessed 9 July 2013). On India, see Khorana and Garcia, 'European Union–India trade negotiations'.

81 European Parliament, 'Study: human rights mainstreaming in EU's external relations', EXPO/B/DROI/2008/66, September 2009, pp. 59–60.

82 European Parliament, 'Study: human rights mainstreaming', p. 36.

83 Council of the European Union, *EU Annual Report on Human Rights and Democracy in the World in 2010* (September 2011), p. 14.

84 Council of the EU, 'EU annual report on human rights 2012', p. 133.

85 Council of the EU and European Commission, 'EU annual report on human rights 2006', p. 20.

86 See Mark Bromley, 'The review of the EU common position on arms exports: prospects for strengthened controls', EU Non-Proliferation Consortium, Non-Proliferation Papers no. 7, January 2012 p. 9. Available at: http://www.sipri.org/research/armaments/transfers/transparency/EU_reports/research/disarmament/eu-consortium/publications/publications/non-proliferation-paper-7 (last accessed 1 August 2013).

87 Bromley, 'The review of the EU common position on arms exports', p. 10.

88 Andrew Rettman, 'Loopholes aplenty in EU "arms ban" on Egypt', *EUObserver.com*, 2 September 2013.

89 Richard Norton-Taylor, 'UK approves £12bn of arms exports to countries with poor human rights', *Guardian*, 17 July 2013.

90 See, for example, Council of the EU, 'Common position of 25 May 1998 concerning human rights, democratic principles, the rule of law and good governance in Africa (98/350/CFSP)', *OJ* L 158, 2 June 1998.

91 Kristina Kausch, 'Morocco', in Richard Youngs, ed., *Is the European Union Supporting Democracy in its Neighbourhood?* Madrid: FRIDE, 2008, p.21.

92 European Commission and High Representative of the European Union for Foreign Affairs and Security Policy, 'Implementation of the agenda for action on democracy support in the EU's external relations', JOIN(2012) 28 final, 11 October 2012, p. 8.

93 See Gordon Crawford, *Foreign Aid and Political Reform: A Comparative Analysis of Democracy Assistance and Political Conditionality*, Houndmills: Palgrave Macmillan, 2001, and Sabine C. Zanger, 'Good Governance and European Aid', *European Union Politics*, 1, 3 (2000).

[94] Sabine C. Carey, 'European aid: human rights versus bureaucratic inertia', *Journal of Peace Research*, 44, 4 (2007): 462.

[95] European Commission and High Representative, 'Delivering on a new neighbourhood policy', JOIN (2012) 14 final (15 May 2012): 3–6.

[96] European Commission, 'Increasing the impact of EU development policy', p. 5.

[97] European Commission, 'European instrument for democracy and human rights (EIDHR) Strategy Paper 2011–13', C(2010)2432, 21 April 2010.

[98] Council of the EU, 'Mainstreaming human rights' (2006), p. 6.

[99] European Parliament, 'Study: human rights mainstreaming', p. 57.

[100] Council of the EU, 'EU strategic framework'.

[101] Martin Fouwels, 'The European Union's common foreign and security policy and human rights', *Netherlands Quarterly of Human Rights*, 15, 3 (1997): 309.

[102] Council Decision 2012/440/CFSP of 25 July 2012 appointing the European Union Special Representative for Human Rights, *OJ* L 200/21, 27 July 2012.

[103] Council of the EU and European Commission, 'EU annual report on human rights 2006', p. 9.

[104] Council of the EU, 'Conclusions on the implementation of EU policy on human rights and democratisation in third countries', document no. 16719/06, 13 December 2006, p. 4.

[105] European Commission, 'The European Union's role in promoting human rights and democratisation in third countries', COM (2001) 252 final, 8 May 2001, p. 9, and Council of the EU, 'Conclusions on the EU's role in promoting human rights' (2001).

[106] The cases include: Cambodia, Egypt, Jordan, Laos, Lebanon, Morocco, Pakistan, Palestinian Authority, Tunisia and Vietnam. European Union, *EU Annual Report on Human Rights and Democracy in the World in 2010* (September 2011), p. 13.

[107] Elgström, 'Lomé and Post-Lomé', p. 191, and Richard Youngs, *Democracy Promotion: The Case of European Union Strategy*, Centre for European Policy Studies Working Document no. 167, Brussels 2001, pp. 41–6.

[108] European Union, *EU Annual Report on Human Rights and Democracy in the World in 2010*, p. 11. The structured human rights dialogues take place with China, Belarus, Armenia, African Union, Kazakhstan, Kyrgyz Republic, Tajikistan, Turkmenistan, Uzbekistan and Iran (suspended since 2006).

[109] See, for example, Council of the European Union, *2009 Annual Report from the High Representative of the Union for Foreign Affairs and Security Policy to the European Parliament on the Main Aspects and Basic Choices of the CFSP* (June 2010), pp. 30–32.

[110] General Affairs Council, 'Conclusions, 20 March 2000', press release no. 6810/00 (Presse 73) and 'Conclusions, 22–3 January 2001', press release no. 5279/01 (Presse 19). Other countries also conduct dialogues on human rights with China, including the USA and Australia.

[111] Council of the EU, 'Conclusions on the implementation of EU policy on human rights' (2006), p. 5.

[112] Council of the EU, 'EU strategic framework' action plan point 32.

[113] Apparently this was because the German military was using an aid base in Uzbekistan as part of its contribution to the International Security Assistance

Force in Afghanistan. Youngs, ed., *Survey of European Democracy Promotion Policies*, pp. 127–8.

[114] EU relations with Cuba provide a classic example of the north–south split, with southern states generally pressing for engagement and northern ones for tougher action. Relations are also complicated by the US embargo, which the EU opposes.

[115] See K. Smith, 'Speaking with one voice?'

[116] European Parliament, 'Study: human rights mainstreaming', p. 52.

[117] Council of the EU, 'Conclusions on the EU's role in promoting human rights' (2001).

[118] Nathalie Tocci, *The EU and Conflict Resolution: Promoting Peace in the Backyard*, London: Routledge, 2007, p. 117.

[119] Appendix this volume, and Youngs, ed., *Survey of European Democracy Promotion Policies*, pp. 149–50, 195–6, 220–1.

[120] Crawford, *Foreign Aid*, pp. 177–81.

[121] Richard Youngs, *The European Union and the Promotion of Democracy: Europe's Mediterranean and Asian Policies*, Oxford: Oxford University Press, 2001, pp. 61, 74, 77. See also K. Smith, 'The limits of "proactive cosmopolitanism"', Brummer, 'Imposing sanctions', pp. 203–5.

[122] Apparent complicity by some EU member states in the US practice of rendition illustrates the extent to which both Europe and the USA have limited civil liberties in the fight against terrorism.

[123] On these two cases, see in particular, Stefania Panebianco, 'Promoting human rights and democracy in European Union relations with Russia and China', in Sonia Lucarelli and Ian Manners, eds, *Values and Principles in European Union Foreign Policy*, London: Routledge, 2007.

[124] Andrew Rettman, 'EU: Magnitsky verdict is "disturbing" sign', *EUobserver.com*, 11 July 2013.

[125] And there has been little evidence of much improvement across the region since. See Neil Melvin, 'The EU Needs a New Central Asia Strategy', EUCAM Policy Brief no. 28, 31 October 2012.

[126] As Nathalie Tocci points out, 'the Union has never exerted any form of conditionality' vis-à-vis Israel. It has criticized some Israeli policies but never imposed negative measures on it. Tocci, *The EU and Conflict Resolution*, p. 117.

[127] Jack Donnelly, 'Human rights and foreign policy', *World Politics*, 34, 4 (1982): 591–2.

Chapter 6   Democracy and good governance

[1] US democracy promotion can be traced back to the late 1890s. See Thomas Carothers, *Aiding Democracy Abroad*, Washington, DC: Carnegie Endowment for International Peace, 1999 and Margot Light, 'Exporting democracy', in Smith and Light, eds., *Ethics and Foreign Policy*.

[2] Council of the European Union, 'EU strategic framework on human rights' (2012).

[3] Arts, *Integrating Human Rights*, p. 40.

[4] Arts, *Integrating Human Rights*, p. 41.

[5] Freedom House, *Freedom in the World 2013: Democratic Breakthroughs in the Balance*.

[6] See in particular Laurence Whitehead, 'Losing "the force"? the "dark side" of democratization after Iraq', *Democratization*, 16, 2 (2011).

[7] COBRA II, the US ground war plan, declared that 'the endstate for this operation is regime change'. Quoted in Thomas Ricks, *Fiasco: The American Military Adventure in Iraq*, New York: Penguin Press, 2006, p. 116.

[8] Thomas Carothers, 'The backlash against democracy promotion', *Foreign Affairs*, 85, 2 (2006).

[9] See for example Pew Global Attitudes surveys on democracy: http://www. pewresearch.org/topics/democracy/ (last accessed 13 January 2014); or the Latinobarometro surveys of public opinion in Latin America: http://www. latinobarometro.org/lat.jsp (last accessed 13 January 2014). One way that regimes have reacted is to prohibit or limit severely the foreign funding of NGOs.

[10] Štefan Füle, Speech on the recent events in North Africa to the Committee on Foreign Affairs, European Parliament, Brussels, SPEECH/11/130, 28 February 2011.

[11] See Michelle Pace, 'Mixed messages from the EU won't help solve Egypt's Crisis', blog posting on The Conversation.com, 6 August 2013: http://the conversation.com/mixed-messages-from-the-eu-wont-help-solve-egypts-crisis-16595 (last accessed 7 August 2013).

[12] See Youngs, ed., *Survey of European Democracy Promotion Policies*.

[13] See David Beetham, *Democracy and Human Rights*, Cambridge: Polity, 1999, pp. 4–5.

[14] Council of the European Union, 'Council conclusions on democracy support in the EU's external relations', 17 November 2009.

[15] Until 2017, a member state can insist that a vote be taken under the Nice Treaty rules (on voting weights) rather than the Lisbon Treaty rules. On 1 April 2017, the double voting system will be obligatory.

[16] There are national variations: in 2009, over 90 per cent turnout in Belgium and Luxembourg, about 35 per cent in the UK, and 25 per cent in Poland. See the European Parliament's website on voter turnout: http://www. europarl.europa.eu/aboutparliament/en/000cdcd9d4/Turnout-(1979-2009). html (last accessed 15 July 2013).

[17] Julie Smith, *Europe's Elected Parliament*, Sheffield: Sheffield Academic Press, 1999, p. 22.

[18] European Commission, Standard Eurobarometer 78, Public Opinion in the European Union, Autumn 2012. Even lower percentages trust national parliaments or governments, however.

[19] European Commission, COM (2001) 252, p. 3.

[20] European Union statement on human rights, *EU Bulletin*, no. 12, 1998, p. 111.

[21] European Political Cooperation, 'Statement by the Twelve on human rights' (1986).

[22] In 1980, the Community concluded a trade agreement with Romania, a reward for its more independent foreign policy and an encouragement to other Warsaw Pact countries to do the same.

[23] H. Smith, 'Actually existing foreign policy', p. 158.

[24] World Bank, *Sub-Saharan Africa: From Crisis to Sustainable Growth*, Washington DC: The World Bank, 1989, pp. 3 and 5.

[25] See Crawford, *Promoting Democracy*, pp. 3–4.

[26] European Council, Luxembourg, 'Declaration on human rights', p. 17.

[27] Youngs, *Democracy Promotion*, pp. 25 and 34; Regulation no. 978 (2012), *OJ* L 1303, 31 October 2012.

[28] Arts, *Integrating Human Rights*, p. 200, fn. 83.

[29] Chris Patten, 'Speech to the European Parliament plenary on the Commission communication on EU election assistance and observation', Speech/01/125, 14 March 2001.

[30] European Commission, 'The European Union and the external dimension of human rights policy: from Rome to Maastricht and beyond', COM (95) 567 final, 22 November 1995, p. 10.

[31] European Commission, COM (2001) 252, p. 4.

[32] Kofi Annan, 'Democracy as an international issue', *Global Governance*, 8, 2 (2002): 136–9.

[33] Crawford, *Foreign Aid*, p. 3.

[34] See Crawford, *Foreign Aid*, pp. 36–9. Furthermore, economic growth fuelled by the exploitation of natural resources (oil, gas) has boosted authoritarian regimes in Russia, Sudan and the Persian Gulf and arguably fuelled the authoritarian tendencies of the Venezuelan government.

[35] European Parliament, Council and Commission, 'The European consensus on development', paragraph 86.

[36] Council of the European Union, 'Council conclusions on democracy support' (2009). Annex on EU Agenda for Action on Democracy Support in the EU's External Relations, p. 3; European Commission, COM (2011) 637, p. 5.

[37] Anne Wetzel and Jan Orbie, 'The EU's promotion of external democracy – in search of the plot', CEPS Policy Brief no. 281, Brussels: Centre for European Policy Studies, 13 September 2012, p. 5. In 2012, donors (such as the UK and Germany) suspended aid to Rwanda – because of its support for violent rebels in neighbouring Democratic Republic of Congo, not any failings with respect to democratic standards.

[38] See Karen Del Biondo, 'Democracy promotion meets development cooperation: the EU as a promoter of democratic governance in sub-Saharan Africa', *European Foreign Affairs Review*, 16, 5 (2011).

[39] Rosa Balfour, *Human Rights and Democracy in EU Foreign Policy: The Cases of Ukraine and Egypt*, London: Routledge, 2012, p. 137.

[40] Wetzel and Orbie, 'The EU's promotion of external democracy', p. 2.

[41] Anne Wetzel and Jan Orbie, 'With map and compass on narrow paths and through shallow waters: discovering the substance of EU democracy promotion', *European Foreign Affairs Review*, 16, 5 (2011): 706.

[42] Carothers, *Aiding Democracy Abroad*, p. 44.

[43] European Parliament, Briefing Paper, 'EU election observation – Achievements, Challenges', EXPO/B/DEVE-AFET/2007/40, PE 385556, June 2008, p. 5.

[44] See Richard Youngs, 'Trends in democracy assistance: what has Europe been doing?', *Journal of Democracy*, 19, 2 (2008); European Parliament, Briefing Paper, 'EU election observation', p. 5.

[45] Del Biondo, 'Democracy promotion meets development cooperation', p. 671.

[46] Youngs, ed., *Survey of European Democracy Promotion Policies*.

[47] Charter of Paris for a New Europe, reprinted in *EC Bulletin*, no. 11, 1990, p. 126.

[48] The vagueness of the concepts caused problems in the Union's relations with the ACP countries, so in March 1998, the Commission issued a communication to try to arrive at 'a shared, practical and operational understanding' of concepts including human rights, democracy, and good governance. European Commission, COM (1998) 146, pp. 2–3.

[49] Council of the EU, 'Common position of 25 May 1998 on human rights in Africa', Article 2.

[50] Council of the European Union, 'Council conclusions on democracy support' (2009), Annex on EU Agenda for Action.

[51] Crawford, *Promoting Democracy*, pp. 60–1.

[52] Crawford, *Foreign Aid*, p. 73.

[53] Development Council et al., 'Resolution on human rights, democracy, and development', p. 122.

[54] See Crawford, *Foreign Aid*, pp. 22–8.

[55] European Commission, COM (1998) 146, pp. 7–8.

[56] European Commission, 'Governance in the European consensus on development: towards a harmonised approach within the European Union', COM (2006) 421 final, 30 August 2006, p. 5. Emphasis added.

[57] European Commission, COM (2006) 421, p. 6.

[58] See Council of the European Union, 'Council Conclusions on democracy support' (2009), Annex on EU agenda for action; and European Commission, COM (2011) 637.

[59] Wetzel and Orbie, 'The EU's promotion of external democracy – in search of the plot', p. 3.

[60] The nine countries were: Benin, Bolivia, Ghana, Lebanon, Indonesia, Kyrgyz Republic, Maldives, Mongolia and the Solomon Islands. See European Commission and High Representative, JOIN (2012) 28 final, p. 3, and Council of the EU, 'EU strategic framework on human rights' (2012), p. 8.

[61] Council of the European Union, 'Council conclusions on democracy support' (2009), paragraph 3.

[62] See the update on Myanmar on the EuropeAid website: http://ec.europa.eu/europeaid/where/asia/country-cooperation/myanmar/myanmar_en.htm (last accessed 5 August 2013).

[63] Milada Vachudova, *Europe Undivided: Democracy, Leverage and Integration after Communism*, Oxford: Oxford University Press, 2005.

[64] There has been debate about the extent to which the questioning of Turkey's membership prospects has affected its compliance with EU conditionality. Beken Saatçioğlu argues that reform efforts have stagnated, but reforms have not been withdrawn. Beken Saatçioğlu, 'Unpacking the compliance puzzle: the case of Turkey's AKP under EU conditionality', KFG Working Paper no. 14, Berlin: Freie Universtität Berlin, 2010.

[65] Muriel Asseburg, 'The Arab spring and the European response', *The International Spectator*, 48, 2 (2013): 59.

[66] In the Ukrainian case, however, there is a substantial lobby within the EU in favour of offering Ukraine membership: several member states (above all Poland), MEPs and commentators have called on the EU to offer Ukraine the clear prospect of membership. See 'Yushchenko seeks EU membership', *BBC News online*, 25 January 2005; Jacek Pawlicki and Robert Soltyk, 'Time to offer more to Ukraine during "birth of a new European nation"', *European Voice*, 16 December 2004 – 12 January 2005. On 13 January 2005, the European Parliament voted by 467 to 19 in favour of a non-binding resolution calling for Ukraine to be given the perspective of EU membership.

[67] Youngs, *The European Union and the Promotion of Democracy*, pp. 129–30.

[68] Peter Burnell, 'Promoting democracy backwards', FRIDE Working Paper no. 28, Madrid: FRIDE, 2006, p. 7.

[69] OECD, Development Assistance Committee, 'Peer review: European Community 2007', p. 89.

[70] Judy Dempsey, 'Inconsistency backfires on European Union in Africa', *The New York Times*, 24 January 2011.

[71] Suzanne Daley, 'Moroccans fear that flickers of democracy are fading', *New York Times*, 10 December 2012. The EU has opened negotiations on a deep and comprehensive free trade agreement with Morocco (the first of the Euro-Med countries) and concluded a mobility partnership with it.

[72] Richard G. Whitman and Ana E. Juncos, 'The Arab spring, the Eurozone crisis and the neighbourhood: a region in flux', *The JCMS Annual Review of the European Union in 2011*, pp. 155–6.

[73] Though some military takeovers are merely condemned rhetorically, as in Thailand in 2006, or Bangladesh in 2007.

[74] Wetzel and Orbie, 'With map and compass on narrow paths and through shallow waters', p. 711.

[75] Youngs, *Democracy Promotion*, p. 22.

[76] Sinikukka Saari, *Promoting Democracy and Human Rights in Russia*, London: Routledge, 2011.

[77] EU Election Observation Mission West Bank and Gaza 2006, press release, Jerusalem, 26 January 2006. The EU softened the impact of the measures through a 'temporary international mechanism' (now called PEGASE), which channelled aid via the Palestinian Authority Presidency (controlled by Fatah) and international organizations. Perversely, this came after years in which the EU had tried to channel aid *away* from the presidency (particularly when Arafat held the post). Tocci, *The EU and Conflict Resolution*, p. 121.

[78] See Tocci, *The EU and Conflict Resolution*, p. 121–2.

[79] Harriet Sherwood, 'Hamas claims increased contact with European countries', *Guardian*, 12 July 2013.

[80] European Commission, C(2010) 2432, pp. 33–6.

[81] Dinorah Azpuru, Steven E. Finkel, Aníbal Pérez-Liñán and Mitcheel A. Sligson, 'Trends in democracy assistance: what has the United States been doing?', *Journal of Democracy*, 19, 2 (2008): 157.

[82] Youngs, *Democracy Promotion*, p. 10.

[83] Federica Bicchi, 'Want funding? Don't mention Islam: EU democracy promotion in the Mediterranean', *CFSP Forum*, 4, 2 (2006), available at: http://www.

lse.ac.uk/internationalRelations/centresandunits/EFPU/FORNETarchive.aspx (last accessed 20 August 2013) ; Youngs, *The European Union*, 81–6.

84 Nicholas Boucher, 'Democracy lobby under siege' *The World Today*, June and July 2012, p. 37; Carothers, 'The backlash against democracy promotion'. These fears largely stem from the support that the USA gave to NGOs in Georgia and Ukraine (EU assistance in the run-up to both 'colour revolutions' was considerably less).

85 Andrew Rettman, 'EU moving to US model on pro-democracy funding', *EUobserver.com*, 19 April 2006.

86 See Solveig Richter and Julia Leininger, 'Flexible and unbureaucratic democracy promotion by the EU?', SWP Comments 26, Berlin: Stiftung Wissenschft und Politik, August 2012.

87 Development Council, 'Conclusions, 31 May 2001', press release no. 8855/01 (Presse 191).

88 Election support measures in conflict-affected countries are also funded by the Instrument for Stability.

89 In 2003, various EU actors (the EU election observation mission, the CFSP High Representative, the Council Presidency) all made contradictory declarations about whether presidential and general elections in Rwanda were free and fair. Federico Santopinto, 'Why the EU needs an institutional reform of its external relations', GRIP Note d'Analyse, 19 June 2007 (http://archive.grip.org/en/siteweb/dev_4569b9db.asp.html; last accessed 13 January 2014).

90 European Commission, 'Communication on EU election assistance and observation', COM (2000) 191 final, 11 April 2000, Annex III, p. 35, 39.

91 This included expelling the head of the mission, a Swedish diplomat, and refusing to accept monitors from northern states (Sweden, Denmark, Finland, Germany, the Netherlands and the UK), who were perceived as biased towards the opposition.

92 European Union Election Observation Mission, Final Report on the Ugandan General Elections 18 February 2011, 5 March 2011.

93 European Parliament, Briefing Paper, 'EU election observation', pp. 11–12, 27.

94 Jonathan Steel, 'Campaign corruption', *Guardian*, 29 June 2000.

95 Council of the EU, 'Declaration by the Presidency on behalf of the European Union on the elections in Nigeria', Press release 8953/07 (Presse 95), 27 April 2007.

96 European Parliament, Briefing Paper, 'EU Election Observation', p. 16.

97 European Commission, COM (2001) 252, p. 9, and Council of the EU, 'Conclusions on the EU's role in promoting human rights' (2001).

98 Richard Youngs, 'European Union democracy promotion policies: ten years on', *European Foreign Affairs Review*, 6, 3 (2001): 359–60.

99 European Commission, COM (2001) 252, p. 8.

100 Youngs, *The European Union*, pp. 193–4.

101 Diplomatic sanctions against Belarus initially included a ban on high-level contacts from 2002, and visa bans and asset freezes on officials responsible for repressing peaceful demonstrations in 2004 and violating international electoral standards in 2006. In 2008, the sanctions were mostly suspended as Belarus made moves to accommodate some of the EU's demands. However,

following a flawed presidential election in December 2010 and a crackdown on protesters, the EU reintroduced the sanctions (and tripled the number of Belarusian officials subject to a visa ban and asset freeze). See Clara Portela, 'The European Union and Belarus: sanctions and partnership?', *Comparative European Politics*, 9, 4/5 (2011).

102 See David Chandler's trenchant critique, *Bosnia: Faking Democracy after Dayton*, 2nd edn, London: Pluto Press, 2000. For a less critical view of the role of the High Representative, see Paddy Ashdown, *Swords and Ploughshares: Bringing Peace to the 21ˢᵗ Century*, London: Weidenfeld and Nicolson, 2007, especially the two appendices, which recount some of his experiences as High Representative in Bosnia and Herzegovina between 2002 and 2006.

103 Burnell, 'Promoting democracy backwards', pp. 5–6.

104 See Amichai Magen, Thomas Risse and Michael McFaul, eds, *Promoting Democracy and the Rule of Law: American and European Strategies*, London: Palgrave Macmillan, 2009.

105 Burnell, 'Promoting democracy backwards', p. 12.

106 Gorm Rye Olsen, 'Europe and the promotion of democracy in post-Cold War Africa: how serious is Europe and for what reason?', *African Affairs*, 97, 388 (1998); Crawford, *Foreign Aid*, pp. 12–14.

107 Gareth Harding, 'Union softens its stance on Pakistan coup', *European Voice*, 10–17 November 1999.

108 Council of the European Union, 'Annual Report CFSP 1999', section II.12.m.

109 Crawford, *Foreign Aid*, p. 221; see also Aylin Güney and Aslihan Çelenk, 'The European Union's Democracy Promotion Policies in Algeria: Success or Failure?', *The Journal of North African Studies*, 12, 1 (2007).

110 Crawford, *Foreign Aid*, p. 223.

111 See Saari, *Promoting Human Rights and Democracy in Russia*.

112 Carothers, *Aiding Democracy Abroad*, p. 308.

113 See Whitehead, 'Losing "the force"?'.

Chapter 7   Conflict prevention

1 ADE, 'Thematic evaluation of European Commission support to conflict prevention and peace-building; Final Report, volume 1: Main report', October 2011, p. 28.

2 Julia Schünemann, 'EU conflict prevention 10 years after Göteberg', Policy Paper no. 1, June 2011, Institut Català Internacional per la Pau, p. 5; European Commission, 'Towards an EU response to situations of fragility – engaging in difficult environment for sustainable development, stability and peace', COM (2007) 643 final, 25 October 2007.

3 Reinhardt Rummel, 'The CFSP's conflict prevention policy', in Martin Holland, ed., *Common Foreign and Security Policy: The Record and Reforms*, London: Pinter, 1997, p. 110. The experience of enlargement to the Republic of Cyprus has to some extent confirmed these fears.

4 Eva Gross and Ana E. Juncos, 'Introduction', in Eva Gross and Ana E. Juncos, eds, *EU Conflict Prevention and Crisis Management: Roles, Institutions, and Policies*, London: Routledge, 2010, p. 5.

[5] Schünemann, 'EU conflict prevention 10 years after Göteberg', pp. 4–5.

[6] Javier Solana, 'Intervention in the open debate on conflict prevention in the General Affairs Council', press release no. 004/01, Brussels, 22 January 2001.

[7] Karl Deutsch, et al., *Political Community and the North Atlantic Area*, Princeton: Princeton University Press, 1957, p. 5.

[8] Maurice Keens-Soper, *Europe in the World: The Persistence of Power Politics*, Houndmills: Macmillan, 1999, p. 11.

[9] Feldman, 'Reconciliation and legitimacy', p. 75.

[10] Norwegian Nobel Committee, 'Announcement: the Nobel Peace Prize for 2012', Oslo 12 October 2012, available at: http://www.nobelprize.org/nobel_prizes/peace/laureates/2012/press.html (last accessed 8 August 2013).

[11] Trading states accept that they will do better through economic development and trade than by trying to conquer territory. Richard Rosecrance, *The Rise of the Trading State: Commerce and Conquest in the Modern World*, New York: Basic Books, 1986.

[12] Waltz, 'Reductionist and systemic theories', pp. 58–9.

[13] Sarah Kneezle, 'EU's Nobel Peace Prize: does NATO deserve it more?', *Time*, 12 October 2012.

[14] European Council, 'A secure Europe in a better world', p. 1.

[15] Christopher Hill, 'The EU's capacity for conflict prevention', *European Foreign Affairs Review*, 6, 3 (2001): 321–2.

[16] See Alan James, 'United Nations preventive diplomacy in an historical perspective', in Jeremy Ginifer, Espen Barth Eide and Carsten Rønnfeldt, eds, *Preventive Action in Theory and Practice: The Skopje Papers*, Oslo: Norwegian Institute of International Affairs, 1999.

[17] Nick Killick and Simon Higdon. 'The cost of conflict', in Peter Cross, ed., *Contributing to Preventive Action. Conflict Prevention Network Yearbook 1997/98*, Baden-Baden: Nomos Verlagsgesellschaft, 1998, pp. 98–101.

[18] Jacques Delors, 'European unification and European security', in *European Security After the Cold War, Part I*, Adelphi Paper no. 284, London: Brassey's for the International Institute of Security Studies, 1994, p. 11.

[19] European Commission, 'Communication on conflict prevention', COM (2001) 211 final, 11 April 2001, p. 7.

[20] Council of the EU, 'Conclusions on preventive diplomacy, conflict resolution and peacekeeping in Africa', 4 December 1995; Common Position of 2 June 1997 concerning conflict prevention and resolution in Africa (97/356/CFSP)', *OJ* L 153, 11 June 1997, 'Common Position of 14 May 2001 concerning conflict prevention, management and resolution in Africa (2001/374CFSP)', *OJ* L 123, 15 May 2001, and 'Common Position 2005/304/CFSP of 12 April 2005 concerning conflict prevention, management and resolution in Africa', *OJ* L 97, 15 April 2005.

[21] European Council, Göteberg, 'EU programme for the prevention of violent conflicts', 15–16 June 2001.

[22] Secretary-General/High Representative and the European Commission, 'Improving the coherence and effectiveness of European Union action in the field of conflict prevention', press release no.14088/00, Brussels, 30 November 2000, p. 2.

[23] General Affairs Council, 'Conclusions, 22–23 January 2001'.

[24] European Council, Göteberg, 'EU programme for the prevention of violent conflicts'.

[25] Council of the European Union, 'Report on the implementation of the European security strategy: providing security in a changing world', S407/08, Brussels, 11 December 2008, p. 9.

[26] Council of the European Union, 'Council conclusions on conflict prevention', Luxembourg, 20 June 2011, paragraph 1.

[27] Secretary-General, 'Improving the coherence and effectiveness', p. 2. A decade later, the Council put it less self-interestedly: 'Violent conflicts cost lives, cause human rights abuses, displace people, disrupt livelihoods, set back economic development, exacerbate state fragility, weaken governance and undermine national and regional security.' Council of the EU, 'Council conclusions on conflict prevention' (2011), paragraph 1.

[28] European Council, 'A secure Europe in a better world', p. 4.

[29] Reinhardt Rummel, *Common Foreign and Security Policy and Conflict Prevention*, London: Saferworld and International Alert, 1996, pp. 10–15.

[30] Alexander Costy and Stefan Gilbert, *Conflict Prevention and the European Union: Mapping the Actors, Instruments and Institutions*, London: Forum on Early Warning and Early Response, and International Alert, 1998, p. 32.

[31] See, for example, Ministry for Foreign Affairs (Sweden), *Preventing Violent Conflict: A Study. Executive Summary and Recommendations*, Stockholm: Ministry for Foreign Affairs, 1994.

[32] Finland has traditionally played a strong role in mediation efforts. See in general, Tanja Tamminen, ed., *Strengthening the EU's Peace Mediation Capacities* FIIA report 34, Helsinki: Finnish Institute for International Affairs, 2012.

[33] See, for example, European Parliament. 'Resolution on developing the Union's capabilities in conflict prevention and civil crisis management', 15 March 2001, B5–172/2001. In March 2013, MEPs and parliamentarians from EU member states met to discuss ways of strengthening the EU's role in conflict prevention and resolution. See the press release http://www.oireachtas.ie/parliament/mediazone/pressreleases/name-16039-en.html (last accessed 8 August 2013).

[34] See International Crisis Group, *EU Crisis Response Capability: Institutions and Processes for Conflict Prevention and Management*, ICG Issues Report no. 2, Brussels, 26 June 2001; Costy and Gilbert, *Conflict Prevention*; and Rummel, *Common Foreign and Security Policy*.

[35] European Commission, COM (2001) 211, p. 6.

[36] See Council of the EU, 'Common position of 14 May 2001', article 2. These definitions have remained pretty stable, and are largely repeated in Council of the EU, 'Common Position of 12 April 2005', article 2.

[37] Secretary-General, 'Improving the coherence and effectiveness', p. 6.

[38] Council of the EU, 'Council conclusions on conflict prevention' (2011), quote from paragraph 4.

[39] European Peacebuilding Liaison Office, 'The EEAS and peacebuilding one year on', April 2012, p. 5; available at: http://www.eplo.org/assets/files/2.%20Activities/Working%20Groups/EEAS/EPLO_Statement_EEASPeacebuildingOne YearOn.pdf (last accessed 9 August 2013).

[40] European Peacebuilding Liaison Office, 'Power analysis' (March 2013).

[41] Ashdown, *Swords and Ploughshares*, p. 188.

[42] Council of the EU, 'Council conclusions on conflict prevention' (2011), paragraph 5.

[43] ADE, 'Thematic evaluation of European Commission support', p. 29, pp. 20–24.

[44] European Peacebuilding Liaison Office, 'The EEAS and Peacebuilding One Year On', p. 3.

[45] Schünemann, 'EU conflict prevention 10 years after Göteberg', p. 4.

[46] Els Vanheusden, 'Overview of the conflict prevention policy of the EU', MICROCON Policy Working Paper 16, Brighton: MICROCON, 2011, p. 15.

[47] Task Force on the EU Prevention of Mass Atrocities, 'The EU and the prevention of mass atrocities: strengths and weaknesses', February 2013, p. 43.

[48] European External Action Service, 'Strategy for security and development in the Sahel', 2011, http://eeas.europa.eu/africa/docs/sahel_strategy_en.pdf (last accessed 15 August 2013). While some observers praised the link made between development and security in this strategy, some NGOs (such as Bond) criticized the prioritization of anti-terrorism and security operations in the Sahel. See UK government, 'Review of the balance of competences between the United Kingdom and the European Union: development cooperation and humanitarian aid report', July 2013, pp. 44 and 56.

[49] Council of the EU, 'Council conclusions on the situation in Mali', 15 October 2012; Nick Witney, 'Where does CSDP fit in European foreign policy?', Policy Paper no. 64, Notre Europe, 13 February 2013, p. 2.

[50] Schünemann, 'EU conflict prevention 10 years after Göteberg', p. 3.

[51] United Nations Secretary-General, 'An agenda for development', report no. A/48/935, 6 May 1994

[52] To cite a few negative experiences: Hutu extremists, responsible for the genocide in Rwanda, were sheltered and fed in the Rwandan refugee camps; the refugee camps in Zaire (now DRC) created security problems for the local population; humanitarian and food aid to Somalia affected political stability there.

[53] European Commission, 'Linking relief, rehabilitation and development, "LRRD"', COM (96) 153 final, 30 April 1996, p. 20.

[54] Costy and Gilbert, *Conflict Prevention*, p. 13; European Commission, COM (2001) 211, p. 10.

[55] Council of the EU, 'Conclusions on preventive diplomacy in Africa' (1995); Development Council, 'Resolution on coherence', 5 June 1997, and 'Conclusions, 30 November 1998', press release no. 13461/98.

[56] Development Council, 'Conclusions, 31 May 2001' and Development Council and the European Commission, 'The European Community's development policy', press release no. 12929/00 (Presse 421), 10 November 2000.

[57] ADE, 'Thematic evaluation of European Commission support', p. 29, pp 7–8.

[58] European Commission, COM (2001) 211, p. 11.

[59] Catriona Gourlay, 'Civil-civil co-ordination in EU crisis management', in Agnieszka Nowak, ed., *Civilian Crisis Management: The EU Way*. Chaillot Paper no. 90, Paris: EU Institute for Security Studies, June 2006, p. 107.

60 Catriona Gourlay, 'The EU's progress in mainstreaming conflict prevention'. *European Security Review* (ISIS Europe), no. 12, May 2002, p. 2.

61 Rummel, 'The EU's involvement in conflict prevention', pp. 80–4.

62 The remainder focused on responses to transnational security threats, and reducing risks related to chemical, biological, radiological and nuclear materials. European Commission, '2012 annual report on the instrument for stability', COM(2013) 563 final, 26 July 2013.

63 European Commission, 'Agenda 2000: for a stronger and wider union', *EU Bulletin Supplement 5/97*, p. 51.

64 European Council, Helsinki, 'Presidency conclusions', 10–11 December 1999, paragraph 4. This condition was aimed at Turkey in the first instance, but builds on previous declarations vis-à-vis the other applicants.

65 On this issue, see Tocci, *The EU and Conflict Resolution*, chapter 3; Oliver Richmond, 'Shared sovereignty and the politics of peace: evaluating the EU's "catalytic" framework in the Eastern Mediterranean', *International Affairs*, 82, 1 (2006).

66 Tocci notes that the EU's stance was perceived to be self-interested: the EU would thus avoid having to negotiate two SAAs, and enlarge to an even higher number of states. Tocci, *The EU and Conflict Resolution*, p. 99.

67 On one estimate, the economic sanctions cost FYROM over $2 billion by 1997. Sophia Clément, *Conflict Prevention in the Balkans: Case Studies of Kosovo and the FYR of Macedonia*, Chaillot Paper no. 30, Paris: Western European Union Institute for Security Studies, 1997, p. 30.

68 Clara Portela, 'The EU's sanctions against Syria: conflict management by other means', Egmont Security Policy Brief no. 38, Brussels: Royal Institute for International Relations, 2012, p. 2.

69 Jonathan Marcus, 'Syria arms embargo: EU divided despite consensus', BBC news online, 28 May 2013.

70 European Council, Luxembourg, 'Presidency conclusions', June 1991; European Council, Lisbon, 'Presidency conclusions', June 1992.

71 CFSP Common Position 2008/944/CFSP, 8 December 2008, in *OJ* L 335, 13 December 2008.

72 Council of the EU, 'EU Strategy to combat illicit accumulation and trafficking of SALW and their ammunition', document no. 5319/06, 13 January 2006, p. 5.

73 Council of the EU, 'Joint action of 17 December 1998 on the European Union's contribution to combating the destabilizing accumulation and spread of small arms and light weapons (1999/34/CFSP)' in *OJ* L 9, 15 January 1999.

74 European Commission, COM (2001) 211, p. 23.

75 Council of the EU, 'Concept on strengthening EU mediation and dialogue capacities', doc. 15779/09, 10 November 2009.

76 Council of the European Union, 'Council conclusions on conflict prevention' (2011), paragraph 6. See also Tamminen, ed., *Strengthening the EU's Peace Mediation Capacities*.

77 On the dispute, see Smith, *The Making of EU Foreign Policy*, pp. 151–5.

78 Council of the EU, 'Common Position of 12 April 2005'.

79 Simon Taylor, 'EU–NATO: room for Improvement', *European Voice*, 7–13 June 2007; Toby Vogel, 'Diplomats warn over poor EU–NATO communication', *European Voice*, 22–28 November 2007.

[80] This language is repeated in the presidency reports to the Helsinki, Feira, and Nice European Councils.

[81] 'EU unlikely to deploy Chad force on time due to dispute over funding, helicopters', *International Herald Tribune*, 28 November 2007; 'Russia "ready to help EU" in Chad', BBC news, 29 September 2008.

[82] 'EU split on Congo troop mission', BBC news, 8 December 2008; Toby Vogel, 'Why Europe is split over troops for Congo', *European Voice*, 11 December 2008.

[83] Richard Gowan, 'Good intentions, bad outcomes', *E! Sharp*, January-February 2009, p. 58.

[84] Sven Biscop and Edith Drieskens, 'Effective multilateralism and collective security: empowering the UN', in Katie Verlin Laatikainen and Karen E Smith, eds, *The European Union at the United Nations: Intersecting Multilateralisms*, London: Macmillan, 2006, pp. 126–7.

[85] Secretary-General, 'Improving the coherence and effectiveness', paragraph 26.

[86] International Crisis Group, *EU Crisis Response Capability*, p. 7.

Chapter 8   The fight against international crime

[1] Council of the EU, 'European Union priorities and objectives for external relations in the field of justice and home affairs', press release no. 7653/00, 6 June 2000.

[2] On the blurring distinction between external and internal security, see Malcolm Anderson and Joanna Apap, *Changing Conceptions of Security and their Implications for EU Justice and Home Affairs Cooperation*, CEPS Policy Brief no. 26, Brussels: Centre for European Policy Studies, 2002.

[3] Elsewhere I have described the 'external dimension of JHA' as a 'policy universe', comprising issues that are dealt with at the EU level under a variety of different institutional set-ups (first pillar, second pillar, and remnants of the third pillar) – and across all of them. Those issues can be summarized as immigration and asylum policy, and combating crime (including terrorism, drug-trafficking, currency forgery and so on). They have an 'internal dimension', involving cooperation, coordination and policy-making which principally relates to within the EU's borders, and an 'external dimension', involving the incorporation of JHA issues in relations with countries outside the EU's borders – though that 'internal–external' distinction can be quite blurry at times. Karen E. Smith, 'The justice and home affairs policy universe: some directions for further research', *European Integration*, 31, 1 (2009): 3.

[4] These are the forms of international crime that Europol deals with.

[5] Council of the EU, 'A strategy for the external dimension of JHA: global freedom, security and justice', document 15446/05, 6 December 2005, p. 5.

[6] See Monar, 'The dynamics of justice and home affairs', pp. 754–6.

[7] Leslie Holmes, 'Crime, corruption and politics: transnational factors', in Alex Pravda and Jan Zielonka, eds, *Democratic Consolidation in Eastern Europe. Volume 2: International and Transnational Factors*, Oxford: Oxford University Press, 2001, pp. 196–203.

[8] Didier Bigo, 'Border regimes, police cooperation and security in an enlarged European Union', in Jan Zielonka, ed., *Europe Unbound: Enlarging and Reshaping the Boundaries of the European Union*, London: Routledge, 2002, p. 229.

[9] European Council, 'A secure Europe in a better world', p. 5. Trafficked women are women smuggled into the EU and forced into prostitution.

[10] European Council, Tampere, 'Presidency conclusions', paragraph 8.

[11] Council of the EU, 'EU priorities and objectives (2000)', p. 1.

[12] Council of the European Union, 'The Hague programme: strengthening freedom, security and justice in the European Union', in *OJ* C 53, 3 March 2005, p. 14.

[13] Council of the EU, 'A strategy for the external dimension of JHA' (2005).

[14] European Council, 'The Stockholm programme – an open and secure Europe serving and protecting citizens', *OJ* C 115, 4 May 2010, pp. 34–5.

[15] Council of the European Union, 'Internal security strategy for the European Union: towards a European security model', document no. 7120/10, 25–26 February 2010, see especially p. 17.

[16] As the Belgian presidency noted in late 2001, 'major differences of approach' have emerged on criminal matters: there are concerns about the level of protection of civil liberties in other states, a reluctance to harmonize penal sanctions, and a reluctance to provide Europol with sensitive information. Belgian Presidency, 'Evaluation of the conclusions of the Tampere European Council', Council of the EU document no. 14926/01, 6 December 2001. This still holds true more than ten years later.

[17] See, for example, Council of the European Union, Note from the Counter-Terrorism Coordinator, 'EU counter-terrorism strategy-discussion paper', document no. 9990/12, 23 May 2012, pp. 5–6.

[18] On the counter-terrorism action plan, see Raphael Bossong, 'The action plan on countering terrorism: a flawed instrument of EU security governance', *Journal of Common Market Studies*, 46, 1 (2008). Two observers have even argued that the next multiannual programme should focus only on implementation of existing policies and priorities. Sergio Carrera and Elspeth Guild, 'Does the Stockholm programme matter? The struggles over ownership and AFSJ multiannual programming', CEPS Paper in Liberty and Security in Europe no. 51, Brussels: Centre for European Policy Studies, 2012, p. 15.

[19] Jörg Monar, 'Justice and home affairs', in Nathaniel Copsey and Tim Haughton, eds, *The JCSM Annual Review of the European Union in 2012*, Oxford: Wiley-Blackwell, 2013, p. 133.

[20] Council of the EU, 'EU priorities and objectives' (2000), p. 4.

[21] See Annex 1, 'Chairmanship and commission attendance in Foreign Affairs Council preparatory working groups', in Helwig, Ivan and Kostanyan, 'The new EU foreign policy architecture'.

[22] Originally, both of these DGs were one (the DG Justice, Liberty and Security) but tensions between two relevant Commissioners (Commissioner for Home Affairs Cecilia Malmström and Commissioner for Justice, Fundamental Rights and Citizenship) led Commission President Barroso to separate them. Carrera and Guild, 'Does the Stockholm programme matter?', pp. 2–3. See also Jörg

Monar, 'Justice and home affairs', *The JCMS Annual Review of the European Union in 2010*, pp. 157–8.

[23] Carrera and Guild, 'Does the Stockholm programme matter?', pp. 2–5.

[24] European Commission, 'The EU internal security strategy in action: five steps towards a more secure Europe', COM (2010) 673 final, 22 November 2010, p. 3.

[25] Events include: the killing of a British policewoman by a gunshot from the window of the Libyan People's Bureau in London (1984); terrorist attacks at the Vienna and Rome airports (1985); the bombing of a Berlin discotheque (1986), for which Libya was implicated; the attempted bombing of a London-Tel Aviv flight (1986), for which Syria was implicated; and the bombing of a Pan Am flight over Lockerbie, Scotland (1988), for which Libya was implicated.

[26] Nuttall, *European Political Co-operation*, pp. 302–3.

[27] 'Statement by the twelve foreign ministers on the combating of international terrorism, Brussels, 27 January 1986', document no. 4b/25, in Hill and Smith, eds, *European Foreign Policy*, pp. 323–5.

[28] On Libya, see 'Statement by the twelve foreign ministers on international terrorism and the crisis in the Mediterranean, The Hague, 14 April 1986', document no. 4b/26, in Hill and Smith, eds, *European Foreign Policy*, pp. 325–6. On Syria, see 'Press statement by the presidency on terrorism, London, 10 November 1986', document no. 4b/28, in Hill and Smith, eds, *European Foreign Policy*, pp. 327–8.

[29] Council of the EU and European Commission, 'Action plan on how best to implement the provisions of the Treaty of Amsterdam establishing an area of freedom, security and justice', 7 December 1998, paragraph 18, pp. 10–12.

[30] European Council, Tampere, 'Presidency conclusions', paragraphs 43–50.

[31] See Heather Grabbe, 'Breaking new ground in internal security', in Edward Bannerman, et al., *Europe after September 11ᵗʰ*, London: Centre for European Reform, 2002, pp. 63–6.

[32] European Council, Brussels, 'Conclusions and plan of action of the extraordinary European Council meeting on 21 September 2001'.

[33] Rik Coolsaet, 'EU counterterrorism strategy: value added or chimera', *International Affairs*, 86, 4 (2010): 871.

[34] See Council of the EU, 'Common position of 27 December 2001 on the application of specific measures to combat terrorism (2001/931/CFSP)', OJ L 344 28 December 2001. The EU list is incorporated into the USA's own list of terrorists. Spanish Presidency, 'Memorandum on the EU's external relations in the field of JHA', Council document no. 10835/02, 9 July 2002, p. 21.

[35] Council of the EU, 'Framework decision of 13 June 2002 on combating terrorism', OJ L 164 22 June 2002, and 'Council framework decision of 13 June 2002 on the European arrest warrant and surrender procedures between member states', OJ L 190, 18 July 2002.

[36] Although the UK government announced in July 2013 that it would opt out of a hundred or so JHA measures, it would still keep the European arrest warrant.

[37] European Council, 'Declaration on combating terrorism', 25 March 2004.

[38] European Council, 'The European Union counter-terrorism strategy', document 14469/4/05 REV 4, 15/16 December 2005.

[39] Sarah Laitner, 'EU Counter-terrorism chief's efforts hampered by Turf Wars', *The Financial Times*, 7 March 2005.

[40] Apparently Solana and his office were too busy to find a replacement. They were seeking, however, to strengthen the role and mandate of the new coordinator. Judith Crosbie, 'Solana steps up effort to fill anti-terrorism post', *European Voice*, 5–11 July 2007.

[41] This includes all attacks considered to be terrorist, whether by religious-inspired groups, left-wing or right-wing groups, lone attackers, or single issue groups such as extremist animal rights groups. Europol, 'EU terrorism situation and trend report 2010' and EU terrorism situation and trend report 2012'.

[42] See Coolsaet, 'EU counterterrorism strategy', pp. 861, 866–70.

[43] European Commission, 'EC external assistance facilitating the implementation of UN Security Council Resolution 1373: An Overview', SEC (2002), 231, 25 February 2002.

[44] European Council, Seville, 'Conclusions of the presidency', Annex V. Of course, one of the biggest controversies in the fight against terrorism is the extent to which human rights and civil liberties are being curtailed *within* EU member states (by, for example, extending the period in which suspects can be detained without being charged, or increasing surveillance of the population by CCTV cameras).

[45] See, for example, European Commission, 'A strategy on the external dimension of the area of freedom, security and justice', COM (2005) 491 final, 12 October 2005, p. 5.

[46] Jef Huysmans, 'The European Union and the securitization of migration', *Journal of Common Market Studies*, 38, 5 (2000): 752.

[47] Zielonka, 'How new enlarged borders', p. 522.

[48] Andrew Geddes, 'International migration and state sovereignty in an integrating Europe', *International Migration*, 39, 6 (2001): 30.

[49] Council of the EU, 'Comprehensive plan to combat illegal immigration and trafficking of human beings in the European Union', document no. 6621/1/02 REV 1, 27 February 2002.

[50] Justice and Home Affairs Council, 'Conclusions, 13 June 2002', press release no. 9620/02 (Presse 175).

[51] David Cronin, 'Immigration – time to see if moderates or extremists are running the show', *European Voice*, 20–6 June 2002.

[52] Judith Sunderland, 'Frontex should respect rights, even on the high seas', *European Voice*, 6 June 2013.

[53] See Brussels European Council, Presidency Conclusions, 15/16 December 2005; Council of the EU, 'Draft conclusions on extending and enhancing the global approach to migration', document no. 10746/07, 13 June 2007.

[54] See William Vlcek, 'Development v terrorism – migrant remittances or terrorist financing?''. LSE Challenge Working Paper, September 2006; available at www.lse.ac.uk/Depts/intrel/EUfoRPUnit.html (last accessed 13 January 2014).

[55] Jörg Monar, 'Justice and home affairs', *The JCMS Annual Review of the European Union in 2011*, p 117.

56   European Commission, 'Communication on migration', COM (2011) 248 final,
     4 May 2011. It was endorsed by the June 2011 European Council.
57   Sergio Carrera, Joanna Parkin and Leonhard den Hertog, 'EU migration policy
     after the Arab spring: the pitfalls of home affairs diplomacy', Notre Europe/
     CEPS Policy Paper 74, 26 February 2013.
58   Council of the European Union, 'EU drugs strategy (2013–20)', OJ C 402, 29
     December 2012.
59   Council of the European Union, 'EU drugs strategy (2013–20)', paragraph 28.
60   Council of the European Union, 'European pact to combat international drug
     trafficking – disrupting cocaine and heroin routes', 3 June 2010, paragraph 4.
61   David Cronin, 'EU human rights push at odds with US "secret war" in Colombia',
     European Voice, 14–20 June 2001.
62   European Commission, 'Proposal for a council framework decision on combat-
     ing terrorism', COM (2001) 521 final, 19 September 2001.These include the
     Council of Europe 1977 convention on the suppression of terrorism, and
     several UN conventions from the 1970 convention on the suppression of
     Unlawful Seizure of Aircraft to the 1999 convention for the suppression of
     financing terrorism.
63   Council of the EU, 'Framework decision of 13 June 2002'. The maximum penal-
     ties range from at least eight to fifteen year's imprisonment.
64   Council of the EU, 'Comprehensive plan to combat illegal immigration' (2002),
     p. 27; 'Council framework decision of 19 July 2002 on combating trafficking
     in human beings', in OJ L 203, 1 August 2002.
65   Council of the EU, 'Council framework decision of 19 July 2002'. It sets a
     maximum penalty of at least eight years' imprisonment for trafficking;
     Directive 2011/36/EU of the European Parliament and of the Council of 5 April
     2011 on preventing and combating trafficking in human beings and protect-
     ing its victims, and replacing Council Framework Decision 2002/629/JHA', in
     OJ L 101, 15 April 2011.
66   European Commission, 'Proposal for a council framework decision laying
     down minimum provisions on the constituent elements of criminal acts and
     penalties in the field of illicit drug trafficking', COM (2001) 259 final, 23 May
     2001, pp 5, 15. The commission suggested imprisonment of five to ten years
     for activities involving large quantities of drugs.
67   The 1961 Single Convention on Narcotic Drugs, the 1971 Vienna Convention
     on Psychotropic Substances, and the 1988 Convention against Illicit Traffic in
     Narcotic Drugs and Psychotropic Substances.
68   See JHA Council, 'Conclusions, 13 June 2002, p. 15; Council of the EU,
     'Framework decision laying down minimum provisions on the constituent
     elements of criminal acts and penalties in the field of drug trafficking', in OJ
     L 335, 11 November 2004. Penalties for serious offences range from five to ten
     years imprisonment; for very serious offences, at least ten.
69   The European Commission pledged to incorporate migration aspects into the
     2003 review of all country strategy papers, which could lead to a reallocation
     of funding within each country programme. European Commission,
     'Integrating migration issues in the European Union's relations with third
     countries', COM (2002) 703 final, 3 December 2002, p. 27.

[70] European Commission, SEC (2002) 231, pp. 4–5. Refugee returns are also funded through the European Refugee Fund, which helps the EU member states deal with refugee influxes and returns.

[71] European Commission, 'Thematic programme: cooperation with third countries in areas of migration and asylum: 2011–2013 Multi-Annual Strategy Paper'; Regulation (EC) no. 491/2004 of the European Parliament and of the Council of 10 March 2004 establishing a programme for financial and technical assistance to third countries in the areas of migration and asylum (AENEAS), *OJ* L 80, 18 March 2004.

[72] European Commission, 'The global approach to migration and mobility', COM (2011) 743 final, 18 November 2011, p. 10.

[73] Ibid.

[74] European Commission, 'Progress report on the implementation of the strategy for the external dimension of the JHA', SEC (2006) 1498, 16 November 2006, p 6.

[75] See Council of the EU, 'Joint action of 13 April 2000 on a European Union assistance programme to support the Palestinian authority', in *OJ* L 97, 19 April 2001 and European Commission SEC (2002) 231.

[76] Council of the EU, 'Multi-annual financial framework 2014–20 – List of Programmes', document no. 8288/13, 9 April 2013.

[77] European Commission, 'Building an open and security Europe: The Home Affairs Budget for 2014–2020', COM (2011) 749 final, 15 November 2011, p. 12.

[78] European Commission, 'Communication on the implementation of the EU action plan on drugs (2000–2004)', COM (2001) 301 final, 8 June 2001, pp. 6–7, 40–4.

[79] European Commission, DG Relex/B2 – Treaties Office, 'Inventory of Agreements Containing the Anti-Terrorism Clause', 7 July 2011 (downloaded 15 August 2013).

[80] Richard Norton-Taylor, 'Secret terror treaty plan raises rights fears', *Guardian*, 3 September 2002.

[81] European Commission, 'Communication on a common policy on illegal immigration', COM (2001) 672 final, 15 November 2001, p. 24.

[82] European Commission, DG RELEX/B2 – Treaties Office, 'Inventory of Agreements Containing the Readmission Clause', 7 July 2011, downloaded 15 August 2013.

[83] Sandra Lavenex, 'Asylum, immigration and Central-Eastern Europe: Challenges to EU Enlargement', *European Foreign Affairs Review*, 3, 2 (1998): 281, 291–2.

[84] European Commission, 'Policy priorities in the fight against illegal immigration of third country nationals', COM (2006) 402 final, 19 July 2006, p. 10.

[85] European Commission, COM (2002) 703, pp. 25–6.

[86] Monar, 'Justice and home affairs', in *The JCMS Annual Review of the European Union in 2012*, pp. 128–9.

[87] European Commission, 'Evaluation of EU readmission agreements', COM (2011) 76 final, 23 February 2011.

[88] Carrera, Parkin and den Hertog, 'EU migration policy after the Arab spring', p. 2.

[89] Council of the EU, 'EU priorities and objectives' (2000), p. 4

[90] Belgian Presidency, 'Evaluation of the conclusions', p. 12.

91 See the explanation on DG Home Affairs' website: http://ec.europa.eu/dgs/ home-affairs/what-we-do/policies/international-affairs/global-approach-to-migration/specific-tools/index_en.htm#1 (last accessed 15 August 2013).

92 European Commission, SEC (2006) 1498, p. 12.

93 European Council, 'Common strategy of the European Union of 14 June 1999 on Russia (1999/14/CFSP', *OJ* L 157, 24 June 1999.

94 European Commission, SEC (2006) 1498, pp. 9–10.

95 The countries are Bolivia, Columbia, Costa Rica, Ecuador, El Salvador, Guatemala, Honduras, Nicaragua, Panama, Peru and Venezuela.

96 Council regulation no 980/2005, *OJ* L 169, 30 June 2005.

97 Council of the EU, 'CFSP Annual Report 2001', p. 14.

98 EEAS, 'EU Launches a need assessment mission for border management in Libya', 2 March 2012, http://eeas.europa.eu/libya/docs/2012_lybia_border_ management_en.pdf (last accessed 13 January 2014).

99 JHA Council, 'Conclusions, 13 June 2002'.

100 European External Action Service, 'EU training mission in Mali (EUTM)', February 2013, available at: http://consilium.europa.eu/media/1892457/ factsheet_eutm_mali_en_.pdf (last accessed 15 August 2013).

101 European External Action Service, 'EU border assistance mission (EUBAM) in Libya', no date; available at: http://www.eeas.europa.eu/csdp/missions_ operations/eubam-libya/eubam_factsheet_en.pdf (last accessed 17 August 2013).

102 See Isabelle Ioannides, 'EU police mission *Proxima*: testing the European approach to building peace', in Agnieszka Nowak, ed., *Civilian Crisis Management: The EU Way*, Chaillot Paper no. 90, Paris: EU Institute for Security Studies, 2006.

103 Agnieska Nowak, 'Civilian crisis management within ESDP', in Novak, ed., *Civilian Crisis Management* (2006), pp. 26–7.

104 Felix Berenskoetter, 'Under construction: ESDP and the "Fight against organised crime"', LSE Challenge working paper, July 2006, available at www.lse. ac.uk/Depts/intrel/EUfoRPUnit.html (last accessed 13 January 2014), pp. 22–4.

105 Monar, 'The dynamics of justice and home affairs', pp. 761–2.

106 See Zielonka, 'How new enlarged borders', pp. 522–6.

Chapter 9   Conclusion

1 Sven Biscop, 'Raiders of the lost art: strategy-making in Europe', Egmont Security Policy Brief no. 40, Brussels: Egmont Royal Institute for International Relations, 2012.

2 See Nathalie Chaban, Ole Elgström and Martin Holland. 'The European Union as others see it', *European Foreign Affairs Review*, 11, 2 (2006); Sonia Lucarelli, ed., 'The external image of the EU', special issue of *European Foreign Affairs Review*, 12, 3 (2007); and Martin Ortega, ed., *Global Views on the European Union*, Chaillot Paper no. 72, Paris: EU Institute for Security Studies, 2004.

3 In a recent series of roundtables on EU foreign policy after Lisbon held at the LSE in 2011–12, numerous speakers highlighted the damaging effect of the euro crisis on the EU's role and image in the world. See http://www2.lse.ac.uk/ internationalRelations/centresandunits/EFPU/EUFPafterLisbon.aspx. See also

European Council on Foreign Relations, 'Introduction', *European Foreign Policy Scorecard 2012*; available at: http://www.ecfr.eu/page/-/ECFR_SCORECARD_2012_ WEB.pdf (last accessed 13 January 2014) and BBC World Service, 'Views of Europe slide sharply in global poll, while views of China improve', 10 May 2012, http://www.worldpublicopinion.org/pipa/articles/views_on_countries regions_bt/717.php (last accessed 13 January 2014).

[4] See, for example, Elisabeth Johansson-Nogués, *The Decline of the EU's 'Magnetic Attraction'? The European Union in the Eyes of Neighbouring Arab Countries and Russia*, LSE European Foreign Policy Unit Working Paper no. 2011–1. London: LSE, March 2011.

References

Addo, Michael. 'Some issues in European Community aid policy and human rights', *Legal Issues in European Integration*, 1 (1988).

ADE. 'Thematic evaluation of European Commission support to conflict prevention and peace-building; Final Report, volume 1: Main report', October 2011.

Allen, David. 'The European rescue of national foreign policy?', in Christopher Hill, ed., *The Actors in Europe's Foreign Policy*. London: Routledge, 1996.

__ ' "Who speaks for Europe?" The search for an effective and coherent external policy', in John Peterson and Helene Sjursen, eds, *A Common Foreign Policy for Europe?* London: Routledge, 1998.

Allen, David and Michael Smith. 'Western Europe's presence in the contemporary international arena', *Review of International Studies*, 16, 1 (1990).

Allen, David and Michael Smith. 'Relations with the rest of the world', in Nathaniel Copsey and Tim Haughton, eds, *The JCMS Annual Review of the European Union in 2010*. Oxford: Wiley-Blackwell, 2011.

__ 'Relations with the rest of the world', in Nathaniel Copsey and Tim Haughton, eds, *The JCMS Annual Review of the European Union in 2011*. Oxford: Wiley-Blackwell, 2012.

Alston, Philip, ed. *The EU and Human Rights*. Oxford: Oxford University Press, 2000.

Amnesty International. 'Annual Report 2006–7: Human Rights and the EU', 23 May 2007.

Anderson, Malcolm and Joanna Apap. *Changing Conceptions of Security and their Implications for EU Justice and Home Affairs Cooperation*. CEPS Policy Brief no. 26, Brussels: Centre for European Policy Studies, 2002.

Annan, Kofi. 'Democracy as an International Issue', *Global Governance*, 8, 2 (2002).

Arts, Karin. *Integrating Human Rights into Development Cooperation: The Case of the Lomé Convention*. The Hague: Kluwer Law International, 2000.

Ashdown, Paddy. *Swords and Ploughshares: Bringing Peace to the 21st Century*. London: Weidenfeld and Nicolson, 2007.

Asseburg, Muriel. 'The Arab spring and the European response', *The International Spectator*, 48, 2 (2013).

Azpuru, Dinorah, Steven E. Finkel, Aníbal Pérez-Liñán and Mitcheel A. Sligson. 'Trends in democracy assistance: what has the United States been doing?', *Journal of Democracy*, 19, 2 (2008).

Baabood, Abdulla. 'Dynamics and determinants of the GCC states' foreign policy, with special reference to the EU', in Gerd Nonneman, ed., *Analyzing Middle East Foreign Policies*. London: Routledge, 2005.

Baabood, Abdulla and Geoffrey Edwards. 'Reinforcing ambivalence: the interaction of Gulf states and the European Union', *European Foreign Affairs Review*, 12, 4 (2007).

Baehr, Peter. *The Role of Human Rights in Foreign Policy*. Houndmills: Macmillan, 1994.

Baldwin, David. *Economic Statecraft*. Princeton: Princeton University Press, 1985.

Bailes, Alyson J. K. 'The role of subregional cooperation in post-Cold War Europe: integration, security, democracy', in Andrew Cottey, ed. *Subregional Cooperation in the New Europe: Building Security, Prosperity and Solidarity from the Barents to the Black Sea*. London: Macmillan, 1999.

Balfour, Rosa. *Human Rights and Democracy in EU Foreign Policy: The Cases of Ukraine and Egypt*. London: Routledge, 2012.

Barbé, Esther. 'Balancing Europe's eastern and southern dimension', in Jan Zielonka, ed., *Paradoxes of European Foreign Policy*. The Hague: Kluwer Law International, 1998.

Barbé, Esther and Benjamin Kienzle. 'Security provider or security consumer? The European Union and conflict management', *European Foreign Affairs Review*, 12, 4 (2007).

Barya, John-Jean. 'The new political conditionalities of aid: an independent view from Africa', *IDS Bulletin*, 24, 3 (1993).

Beetham, David. *Democracy and Human Rights*. Cambridge: Polity Press, 1999.

Belgian Presidency. 'Evaluation of the conclusions of the Tampere European Council', Council document no. 14926/01, 6 December 2001.

Bendiek, Annegret and Hannah Whitney-Steele. 'The financing of the EU's common foreign and security policy', SWP Comments 16, Berlin: Stiftung Wissenschaft und Politik, June 2006.

Bendiek, Annegret, Hannah Whitney-Steele and Heinz Kramer. 'The EU as a "strategic" international actor: substantial and analytical ambiguities', *European Foreign Affairs Review*, 15, 4 (2010).

Berenskoetter, Felix. 'Under construction: ESDP and the "fight against organised crime"', LSE Challenge working paper, July 2006; available at: www.lse.ac.uk/Depts/intrel/EUroFPUnit.html (last accessed 13 January 2014).

Bicchi, Federica. 'Want funding? Don't mention Islam: EU democracy promotion in the Mediterranean', *CFSP Forum*, 4, 2 (2006); available at: http://www.lse.ac.uk/internationalRelations/centresandunits/EFPU/FORNETarchive.aspx (last accessed 13 January 2014).

Bigo, Didier. 'Border regimes, police cooperation and security in an enlarged European Union', in Jan Zielonka, ed., *Europe Unbound: Enlarging and Reshaping the Boundaries of the European Union*. London: Routledge, 2002.

Birnbaum, Karl and Ingo Peters. 'The CSCE: a reassessment of its role in the 1980s', *Review of International Studies*, 16, 4 (1990).

Biscop, Sven. 'Raiders of the lost art: strategy-making in Europe', Egmont Security Policy Brief no. 40, Brussels: Egmont Royal Institute for International Relations, 2012.

Biscop, Sven and Edith Drieskens. 'Effective multilateralism and collective security: empowering the UN', in Katie Verlin Laatikainen and Karen E. Smith, eds, *The European Union at the United Nations: Intersecting Multilateralisms*. London: Palgrave, 2006.

Blockmans, Steven. 'The European external action service one year on: first signs of strengths and weaknesses', CLEER Working Paper 2012/2, The Hague: TMC Asser Institute, 2012.

BOND. 'Renewing Europe's role as a global development actor: BOND submission to the future of Europe convention', London, 2002.

Bossong, Raphael. 'The action plan on countering terrorism: a flawed instrument of EU security governance', *Journal of Common Market Studies*, 46, 1 (2008).

Bossuyt, Fabienne. 'The social dimension of the new generation of EU FTAs with Asia and Latin America: ambitious continuation for the sake of policy coherence', *European Foreign Affairs Review*, 14, 5 (2009).

Boucher, Nicholas. 'Democracy lobby under siege' *The World Today*, June and July 2012.

Boutros-Ghali, Boutros. *An Agenda for Peace*. New York: United Nations, 1992.

Bradley, Andrew. 'An ACP perspective and overview of Article 96 cases', ECDPM (European Centre for Development Policy Management) Discussion Paper no. 64D, Maastricht, August 2005.

Bretherton, Charlotte and John Vogler. *The European Union as a Global Actor*. 2nd edn, London: Routledge, 2006.

__ 'Towards an EU policy for sustainable development?', in Stefan Gänzle, Sven Grimm and Davina Makhan, eds, *The European Union and Global Development*. Houndmills: Palgrave Macmillan, 2012.

Bromley, Mark. 'The review of the EU common position on arms exports: prospects for strengthened controls', EU Non-Proliferation Consortium, Non-Proliferation Papers no. 7, January 2012; available at: http://www.sipri.org/research/armaments/transfers/transparency/EU_reports/research/disarmament/eu-consortium/publications/publications/non-proliferation-paper-7 (last accessed 1 August 2013).

Brummer, Klaus. 'Imposing sanctions: the not so "normative power Europe"', *European Foreign Affairs Review*, 14, 2 (2009).

Bull, Hedley. 'Civilian power Europe: a contradiction in terms?', *Journal of Common Market Studies*, 21, 1–2 (1982).

Burnell, Peter. 'Promoting democracy backwards', FRIDE Working Paper no. 28, Madrid, November 2006.

Carey, Sabine C. 'European aid: human rights versus bureaucratic inertia', *Journal of Peace Research*, 44, 4 (2007).

Carrera, Sergio and Elspeth Guild. 'Does the Stockholm programme matter? The struggles over ownership and AFSJ multiannual programming', CEPS Paper in Liberty and Security in Europe no. 51, Brussels: Centre for European Policy Studies, 2012.

Carrera, Sergio, Joanna Parkin and Leonhard den Hertog, 'EU migration policy after the Arab spring: the pitfalls of home affairs diplomacy', Notre Europe/CEPS Policy Paper 74, 26 February 2013.

Carothers, Thomas. *Aiding Democracy Abroad*. Washington, DC: Carnegie Endowment for International Peace, 1999.

__ 'The backlash against democracy promotion', *Foreign Affairs*, 85, 2 (2006).

Chaban, Nathalie, Ole Elgström and Martin Holland. 'The European Union as others see it', *European Foreign Affairs Review*, 11, 2 (2006).

Chandler, David. *Bosnia: Faking Democracy After Dayton*. 2nd edn, London: Pluto Press, 2000.

___ *From Kosovo to Kabul: Human Rights and International Intervention*. London: Pluto Press, 2002.

Clapham, Andrew. *Human Rights and the European Community: A Critical Overview*. Baden-Baden: Nomos Verlagsgesellschaft, 1991.

Clément, Sophia. *Conflict Prevention in the Balkans: Case Studies of Kosovo and the FYR of Macedonia*. Chaillot Paper no. 30. Paris: Western European Union Institute for Security Studies, 1997.

Concord. 'Hold the applause! EU Governments risk breaking aid promises', April 2007; available at www.concordeurope.org (last accessed 13 January 2014).

___ 'Spotlight on EU policy coherence for development', 2011 Report.

Coolsaet, Rik. 'EU counterterrorism strategy: value added or chimera', *International Affairs*, 86, 4 (2010).

Cooper, Robert. *The Breaking of Nations: Order and Chaos in the Twenty-First Century*. London: Atlantic Books, 2003.

Costy, Alexander and Stefan Gilbert. *Conflict Prevention and the European Union: Mapping the Actors, Instruments and Institutions*. London: Forum on Early Warning and Early Response, and International Alert, 1998.

Council of the European Union. 'Annual Report on CFSP', various years since 1997 (available at www.consilium.europa.eu; last accessed 13 January 2014).

___ 'Annual EU Report on human rights', various years since 1999 (available at www.consilium.europa.eu).

___ 'Conclusions on the principle of conditionality governing the development of the European Union's relations with certain countries of south-east Europe', 29 April 1997, *EU Bulletin*, no. 4, 1997.

___ 'Common position of 2 June 1997 concerning conflict prevention and resolution in Africa (97/356/CFSP)', in *OJ* L 153, 11 June 1997.

___ 'Common position of 25 May 1998 concerning human rights, democratic principles, the rule of law and good governance in Africa (98/350/CFSP)', in *OJ* L 158, 2 June 1998.

___ 'Joint action of 17 December 1998 on the European Union's contribution to combating the destabilizing accumulation and spread of small arms and light weapons (1999/34/CFSP)', in *OJ* L 9, 15 January 1999.

___ 'Common position 1999/345/PESC of 17 May 1999 concerning the launching of the stability pact of the EU in south-eastern Europe', *OJ* L 133, 28 May 1999.

___ 'Joint action of 13 April 2000 on a European Union assistance programme to support the Palestinian Authority in its effort to counter terrorist activities emanating from the territories under its control (2000/298/CFSP)', in *OJ* L 97, 19 April 2000.

___ 'European Union priorities and objectives for external relations in the field of justice and home affairs: fulfilling the Tampere remit', press release no. 7653/00, 6 June 2000.

___ 'Common position of 14 May 2001 concerning conflict prevention, management and resolution in Africa (2001/374/CFSP)', in *OJ* L 132, 15 May 2001.

___ 'Common position of 11 June 2001 on the International Criminal Court (2001/443/CFSP)', in *OJ* L 155, 12 June 2001.

__ 'Council conclusions on the European Union's role in promoting human rights and democratisation in third countries', Luxembourg, 25 June 2001.

__ 'Common position of 27 December 2001 on the application of specific measures to combat terrorism (2001/931/CFSP)', in *OJ* L 344, 28 December 2001.

__ 'Comprehensive plan to combat illegal immigration and trafficking of human beings in the European Union', document no. 6621/1/02 REV 1, 27 February 2002.

__ 'Council framework decision of 13 June 2002 on combating terrorism', in *OJ* L 164, 22 June 2002.

__ 'Council framework decision of 13 June 2002 on the European arrest warrant and the surrender procedures between member states', in *OJ* L 190, 18 July 2002.

__ 'Common position of 17 June 2002 updating common position 2001/931/CFSP', in *OJ* L 160, 18 June 2002.

__ 'Council framework decision of 19 July 2002 on combating trafficking in human beings', in *OJ* L 203, 1 August 2002.

__ 'Framework decision laying down minimum provisions on the constituent elements of criminal acts and penalties in the field of drug trafficking', *OJ* L 335 11 November 2004.

__ 'Action plan for ESDP support to peace and security in Africa', document no. 10538/4/04, 16 November 2004.

__ 'The Hague programme: strengthening freedom, security and justice in the European Union', in *OJ* C 53, 3 March 2005.

__ 'Common position 2005/304/CFSP of 12 April 2005 concerning conflict prevention, management and resolution in Africa', *OJ* L 97, 15 April 2005.

__ 'Council regulation (EC) no. 980/2005 of 27 June 2005 applying a scheme of generalised tariff preferences', *OJ* L 169, 30 June 2005.

__ 'A strategy for the external dimension of JHA: global freedom, security and justice', document 15446/05, 6 December 2005.

__ 'The EU and Africa: towards a strategic partnership', document no. 15961/05 (Presse 367), 18 December 2005.

__ 'EU strategy to combat illicit accumulation and trafficking of SALW and their ammunition', document 5319/06, 13 January 2006.

__ 'Mainstreaming human rights across CFSP and other EU policies', document no. 10076/06, 7 June 2006.

__ 'Council conclusions on the implementation of the EU policy on human rights and democratisation in third countries', document no. 16719/06, 13 December 2006.

__ 'The EU and Central Asia: strategy for a new partnership', document no. 10113/07, 31 May 2007.

__ 'Draft council conclusions on extending and enhancing the global approach to migration', document 10746/07, 13 June 2007.

__ The Africa–EU strategic partnership: a joint Africa–EU strategy', document 16344/07, 9 December 2007.

__'Report on the Implementation of the European security strategy: providing security in a changing world', S407/08, Brussels, 11 December 2008.

__ 'Concept on strengthening EU mediation and dialogue capacities', doc. 15779/09, 10 November 2009.

__ 'Council conclusions on democracy support in the EU's external relations', 17 November 2009.

__ 'Internal security strategy for the European Union: towards a European security model', document no. 7120/10, 25–6 February 2010.

__ 'European pact to combat international drug trafficking – disrupting cocaine and heroin routes', 3 June 2010.

__ 'Joint progress report by the Council and the European Commission to the European Council on the implementation of the EU Central asia strategy', document no. 11402.10, Brussels, 28 June 2010.

__ 'Council conclusions on conflict prevention', Luxembourg, 20 June 2011.

__ 'Council conclusions on increasing the impact of EU development policy: an agenda for change', Foreign Affairs Council meeting 14 May 2012.

__ Note from the Counter-terrorism coordinator, 'EU counter-terrorism strategy-discussion paper', document no. 9990/12, 23 May 2012.

__ 'EU strategic framework and action plan on human rights and democracy', document no. 11855/12, 25 June 2012.

__ 'Council conclusions on the situation in Mali', 15 October 2012.

__ 'EU drugs strategy (2013–20)', in *OJ* C 402, 29 December 2012.

Council of the European Union and European Commission. 'Action plan on how best to implement the provisions of the Treaty of Amsterdam establishing an area of freedom, security and justice', 7 December 1998.

Council of Foreign Ministers. 'Report to the European Council in Lisbon on the likely development of the common foreign and security policy (CFSP) with a view to identifying areas open to joint action vis-à-vis particular countries or groups of countries', Annex to the Conclusions of the Presidency, Lisbon European Council, 26–27 June 1992, *EC Bulletin*, no. 6, 1992.

Cox, Aidan and Jenny Chapman. *The European Community External Cooperation Programmes: Policies, Management and Distribution*. London and Brussels: Overseas Development Institute and European Commission, 1999.

Crawford, Gordon. *Promoting Democracy, Human Rights and Good Governance Through Development Aid: A Comparative Study of the Policies of Four Northern Donors*. Working Paper on Democratization no. 1. Leeds: University of Leeds Centre for Democratization Studies, 1996.

__ *Foreign Aid and Political Reform: A Comparative Analysis of Democracy Assistance and Political Conditionality*. Houndmills: Palgrave, 2001.

de Búrca, Gráinne. 'The road not taken: the European Union as a global human rights actor', *American Journal of International Law*, 105, 4 (2011).

Del Biondo, Karen. 'Democracy promotion meets development cooperation: the EU as a promoter of democratic governance in sub-Saharan Africa', *European Foreign Affairs Review*, 16, 5 (2011).

__ 'EU aid conditionality in ACP countries: explaining inconsistency in EU Sanctions Practice', *Journal of Contemporary European Research*, 7, 3 (2011).

Delevic, Milica, *Regional Cooperation in the Western Balkans*, Chaillot Paper no. 104. Paris: EU Institute for Security Studies, July 2007.

Delors, Jacques. 'European unification and European security', in *European Security After the Cold War, Part I*, Adelphi Paper no. 284. London: Brassey's for the International Institute of Security Studies, 1994.

Delputte, Sarah and Fredrik Söderbaum. 'European aid coordination in Africa: Is the commission calling the tune?', in Stefan Gänzle, Sven Grimm and Davina Makhan, eds, *The European Union and Global Development*. Houndmills: Palgrave Macmillan, 2012.

del Sarto, Raffaella, and Tobias Schumacher. 'From EMP to ENP: what's at stake with the European neighbourhood policy towards the southern Mediterranean?', *European Foreign Affairs Review*, 10, 1 (2005).

de Schoutheete, Philippe. *La coopération politique européenne*. Brussels: Editions Labour, 1980.

Deutsch, Karl, et al., *Political Community and the North Atlantic Area: International Organization in the Light of Historical Experience*. Princeton: Princeton University Press, 1957.

Development Council. 'Resolution on coherence', 5 June 1997.

__ 'Conclusions, 30 November 1998', press release no. 13461/98.

Development Council and European Commission. 'The European Community's development policy', press release no. 12929/00 (Presse 421), 10 November 2000.

__ 'Conclusions, 31 May 2001', press release no. 8855/01 (Presse 191).

Development Council and the member states. 'Resolution on human rights, democracy and development', *EC Bulletin*, no. 11, 1991.

Dijkstra, Hylke. 'European external action service: towards the 2013 review', *Studia Diplomatica*, LXV-4 (2012).

Dinan, Desmond. 'Governance and Institutions: implementing the Lisbon Treaty in the shadow of the Euro crisis', in Nathaniel Copsey and Tim Haughton, eds, *The JCMS Annual Review of the European Union in 2010*. Oxford: Wiley-Blackwell, 2011.

Doctor, Mahrukh. 'Why bother with inter-regionalism? Negotiations for a European Union–Mercosur agreement', *Journal of Common Market Studies*, 45, 2 (2007).

Donnelly, Jack. 'Human rights and foreign policy', *World Politics*, 34, 4 (1982).

__ 'An overview', in David Forsythe, ed., *Human Rights and Comparative Foreign Policy*. Tokyo: United Nations University Press, 2000.

Duchêne, François. 'The European Community and the uncertainties of interdependence', in Max Kohnstamm and Wolfgang Hager, eds, *A Nation Writ Large? Foreign-Policy Problems Before the European Community*. London: Macmillan, 1973.

Dyson, Kenneth. 'The Conference on Security and Cooperation in Europe: Europe before and after the Helsinki final act', in Kenneth Dyson, ed., *European Détente: Case Studies in the Politics of East-West Relations*. London: Frances Pinter, 1986.

Edwards, Geoffrey and Eric Philippart. 'The Euro-Mediterranean partnership: fragmentation and reconstruction', *European Foreign Affairs Review*, 2, 4 (1997).

Elgström, Ole. 'Lomé and Post-Lomé: asymmetric negotiations and the impact of norms', *European Foreign Affairs Review*, 5, 2 (2000).

European Commission [COM (94) 42]. 'Report on the implementation in 1993 of the Resolution of the Council and of the Member States meeting in the Council on human rights, democracy and development, adopted on 28 November 1991', COM (94) 42 final, 23 February 1994.

___ 'Report to the General Affairs Council on the promotion of intra-regional cooperation and "bon voisinage" ', 6 March 1995.

___ [COM (95) 216]. 'Communication on the inclusion of respect for democratic principles and human rights in agreements between the community and third countries', COM (95) 216 final, 23 May 1995.

___ [COM (95) 219]. 'Communication on European Community support for regional economic integration efforts among developing countries', COM (95) 219 final, 16 June 1995.

___ [COM (95) 567]. 'The European Union and the external dimension of human rights policy: from Rome to Maastricht and beyond', COM (95) 567 final, 22 November 1995.

___ [COM (96) 153]. 'Linking relief, rehabilitation and development (LRRD)', COM (96) 153 final, 30 April 1996.

___ 'Agenda 2000: For a stronger and wider union', *EU Bulletin Supplement* 5/97.

___ [COM (1998) 146]. 'Democratisation, the rule of law, respect for human rights and good governance: the challenges of the partnership between the European Union and the ACP states', COM (1998) 146 final, 12 March 1998.

___ [COM (2000) 191]. 'Communication on EU election assistance and observation', COM (2000) 191 final, 11 April 2000.

___ [COM (2001) 211]. 'Communication on conflict prevention', COM (2001) 211 final, 11 April 2001.

___ [COM (2001) 252]. 'The European Union's role in promoting human rights and democratisation in third countries', COM (2001) 252 final, 8 May 2001.

___ [COM (2001) 259]. 'Proposal for a council framework decision laying down minimum provisions on the constituent elements of criminal acts and penalties in the field of illicit drug trafficking', COM (2001) 259 final, 23 May 2001.

___ [COM (2001) 301]. 'Communication on the implementation of the EU action plan on drugs (2000–4)', COM (2001) 301 final, 8 June 2001.

___ [COM (2001) 521]. 'Proposal for a council framework decision on combating terrorism', COM (2001) 521 final, 19 September 2001.

___ 'Euro-Med partnership: regional strategy paper 2002–6 and regional indicative programme 2002–4', 2001.

___ [COM (2001) 672]. 'Communication on a common policy on illegal immigration', COM (2001) 672 final, 15 November 2001.

___ [SEC (2002) 231]. 'EC external assistance facilitating the implementation of UN Security Council Resolution 1373: an overview', SEC (2002) 231, 25 February 2002.

___ [COM (2002), 703]. 'Integrating migration issues in the European Union's relations with third countries', COM (2002) 703 final, 3 December 2002.

___ [COM (2003), 104] 'Wider Europe – neighbourhood: a new framework for relations with our southern and eastern neighbours', COM (2003) 104 final, 11 March 2003.

___ 'Civilian instruments for EU crisis management', April 2003.

___ [COM (2005) 491]. 'A strategy on the external dimension of the area of freedom, security and justice', COM (2005) 491 final, 12 October 2005.

___ [COM (2006) 86]. 'An EU–Caribbean partnership for growth, stability and development', COM (2006) 86 final, 2 March 2006.

__ [COM (2006) 402]. 'Policy priorities in the fight against illegal immigration of third country nationals', COM (2006) 402 final, 19 July 2006.

__ [COM (2006) 421]. 'Governance in the European consensus on development: towards a harmonised approach within the European union', COM (2006) 421 final, 30 August 2006.

__ [COM (2006) 567]. 'Global Europe: competing in the world. a contribution to the EU's growth and jobs strategy', COM (2006) 567 final, 4 October 2006.

__ [SEC (2006) 1498]. 'Progress report on the implementation of the strategy for the external dimension of the JHA: global freedom, security and justice', SEC (2006) 1498, 16 November 2006.

__ 'Regional strategy paper (2007–13) for the Euro-Mediterranean partnership'.

__ [COM (2007) 643]. 'Towards an EU response to situations of fragility – engaging in difficult environment for sustainable development, stability and peace', COM (2007) 643 final, 25 October 2007.

__ [C(2010) 2432]. 'European instrument for democracy and human rights (EIDHR) strategy paper 2011–13', C(2010) 2432, 21 April 2010.

__ [COM (2010) 612]. 'Trade, growth and world affairs: trade policy as a core component of the EU's 2020 strategy', COM (2010) 612 final, 9 November 2010.

__ [COM (2010) 673]. 'The EU internal security strategy in action: five steps towards a more secure Europe', COM (2010) 673 final, 22 November 2010.

__ [COM (2011) 76]. 'Evaluation of EU readmission agreements', COM (2011) 76 final, 23 February 2011.

__ [COM (2011) 200]. 'A partnership for democracy and shared prosperity with the southern Mediterranean', COM (2011) 200 final, 8 March 2011.

__ [COM (2011) 248]. 'Communication on migration', COM (2011) 248 final, 4 May 2011.

__ [COM (2011) 637]. 'Increasing the impact of EU development policy: an agenda for change', COM (2011) 637 final, 13 October 2011.

__ [COM (2011) 749]. 'Building an open and secure Europe: The Home Affairs budget for 2014–20', COM (2011) 749 final, 15 November 2011.

__ [COM (2011) 743]. 'The global approach to migration and mobility', COM (2011) 743 final, 18 November 2011.

__ 'Thematic programme: cooperation with third countries in areas of migration and asylum: 2011–13 multi-annual strategy paper'.

__ 'Budget 2012 in figures', http://ec.europa.eu/budget/figures/2012/2012_en.cfm (last accessed 3 May 2013).

__ [COM (2012) 339]. 'Report on the implementation of macro-financial assistance to third countries in 2011'. COM (2012) 339 final, 28 June 2012.

__ [COM(2013) 562]. '2012 Annual report on the instrument for stability', COM(2013) 563 final, 26 July 2013.

__ 'The EU's new generalised scheme of preferences (GSP)', December 2012; available at: http://trade.ec.europa.eu/doclib/docs/2013/february/tradoc_150582. pdf (last accessed 10 June 2013).

__ 'Memo: The EU's free trade agreements – where are we?', Reference MEMO/13/282, 25 March 2013.

__ '2012 Report on the application of the EU charter of fundamental rights' (Luxembourg: Office of the Official Publications of the EU, 2013).

European Commission and High Representative of the EU for Foreign Affairs and Security Policy. 'Human rights and democracy at the heart of EU external action – towards a more effective approach', COM (2011) 886 final, 12 December 2011.

__ 'Delivering on a new neighbourhood policy', JOIN (2012) 14 final, 15 May 2012.

__ 'Implementation of the agenda for action on democracy support in the EU's external relations', JOIN (2012) 28 final, 11 October 2012.

European Council, 'Presidency conclusions' (various years) (available at: www.consilium.europa.eu; last accessed 13 January 2014)

__ Copenhagen. 'Declaration on democracy', *EC Bulletin* no. 3, 1978.

__ Luxembourg. 'Declaration on human rights', *EC Bulletin*, no. 6, 1991.

__ 'Common strategy of 19 June 2000 on the Mediterranean region (2000/458/CFSP)', in *OJ* L 183, 22 July 2000.

__ Göteberg. 'EU programme for the prevention of violent conflicts', 15–16 June 2001.

__ Brussels. 'Conclusions and plan of action of the extraordinary European council meeting on 21 September 2001'.

__ 'A secure Europe in a better world: European security strategy', Brussels, 12 December 2003.

__ 'Declaration on combating terrorism', 25 March 2004.

__'The European Union counter-terrorism strategy', document 14469/4/05 REV 4, 15/16 December 2005.

__ 'The Stockholm Programme – an open and secure Europe serving and protecting citizens', in *OJ* C 115, 4 May 2010.

European External Action Service, 'Strategy for security and development in the Sahel', 2011, http://eeas.europa.eu/africa/docs/sahel_strategy_en.pdf (last accessed 15 August 2013).

European External Action Service and European Commission. 'Progress report on the implementation of the EU strategy for Central Asia: implementation review and outline for future orientations', doc 11455/12, 28 June 2012.

European Council on Foreign Relations, 'Introduction', *European Foreign Policy Scorecard 2012*; available at: http://www.ecfr.eu/page/-/ECFR_SCORECARD_2012_WEB.pdf (last accessed 13 January 2014).

European Investment Bank. *Activity Report 2012*, available at: http://www.eib.org/attachments/general/reports/ar2012en.pdf (last accessed 3 May 2013).

European Parliament. 'Resolution for the year 1983/1984 on human rights in the world and Community policy on human rights', in *OJ* C 172, 2 July 1984.

__ *The European Parliament and Human Rights*. Luxembourg: OOPEC, 1994.

__ 'Resolution on developing the union's capabilities in conflict prevention and civil crisis management', 15 March 2001, B5–172/2001.

__ 'Resolution on the human rights and democracy clause in European Union agreements (2005/2057(INI))', P6_TA(2006)0056, 14 February 2006.

__ Briefing Paper, 'EU election observation – achievements, challenges', EXPO/B/DEVE-AFET/2007/40, PE 385556, June 2008.

__ 'Study: human rights mainstreaming in EU's external relations', EXPO/B/DROI/2008/66, September 2009.

European Parliament, Council and Commission. 'Joint declaration by the European Parliament, the Council and the Commission concerning the protection of fundamental rights', *OJ* C 103, 27 April 1977.

__ 'The European consensus on development', *OJ* C 46, 24 February 2006.

European Peacebuilding Liaison Office. 'The EEAS and peacebuilding one year on', April 2012; available at: http://www.eplo.org/assets/files/2.%20Activities/ Working%20Groups/EEAS/EPLO_Statement_EEASPeacebuildingOneYearOn.pdf (last accessed 9 August 2013).

__ 'Power analysis: the EU and peacebuilding after Lisbon', March 2013; available at http://www.eplo.org/assets/files/2.%20Activities/Working%20Groups/EEAS/ EPLO_Peacebuilding%20after%20Lisbon_March2013.pdf (last accessed 9 August 2013).

Europol. 'EU terrorism situation and trend report 2010'.

__ 'EU terrorism situation and trend report 2012'.

European Political Cooperation. 'Statement by the Twelve on human rights', Brussels, 21 July 1986, reprinted in Press and Information Office of the Federal Republic of Germany, *European Political Co-operation (EPC)*, 5th edn (1988).

European Union External Action. *EEAS Review*, July 2013.

Farrell, Mary. 'A triumph of realism over idealism? Cooperation between the European Union and Africa', *Journal of European Integration*, 27, 3 (2005).

Feldman, Lily Gardner. 'Reconciliation and legitimacy: foreign relations and enlargement of the European Union', in Thomas Banchoff and Mitchell P. Smith, eds, *Legitimacy and the European Union: The Contested Polity*. London: Routledge: 1999.

Finnish Presidency and the European Commission. 'Report to the European Council on EU action in support of the stability pact and south-eastern Europe', press release no. 13814/99, 6 December 1999.

Flaesch-Mogin, Catherine. 'Competing frameworks: the dialogue and its legal bases', in Geoffrey Edwards and Elfriede Regelsberger, eds, *Europe's Global Links: The European Community and Inter-Regional Cooperation*. London: Pinter, 1990.

Florini, Ann. 'The evolution of international norms', *International Studies Quarterly*, 40, 3 (1996).

Flynn, Gregory and Henry Farrell. 'Piecing together the democratic peace: the CSCE, norms, and the "construction" of security in post-Cold War Europe', *International Organization*, 53, 3 (1999).

Fouwels, Martine. 'The European Union's common foreign and security policy and human rights', *Netherlands Quarterly of Human Rights*, 15, 3 (1997).

Franck, Thomas. 'Are human rights universal?', *Foreign Affairs*, 80, 1 (2001).

Freedom House, *Freedom in the World 2013: Democratic Breakthroughs in the Balance*.

Füle, Štefan. Speech on the recent events in North Africa to the Committee on Foreign Affairs, European Parliament, Brussels, SPEECH/11/130, 28 February 2011.

Galtung, Johann. *The European Community: A Superpower in the Making*. London: George Allen and Unwin, 1973.

Gebert, Constanty. 'Shooting in the dark? EU sanctions policies', European Council on Foreign Relations, Policy Brief, 15 January 2013.

Gebhard, Carmen. 'Coherence', in Christopher Hill and Michael Smith, eds, *International Relations and the European Union*. 2nd edn, Oxford: Oxford University Press, 2011.

Geddes, Andrew. 'International migration and state sovereignty in an integrating Europe', *International Migration*, 39, 6 (2001).

General Affairs Council. 'Conclusions, 20 March 2000', press release no. 6810/00 (Presse 73).

__ 'Conclusions on European Union lines of action towards North Korea', press release no. 1343/00 (Presse 435), 20 November 2000.

__ 'Conclusions, 22–3 January 2001', press release no. 5279/01 (Presse 19).

Gillespie, Richard. 'The Union for the Mediterranean: an intergovernmentalist challenge for the European Union?', *Journal of Common Market Studies*, 49, 6 (2011).

Gilson, Julie. 'New interregionalism? The EU and East Asia', *Journal of European Integration*, 27, 3 (2005).

Ginsberg, Roy. *Foreign Policy Actions of the European Community: The Politics of Scale*. Boulder: Lynne Rienner, 1989.

__ 'Conceptualizing the European Union as an international actor: narrowing the theoretical capability–expectations gap', *Journal of Common Market Studies*, 37, 3 (1999).

Goldstein, Judith and Robert Keohane. 'Ideas and foreign policy: an analytical framework', in Judith Goldstein and Robert Keohane, eds. *Ideas and Foreign Policy: Beliefs, Institutions and Political Change*. Ithaca: Cornell University Press, 1993.

Gourlay, Catriona. 'The EU's progress in mainstreaming conflict prevention'. *European Security Review* (ISIS Europe) 12 (May 2002).

__ 'Civil–civil co-ordination in EU crisis management', in Agnieszka Nowak, ed., *Civilian Crisis Management: The EU Way*. Chaillot Paper no. 90. Paris: EU Institute for Security Studies, June 2006.

Grabbe, Heather. 'Breaking new ground in internal security', in Edward Bannerman, et al., *Europe After September 11ᵗʰ*. London: Centre for European Reform, 2002.

Grevi, Giovanni. *The Interpolar World: A New Scenario*, Occasional Paper no. 79. Paris: European Union Institute for Security Studies, June 2009.

Grilli, Enzo. *The European Community and the Developing Countries*. Cambridge: Cambridge University Press, 1993.

Gross, Eva and Ana E. Juncos. 'Introduction', in Eva Gross and Ana E. Juncos, eds, *EU Conflict Prevention and Crisis Management: Roles, Institutions, and Policies*. London: Routledge, 2010.

Guehenno, Jean-Marie. 'A foreign policy in search of a polity', in Jan Zielonka, ed., *Paradoxes of European Foreign Policy*. The Hague: Kluwer Law International, 1998.

Güney, Aylin and Aslihan Çelenk. 'The European Union's democracy promotion policies in Algeria: success or failure?', *The Journal of North African Studies*, 12, 1 (2007).

Haas, Ernst. *The Uniting of Europe: Political, Economic and Social Forces 1950–1957*. London: Stevens and Sons, 1958.

Haas, Peter. 'Introduction: epistemic communities and international policy coordination', *International Organization*, 46, 1 (1992).

Hatzigeorgopoulos, Myrto. 'The role of EU battlegroups in european defence', *European Security Review*, 56, ISIS Europe, June 2012. http://www.isis-europe.eu/sites/default/files/publications-downloads/esr56_EUBattlegroups-June2012%20MH_2.pdf (last accesed 13 January 2014).

Hazelzet, Hadewych. 'Suspension of development cooperation: an instrument to promote democracy?', ECDPM (European Centre for Development Policy Management) Discussion Paper no. 64B, Maastricht, August 2005.

Helwig, Niklas, Paul Ivan and Hrant Kostanyan. *The New EU Foreign Policy Architecture: Reviewing the First Two Years of the EEAS*. Brussels: Centre for European Policy Studies, 2013.

Hill, Christopher. 'European foreign policy: power bloc, civilian model – or flop?', in Reinhardt Rummel, ed., *The Evolution of an International Actor: Western Europe's New Assertiveness*. Boulder: Westview, 1990.

__ 'The capability–expectations gap, or conceptualizing Europe's international role', *Journal of Common Market Studies*, 31, 3 (1993).

__ 'The EU's capacity for conflict prevention', *European Foreign Affairs Review*, 6, 3 (2001).

__ *The Changing Politics of Foreign Policy*. Houndmills: Palgrave, 2003.

Hill, Christopher and Karen E. Smith, eds. *European Foreign Policy: Key Documents*. London: Routledge, 2000.

Hill, Christopher and William Wallace. 'Introduction', in Christopher Hill, ed., *The Actors in Europe's Foreign Policy*. London: Routledge, 1996.

Hill, Dilys. 'Human rights and foreign policy: theoretical foundations', in Dilys Hill, ed., *Human Rights and Foreign Policy: Principles and Practice*. Houndmills: Macmillan, 1989.

Hoffmann, Stanley. 'Obstinate or obsolete? The fate of the nation state and the case of Western Europe', *Daedalus*, 95 (1966).

__ 'Towards a common European foreign and security policy?', *Journal of Common Market Studies*, 38, 2 (2000).

Holland, Martin. *The European Union and the Third World*. Houndmills: Palgrave, 2002.

Holmes, Leslie. 'Crime, corruption, and politics: transnational factors', in Alex Pravda and Jan Zielonka, eds, *Democratic Consolidation in Eastern Europe. Volume 2: International and Transnational Factors*. Oxford: Oxford University Press, 2001.

Holsti, K. J. *International Politics: A Framework for Analysis*. 7th edn, Englewood Cliffs, NJ: Prentice-Hall, 1995.

House of Commons (UK). *Foreign Affairs Committee – Seventh Report: The role of the FCO in UK government*, 27 April 2011.

Howorth, Jolyon. 'European defence and the changing politics of the EU: hanging together or hanging separately?', *Journal of Common Market Studies*, 39, 4 (2001).

Hurrell, Andrew and Louise Fawcett. 'Conclusion: regionalism and international order?', in Louise Fawcett and Andrew Hurrell, eds, *Regionalism in World Politics*. Oxford: Oxford University Press, 1995.

Huysmans, Jef. 'The European Union and the securitization of migration', *Journal of Common Market Studies*, 38, 5 (2000).

International Crisis Group. *EU Crisis Response Capability: Institutions and Processes for Conflict Prevention and Management*. ICG Issues Report no. 2, Brussels, 26 June 2001.

Ioannides, Isabelle. 'EU police mission *Proxima*: testing the 'European' approach to building peace', in Agnieszka Nowak, ed. *Civilian Crisis Management: The EU Way*. Chaillot Paper no. 90. Paris: EU Institute for Security Studies, June 2006.

James, Alan. 'United Nations preventive diplomacy in an historical perspective', in Jeremy Ginifer, Espen Barth Eide and Carsten Rønnfeldt, eds, *Preventive Action in Theory and Practice: The Skopje Papers*. Oslo: Norwegian Institute of International Affairs, 1999.

Jenkins, Carolyn and Lynne Thomas. 'African regionalism and the SADC', in Mario Telò, ed., *European Union and New Regionalism: Regional Actors and Global Governance in a Post-Hegemonic Era*. Aldershot: Ashgate, 2001.

Jepperson, Ronald, Alexander Wendt and Peter Katzenstein. 'Norms, identity and culture in national security', in Peter Katzenstein, ed., *The Culture of National Security: Norms and Identity in World Politics*. New York: Columbia University Press, 1996.

Jetschke, Anja and Clara Portela. 'ASEAN–EU relations: from regional integration assistance to security significance?', GIGA Focus no. 3, 2013. Hamburg: German Institute of Global and Area Studies.

Joergensen, Knud Erik. 'PoCo: The diplomatic republic of Europe', in Knud Erik Joergensen, ed., *Reflective Approaches to European Governance*. London: Macmillan, 1997.

Johansson-Nogués, Elisabeth. *The Decline of the EU's 'Magnetic Attraction'? The European Union in the Eyes of Neighbouring Arab Countries and Russia*, LSE European Foreign Policy Unit Working Paper no. 2011-1. London: LSE, March 2011.

Juncos, Ana E. and Karolina Pomorska. 'Invisible and unaccountable? National representatives and council officials in EU foreign policy', *Journal of European Public Policy*, 18, 8 (2011).

Justice and Home Affairs Council. 'Conclusions, 13 June 2002', press release no. 9620/02 (Presse 175).

Kagan, Robert. *Of Paradise and Power: America and Europe in the New World Order*. London: Atlantic Books, 2003.

Kausch, Kristina. 'Morocco', in Richard Youngs, ed., *Is the European Union Supporting Democracy in its Neighbourhood?* Madrid: FRIDE, 2008.

Keens-Soper, Maurice. *Europe in the World: The Persistence of Power Politics*. Basingstoke: Macmillan, 1999.

Kennan, George. 'Morality and foreign policy', *Foreign Affairs*, 64, 2 (1985).

Keohane, Robert and Joseph S. Nye. *Power and Interdependence*. 2nd edn, Glenview, IL: Scott, Foresman and Co., 1989.

Keukeleire, Stephan. 'The European Union as a diplomatic actor: internal, traditional and structural diplomacy', *Diplomacy and Statecraft*, 14, 3 (2003).

Khorana, Sangeeta and Maria Garcia. 'European Union–India trade negotiations: one step forward, one back?, *Journal of Common Market Studies*, 51, 4 (2013).

Killick, Nick and Simon Higdon. 'The cost of conflict', in Peter Cross, ed., *Contributing to Preventive Action. Conflict Prevention Network Yearbook 1997/98*. Baden-Baden: Nomos Verlagsgesellschaft, 1998.

Koch, Christian. 'GCC-EU relations: the news again is "no news"', *Gulf Research Center: GCC-EU Research Bulletin*, no. 5, July 2006.

__ 'A union in danger: where the GCC is headed is increasingly questionable', Gulf Research Center Foundation, 10 December 2012.

Korski, Daniel and Richard Gowan, 'Can the EU rebuild failing states? A review of Europe's civilian capacities', European Council on Foreign Relations, October 2009.

Krotz, Ulrich. 'Momentum and impediments: why Europe won't emerge as a full political actor on the world stage soon', *Journal of Common Market Studies*, 47, 3 (2009).

Laatikainen, Katie Verlin. 'Multilateral leadership at the UN after the Lisbon Treaty', *European Foreign Affairs Review*, 15, 4 (2010).

Larsen, Henrik. 'Concepts of security in the European Union after the Cold War', *Australian Journal of International Affairs*, 54, 3 (2000).

Lavenex, Sandra. 'Asylum, immigration, and Central-Eastern Europe: challenges to EU enlargement', *European Foreign Affairs Review*, 3, 2 (1998).

Lehne, Stefan. 'The role of sanctions in EU foreign policy', Carnegie Endowment for International Peace, 14 December 2012.

Leonard, Mark. *Why Europe Will Run the 21st Century*. New York: Fourth Estate, 2005.

Lerch, Marika and Guido Schwellnus. 'Normative by nature? the role of coherence in justifying the EU's external human rights policy', in Helene Sjursen, ed., *Civilian or Military Power? European Foreign Policy in Perspective*. London: Routledge, 2007.

Light, Margot. 'Exporting democracy', in Karen E. Smith and Margot Light, eds, *Ethics and Foreign Policy*. Cambridge: Cambridge University Press, 2001.

Lindberg, Leon. *The Political Dynamics of European Economic Integration*. Stanford: Stanford University Press, 1963.

Lucarelli, Sonia, ed. 'The external image of the European Union', Special Issue. *European Foreign Affairs Review*, 12, 3 (2007).

Lundestad, Geir. *'Empire' By Integration: The United States and European Integration, 1945–1997*. Oxford: Oxford University Press, 1998.

Magen, Amichai, Thomas Risse and Michael McFaul, eds. *Promoting Democracy and the Rule of Law: American and European Strategies*. London: Palgrave Macmillan, 2009.

Manners, Ian. 'Normative power Europe: a contradiction in terms?', *Journal of Common Market Studies*, 40, 2 (2002).

Marantis, Demetrios James. 'Human rights, democracy and development: the European Community model', *Harvard Human Rights Journal*, 7 (1994).

Maull, Hanns W. 'Germany and Japan: The new civilian powers', *Foreign Affairs*, 69, 5 (1990).

__ 'Europe and the new balance of global order', *International Affairs*, 81, 4 (2005).

McCormick, John. *The European Superpower*. Houndmills: Palgrave Macmillan, 2007.

Melvin, Neil. 'The EU needs a new Central Asia strategy', EUCAM Policy Brief no. 28, 31 October 2012.

Milward, Alan. *The European Rescue of the Nation State*. London: Routledge, 1992.

Ministry for Foreign Affairs (Sweden). *Preventing Violent Conflict: A Study. Executive Summary and Recommendations*. Stockholm: Ministry for Foreign Affairs, 1994.

Mitrany, David. 'The prospect of integration: federal or functional?', in Joseph S. Nye, Jr, ed., *International Regionalism*. Boston: Little, Brown and Co., 1968.

Moïsi, Dominique. 'French policy toward Central and Eastern Europe', in William Griffith, ed., *Central and Eastern Europe: The Opening Curtain?* Boulder: Westview, 1989.

Monar, Jörg. 'Political dialogue with third countries and regional political groupings: the fifteen as an attractive interlocutor', in Elfriede Regelsberger, Phillipe de Schoutheete de Terverant and Wolfgang Wessels, eds, *Foreign Policy of the European Union: From EPC to CFSP and Beyond*. Boulder: Lynne Rienner, 1997.

___ 'The dynamics of justice and home affairs: laboratories, driving factors and costs', *Journal of Common Market Studies*, 39, 4 (2001).

___ 'Justice and home affairs', in Nathaniel Copsey and Tim Haughton, eds, *The JCMS Annual Review of the European Union in 2010*. Oxford: Wiley-Blackwell, 2011.

___ 'Justice and home affairs', in Nathaniel Copsey and Tim Haughton, eds, *The JCMS Annual Review of the European Union in 2011*. Wiley and Blackwell, 2012.

___ 'Justice and home affairs', in Nathaniel Copsey and Tim Haughton, eds, *The JCSM Annual Review of the European Union in 2012*. Oxford: Wiley-Blackwell, 2013.

Monshipouri, Mahmood. *Democratization, Liberalization and Human Rights in the Third World*. Boulder: Lynne Rienner, 1995.

Moravcsik, Andrew. *The Choice for Europe: Social Purpose and State Power from Messina to Maastricht*. London: UCL Press, 1998.

___ 'The quiet superpower', *Newsweek*, 17 June 2002.

Müller-Brandeck-Bocquet, Gisela. 'Perspectives for a new regionalism: relations between the EU and MERCOSUR', *European Foreign Affairs Review*, 5, 4 (2000).

___ 'The new CFSP and ESDP decision-making system of the European Union', *European Foreign Affairs Review*, 7, 3 (2002).

Müller-Brandeck-Bocquet, Gisela and Carolin Rüger, eds. *The High Representative for the EU Foreign and Security Policy – Review and Prospects*. Baden-Baden: Nomos, 2011.

Murray, Philomena and Edward Moxon-Browne. 'The EU as a template for regional integration? The Case of ASEAN and its Committee of Permanent Representatives', *Journal of Common Market Studies*, 51, 3 (2013).

North Atlantic Treaty Organization. 'Active engagement, modern defence: strategic concept for the defence and security of the members of the North Atlantic Treaty Organization', adopted by heads of state and government at the NATO Summit in Lisbon, 19–20 November 2010.

Nowak, Agnieszka. 'Civilian crisis management within ESDP', in Agnieszka Nowak, ed., *Civilian Crisis Management: The EU Way*. Chaillot Paper no. 90. Paris: EU Institute for Security Studies, June 2006.

Nuttall, Simon. *European Political Co-operation*. Oxford: Clarendon Press, 1992.

___ *European Foreign Policy*. Oxford: Oxford University Press, 2000.

Nye, Joseph S., Jr. *Soft Power: The Means to Success in World Politics*. New York: Public Affairs, 2004.

Olsen, Gorm Rye. 'Europe and the promotion of democracy in post Cold War Africa: how serious is Europe and for what reason?', *African Affairs*, 97, 388 (1998).

Organisation for Economic Cooperation and Development (OECD), Development Assistance Committee, 'Peer review: European Community 2007' (available at www.oecd.org/dac; last accessed 13 January 2014).

__ 'Peer Review: European Union 2012'.

Ortega, Martin, ed., *Global Views on the European Union*. Chaillot Paper. no. 72. Paris: EU Institute for Security Studies, 2004.

Panagariya, Arvind. 'The regionalism debate: an overview', *The World Economy*, 22, 4 (1999).

Panebianco, Stefania. 'Promoting human rights and democracy in European Union relations with Russia and China', in Sonia Lucarelli and Ian Manners, eds, *Values and Principles in European Union Foreign Policy*. London: Routledge, 2007.

Patel, Mayur. 'Economic partnership agreements between the EU and African countries: potential development implications for Ghana', report for Realizing Rights, June 2007; available at http://www.realizingrights.org/pdf/EPAs_between_the_EU_and_African_Countries_-_Development_Implications_for_Ghana.pdf (last accessed 20 August 2013).

Patten, Chris. 'Speech to the European Parliament plenary on the Commission communication on EU election assistance and observation', Speech/01/125, 14 March 2001.

Picken, Margo. 'Ethical foreign policies and human rights: dilemmas for non-governmental organisations', in Karen E. Smith and Margot Light, eds, *Ethics and Foreign Policy*. Cambridge: Cambridge University Press, 2001.

Piening, Christopher. *Global Europe: The European Union in World Affairs*. London: Lynne Rienner, 1997.

Pijpers, Alfred. 'European political co-operation and the CSCE process', *Legal Issues of European Integration*, 10, 1 (1984).

Pomorska, Karolina and Sophie Vanhoonacker. 'Poland in the driving seat: a mature presidency in turbulent times', in Nathaniel Copsey and Tim Haughton, eds, *The JCMS Annual Review of the European Union in 2011*. Oxford: Wiley Blackwell, 2012.

Portela, Clara. *European Union Sanctions and Foreign Policy: When and Why Do They Work?* London: Routledge, 2010.

__ 'The European Union and Belarus: sanctions and partnership?', *Comparative European Politics*, 9, 4/5 (2011).

__ 'The EU's sanctions against Syria: conflict management by other means', Egmont Security Policy Brief no. 38, Brussels: Royal Institute for International Relations, 2012.

Puetter, Uwe and Antje Wiener. 'Accommodating normative divergence in European foreign policy co-ordination: the example of the Iraq Crisis', *Journal of Common Market Studies*, 45, 5 (2007).

Regelsberger, Elfriede. 'The EU as an actor in foreign and security policy: Some key features of CFSP in an historical perspective', *CFSP Forum*, 5, 4 (2007); available at: http://www.lse.ac.uk/internationalRelations/centresandunits/EFPU/FORNETarchive.aspx (last accessed 13 January 2014).

Richmond, Oliver. 'Shared sovereignty and the politics of peace: evaluating the EU's "catalytic" framework in the Eastern Mediterranean', *International Affairs*, 82, 1 (2006).

Richter, Solveig and Julia Leininger. 'Flexible and unbureaucratic democracy promotion by the EU?', SWP Comments 26, Berlin: Stiftung Wissenschft und Politik, August 2012.

Ricks, Thomas. *Fiasco: The American Military Adventure in Iraq*. New York: Penguin Press, 2006.

Riedel, Eibe and Martin Will. 'Human rights clauses in external agreements of the EC', in Philip Alston, ed., *The EU and Human Rights*. Oxford: Oxford University Press, 1999.

Rosecrance, Richard. *The Rise of the Trading State: Commerce and Conquest in the Modern World*. New York: Basic Books, 1986.

Roth, Kenneth. 'A façade of action: the misuse of dialogue and cooperation with rights abusers', in Human Rights Watch, *World Report 2011*.

Rummel, Reinhardt. *Common Foreign and Security Policy and Conflict Prevention: Priorities for the Intergovernmental Conference*. London: Saferworld and International Alert, 1996.

___ 'The CFSP's conflict prevention policy', in Martin Holland, ed., *Common Foreign and Security Policy: The Record and Reforms*. London: Pinter, 1997.

Saari, Sinikukka. *Promoting Democracy and Human Rights in Russia*. London: Routledge, 2011.

Saatçioğlu, Beken. 'Unpacking the compliance puzzle: the case of Turkey's AKP under EU Conditionality', KFG Working Paper no. 14. Berlin: Freie Universtität Berlin, 2010.

Santopinto, Federico. 'Why the EU needs an institutional reform of its external relations', GRIP Note d'Analyse, 19 June 2007; www.grip.org. http://archive.grip.org/en/siteweb/dev_4569b9db.asp.html (last accessed 13 January 2014).

Schmitter, Philippe. 'Three neofunctional hypotheses about international integration', *International Organization*, 33, 2 (1969).

Schnabel, Rockwell. *The Next Superpower? The Rise of Europe and its Challenge to the United States*. Rowan and Littlefield, 2005.

Schünemann, Julia. 'EU conflict prevention 10 years after Göteberg', Policy Paper no. 1, June 2011, Institut Català Internacional per la Pau.

Secretariat of the African, Caribbean and Pacific Group of States. 'Press release: consensus on economic partnership agreements between EU and ACP Countries', Berlin, 14 March 2007.

Secretary-General/High Representative and the European Commission. 'Improving the coherence and effectiveness of European Union action in the field of conflict prevention', press release no.14088/00, Brussels, 30 November 2000.

Sikkink, Kathryn. 'The power of principled ideas: human rights policies in the United States and Western Europe', in Judith Goldstein and Robert Keohane, eds, *Ideas and Foreign Policy: Beliefs, Institutions and Political Change*. Ithaca: Cornell University Press, 1993.

Sjöstedt, Gunnar. *The External Role of the European Community*. Westmead: Saxon House, 1977.

Sjursen, Helene. 'What kind of power?', in Helene Sjursen, ed., *Civilian or Military Power? European Foreign Policy in Perspective*. London: Routledge, 2007.

Smith, Hazel. 'Actually existing foreign policy – or not? The EU in Latin and Central America', in John Peterson and Helene Sjursen, eds, *A Common Foreign Policy for Europe?*. London: Routledge, 1998.

__ *European Union Foreign Policy: What It Is and What It Does*. London: Pluto Press, 2002.

Smith, Julie. *Europe's Elected Parliament*. Sheffield: Sheffield Academic Press, 1999.

Smith, Karen E. *The Making of EU Foreign Policy: The Case of Eastern Europe*. 2nd edn, London: Macmillan, 2004.

__ 'Beyond the civilian power debate', *Politique Europeénne*, no. 17, automne 2005.

__ 'The limits of "proactive cosmopolitanism": EU Policy towards Burma, Cuba and Zimbabwe', in Ole Elgström and Michael Smith, eds, *The European Union's Roles in International Politics: Concepts and Analysis*. London: Routledge, 2006.

__ 'Speaking with one voice? European Union coordination on human rights issues at the United Nations', *Journal of Common Market Studies*, 44, 1 (2006).

__ 'The justice and home affairs policy universe: some directions for further research', *European Integration*, 31, 1 (2009).

__ 'The European Union and the politics of legitimization at the United Nations', *European Foreign Affairs Review*, 18, 1 (2013).

Smith, Michael. 'The European Union, foreign economic policy and the changing world arena', *Journal of European Public Policy*, 1, 2 (1994).

__ 'Does the flag follow trade? "Politicisation" and the emergence of a European foreign policy', in John Peterson and Helene Sjursen, eds, *A Common Foreign Policy for Europe?*. London: Routledge, 1998.

Smith, Michael E. 'The legalization of EU foreign policy', *Journal of Common Market Studies*, 39, 1 (2001).

__ *Europe's Foreign and Security Policy: The Institutionalization of Cooperation*. Cambridge: Cambridge University Press, 2004.

Söderbaum, Fredrik, Patrik Stålgren and Luk Van Langenhove. 'The EU as a global actor and the dynamics of interregionalism: a comparative analysis', *Journal of European Integration*, 27, 3 (2005).

Solana, Javier. 'Intervention in the open debate on conflict prevention in the general affairs council', press release no. 004/01, Brussels, 22 January 2001.

Spanish Presidency. 'Memorandum on the EU's external relations in the field of JHA', Council document no. 10835/02, 9 July 2002.

Spencer, Claire. 'The EU and common strategies: the revealing case of the Mediterranean', *European Foreign Affairs Review*, 6, 1 (2001).

Stavridis, Stelios. 'Why the "militarising" of the European Union is strengthening the concept of a *"Civilian Power Europe"* ', Robert Schuman Centre Working Paper no. 2001/17. Florence: European University Institute, 2001.

Stirk, Peter M. R. and David Weigall. *The Origins and Development of European Integration*. London: Pinter, 1999.

Szymanski, Marcela and Michael E. Smith. 'Coherence and conditionality in European foreign policy: negotiating the EU–Mexico global agreement', *Journal of Common Market Studies*, 43, 1 (2005).

Tamminen, Tanja, ed. *Strengthening the EU's Peace Mediation Capacities*. FIIA report 34. Helsinki: Finnish Institute for International Affairs, 2012.

Task Force on the EU Prevention of Mass Atrocities. 'The EU and the prevention of mass atrocities: strengths and weaknesses', February 2013.

Telò, Mario.'Reconsiderations: three scenarios', in Mario Telò, ed., *European Union and New Regionalism: Regional Actors and Global Governance in a Post-hegemonic Era*. Aldershot: Ashgate, 2001.

__ *Europe: A Civilian Power?* Palgrave, 2005.

Thatcher, Margaret. *The Downing Street Years*. London: HarperCollins, 1993.

Therborn, Göran. 'Europe in the twenty-first century: the world's Scandinavia?', in Peter Gowan and Perry Anderson, eds, *The Question of Europe*. London: Verso, 1997.

Thomas, Daniel C. 'Still punching below its weight? Coherence and effectiveness in European Union foreign policy', *Journal of Common Market Studies*, 50, 3 (2012).

Tocci, Nathalie. *The EU and Conflict Resolution: Promoting Peace in the Backyard*. London: Routledge, 2007.

Tonra, Ben. *The Europeanisation of National Foreign Policy: Dutch, Danish and Irish Foreign Policy in the European Union*. Aldershot: Ashgate, 2001.

United Kingdom government. 'Review of the balance of competences between the United Kingdom and the European Union: development cooperation and humanitarian aid report', July 2013.

United Nations Secretary-General. 'An agenda for development', report no. A/48/935, 6 May 1994.

Vachudova, Milada Anna. *Europe Undivided: Democracy, Leverage and Integration after Communism*. Oxford: Oxford University Press, 2005.

Vanheusden, Els. 'Overview of the conflict prevention policy of the EU', MICROCON Policy Working Paper 16. Brighton: MICROCON, 2011.

Vanhoonacker, Sophie, Petar Petrov and Karolina Pomorska, eds. Special Issue on 'The emerging EU diplomatic system', *The Hague Journal of Diplomacy*, 7, 1 (2012).

van Praag, Nicholas. 'European political cooperation and Southern Africa', in David Allen, Reinhardt Rummel and Wolfgang Wessels, eds, *European Political Cooperation: Towards a Foreign Policy for Western Europe*. London: Butterworth Scientific, 1982.

Vlcek, William. 'Development v terrorism – migrant remittances or terrorist financing?', LSE Challenge Working Paper, September 2006 (available at: www.lse.ac.uk/Depts/intrel/EUroFPUnit.html; last accessed 13 January 2014).

Vincent, R. J. 'Human rights in foreign policy', in Dilys Hill, ed., *Human Rights and Foreign Policy: Principles and Practice*. Houndmills: Macmillan, 1989.

Waltz, Kenneth. 'Reductionist and systemic theories', in Robert Keohane, ed., *Neorealism and its Critics*. New York: Columbia University Press, 1986.

Ward, Benjamin. 'Europe's own human rights crisis', in Human Rights Watch, *World Report 2012*.

Weiler, Joseph. 'The evolution of mechanisms and institutions for a European foreign policy: reflections on the interaction of law and politics', European University Institute Working Paper no. 85/202. Florence: European University Institute, 1985.

Wendt, Alexander. 'Anarchy is what states make of it: the social construction of power politics', *International Organization*, 46, 2 (1992).

__ 'Collective identity formation and the international state', *American Political Science Review*, 88, 2 (1994).

Wetzel, Anne and Jan Orbie. 'With map and compass on narrow paths and through shallow waters: discovering the substance of EU democracy promotion', *European Foreign Affairs Review*, 16, 5 (2011).

__ 'The EU's promotion of external democracy – in search of the plot', CEPS Policy Brief no. 281, Brussels: Centre for European Policy Studies, 13 September 2012.

Whitehead, Laurence. 'Losing "the force"? The "dark side" of democratization after Iraq', *Democratization*, 16, 2 (2011).

Whitman, Richard. *From Civilian Power to Superpower? The International Identity of the European Union*. London: Macmillan, 1998.

Whitman, Richard and Ana E. Juncos. 'Relations with the wider Europe', in Nathaniel Copsey and Tim Haughton, eds, *The JCMS Annual Review of the European Union in 2010*. Oxford: Wiley-Blackwell, 2011.

__ 'The Arab spring, the Eurozone crisis and the neighbourhood: a region in flux', in Nathaniel Copsey and Tim Haughton, eds, *The JCMS Annual Review of the European Union in 2011*. Oxford: Wiley-Blackwell, 2012.

Williams, Andrew. *EU Human Rights Policies: A Study in Irony*. Oxford: Oxford University Press, 2004.

Witney, Nick. 'Where does CSDP fit in European foreign policy?', Policy Paper no. 64, Notre Europe, 13 February 2013.

Wolfers, Arnold. *Discord and Collaboration: Essays on International Politics*. Baltimore: Johns Hopkins University Press, 1962.

Wong, Reuben. 'Model power or reference point? The EU and the ASEAN Charter', *Cambridge Review of International Affairs*, 25, 4 (2012).

World Bank. *Sub-Saharan Africa: From Crisis to Sustainable Growth: A Long-Term Perspective Study*. Washington, DC: The World Bank, 1989.

Youngs, Richard. *Democracy Promotion: The Case of European Union Strategy*. Centre for European Policy Studies Working Document no. 167, Brussels, 2001.

__ 'European Union democracy promotion policies: ten years on', *European Foreign Affairs Review*, 6, 3 (2001).

__ *The European Union and the Promotion of Democracy: Europe's Mediterranean and Asian Policies*. Oxford: Oxford University Press, 2001.

__ *Europe and the Middle East: In the Shadow of September 11*. London: Lynne Rienner, 2006.

__ ed. *Survey of European Democracy Promotion Policies 2000–2006*. Madrid: FRIDE, 2006.

__ 'Trends in democracy assistance: what has Europe been doing?', *Journal of Democracy*, 19, 2 (2008).

Zanger, Sabine C. 'Good governance and European aid', *European Union Politics*, 1, 3 (2000).

Zielonka, Jan. 'How new enlarged borders will reshape the European Union', *Journal of Common Market Studies*, 39, 3 (2001).

Zwagemakers, Fabienne. 'The EU's conditionality policy: a new strategy to achieve compliance', IAI Working Papers 12/03, Rome: Istituto Affari Internazionali, January 2012.

Zwanborn, Michael. 'Human rights promotion and protection through the external relations of the European Community and the Twelve', *Netherlands Quarterly of Human Rights*, 7, 1 (1989).

Index